The Tyndale New Testament Commentaries

General Editor:
THE REV. CANON LEON MORRIS, M.Sc., M.Th., Ph.D.

MARK

THE GOSPEL ACCORDING TO MARK

AN INTRODUCTION AND COMMENTARY

by

THE REV. CANON R. A. COLE, M.Th., Ph.D.

Church Missionary Society of Australia
Lecturer, Trinity Theological College, Singapore

Inter-Varsity Press
Leicester, England

William B. Eerdmans Publishing Company
Grand Rapids, Michigan

Inter-Varsity Press
38 De Montfort Street, Leicester LE1 7GP, England

Wm. B. Eerdmans Publishing Company
255 Jefferson S.E., Grand Rapids, MI 49503

Published and sold only in the USA and Canada by Wm. B. Eerdmans Publishing Co.

1st edition 1961
2nd edition 1989

Reprinted 1997

Unless otherwise stated, quotations from the Bible are taken from the Revised Standard Version, copyrighted 1946, 1952, © 1971, 1973 by the Division of Christian Education, National Council of the Churches of Christ in the USA, and used by permission.

British Library Cataloguing in Publication Data

Cole, Alan, *1923–*
    The Gospel according to Mark. 2nd ed.
    1. Bible. N.T. Mark Critical studies
    I. Title.   II. Series
    226'.306

    IVP ISBN 0-85111-871-2

Library of Congress Cataloging-in-Publication Data

Cole, R. A. (R. Alan), 1923-
    The Gospel according to Mark : an introduction and commentary /
    R. A. Cole. — 2nd ed.
    p.   cm. — (The Tyndale New Testament commentaries : 2)
    Includes bibliographical references.
    1. Bible. N.T. Mark—Commentaries. I. Title. II. Series.
    BS2585.3.C6 1989
    226.3'07—dc20   89-28136
                                                      CIP
    Eerdmans ISBN 0-8028-0481-0

Set in Palatino
Typeset in Great Britain by Parker Typesetting Service, Leicester
Printed in USA by Eerdmans Printing Company, Grand Rapids, Michigan

Inter-Varsity Press is the book-publishing division of the Universities and Colleges Christian Fellowship (formerly the Inter-Varsity Fellowship), a student movement linking Christian Unions in universities and colleges throughout the United Kingdom and the Republic of Ireland, and a member movement of the International Fellowship of Evangelical Students. For information about local and national activities write to UCCF, 38 De Montfort Street, Leicester LE1 7GP.

GENERAL PREFACE

The original *Tyndale Commentaries* aimed at providing help for the general reader of the Bible. They concentrated on the meaning of the text without going into scholarly technicalities. They sought to avoid 'the extremes of being unduly technical or unhelpfully brief'. Most who have used the books agree that there has been a fair measure of success in reaching that aim.

Times, however, change. A series that has served so well for so long is perhaps not quite as relevant as when it was first launched. New knowledge has come to light. The discussion of critical questions has moved on. Bible-reading habits have changed. When the original series was commenced it could be presumed that most readers used the Authorized Version and one could make one's comments accordingly, but this situation no longer obtains.

The decision to revise and up-date the whole series was not reached lightly, but in the end it was thought that this is what is required in the present situation. There are new needs, and they will be better served by new books or by a thorough up-dating of the old books. The aims of the original series remain. The new commentaries are neither minuscule nor unduly long. They are exegetical rather than homiletic. They do not discuss all the critical questions, but none is written without an awareness of the problems that engage the attention of New Testament scholars. Where it is felt that formal consideration should be given to such questions, they are discussed in the Introduction and sometimes in Additional Notes.

But the main thrust of these commentaries is not critical. These books are written to help the non-technical reader to understand the Bible better. They do not presume a knowledge of Greek, and all Greek words discussed are transliterated; but the authors have the Greek text before them and their comments are made on the basis of the originals. The authors are free to choose their own modern translation, but are asked to bear in mind the variety of translations in current use.

The new series of *Tyndale Commentaries* goes forth, as the former series did, in the hope that God will graciously use these books to help the general reader to understand as fully and clearly as possible the meaning of the New Testament.

LEON MORRIS

CONTENTS

AUTHOR'S PREFACE TO THE FIRST EDITION

This little book cannot pretend to be scholarly, but it does at least attempt to be theological. There are many excellent commentaries on Mark already in existence, but perhaps this slender volume may yet find a place on the shelves of those who are too busy to read the larger volumes, or who feel themselves to be too ill equipped to enjoy the scholastic riches available elsewhere in such embarrassing abundance. It is an attempt at a practical work-a-day commentary for the use of those engaged in the humbler levels of Christian service, and it has at least the merit of being produced by such a one himself. The absence of reference to many works of proven value does not correspond to scorn for their contents, but simply to the limitations of library necessary to one whose calling has been to work with his fellow Christians in the Church of South East Asia. For inadvertent lack of acknowledgment, if such there be in places, the author apologizes humbly. It, too, is not intentional, but the result of assimilation so complete that the material has become part of the author: and, rightly seen, there could be no truer compliment to the now forgotten original authors. This book now goes forth with the prayer that it may lead the readers into as much blessing as it led the writer, through the same means of the careful study of the actual text of Scripture. If it had a dedication it would be to his brethren in the Church of South East Asia, to whom the author has given so little, but from whom he has learnt so much.

R. A. C.

9

PREFACE TO THE
SECOND EDITION

It is not given to many to revise a book first written twenty five years ago, and I thank the Inter-Varsity Press for the opportunity. The question is: would the same sort of commentary have been written today? Would there have been any major changes of approach? Those who compare this edition with the first will find the answers, as far as the present author at least is concerned, from the fact that the major changes are in the Introduction, which has been completely re-written, rather than in the main body of the commentary, although many additions and references to the views of other writers have been included there. It is to be hoped that this will show that, even if the author has not changed his basic position, it is not through ignorance of those who think otherwise, and that their views have been carefully taken into account throughout. Nor is it a claim that the exegesis could not be improved, but merely the view that, given the necessary limits and given the public in view, it still seems on the whole to be rightly directed. The basic approach, of the wisdom of which the author is more and more convinced, is to let the text in its present form speak for itself, and to read it in its own light. To some this may seem simplistic; but perhaps the whole approach of Mark's Gospel was simplistic too, compared with other later gospels, especially if it represents either a compilation of Petrine testimony (which not many scholars would hold in this form today) or a record of general early Christian tradition (which seems more tenable) or a combination of both. This 'simplicity' of Mark's Gospel was widely held by earlier commentators like Turner, Bartlett and Taylor; as we shall see, it has been widely challenged by later commentators influenced by some aspects of the 'redaction criticism' school. To them, this gospel is highly theological, sophisticated, controversial and even tendentious; but the evidence for any of these characteristics is very doubtful and the present commentator cannot share their views.

If we do not share these views then it means that we should try to see Mark's Gospel, not through traditional eyes, not even through the eyes of the other evangelists, but as it is in itself, and assess its evidence accordingly. This is a plea very strongly made by Belo, not from a conservative position but for 'structuralist' reasons, and by many of the 'new literary criticism' school for other reasons. As neither of these two groups is concerned with the historicity of the account, however, they are doubtful allies to claim in a commentary written from a conservative viewpoint.

If the text of the Commentary itself has remained basically the same (although minor additions have been made on every page and irrelevancies removed), with the Introduction it is quite another matter. It has been totally re-written, not because the basic material available for study, whether manuscript or otherwise, has altered or increased significantly, but because the approach of biblical scholarship and, in particular, of New Testament criticism, continually changes, as can easily be seen by consulting Hunter, Neill, Marshall and most recently Telford, for a good summary of recent views. Indeed, Telford well speaks of the 'literary explosion' of the last thirty years, when literally hundreds of books and articles on Mark have been written, as opposed to the paucity of treatments in earlier years. It is not the approach of scholarship alone which has changed: it is also the interests of scholars which have altered. Different questions are asked, so that it is natural that different answers are obtained.

So three typical modern scholars and their approaches have been selected and studied in some detail, against the background of a brief mini-history of earlier gospel criticism. Of these, two are well known and would be regarded by any commentator as significant. The third is not so well known (certainly not to traditional western scholars), but is chosen as typical of one school of modern exegesis, widespread both in the third world in general and behind the 'Iron' or 'Bamboo' Curtains in particular, where not inconsiderable numbers of Christians are to be found.

The basic questions of Christianity are always the same: Who is Jesus? What is salvation? What is the good news? Why should we preach it? Perhaps, if we look carefully at Mark, we shall find the answers to some of these questions given all the more clearly because presented without the later, though perfectly valid, theological explanations to be found in the other gospels. So we shall consider those points, along with several new questions that are burning issues today. We shall also look squarely at the so-called 'deficiencies' of Mark's Gospel and try to see the reasons for them. We shall see that, rightly considered, these very 'deficiencies' are the surest guarantee of reliable early evidence. Indeed, the very simplicity and directness of Mark is a great theological safeguard; if we laboriously reconstruct some complex theory of Messiahship, let us say, that does not find support in Mark, we are clearly on the wrong road. This is undoubtedly what the earliest Christians believed; none can deny that, not even those scholars who see the Gospel more as a record of early Christian belief than of the teaching of Jesus Himself. Whether Mark's Gospel is Peter's preaching, or a record of general early tradition, or Mark's own compilation based on the two, the result is the same – it is still an invaluable testimony to the beliefs of the earliest Christians about Jesus Christ; and, naturally, they believed these things because they held them to be true and factual.

The most urgent of all these questions racking the church today is: What is the good news? We are not talking here of the literary form of the gospel, or its origins, but its determinative content. Here we shall try to see what the good news meant to Mark and his first readers.

On the one hand, evangelicals have increasingly and rightly seen over the past few decades that the fruits and effects of the gospel cannot be restricted to a purely spiritual area. Here 'left wing' commentators like Belo would heartily agree. Luke, of all the evangelists, has shown us this particularly clearly, but it is equally clear in Mark, says Belo, if we take Mark at his face value without artificial 'spiritualizing'. A gospel that does not affect every aspect of the Christian's life is a shallow faith, if not a dead orthodoxy.

On the other hand, to make salvation entirely physical, to see the kingdom of God as entirely this-worldly, and to see it as produced entirely by human efforts, is foreign to the whole message of the New Testament, and especially foreign to the Gospel of Mark, in spite of all his obvious 'earthiness'. Here is where we must part company with commentators like Belo and his group. Privatizing, individualizing, and spiritualizing of the gospel (to use modern terminology), may well be dangers; but so are materializing and politicizing the gospel, and they are far greater dangers for us today because they agree with the spirit of our times.

Perhaps, however, the greatest danger of all that we face is a false polarisation of two aspects of the gospel (rather like a polarisation of faith and works) instead of seeing both aspects as integrally and necessarily related. There is a tendency today in some quarters, perhaps especially in North America and parts of East Asia, to associate the blessings of the Kingdom with material wealth and 'capitalist' prosperity; we rightly reject this as shallow and humanistic. But equally shallow and mistaken is another modern tendency to associate the Kingdom of God with some kind of utopian socialist world state. The Bible is very even-handed: sin is regarded as a universal human phenomenon, and every type of political system, whether of the 'left' or of the 'right', is therefore regarded as carrying within itself the seeds of its own decay and being subject to God's judgment. The Christian cannot give total unquestioning allegiance to any one political system, for the Christian hope is not placed in political systems. Mark's Gospel certainly makes plain the special concern that Jesus has for the poor and the sick and the afflicted, although it never goes so far as to say, with some modern scholars, that God 'has a bias to the poor'. It is impossible, in spite of all Belo's attempts, to prove that Jesus, in Mark, attacks the rich, and encourages 'class struggle'. True, in Mark's Gospel the dangers of wealth, influence and power are pointed out very clearly, and the divergence between the values of the kingdom and the values of this world is stressed; but that is not the same thing. In other words, Mark's Gospel was written to show us a way of salvation which is fundamentally spiritual, not to give us an economic or political blueprint for a new social order. To that extent, the 'good news' as outlined in Mark may fairly be described as 'apolitical'. But it does contain great principles which must be embodied in any socio-political order, and so it is not 'neutral' in this area. 'Liberation theologians' sometimes turn (rightly or wrongly) to Luke for inspiration, but rarely to Mark. If Mark's Gospel is the earliest, this is highly significant, for in Mark we see how the earliest Christians viewed the gospel. Jesus is no zealot: even Belo admits that Christ rejected violence as a means to achieve His goals, though Belo maintains that Jesus strove for the same goals as the zealots by what he calls 'quiet subversion'.

Further, we must never lose sight of the clear eschatology of Mark, that is to say his doctrine of the 'last things'. It is not human struggle but God Himself (sometimes, in Mark, through His 'agent', the Son of man) who will finally introduce His kingdom with power at the last day. This does not mean that the Christian must not strive to obey Christ in every way in the present age, to make real those aspects of the kingdom that we can, in this material world. 'The coming kingdom', it has been well said, 'casts its shadow before it'. Once the good seed has been sown, there is a steady, unseen growth, until the harvest (4:29): both aspects are equally stressed in this gospel. But ultimately our final hope and triumph (if we follow Mark) is not within this world but beyond it. That is precisely why we have courage to work for God's kingdom in the here and now; even if we seem at times to fail here, we cannot ultimately be defeated, because God will finally win the victory (1 Cor. 15:57–58). This type of eschatology we may think of as typically Pauline, but it is just as distinctively Marcan. There is incidentally no need to assume that Mark derived this eschatology directly from Paul rather than from Christ Himself, whether the knowledge came through Peter or through the common Christian tradition, as Johnson shows to be more likely.

Finally, the good news in Mark is never seen as some process of self-understanding, self-development, and self-fulfilment. These concepts, so congenial to what is often called the 'me age', are utterly alien to the gospel of Jesus as recorded in Mark:

if there is a self-fulfilment (10:30), it is only on the other side of a death to self (8:35). This, in Mark, is the path that Jesus trod and is equally clearly laid down as the path for His followers (10:39). We are told to love God with heart and soul and mind and strength (12:30): we are never told anywhere in Mark to love ourselves, although he does not go as far as Luke does (14:26) in recording Jesus as saying that we should hate ourselves (where the word must of course be understood in the Semitic sense of a strong contrast to 'love'). He assumes, with the law of Moses, that, like all humanity, we will 'love ourselves' in the Semitic sense of caring activity, not emotion, and tells us to care for our neighbour in the same way (12:31). Blunt Mark will never encourage us to wallow in emotion, although, in his matter of fact way, he will record, without comment, very human emotions, displayed and expressed by Jesus (e.g. 8:12; 9:19; 10:14; 14:33). To him, love is shown in action and sacrifice (14:3), as indeed it was to be in the case of Christ Himself (10:45). These may be hard sayings, but they are refreshingly clear and challenging: this is the voice of the martyr-church of the first century speaking to the martyr-churches of the twentieth century.

R. A. C.

CHIEF ABBREVIATIONS

AV   English Authorized Version (King James).

BAGD   *A Greek-English Lexicon of the New Testament and Other Early Christian Literature* (a translation and adaptation of Walter Bauer's *Griechisch-Deutsches Wörterbuch zur den Schriften des neuen Testaments und der übrigen urchristlichen Literatur*), by William F. Arndt and F. Wilbur Gingrich; second edition revised and augmented by F. Wilbur Gingrich and F. W. Danker (University of Chicago Press, 1979).

BDB   *A Hebrew-English Lexicon to the Old Testament*, edited by F. Brown, S. R. Driver and C. A. Briggs (Oxford: OUP, 1907).

E.T.   English Translation.

IBD   *The Illustrated Bible Dictionary*, 3 vols. (Leicester: Inter-Varsity Press, 1980).

IDB   *The Interpreter's Dictionary of the Bible* (Nashville: Abingdon, 1979).

IDB Sup. Supplementary Volume to *The Interpreter's Dictionary of the Bible* (Nashville: Abingdon, 1979).

IOM   *The Interpretation of Mark*, edited by William R. Telford (SPCK, 1985).

JB   Jerusalem Bible, 1985.

JBC   *The Jerome Biblical Commentary*, 2 vols., edited by R. Brown *et al.* (Chapman, 1968).

KB   *A Hebrew and Aramaic Lexicon to the Old Testament*, edited by L. Koehler and W. Baumgartner (Leiden: Brill, 1967).

LXX   The Septuagint (pre-Christian Greek version of the Old Testament).

MM   *The Vocabulary of the Greek New Testament*, by J. H. Moulton and George Milligan (Grand Rapids: Eerdmans, 1980).

MS(S)   Manuscript(s).

NEB   New English Bible, 1961.

NICNT   The New International Commentary on the New Testament.

NIV   New International Version, 1973.

NT   New Testament.

NTS   *New Testament Studies*.

OT   Old Testament.

PCB   *Peake's Commentary on the Bible*, edited by Matthew Black and H. H. Rowley (Van Nostrand Reinhold, 1982).

RSV   American Revised Standard Version, 1946.

RV   English Revised Version, 1881.

TDNT   *Theological Dictionary of the New Testament*, a translation by Geoffrey W. Bromiley of *Theologisches Wörterbuch zum neuen Testament*, vols. 1–4 edited by G. Kittel, 5–10 edited by G. Friedrich (Grand Rapids: Eerdmans, 1964–76).

TNTC   Tyndale New Testament Commentary.

SELECT BIBLIOGRAPHY

Aland, K., *Synopsis Quattuor Evangeliorum* (Württemberg: Württemberg Bible Society, 1964).

Anderson, H., *The Gospel of Mark* (Marshall, Morgan & Scott, 1976).

Beasley-Murray, G. R., *Jesus and the Future* (1954).

Belo, F., *A Materialist Reading of the Gospel of Mark* (New York: Orbis, 1984).

Black, M., *An Aramaic Approach to the Gospels and Acts* (Oxford: Clarendon Press, 1954).

Brown, C., *That You May Believe: Miracles and Faith Then and Now* (US ed. Grand Rapids: Eerdmans, 1985. UK ed. Paternoster Press, 1986).

Butler, B. C., *The Originality of St. Matthew* (Cambridge: 1951).

Carrington, P., *The Primitive Christian Calendar* (Cambridge: 1940).

Carson, D. A. and Woodbridge, John D. (eds.), *Hermeneutics, Authority, and Canon* (Leicester: IVP, 1986).

Cole, R. A., *The New Temple* (Tyndale Press, 1950).

Cranfield, C. E. B., *The Gospel According to St. Mark* (Cambridge: Cambridge University Press, 1959).

Cullmann, O., *The Christology of the New Testament* (SCM, 1971).

Dodd, C. H., *The Apostolic Preaching and its Developments* (1936).

Farmer, W. R., *The Synoptic Problem* (1964).

France, R. T., *The Gospel According to Matthew: . . .*, TNTC (Leicester: IVP, 1985).

Funk, R. W., *A Greek Grammar of the New Testament* (Cambridge: Cambridge University Press, 1961).

Green, Joel B., *How to read the Gospels and Acts* (Leicester: IVP, 1987).

Grollenberg, L. H., *Atlas of the Bible* (Nelson, 1957).

Guarducci, M., *The Tomb of St. Peter* (Harrap, 1964).

Hengel, Martin, *Crucifixion* (E.T., Philadelphia: Fortress Press, 1977).

Hunter, A. M., *Interpreting the New Testament, 1900–1950* (SCM, 1951).

Johnson, S. E., *The Gospel According to St. Mark* (Black, 1977).

Kirschbaum, E., *The Tombs of St. Peter and St. Paul* (Seeker & Warburg, 1959).

Kline, M., *By Oath Consigned* (Grand Rapids: Eerdmans, 1986).

Kümmel, W. G., *Introduction to the New Testament* (SCM, 1966).

Lane, W. L., *The Gospel According to St. Mark* (Grand Rapids: Eerdmans, 1974).

Lightfoot, R. H., *The Gospel Message of St. Mark* (Oxford: Oxford University Press, 1950).

Manson, T. W., *The Sayings of Jesus* (Norwich: SCM, 1949).

Marshall, I. H. (ed.), *New Testament Interpretation* (Exeter: Paternoster Press, 1977).

Martin, R. P., *Mark, Evangelist and Theologian* (Paternoster Press, 1979).

Marxsen, W., *Mark the Evangelist: Studies on the Redaction History of the Gospel* (Nashville: 1969).

Minear, P. S., *Mark* (Atlanta: John Knox Press, 1962).

Morris, L., *Luke, an Introduction and Commentary*, 2nd rev. ed., TNTC (Leicester: IVP, 1988).

Morris, L., *New Testament Theology* (Grand Rapids: Eerdmans, 1988).

Moule, C. F. D., *The Birth of the New Testament* (Black, 1981).

Moule, C. F. D., *Idiom Book of New Testament Greek* (Cambridge: Cambridge University Press, 1953).

Neill, S., *The Interpretation of the New Testament, 1861–1961* (Oxford University Press, 1964).

Nineham, D. E., *Saint Mark* (Penguin Books 1969).

Ogg, G., *The Chronology of the Life of Paul* (Epworth Press, 1968).

Robinson, J. A. T., *The Problem of History in Mark* (1957).

Schmoller, A., *Concordantiae Novi Testamenti Graeci* (Wurttemberg: Württemberg Bible Society, 1973).

Schweizer, E., *The Good News According to Mark* (SPCK, 1987).

Singer, S., *Daily Jewish Prayerbook* (Eyre & Spottiswoode, 1949).

SELECT BIBLIOGRAPHY

Taylor, V., *The Gospel According to St. Mark* (Macmillan, 1966).
Telford, W. (ed.), *The Interpretation of Mark* (SPCK, 1985).
Trocmé, E., *The Formation of the Gospel According to Mark* (SPCK, 1975).
Turner, C. H., 'The Gospel According to St. Mark' in *A New Commentary on Holy Scripture* (1928).
Westminster, *Westminster Historical Atlas to the Bible* (SCM, 1946).
Wikenhauser, A., *New Testament Introduction* (Nelson, 1958).
Wikgren, A., *Hellenistic Greek Texts* (Chicago: University of Chicago Press, 1947).
Wimber, J., *Power Healing* (Hodder & Stoughton, 1986).

INTRODUCTION

I. WHO WAS 'MARK'?

At first sight this might seem a simple question, but it is far from that, as a study of the brief and helpful summaries in Johnson, Schweizer and Anderson, among other modern commentators will at once show. All that we can do is to give a tentative answer based on such evidence as we have.

In one sense, the answer given does not matter greatly, although of course it is interesting to us today. The gospel itself does not claim to be written by Mark: no person named Mark is mentioned anywhere in the book, and the attribution to Mark in the title, although contained in all manuscripts, is probably a later, though still primitive, addition to the gospel. Indeed, the book contains no internal reference to any author at all, and is certainly not 'personalized' in the way that Luke's Gospel is (Lk. 1:3) or Paul's letters (Rom: 1:1). Mark's Gospel does not even insist that it is directly dependent on the testimony of some particular, well-known and trusted eyewitness, as John's Gospel does (Jn. 21:24), nor does it claim that it is based on a careful second-hand compilation of all available first-hand evidence, as Luke's Gospel does (Lk. 1:3).

Perhaps indeed both of these are self-conscious aspects that would not have occurred naturally to an earlier evangelist; they are a sign that the truth of the gospel is somehow already being challenged, either by critics or by false gospels. Indeed, earlier scholars went so far as to say that the reason for this 'anonymity of Mark' is that he is simply recording either the preaching of Peter or the common and generally-held tradition of one particular church; he is not writing as an individual at all (*e.g.* Dibelius). Most modern scholars since Marxsen would reject this view, however, and allow Mark a strongly individual role, whether as editor or author.

True, it is sometimes held that the account of the young man who fled naked in Gethsemane to escape arrest (14:51–52) is a concealed 'personal touch' added by the author, who in this way was identifying himself anonymously. This may well be correct: but, if so, since no such identification is specifically made (unlike Jn. 21:24), the secret would be plain only to those already 'in the know'. The anonymity of the youth himself would, however, be explicable enough on other grounds. No identification is made in Mark either of the wounded servant of the high priest or of the disciple who struck the blow which wounded him (14:47) and presumably for exactly the same reason; it was not safe at the time. Not until John's Gospel, probably written long afterwards (with apologies to those who believe in an early date for John) will it be safe to identify both servant and disciple (Jn. 18:10). Unfortunately John does not mention the incident of the young man in the garden, or the mystery might be solved by the giving of a name.

All that this proves is early dating for Mark's Gospel, irrespective of whoever wrote it. The detail certainly shows that the author of the gospel had access to genuine eye-witness accounts of these last days in Jerusalem; but even so, it is more likely to be accidental rather than deliberate witness; a vivid and inconsequential memory of an insignificant fact is a hallmark of truth. Nevertheless, even if it were proved that this young man in the garden was Mark (which is uncertain), it still would not prove that he had written the gospel now associated with his name: it would prove only that he had been present during the events.

As far as any solid proof goes, we are therefore left with an 'orphan gospel'. But then, a first gospel does not need an author's name to distinguish it and guarantee it, if there are as yet no other gospels, whether orthodox or heretical. Of course, if we are part of the dwindling group who still reject Marcan priority (*e.g.* Butler and Farmer) the problem still remains, for we must assume that other gospels like Matthew were already in existence.

We shall later consider the relationship of this gospel to the other gospels, and also consider in detail the evidence of tradition, for what it is worth. Enough here to say briefly that internal comparison suggests to most scholars that this was the first of the gospels to be written, and that tradition unanimously ascribes this gospel to Mark. Tradition is also unanimous that this Mark was the John Mark mentioned in several places in the New Testament (e.g. Acts 12:25) – perhaps not surprisingly since no other Mark is mentioned in Scripture, although the name was fairly common. Now, in view of the comparative unimportance of this particular Mark, it is hard to see why an 'orphan gospel' should be fathered on him in the absence of any internal evidence pointing to him. Had it been fathered on a well-known apostolic figure like Peter, that would have been another matter, and good reason could be seen for it. Since (as we shall see) the same church tradition, rightly or wrongly, considered Peter to be the ultimate source of information contained in Mark's Gospel, the failure to credit the gospel directly to Peter is even more remarkable. Later apocryphal gospel-writers had no such scruples and cheerfully attributed another gospel to Peter. The only explanation of the failure to do the same here must be a strong early tradition to the contrary, and this should therefore not be rejected lightly.

Leaving this aside for the moment, however, if the gospel was written or compiled by Mark, what do we know of him? Barnabas, his cousin (Col. 4:10, see BAGD and MM for the meaning of *anepsios*), was a 'Hellenist', a wealthy Greek-speaking Jew from Cyprus, of Levitical family (Acts 4:36), so it is highly likely that Mark had shared this Greek-speaking overseas background too. Admittedly, Mary, John Mark's mother (probably a widow, since in charge of a household), appears as living in Jerusalem, where sometimes at least the church gathers at her home (Acts 12:12). But it was not unusual for wealthy and pious Hellenist widows to move to Jerusalem in the later years of life, in order to die in the holy city. For the presence of numerous 'Hellenist' widows in Jerusalem we may also compare the account of the rift between two groups of widows, Hebrews and 'Hellenists', in the early church (Acts 6:1). Barnabas of Cyprus also appears as living at Jerusalem (Acts 4:36; 11:22), like Simon of Cyrene (Mt. 27:32), showing that overseas Jews were not uncommon residents of the city. John Mark may therefore have actually grown up in Jerusalem; in any case, he would have been familiar with the city and the apostolic figures of the church there, although he was not apparently a direct disciple of Jesus. The seeming lack of close knowledge of Palestinian geography in the gospel is, however, a problem here.

Barnabas had apparently donated all his property to the infant church (Acts 4:37). It is possible that Mary had done the same, and that may be why we find the church meeting in her house; but it is a pure assumption to suggest that therefore this home must have held the 'upper room' where the Last Supper had taken place (14:15). Like several other events recorded in Mark, the supper is anonymous in point of place, and possibly for the same reason – the secrecy necessary in days of persecution. Of course it is more probable that Mark's 'reading public' did not share our modern interest in location, rather than an indication that Mark did not know the place himself.

Cypriots had been among the first evangelists of Gentile Antioch (Acts 11:20), a type of work to which they had perhaps become accustomed long before, through Jewish proselytization of Gentiles in Cyprus. Barnabas and Mark had both already shared in Gentile missionary outreach at Antioch in any case, (Acts 12:25), Barnabas from early days (Acts 11:22), and Mark from much later, when Barnabas fetched him from Jerusalem (Acts 12:25). Mark had even shared with Barnabas and Saul one 'leg' of the first missionary journey (Acts 13:2–5, to Cyprus) until he turned back in Cilicia (Acts 13:13) and returned to Jerusalem, where he presumably remained. After the split between Barnabas and Paul over Mark, Barnabas took Mark back with him to Cyprus (Acts 15:39) and possibly elsewhere, on his own 'second missionary journey'. Whatever Paul felt about Mark's departure at the time (Acts 15:38), in much later years Mark appears as associated with Paul (Col. 4:10 and 2 Tim. 4:11), and also as a close junior colleague of Peter (1 Pet. 5:13), presumably in both cases at Rome.

John Mark, whether or not he wrote this gospel, was therefore closely linked with at least three major apostolic figures (Paul, Barnabas and Peter), and also associated with several early centres of Christian tradition, (Jerusalem, Antioch and Rome), while from the start he had been involved in missionary work among Gentiles. John Mark therefore would have had ready access to much early gospel material, and an obvious interest in producing a 'Gentile gospel'.

So much we can say with safety about John Mark from the evidence of the New Testament; for anything more definitely linking him with the gospel that now bears his name, we must turn to traditions of the early church.

WHAT DOES TRADITION SAY?

The evidence here is clearly, if briefly, summarized by Taylor in his commentary and also by Cranfield in *IDB*. Early traditions may or may not be correct, but it is always wise to examine and evaluate them. Certainly they should not be rejected out of hand, for, even if they do not reproduce the truth in detail, they may point to it in broad outline. Alternatively, if we can see the reasons why these traditions arose, we may learn as much as if they were true, at least concerning the questions that they were designed to explain. This is doubly so in any area where there are no variants, but only one consistent tradition, for, had there been major problems left unsolved by this first explanation, other traditions would certainly have survived or been invented. Again, while the existence of a unified tradition does not necessarily mean that it is correct, it does mean that this tradition was generally accepted as a satisfactory explanation of the known phenomena. The other side to this is that, if some tradition survives which cannot be deduced from the facts, or even poses problems when confronted with the facts, it is all the more likely to be true; for why should such a tradition have been invented? The same, of course, is true of the preservation of picturesque but irrelevant details; why should anyone bother to invent details if they are irrelevant? A modern novelist might deliberately insert fictitious 'local colour', but hardly a first-century evangelist – certainly not one as matter of fact as Mark seems to have been.

In the case of Mark's Gospel, there is remarkable unanimity of tradition as far as the broad outline is concerned. That may well be so simply because there seems to have been only one basic source of the tradition: Papias (c. 60–130), a second-century Bishop of Hierapolis. Various snippets of a lost work of his composed in five books and entitled *An Account of the Lord's Sayings*, have been preserved, especially by Eusebius in his *History of the Church*. As these and various other patristic references are conveniently to be found in appendix 2 of Aland, they will be quoted from there in a free translation, using the paragraph or line numbers of Aland for reference purposes. Seeing that Papias, however, is the only primary authority for the origins of Mark's Gospel, it may be helpful to quote him in full, whether we believe him or not. Eusebius, who preserves him, does not apparently have a high intellectual opinion of him.

This also the presbyter used to say: Mark indeed, who became the interpreter of Peter, wrote accurately, as far as he remembered them, the things said or done by the Lord, but not however in order. For he had neither heard the Lord nor been his personal follower, but at a later stage, as I said, he had followed Peter, who used to adapt his teachings to the needs of the moment, but not as though he were drawing up a connected account of the oracles of the Lord: so that Mark committed no error in writing certain matters just as he remembered them. For he had one object only in view, viz to leave out nothing of the things which he had heard, and to include no false statement among them.

Papias refers to someone whom he calls 'the Elder', probably 'John the Elder' (Aland 3), who is described as being a 'disciple of the Lord', but who is apparently not the same as the apostle John, since the latter seems to be mentioned quite separately, although not all scholars would agree on this. 'The Elder' is quoted as saying that Mark was the 'interpreter' of Peter (Aland 15). Papias is here clearly dealing with the source of Mark's tradition. 'Interpreter' can hardly mean 'translator' of an Aramaic original, for it is most unlikely that Peter was unable to speak Greek and, if he had done any Gentile preaching whether in Rome or elsewhere, it would have required the use of Greek. The word should rather be understood in the sense of 'explainer', the sense in which the same root is used by Papias in his foreword, also preserved by Eusebius (Aland 2). Here Papias talks of setting down all he himself had learnt from the Elders, 'along with the interpretations' which, in the context, must mean something like 'along with the explanations'. It is, however, true that just below (Aland 16), when speaking of the origins of Matthew's Gospel, the Elder, again as quoted by Papias, uses the same verb 'interpret' in a more literal and restricted sense. Matthew, he says, drew up his 'sayings' in Hebrew, by which he presumably means 'Aramaic', and everybody 'interpreted' them as best he could. But here there has been a specific reference to the involvement of another language, a factor which is nowhere implied in the case of Peter's preaching. Therefore, if there is anything in this traditional link between Mark and Peter, Mark is portrayed not as a translator of Peter from Aramaic to Greek, but as an explainer of Peter. If the Petrine authorship of 1 Peter is accepted, then the relationship between Silvanus (Silas) and Peter there may have been somewhat similar to that assumed between Mark and Peter here (1 Pet. 5:12), for Peter is not likely to have used such polished Greek as we now find in the Epistle. There is little polish in Mark's Greek, however, so that any 'editorial' activity performed on Petrine material by Mark must have been of another nature.

Papias, or rather John the Elder as quoted by Papias, goes on to say that Mark wrote down (Aland, 15) 'carefully, but not in order, as many of the sayings and doings of Jesus as he (? Peter) remembered' (or possibly 'related'). This may be a defence of Mark against current charges of inaccuracy, or of paucity of material, or of lack of strict chronological sequence. It is interesting that most of these very criticisms are still made today. They were, however, not likely to arise initially in the ancient world, until after the production of other gospels, when Mark might well suffer by comparison.

The reason for these apparent 'deficiencies' is next given by Papias very simply, by pointing out that Mark had neither heard nor followed the Lord himself, but had simply followed Peter, at a later date (Aland 15). The implication therefore is that, if Mark was deficient, it was purely through a lack of direct personal knowledge of the events. Of course, we must remember that Papias is trying to prove a point in all this – that written documents like the gospels are not really as valuable as first hand oral tradition, which Papias championed.

The question could still be raised, however, if Peter was indeed Mark's source, and if Mark was following him, as to why these same three criticisms could not be applied more properly to Peter. The answer given by the Elder is that even Peter was not simply listing the Lord's sayings (Aland 15) but that he was adapting his teaching material according to the needs of his hearers – exactly as 'redaction criticism' says that every evangelist did later. So, says John the Elder, Mark should not be blamed; his only concern was neither to omit material deliberately nor to falsify it; Mark simply 'wrote down some things as he' (presumably Peter) 'remembered (or mentioned) them'. Whether the Elder was correct in his view or not is, of course, quite another matter.

The later Patristic traditions add little to this, except some refinements in detail. The old Latin prologue to Mark (Aland p. 532), however, does add that the gospel itself was written in Italy, after the death of Peter. It also adds the irrelevant (and therefore probably true) detail that Mark was nicknamed 'stumpy-fingered' because of a physical peculiarity. The foolish story that he cut his own thumb off, which is to be found in the Monarchian Prologue to Mark (Aland p. 539) may safely be rejected as a late explanation of the nickname. Whether the original nickname was ever meant to be taken in a literal sense at all is another question. Various minor additions or corrections to the main tradition are made by other Fathers: some say that the work was written during the lifetime of Peter and not after his death; some say that Peter approved it; others say that he neither opposed nor commended it, and so on (Clement of Alexandria, Aland p. 539). These variants, however, do not affect the main tradition as to the Petrine source and Roman origin of the gospel. The only major departure (a suggestion that the work was produced in Alexandria) is late, and is probably connected with the tradition that Mark later became Bishop

of Alexandria (Monarchian Prologue, Aland p. 539), or even that
he was finally martyred there. We may have only some confusion of names here.

There is therefore a general consistent view in the early
church that Mark's Gospel was produced in Italy (almost certainly in Rome), and that it was dependent in some sense on a
Petrine source, being written towards the end, or shortly after
the end, of Peter's life, which came presumably in the AD 64
persecution (see Guarducci and Kirschbaum). This comes with a
full recognition by the early church of the 'flaws' in the gospel,
which were therefore as clearly perceived by ancient as by
modern critics, and allows for selection of material and adaptation to teaching needs on the part of both Peter and Mark.

Nevertheless, there still remain two questions. The first is
whether the evidence contained within Mark's Gospel itself is
consistent with the explanation of a Petrine source. The second
is whether the evidence for a Petrine source is so compelling as
to demand this explanation and no other. Here, every thoughtful reader must make up his or her own mind. Most would
agree that the answer to the first question is 'yes', while the
answer to the second question is 'no'. So, while we may cautiously use the possibility of a Petrine source and a Roman origin
(though the two do not necessarily hang together) to aid our
understanding and exegesis of the gospel, we must not make
them essential factors in its interpretation. However possible,
and even tempting they are, either or both may be incorrect, and
exegesis must never be made to depend on an unprovable
hypothesis. Besides, even if Mark is partially dependent on a
Petrine source, he must also have used other sources, so that
this possible Petrine source cannot be exclusive. It may also be
worth noting that, even if the source of Mark's Gospel was only
the general teaching tradition of the early Roman church, this
almost certainly depended in no small part on Petrine tradition
also. Therefore, if direct dependence on Peter is ruled out as
incapable of proof, some indirect dependence on Peter may be
granted as not only possible but probable, for none other of the
twelve (so far as we know) had direct contact with the west.
Obviously, to judge from the Fathers, such a living source of
tradition would be highly valued. Nevertheless, most modern

scholars prefer the view that Mark is dependent, not on Peter, but on common early tradition. As to the question of who the evangelist was, it is not unfair to say that interest has simply shifted from that to the question as to how he handled his materials. The battle has not been won: it is the battleline that has shifted.

II. PRIORITY OF MARK AMONG THE SYNOPTISTS

This view, so far as we know, was never held in the ancient world: but the question, in this particular form, was not one which would have greatly interested ancient scholars. It is therefore a comparatively modern view, still not universally held. For a useful modern summary of evidence in its favour, see Styler's article in Moule and also see Neirynck in *IDB Sup*.: for the grounds for the opposing view, see Butler and Farmer.

Augustine was probably the first to actually write in detail about the literary relationships of the four gospels ('On the Harmony of the Evangelists', quoted in Kümmel). He maintains that the four gospels were actually produced and written in the order in which they usually appear in our manuscripts today (Matthew, Mark, Luke, John), which is a view that may seem simplistic to us. He further maintains that each evangelist knew of, and used, his literary predecessors, which is a view that in principle most scholars today would hold, except possibly with reference to John. On Mark, Augustine is particularly scathing: 'Mark comes tagging along behind him (Matthew) like a servant, and seems to be his abbreviator.' Of course, if Mark had really been written after Matthew, that would be a perfectly reasonable viewpoint to take, and indeed has been taken (although not so crudely), by scholars like Butler and Farmer. Such modern scholars would of course agree that at times Mark amplified as well as abbreviated the material that he found in other gospels, but it cannot be denied that Mark contains much less material in all.

Before, however, we simply dismiss the views of Augustine as naive and based on the mere fact of the order of the gospels, it would be interesting to speculate why the gospels were originally arranged in their present order. Perhaps it was because there were others in the early church besides Augustine, and indeed before him, who shared his belief, rightly or wrongly, as to the primacy of Matthew. Indeed, as we shall see, there are some who still hold this view today. But in any case, in view of the increasing conservatism of the Roman Church, it is not surprising that Augustine's view, once expressed, gradually became universal and indeed ultimately mandatory in the Roman Catholic Church until the present century. Nevertheless, in Protestantism since the eighteenth century, the view has steadily gained ground that both Matthew and Luke knew and used Mark's Gospel, whatever other sources, written or oral, they may have used as well. With various modifications, this is almost universally held today. Usually (but not always), the view is held as part of the 'two-document hypothesis', one document being Mark and the other a collection of Sayings of Jesus, often known as 'Q'. These two documents, with the addition of special material in either case, are seen as the basic sources of Matthew and Luke. Naturally, this involves the priority of Mark as a corollary.

The reasons for this view are simple and attractive. Both Matthew and Luke follow the general order of Mark. Where they differ from Mark in order, it is only one of the two who differs, but never both at the same time. The material of all three gospels is very similar in wording, often strikingly so. Wherever this wording is altered in Matthew or Luke from the wording of Mark, there is usually an obvious reason – to remove a difficulty, or to smooth over something felt to be crude or theologically offensive to later and more sophisticated Christian ears. The theology of Matthew and Luke, for example, is more reflective and developed as compared with the somewhat curt statements of Mark. As regards contents, over 90% of the material in Mark appears in either Matthew or Luke: to be exact, about 90% of Mark has parallels in Matthew, and 50% has parallels in Luke. Since both these other gospels are much longer than Mark, they obviously contain much additional material, sometimes in great blocks, drawn from a source common to both (the so called 'Q') and other sources independent to each; but this does not affect their general dependence on Mark wherever he is available to them.

Nor can it be seriously maintained, with Augustine, that Mark is a mere abbreviator of Matthew, although he certainly contains much less material than Matthew, if considered as a whole. If he was an abbreviator, how could we explain the fact that, where Mark and Matthew do tell a common story, Mark often contains far more detail than Matthew? He would in these cases be an amplifier, not an abbreviator; and Mark's crisp story-telling style seems to make that an impossibility. Now, while these statistics can be presented from another perspective (as by Butler and Farmer), and it would be most unwise to over-simplify the relationship between the gospels (as Styler, in Moule, shows), there seems to most scholars little doubt that Matthew and Luke are partially dependent on Mark, or upon some other source so close to our Mark in form that it would be hair-splitting to deny it the name. We may therefore safely consider Mark in isolation from the other Synoptics, for he did not use them as sources. Of course this does not mean that Mark may not himself have used earlier sources, whether written or oral or both, and some of these may have equally been known to and used by Matthew and Luke. Mark seems nevertheless to have been the earliest written gospel, in our sense of the word; and this view seems so firmly established today that longer discussion is unnecessary here.

For a fuller treatment of the synoptic problem, readers are directed to Morris on Luke, in this series of commentaries, or to Kümmel or to any other of the standard New Testament introductions. For a spirited defence of Matthaean priority, see, among modern scholars, Butler and Farmer. Their main arguments are that Matthew's Gospel, which is of course far longer than Mark, contains all of Mark's material but for some forty verses, in addition to much extra material: that Matthew and Luke share numerous agreements as against Mark: that Matthew retains Palestinian touches, as against Mark's alleged signs of Pauline influence, and his adaptations of the tradition to Graeco-Roman readers. None of these are convincing arguments, however, and most can be turned in the other way. For a useful discussion, see 'Excursus IV' in Moule. There has also been some revival in recent years of the much earlier 'Griesbach hypothesis', a theory which postulates a direct relationship between Matthew and Luke, with Mark conflating the two (see conveniently Neirynck and Furnish in *IDB Sup.* and Styler in Moule), but this has not commended itself widely. The fact that it has been revived at all, however, is of some significance. It had been the dominant view before the rise of the two document hypothesis. If it has reappeared, it is because not all scholars believe that the two document hypothesis has solved all the problems.

III. MINI-HISTORY OF GOSPEL CRITICISM

This section is, like the section above, presented with apologies to the professional New Testament scholar. Its sole purpose is to present to the general reader of this book the bare essentials for understanding the general position, of which Lane and Anderson both contain short and clear summaries.

The early approach to the study of the New Testament documents (in this case, the gospels) is usually described as 'precritical', or, more unfairly 'uncritical'. This is not altogether true, for many of the church Fathers were, in their way and up to their lights, acute and observant biblical scholars dealing with the facts that they had, although their interests were usually very different from ours today. For centuries this 'non-critical' approach (as it is fairer to call it), persisted, dealing with the text that lay immediately and obviously before it, a type of study which, as has been pointed out (Anderson) led to just as deep spirituality, even if it is not equally possible to us today. Then came the gradual development of 'textual' (or 'lower') criticism, the attempt to establish the 'original' text of the New Testament by rigorous comparison of all available early manuscripts and translations. This laudable but impossible quest led naturally in due course to 'literary' (or 'higher') criticism. It had been realized long before that 'manuscripts must be weighed, not counted'. This judicial 'weighing' involved also the comparison, not only of whole manuscripts, but of literary units, like the gospels, with attempts to explain their similarities, differences and possible relationships. Attempts were also made to suggest how the gospels came into being, and what different sources were used. This is turn led to 'form criticism' – the isolation, study and classification of the numerous separate 'forms' or 'units of tradition' found embedded in the gospels and therefore presumed to lie behind them. Each saying or story was carefully considered in the light of the assumed 'real-life situation' from which it had come, or for use in which it had been preserved. Like every type of study, this had value. It lay in the intense scrutiny given to each individual unit, but it tended by doing so, to atomize the gospels. Each gospel became a mere 'bag of marbles', containing many such disconnected units, each unit smooth and well-worn with use, but rattling together in hopeless and haphazard disunity, while the gospel-writer became a mere collector and recorder of units preserved and already moulded by the tradition of the church.

It is not therefore surprising that the next step was 'redaction criticism', based on the belief that these isolated units must have been somehow collected, shaped and arranged for a particular purpose by a final author or 'redactor'. Along with this there goes the attempt to find out what changes (if any) the redactor may have made to the raw material in the course of the process and, if so, for what reasons. From this, attempts are made to pin-point the 'life situation' of the final redactor, his hearers, or his local church. Of the three modern scholars whose contribution to the study of Mark's Gospel will be considered briefly, Marxsen belonged to this school. Indeed, it could be argued that he pioneered it, for he is credited with the invention of the term. Trocmé, whose contribution we shall also try to assess, followed broadly speaking in his footsteps, though without totally agreeing with Marxsen, and indeed with considerable further development of the theory.

It is not surprising that, as a reaction to this over-analysis, with the original narrative receding further and further from sight, a so called 'new literary criticism' arose. This saw the Bible primarily as literature, not as history or theology, and sought to treat it accordingly, by the rules of literature. Scholars of this school owe a great deal to modern theories of linguistics, semantics and sociology – which means that, at times, their work is very complex and difficult. One major branch of this 'new literary criticism' (although not the only one) is 'structuralism', and of this, Fernando Belo, whose work will be considered briefly, is an example. Put briefly and baldly, 'structuralists' consider any text as a whole, and as it is in its final form. The parts to them have meaning and significance only in relation to the whole. But, deep beneath this unified text before us also lie hidden 'structures' (hence the name of the school) that alone can explain the text. These 'structures' are expressed in 'codes'. Structuralism is continually interested in moving to larger and larger wholes: the isolated instance is therefore only valuable as illustrating this whole. It is not necessary to master this forbidding theory (or even to accept its validity), however, in order to appreciate some of its insights.

IV. HOW SHOULD MARK'S GOSPEL BE VIEWED?

A. MODERN VIEWS OF MARK

i. Marxsen

Form criticism as has been said, when carried out rigorously, had left to Biblical scholars only an infinity of isolated pieces of tradition, totally unrelated. It was therefore left to redaction criticism, as introduced by Marxsen, to explain how these isolated units were welded together into a whole. This could be done (as mentioned) only by a definite author with a definite purpose. Even if the existing isolated units of tradition had been deliberately strung together consecutively by them like 'pearls on a string' (instead of chance 'marbles in a bag' recorded at random with no connection whatsoever between them) then the evangelists would still have been only collectors and mechanical reproducers of the units of tradition, and so indeed earlier scholars had seen them (e.g. Dibelius). Some even assumed that the evangelists found their raw material already assembled in small complexes: they were thus faced with strings of 'pre-strung pearls', and were even less innovative. But if redaction criticism is correct even in broad outline, the evangelists were authors in the full modern sense of the word. Units, Marxsen held, were not only collected and carefully arranged by them; they were reshaped and moulded (some even said, created), for a special purpose that the author had in view. Collection and arrangement of sayings by an author, for a particular purpose, posed no problem to conservative scholars; further than this, they were usually reluctant to go, since they certainly could not agree that material had been created with this aim. Particular interest is directed by scholars towards any supposed changes made to the tradition by the redactors, and the possible reasons for them, in terms of a 'life situation' that can explain and justify these changes. Marxsen was a pioneer in this area of redaction criticism, although the idea itself was not totally new. His book, 'Mark the Evangelist', represented for this reason a turning-point in Marcan studies. For a convenient, if brief, summary of his views see Lane, and also Perrin in *IDB Sup*. Previously, Mark had been considered to be a somewhat pedestrian composition, woodenly reproducing early traditions, whether they were Petrine or not; not so however, according to Marxsen.

Marxsen sees in Mark an elaborate mosaic, not a bag of unrelated marbles nor even a string of connected pearls, and for him this mosaic forms a picture, difficult though some of the individual pieces may still be to fit in. The authors of the original units may be faceless, but not the final redactor: he becomes a real person with real views, aims and even prejudices. His aims, according to Marxsen, arise from a particular situation at a particular place and time.

Whether this situation can be reconstructed with any more certainty than the background of the isolated units is a very good question. Marxsen believes that it can be done, however, because of the larger body of continuous evidence available. This is aided by careful comparison with the later Gospels of Matthew and Luke. If from this comparison we can establish Mark's particular interests, we may be able to turn, in Marxsen's view at least, to find out what the 'original' form of the material was, on which Mark worked.

It will be obvious that the situation is becoming more and more hypothetical. Redaction criticism is certainly valuable in the sense that it looks at the gospel as a whole, not merely as a chance collection of isolated units. It is helpful too in asking the question as to why a gospel was written in its particular form and in allowing to the author a personality, but it seems to tend inevitably to the 'dehistoricisation' of the facts of the gospel. If the gospel cannot really tell us of what Jesus did or said, what value has it for us today?

After all, we may be studying only the mind of the author, or the mind of his church. We may not be studying Jesus and His gospel at all, but only the proclamation of Jesus by others, in the case of extreme exponents of this view. For Marxsen accepts not one but three levels of 'real-life situations' as determinative of the presentation – the original time of Jesus, the time when the oral tradition was still circulating and the actual time of the evangelist himself. So we are at best two removes from reality, unless we are prepared to postulate (with conservative scholars) that it is throughout all these shifts one and the same gospel, even if told against the background of different situations, as is quite possible. Otherwise, the original narrative disappears further and further over the horizon.

Nevertheless, a rejection of Marxsen's views does not necessarily mean the rejection of all forms of redaction criticism. By examining the way in which Mark assembles and puts together sayings and doings of Jesus (which we accept as genuine), we can form some idea of his purpose in writing the gospel, and this can be very helpful. This is roughly the position of Lane, for instance, who uses redaction criticism in a more positive, as well as a more conservative way, to understand the text before us.

There are many interesting (though not necessarily convincing) suggestions made by Marxsen. He sees the gospel as composed not in Rome, but in Galilee, probably before AD 70; it is to him an exhortation to local Christians to hold fast, during the persecution and troubles of the Jewish wars of AD 66–70. At least this has the merit of setting an early date and a Palestinian background for the gospel. He sees Mark as influenced directly by Paul, as shown by his use of the word 'euangelion' or 'gospel', as compared with other evangelists; this is possible but not necessary. Less convincing in his view that the absence in Mark's Gospel of the standard synoptic gospel conclusion, with record of resurrection appearances, shows that the Lord's promise to precede his disciples to Galilee and meet them there (14:28) is merely a prophecy of his second coming or 'parousia'. This, to Marxsen, is only one part of a stress on Galilee and

Galileans, which he sees throughout the whole book: but, as he interprets 'Galilee' theologically rather than geographically (as meaning 'ministry among Gentiles' opposed to 'ministry among Jews'), this does not have the significance which we might expect.

Marxsen was not of course writing a full-blown commentary on Mark: his aim was only to show how in his view the evangelist shaped and edited the traditional material that had come down to him from others. To illustrate this thesis, he isolated and studied the Marcan account of John the Baptist; the significance of the geographical references in the book; Mark's use of the word 'euangelion'; and the Marcan treatment of the apocalyptic matter in chapter 13. From the different manner in which all this material was handled in other gospels, Marxsen drew his own conclusions; although not every scholar would share them. Nor is he convincing when he assumes that Mark confuses the 'past' and 'present' Jesus, reading back into the lifetime of the earthly Jesus aspects which were actually 'post resurrection' in the faith of the church. Nevertheless, this is an important book, perhaps more for the questions raised about Mark than for the answers given, and for its introduction of redaction criticism as a tool for the study of Mark, a tool which has been used consistently since his time by most commentators. Lightfoot, Nineham and Lane, in different ways, show his influence, as does Anderson, but with several penetrating criticisms.

ii. Trocmé

Trocmé's influence on Marcan studies can be seen by the number of references to him in modern commentaries. It is tempting, and not altogether unfair, to say that, if Marxsen is Germanic and 'thorough' (if uninspiring) in his approach to Mark, Trocmé is French and imaginative. In one sense, Trocmé is a follower of Marxsen, since, in his eyes too, Mark's Gospel is a closely constructed work, highly individualistic, and indeed to him essentially controversial. He, like Marxsen, sees the author as the creator of the gospel-form. But he goes further, for he sees Mark as an 'audacious Christian, prompted to confront tradition, and those who transmitted it, with a statement of the real ecclesiological intentions of Jesus' (p. 85). Belo, as we shall see, objects violently to this definition. The question before the thoughtful reader is: Is this really a true picture of Mark or only a picture of Trocmé? The reconstruction made by Trocmé is undoubtedly imaginative and brilliant, but not convincing. When he says that Mark is 'an appeal to history against the institution', he may well be projecting the ideas of a later age. He sees Mark as highly critical of the traditions of the Jerusalem church and as the writer of a polemic against some individuals at Jerusalem (such as Peter and James) in support of the mission of the church, especially of its Gentile mission, which he thinks Jerusalem ignored. But we can admit Marcan enthusiasm for the Gentile mission without necessarily importing the idea of a polemic against Jerusalem. Otherwise, we shall be left with a new version of the old Tübingen theory of a conflict between Peter and Paul, and a theory just as unwarranted from the biblical evidence. It may be true that the Jerusalem church was not as active in the gentile mission as 'Hellenist' Christians were, but there is no Biblical data to suggest that Jerusalem as a whole opposed the gentile mission (see Acts ch. 15), though the 'Judaizers' may have desired to limit its effects.

Trocmé sees Mark chapters 1–13 as a 'little ecclesiological treatise' (a phrase which again particularly irritates scholars like Belo), rather than as a strict biography of Jesus, which it manifestly is not, in our sense of the word. He therefore sees this section of Mark as being in itself the earliest gospel; but we may well ask what function it could possibly have had as a gospel in such a truncated form. The passion narrative, so far from being the climax of the gospel, is to Trocmé only a later addition by a 'humdrum Roman ecclesiastic', using an existing Holy Week lectionary. If this 'Roman ecclesiastic' were to prove to be Mark himself (certainly not 'humdrum'), would Trocmé be satisfied? For the gospel certainly was produced in some such Latinized milieu as Rome, and most scholars would agree that a Passion narrative in some form or other already existed before Mark's Gospel. In that case, we could accept that chapters 1–13 of Mark were Palestinian in origin, possibly even Galilean (especially if

Peter was one source), and 14–16:8 a Roman addition, without necessarily drawing from this all of Trocmé's conclusions. We may well agree with Trocmé that there is a strong missionary interest in Mark, even an interest in a full Gentile mission, without necessarily postulating his cleavage on the matter between the Christians of Galilee and the church at Jerusalem.

The 'downplaying' of Peter in the gospel, on which Trocmé lays great stress, need not be a deliberate theological attack on Peter, made at a later date. It is not something in isolation but is part of the general 'downplaying' of the twelve which characterizes the whole gospel. It could either be Petrine modesty (if we hold to a Petrine source) or primitive frankness (if we do not). Apostles, it has been well said, did not acquire haloes or superhuman stature until well after the first century. Mark or his source may simply have described the apostles as they really were, to the horror of later Christians, who tried to soften the hard facts here too, as they did in other areas of Mark's Gospel. Some editors hold that Mark was motivated by a strongly 'paraenetic' or instructional interest in portraying the apostles in this light (Schweizer); he wanted to warn us of the dangers that face all Christians. This may well be so: but how could he do this better than by showing the apostles as they actually were in all their weakness?

To say, with Trocmé, that the gospel is 'deficient in ethical teaching' is quite unfair, while it is true that long continuous collections of the ethical teaching of Jesus do not appear in Mark, as they do in other synoptists. Perhaps such collections were preserved separately in early days in 'teaching collections'. We should, however, be grateful to Trocmé for setting the gospel material early in date, and therefore closer to the events it describes, even if at the same time he somewhat downgrades the historical and biographical value of the Marcan narratives. His concept of Mark as a rugged individualist rather than as a gifted literary figure is interesting and provocative, but could he not have been merely a typical early Christian? Few would agree with him when he describes Mark as 'neither an ordinary nor a peaceable Christian', even if we were to accept his picture of a Marcan divergence from Jerusalem views. We should of course have to ask – which of the Jerusalem views? Acts makes plain that there were at least three different groups at Jerusalem – James' supporters (Gal. 2:12), the Pharisees (Acts 15:5), and the Hellenists (Acts 6:1). These last were represented by Stephen, who certainly would have had much sympathy with Mark; and Peter's views were very close to Mark's too (Acts 15:7–11). Trocmé's general emphasis on the conservatism of Mark shown by his preservation of early titles for Jesus (like 'Master' or 'Son of Man') rather than the use of later and more developed Christological titles, however, is both true and welcome. This means only that Mark is preserving faithfully the usage of his sources, not that he is ignorant of later usage – how could he be? Trocmé's basic thesis that the 'real life background' of Mark was a church with major problems, both in the form of persecution and in the form of those who had lapsed and denied their Lord, may well be true, even if the place of origin should prove not to be Rome. Such problems were almost universal in the first century, before Christianity had won toleration and even acceptance in the Empire.

To sum up, Trocmé's imaginative historical reconstructions are always interesting and challenging, and always bear consideration. Perhaps his chief contribution has been to develop still further Marxsen's concept of the individuality of the author of Mark's Gospel, and his activity as an editor of his traditional material, even if the motives suggested by Trocmé do not always commend themselves.

iii. Belo

For a third Marcan commentator, Belo has been chosen, not because he is well known (comparatively few traditional New Testament scholars will have even heard of him, let alone read his book), but because he is typical of a widespread modern movement. He does gain passing mention in a footnote in Telford, but this is unusual: nevertheless, Belo and his group should be taken seriously, even if we reject their viewpoint and interpretations.

Just as Marxsen and Trocmé were typical of new approaches to Mark's Gospel, so is Fernando Belo, although in his case, typical of an approach new not only in one particular direction (the socio-political), but in several others also. Increasingly today the whole structure of traditional 'western' biblical exegesis is coming under attack, particularly in countries of the so called 'eastern bloc' and China. Outside these areas, the pressure comes primarily from third world theologians, especially in South and Central America, and secondarily from an increasing group of younger western scholars who are influenced by their views. Starting from the truism that all biblical exegesis is unconsciously coloured by the background and culture of the exegetes, they dismiss traditional western exegesis as wrong-headed. A firm belief of this school is that the Bible was written for and by the poor and the oppressed, and therefore that it can be understood and interpreted only from their viewpoint. This, to them, rules out virtually all past exegesis, and demands a fresh start.

To complicate this, Belo is also a 'structuralist', as well as being a sociologist. All this combines to make his commentary extraordinarily difficult, yet at the same time challenging, with flashes of insight into matters to which more traditional scholars may have been blind. One does not have to accept his political or philosophical terms of reference to appreciate these insights, which may well preserve us from 'pietistic' and 'over-spiritualized' interpretations of Mark. Of course, Belo, just as much as the 'traditional scholars' whom he attacks, is working from his own fixed (and fallible) presuppositions, as future generations of scholars will no doubt be quick to see.

But, for Belo, his terms of reference are fundamental. He scourges those who are preoccupied in exegesis of Mark with the metaphysical problems of evil and suffering (about which he says that we can do nothing) and ignore the practical problems of poverty and oppression (where he says that we could and should do so much). Study of 'forms' and 'redaction history' alike are rejected by him as 'bourgeois', his ultimate adjective of abuse. His 'structuralist' views, as well as his political background, show clearly here. He is more concerned with the finished product in the text before us than with its past history. This is a healthy emphasis, but not when it leads him to be equally impatient with scholarly concern about the 'historicity' of any incident or saying of Jesus. He has no patience with a 'kingdom not of this world', a kingdom which ignores what he calls the 'economic component' of the gospel. The 'interiorizing' and 'personalizing' of salvation are unpardonable sins to him; and 'liberal' and 'conservative' scholars in his eyes have been equally guilty of these sins in the past. Exegetical erudition he says, quite correctly, can easily miss the plain meaning of the text. Trocmé and other commentators therefore come in for stern words of criticism on these grounds. Belo rightly stresses the physical nature of many of Christ's 'deeds of power' as recorded in Mark's Gospel – healings, feedings and so on. We can, he maintains, too easily ignore or 'spiritualize away' these in a commentary, looking only at some presumed 'metaphysical significance' of the text. He will have nothing of the common theological understanding of the word 'poor' in Scripture as meaning 'not only a social class, but also those whose submissive, trusting, joyous faith is summed up in an attitude of religious expectation'. This, to him, is the ultimate extreme of 'bourgois exegesis' and totally mistaken, although to many scholars it may seem the plain biblical meaning. Here, as often, Belo reacts too strongly to a perceived abuse, and is creating a false antithesis.

What are we to make of all this, and what are the positive values of Belo's approach? Evangelical scholars of recent years would gladly agree with Belo that there is always a danger of divorcing the gospel, whether in Mark or the other evangelists, from its practical this-worldly consequences (in this case, a danger of evacuating the word 'poor' of any real meaning), although it is also true that the danger was far greater in former years than it is today. We can also recognize, with Belo, the primarily physical nature of many of Christ's miracles as recorded in Mark, without necessarily restricting either the miracles or salvation to the physical, as he seems tempted to do at times.

This same 'earthiness', however, also leads Belo steadfastly to refuse to 'demythologize' and explain away either the miracles of Jesus, or even the resurrection, although he cautiously regards this as an 'open ended' question. This is certainly a healthy reaction to the scepticism of some other scholars. Less happy is his distinction between a supposed original 'Messianism' of Jesus, and later 'theologizing' about Jesus, of which, to Belo, the other Evangelists and Paul, if not the editor Mark himself, are examples. The doctrine of Christ and the doctrine of salvation are both involved in this, and no conservative scholar could agree with him here. In any case, if Paul was converted within a year or two of the crucifixion of Jesus (so both Ogg and Hengel), and was writing his letter to the churches within twenty years of it, he can hardly be accused of 'late' views.

There are, however, many other insights in Belo which are also valuable and refreshing. He rightly stresses the small first-century 'ecclesial communities' as being Mark's background, rather than the great formal 'Ecclesia' of later days. This is important when considering the origins of Mark's Gospel in and for such small groups or 'house churches'. Too many modern commentators are anachronistic in their concept of the early church, which must have been more like the church of China today than a highly organized western church. When he recalls us to the study of the 'Messianic narrative of Jesus', and calls us, as exegetes, to situate ourselves within the texts and not outside them, we would all agree, even if 'Messiah' for him does not always mean all that 'Christ' means for us. He is, in addition a 'structuralist', and therefore calls us to deal with the text of Mark as a whole, and as it now is. This is a welcome move away from the piecemeal approach of the past, with its engrossment in questions of origins and development of material.

Above all, the conservative scholar will be grateful to Belo for his warning against a selfish and personalized pietism, which ignores the practical demands of Jesus as presented in Mark, and smoothes over His plain teaching on wealth and poverty, although few of us could agree with Belo that Jesus preached 'class struggle' or had no place for the rich. If Fernando Belo has passionately over-reacted to error, none of us can blame him, for he speaks with faith, passion and naivety, out of his own agonized experience.

iv. What can we learn from these modern approaches?

If a study of modern views of, and approaches to, Mark is to be

anything other than an interesting form of theological archae-
ology, it must affect our approach and exegesis today. What
then have these three scholars to teach us? Many of the positive
insights of Marxsen and those redaction critics who followed
him will be found embodied in Lane, Anderson and Schweizer.
Redaction criticism has rightly taught us to consider the personality and situation of the evangelist as well as of his sources
and hearers. Of course every new theory tends to 'over compen-
sate', and redaction criticism is no exception to this rule. Nevertheless, the concept of an individual moulder of the gospel
material, with a particular purpose in view, is the abiding legacy
of redaction criticism. We may take this thought further, and
accept that the author selected and arranged, and perhaps even
himself explained, already existing material in order to achieve
this purpose. But as we have no gospel material earlier in date
than Mark, this would be difficult to prove, and comparisons
with Matthew and Luke may only be misleading. That Mark
edited his work with reference to the needs of some local church
also seems reasonable enough, although it would be dangerous
to draw from the Marcan material anything more than tentative
and general conclusions about the locale, circumstances and
problems of that local church.

There is good reason, however, for not being prepared to go
any further; there is certainly no need to accept any theory of the
creation of material by the redactor to further his supposed
theological purposes. But, having said all this, it is only fair to
point out that this process of 'redaction' is, in broad outline,
only what the early church had always held (perhaps in a
somewhat simplistic form) about Mark and his gospel, or even
about Peter, Mark's assumed source. We do not have to accept
Marxsen's more extreme views to agree with this type of
redaction.

As regards Trocmé, if Marxsen made the author of Mark a
person for us, then Trocmé individualized him still further by
what may seem to some to be an over-subjective and over-
imaginative exegesis. His theories are fascinating, but intel-
lectually and theologically unconvincing. His mistake is to
import a level of sophistication into first-century Christendom
which is most unlikely to have existed in the case of Mark,

whatever of Paul. That Mark and Paul were contemporaries or even colleagues by no means proves that they were of equal theological stature. It may well be that (as Trocmé claims) the place and mission of the church and of its 'shepherds' are in fact the two great themes of Mark. But if so, these themes may simply have been unself-consciously adopted by Mark as being two themes that arose naturally in the life of the early Gentile church. There is no hint in Mark's Gospel that either of them were controversial topics. Trocmé, in spite of all his presentation of Mark as an 'audacious Christian, boldly confronting Jerusalem church tradition', rightly says that we must not yield to the modern romantic notion of an individual standing alone against the whole. He sees Mark rather as spokesman of a minority group. But why can he not be a spokesman of the whole group, in early days, especially since his approach is so similar to that to be found in the pre-Pauline Jerusalem speeches of the early chapters of Acts? Trocmé, to prove his point, must first prove that, at an early date, there were ideas circulating at Jerusalem which conflicted with those expressed in Mark. True, some of Paul's letters were circulating before Mark's Gospel, but, while perhaps more developed theologically, they in no sense conflict with Mark. Nevertheless, while Trocmé's hope that his 'cautious circling around the problem' (of Jesus) 'has prepared the ground for a frontal attack' may be vain, yet we can learn from him the need for a sensitive and imaginative probing of the gospel materials contained in Mark, even if Trocmé's own particular conclusions seem at times far-fetched and unlikely. His influence can be seen in the careful consideration given to his views by later commentators, even by those who reject them.

With Fernando Belo, it is very different, although, because he is less known to orthodox scholarship, his influence has been more limited. His challenge is probably the deepest of all. At the moment when we most disagree with him, he has most to teach us, though not perhaps in the way that he intends. He represents a serious, if perhaps at times mistaken, attempt to escape from modern western presuppositions and assumptions, and to look at the gospel material through new eyes and in a fresh way. We can all learn from this, even if we do not necessarily agree with him when he insists that his was the way in which the early Christians saw and interpreted gospel events. After all, his frame of reference is a just as 'modern' and 'western' as any other form of twentieth-century thought, as indeed Belo himself admits, when turning to analyse first-century Palestinian society. To that extent, we are both of us alike applying alien and external 'grids' to the gospel material; but at least we have been well and truly warned by him of the dangers of our own particular 'grid'. When he urges us to use the gospel itself as a 'grid' to read the events of the gospel, we can only add our hearty amen. Above all, we must attempt, in our exegesis as well as in our Christian living, to be fair to the gospel, and to avoid 'spiritualizing' it to the extent where we evacuate it of any concrete this-worldly demands. Belo may have over-tipped the balance to one side; that does not excuse us from over-tipping it to the other side, as we have sometimes done in the past.

In a world where thousands of millions perish for want of Christians to preach the love of God that alone can bring eternal life, and yet where, as well, millions still starve and suffer for want of Christians to show the same love of God in action, this biblical balance between faith and loving action may well be for Christians today 'the article of a standing or falling church', as our ancestors centuries ago described the doctrine of justification by faith. Belo, even if by over-emphasis, shows us that this is the balance maintained by Mark, the first and greatest of the missionary gospels of the early church. We may not 'spiritualize away' the miracles or the practical implications of the teaching of Jesus recorded in the gospel, any more than we may 'materialize away' (or 'politicize away') salvation and the gospel. This is the balance that we must maintain today at all costs, without allowing any polarization between the two.

B. SIGNS OF PETER'S INFLUENCE

Older commentators, like Turner, took this for granted, presumably on the basis of the patristic tradition. Now, it is not seen by most commentators to be so obvious; indeed, as the Jerusalem Bible says, it is now 'widely maintained that the tradition radically oversimplifies the relationship of Mark's Gospel to Peter's preaching; at most, the connection is remote and tenuous.' It has been already noted that there are basically two questions involved here: the first is whether the material found in Mark's Gospel allows the possibility that it had a Petrine source; the second is whether the evidence is so compelling as to demand such a conclusion. The answer to the first question was given as 'yes' and the answer to the second question as 'no'. Certainly we should not assume Petrine influence too widely, as perhaps the first edition of this commentary did: that would be unwarranted. But in view of the universal early tradition of a Petrine source, and the fact that internal evidence certainly does not rule it out, we should not reject it out of hand in every instance.

Lane makes a good point in demonstrating that the outline of Mark's Gospel follows fairly closely the 'skeleton' of the Petrine preaching, as preserved in Acts 10:36–41. But Dodd was probably more correct in describing this as the general apostolic preaching, rather than merely Petrine, for we have no reason to suppose that Peter's preaching was in any significant way different from that of the other apostles. All that has been proved in fact is that Marcan theology is thoroughly consistent with that of the early apostolic community at Jerusalem, of which Peter is a representative. That we would have already expected, on other grounds, especially if Mark had lived in Jerusalem in early days (Acts 12:12). But it does refute Trocmé's view that there was a deep theological rift between two groups, the Marcan (presumably Trocmé means 'Galilean'), and Jerusalem churches. Nevertheless, to this limited extent at least, the evidence is consistent with the tradition of a Petrine source, although we must distinguish between broad outline and detail.

When we come to the material actually contained in the gospel, the evidence is equally general rather than specific. Certainly there are stories in Mark in which Peter plays a prominent part (e.g. 8:29); but then, if we accept Matthew's evidence (Mt. 16:18), Peter played a leading role among the disciples in any case. Whoever wrote the gospel would have to acknowledge this leading position of Peter, whatever his own particular source or sources, if he was to hold to the truth. There are also accounts of incidents like the transfiguration (9:2), or the prayer in Gethsemane (14:33), where only the 'inner three' were present (Peter, James and John) and where any account of these incidents must have come from one of the three, initially at least. It need not have come directly, however; the three must surely have told their fellow-apostles (but see 9:9-10). One might just as well argue that the source behind Mark's Gospel was Jesus Himself because the gospel contained accounts of incidents like the temptation, for instance (1:13), of which only Jesus initially had first hand knowledge. Nevertheless, none of these aspects are at all inconsistent with a Petrine source, and may well indicate it.

We are on far more uncertain ground when we attribute vivid details in Mark (found in descriptions of events at which Mark could not himself have been present) to Peter. Such details are certainly attributable to some eyewitness present on the occasion, but not necessarily to Peter. Also somewhat subjective is the view that, if Peter is shown in a very human light in this gospel, it is a necessary sign that Peter himself stands behind the story. It may well be so; but it may be only another sign of early date, when any idealization was still far from the thoughts of the disciples. This is strengthened when we remember that many of these realistic aspects are either omitted or 'softened down' in later gospels, when veneration of the apostles was presumably increasing. The position is therefore identical here; the argument for a Petrine source is possible, perhaps even attractive, but not compelling.

Perhaps, as many commentators have noted, the most likely of all the stories in Mark to be 'Petrine' in origin is the account of the healing by Jesus of Peter's mother-in-law (1:29-31). But even here, it seems a total mistake to try (with Lane) to recast the anecdote into the first person, as being an example of Peter's preaching. After all, we could equally well do this with any incident in which Peter appears, particularly if he appears prominently. This does not mean that Mark may not rely here, either in part or largely, on a Petrine source; it does, however, mean that we should not make our exegesis dependent upon the hypothesis. It is more likely that here, as elsewhere, Mark is recording a local church tradition that took its origins largely but not exclusively from the preaching of Peter. If the gospel was indeed written in Rome, this would be very natural, but this again is an unproved assumption.

For those who accept the Petrine authorship of 2 Peter, it is clear that he was intending to make some attempt to record his line of tradition in writing before his own death (2 Pet. 1:15). Whether he ever did so record it, we do not know: even if he did, we have no proof that Mark was the agent, although this was obviously the belief of the early church, perhaps drawn from this very verse in 2 Peter. Nevertheless, while this may not be a proof, it is at least another 'pointer' in the same general direction.

C. SOME EARLY CRITICISMS

We must not think that Mark was universally and highly esteemed by the early church as a gospel. On the contrary, Mark was often either criticized or neglected on several clearly stated grounds, which still remain valid today. For a spirited defence of Mark in some of these areas, see Johnson and Andersen: yet the questions still remain, and should therefore be considered briefly.

Why should anyone want to read Mark's Gospel? That was certainly the reaction of many in the early centuries, as can be seen from the almost total lack of commentaries on Mark, as compared with the number of commentaries written on other Synoptic Gospels. The reason for this neglect was simple; Mark's material was largely repeated in the other longer gospels, which also contained much additional matter. Augustine, it will be remembered, had crushingly said that Mark was only a follower and an abbreviator of Matthew, so it was natural that Matthew rapidly became the favourite church gospel, to judge from its use in early church lectionaries. Modern scholars would not take this low view of the value of Mark's Gospel. Indeed, they would value Mark highly as a primary synoptic source, but they too would be the first to admit that he is limited in certain areas, often those to which attention was drawn by the early church.

It is not until Mark is directly compared with the other gospels, however, that the extent of his so-called limitations, whatever their explanation may be, can be seen. For instance, Mark has no birth stories and no record of resurrection appearances; in that sense, Mark's is a gospel with neither beginning nor ending. There may well be good theological reasons for the apparent total omission of the resurrection appearances; but either Mark did not know of the virgin birth (which seems strange to us) or he did not think it necessary to record it in his gospel, as both Matthew and Luke did. Unlike Luke, Mark has no elaborate cross-dating of important events; indeed, in the whole gospel, there are only the vaguest and most general references to time. His geographical references are often equally vague. He does not seem therefore to have been concerned to set Jesus firmly in history, as Luke was. Further, although Mark frequently mentions Jesus as teaching (1:21), and must surely have known the content, he nowhere gives a long connected account of Christ's teaching, like Matthew's sermon on the mountain (Mt. chs. 5–7) or Luke's parallel sermon on the plain (Lk. 6:17–49), or even John's 'discourses' (Jn. chs. 14–16). Was the content of Jesus' teaching not so important to Mark as it was to other evangelists, or is there some other explanation for its omission in the gospel?

If we turn to doctrine, the Holy Spirit is mentioned only half a dozen times in the whole of the gospel, and then usually in connection with Jesus Himself (1:10, 12 etc.) and more in the sense of a divine power than of a divine person (13:11). It almost seems as if the doctrine of the personality of the Holy Spirit is not fully expressed in the material recorded in Mark.

When we come to the titles of Jesus, they seem very restricted in Mark, compared with the wider range found in later gospels. For instance, in Mark Jesus accepts the title of 'prophet' for Himself (6:4, 15). He is often called 'rabbi' or 'teacher' by others (9:5 NIV; 10:17), and frequently He uses the title 'Son of man' to describe Himself (2:10; 8:38). But He is not called 'Lord', the great New Testament title for Christ, except in polite address by others (e.g. 7:28) where the word probably means only 'sir', as in modern Greek (11:3 should perhaps be translated 'the owner', not 'the Lord'). As for the title 'Christ' or 'Messiah', in Mark's

Gospel it seems as if Jesus deliberately avoided using it of Himself and discouraged its use on the part of others (8:29–30), until His trial before the high priest (14:61–62). There may well be good reason for this 'messianic secret', as theologians of the past have called it; but the stubborn fact still remains. The same is true of a title like 'Son of God', in the body of the gospel. Demons (3:11) and Gentiles (15:39) might use it of Jesus, but not disciples; indeed it seems as if Jesus Himself actively discouraged its use (1:34). Again, there may well be a good reason, but the facts remain the same: what is the explanation?

All this proved somewhat of an embarrassment, to say the least of it, to the early Fathers, but there was worse still to come. In Mark's Gospel, Jesus openly proclaims His ignorance of the exact date of the last days (13:32), although aware that they are to come soon (13:30). In some manuscripts of Mark, Jesus is described, admittedly by Galileans who do not believe in Him, as 'the carpenter's son', (6:3) a phrase which later orthodoxy would never have tolerated: indeed, perhaps that is why other manuscripts read at this point 'the carpenter'. Mary herself, in Mark, seems to have been as unbelieving as the brothers of Jesus (3:21,31); certainly, she is never held up in this gospel as an example of faith. Jesus Himself, in Mark, displays strong and very human emotions, such as anger (1:43; 3:5) and grief (14:33–34). The Samaritans, who appear frequently in other gospels, might as well not have existed, as far as Mark is concerned; he also records much less of Jesus' concern for Gentiles, women, or children. As for the disciples, they all make a poor show in Mark: their faults are obvious, including Peter's (8:33; 14:37). They take only a minor share in the preaching activity of Jesus (6:7–13) when compared with Luke's account (Luke 10:1–12). Indeed, apart from 6:30, Mark does not even call them by the honoured name of 'apostles', used frequently later in the New Testament, though he does describe them as 'the twelve' (6:7 etc.). True, in Mark, Jesus speaks of the kingdom of God (1:15), but he never defines it at all, let alone in terms of Jesus' concern for the poor and oppressed, as recorded in Luke (6:20–21). Mark does mention John the Baptist (1:4–8), but only in the briefest terms, from which one would hardly guess John's true greatness. Mark rarely quotes from the Old Testament to show how

Jesus fulfilled it as, say, Matthew does. Contrariwise, when
Mark records Jesus' description of the last days (ch. 13), all is put
in general terms, and couched in Old Testament apocalyptic
imagery; there is none of the allusion to later historical events
which we find in Luke's version (Lk. ch. 21).

When Mark talks about 'faith' and 'salvation', he usually
means, by the first word, trust in an earthly Jesus, and, by the
second, healing from some physical illness (5:34), or rescue from
some physical danger (13:13), just as, to Mark, 'following' Jesus
means a literal following (2:14). There are as yet no immediate
and obvious theological overtones to these words, as in later
gospels. In Mark, baptism is nowhere clearly enjoined (except
in the late non-Marcan ending, 16:16); the Last Supper seems
portrayed as a Passover meal (14:14), and the disciples are not
specifically told to re-enact it. Although Jesus is certainly shown
in Mark's Gospel as engaging in prayer (e.g. 1:35), there is no
'pattern prayer' given for disciples to follow. Yet Mark certainly
lived in a church where baptism and the Lord's Supper were
observed, and where such prayer was practised.

How are we to understand all this? Mark cannot have been
ignorant of these facts. Was he not greatly concerned with
them? Did he deliberately omit them for some purpose of his
own? All these seem unlikely, but there may still be an explanation. The picture of Jesus given by Mark is not a popular one
today, for the simple reason that many of the theological
interests of modern Christianity do not appear in it. But that
does not in itself prove that it is an untrue picture, although it
may well be an incomplete picture, without the additions found
in the later gospels. A Christian social activist, for example,
would search in vain here for evidence that God's rule means a
restructured society: where in Mark is the cry for justice for the
poor? On these grounds, it might be seen as a 'privatized'
gospel. At least it cannot be accused of being a 'spiritualized'
gospel; it is too 'earthy' for that – too 'earthy' for the taste of
those who see John as a truly 'spiritual' gospel. A Christian
feminist might seek in vain for the deep concern for women that
we find shown by Christ in Luke; does Mark then accept the
'status quo' of a patriarchal society? A charismatic Christian will
miss the stress on the person and work of the Spirit and the

stress on signs and wonders (except in the disputed verses of chapter 16) which is to be found in Acts; a theologian may see a limited Christology in Mark (where is Christ's pre-existence?), as compared with Paul; a mystic will miss the sacramental over- tones to be found in John. But, even admitting all of this, the explanation may still be found in Mark's concept of a gospel.

D. THE ANSWER: MARK'S CONCEPT OF A GOSPEL

What was Mark attempting to do when he wrote his gospel? What aims had he in view? Mark may not have seen any of these omitted factors as being necessarily part of a gospel at all. Seeing that he was probably the first to write a gospel, there were no existing criteria, either to aid him or by which to judge him. He may have believed that the function of a gospel was simply to record the doings and sayings of Jesus in the actual language of their time, without the later and quite legitimate theological interpretations which he must surely have known. In that case, Mark's treatment of his material would be analog- ous to Luke's treatment of early material in the opening chapter of Acts. We may therefore have been asking Mark the wrong questions. Perhaps Mark was right; perhaps he correctly saw the essential scope and function of a gospel, and especially of a missionary gospel. It may also be that he, from his situation, assumes considerable knowledge of some facts in his hearers, much of which a later gospel would be compelled to spell out in detail, because by then the living sources of tradition would have begun to dry up: for Papias shows us that oral sources were more highly valued than written records in his estimation at least.

Mark is the earliest surviving written gospel, probably the first real gospel to be written, as distinct from various shorter collections of sayings or doings of Jesus (cf. Lk. 1:1), and pos- sibly a passion story. It is therefore hardly fair to contrast Mark adversely with his own successors, just because they have refined and modified Mark's gospel-form, a fact which seems undeniable. For instance, Mark apparently saw that a gospel must be 'a Passion story with an extended introduction', but he was probably the first to see this. It is possible, and often assumed, that because of its centrality and importance, Mark's unknown predecessors had seen only the necessity of writing a passion story by itself, without any introduction (although no such isolated passion narrative has survived). All else could be taught verbally, and so was not recorded in writing. In that case, Mark would have 'worked backwards' from this 'set story' to his full 'set gospel'. Apparently he did not see any reason to preface this gospel by birth or infancy narratives; but then neither did John, writing much later. For Mark, the 'good news of Jesus Christ' clearly began with the public preaching of Jesus (1:14) and culminated with the cross (ch. 15). The question of the somewhat abrupt ending of Mark's Gospel and the lack of resurrection appearances is more difficult, and discussion of it belongs more properly to the Commentary. But even assuming that originally the Gospel did end with 16:8 ('they were afraid'), it still would have contained an angelic proclamation of the resurrection (16:6), admittedly without a full resurrection appearance, although this was promised to come in Galilee later (16:7, *cf.* the promise of Jesus in 14:28). It may be that in the first Christian generation, witness to the resurrection was felt to be more appropriately delivered orally by the apostles themselves. They, after all, had been chosen to be the primary witnesses of that event (Acts 1:22; 2:32, and especially 10:41). Not every ordinary Christian had actually seen the risen Lord, even in the early days. Possibly not even Mark had done so himself, although Paul records a 'mass appearance' to five hundred disciples at once, perhaps in Galilee (1 Cor. 15:6).

As to the teachings of Jesus, Mark may well have omitted any extended record of them in his gospel because he assumed that they were already well known to the church of his day, in the form of the codes of instruction for catechumens, usually delivered orally in the ancient world, even if of a set form (see Carrington, and compare the very similar lists of 'family duties' to be found in most epistles). After all, in Mark's Gospel, we stand at the transition point between the oral and the written. It would be strange if at such a time all types of oral tradition were written down initially and simultaneously. We may hazard the guess that it was owing to the subsequent appearance of 'secret teachings' of Jesus, like the so-called 'Secret Gospel of Mark' (for which see Furnish, in *IDB Sup*. who considers it a version of Mark, not an earlier work), usually of a heretical if not a gnostic nature, that it was felt necessary to record in writing the genuine teachings of Jesus, as distinct from narrative, in a fuller, and therefore definitive, form. The second reason for the fuller nature of the record in later gospels is obvious: it was the drying-up of the apostolic sources of living oral tradition, and indeed their total unavailability in many Gentile churches overseas. Even those who do not accept 2 Peter as truly Petrine must agree that it states this point as a known principle (2 Pet. 1:15), and shows a clear knowledge of the need. If, however, the Petrine authorship of 2 Peter is accepted, then Mark's Gospel may be itself the first step in this codifying process.

As regards many other of the omitted topics, Mark may not have regarded them as relevant to his main missionary purpose. This is particularly true if his gospel was indeed somehow (directly or indirectly,) based on the preaching of Peter, which was presumably, in early days at least, preaching of an evangelistic nature. If Mark's Gospel is an 'evangelist's gospel', many questions resolve themselves at once. An evangelist is rarely a careful dogmatic theologian, although Paul is a striking exception. The task of the evangelist is to present the 'bones' of the gospel clearly and compellingly, not necessarily fully or in exact chronological sequence. An evangelist, in short, assumes much, without necessarily spelling it out in detail, an operation which would only confuse his audience at that stage. The time for teaching and theologizing would be later, as we can see from the other gospels.

Let us return to what we have postulated – that Mark is designed to give a simple factual account of such events as were necessary for his purpose, within the loosest possible of chronological and geographic frameworks. He knew that John's baptism, Jesus' temptation, and the call of the twelve came at the beginning of the ministry, and that the passion narrative came at the end; all else has been roughly grouped between them. He knew of a Galilean ministry, and of a Jerusalem ministry, culminating in the cross. This is not to say that in so doing, he has adopted a conscious position, in opposition to others; there were as yet no others to oppose and his choice is probably quite instinctive and unself-conscious, under (if we will) the Spirit's guidance. Indeed, it probably never entered his head to do otherwise. But, precisely because of this, Mark's evidence is invaluable. He gives us an insight into the still unreflective, perhaps at times almost simplistic, mind of the first generation of Christians, and, through that, into the oral tradition that reaches back to the days of the earthly ministry of Jesus. The same can be said, as Dodd acutely saw, of the outline of apostolic preaching recorded in the early chapters of Acts. Luke has faithfully preserved this in Acts, as he has preserved other early Jewish-Christian material in this section, although his own understanding of the gospel is much more developed, thanks to the theological depth brought out of the gospel by Paul. If Mark's Gospel was written by John Mark of Jerusalem, then of course he too cannot have been ignorant of Paul's theologizing, but, true to his editorial principles, it does not appear in his earlier material. Marxsen finds evidence of it in Mark's use of *euangelion*, 'gospel': others find it in his use of *lytron* 'ransom' (10:45): but there is no reason to suppose that both of these words do not go back to Jesus Himself.

If Mark restricted himself to using a few simple titles for Jesus, it may well have been because these were the only titles actually in use during the earthly ministry of Jesus. It is also possible that they were, in the main, the titles still used by the small 'ecclesial communities' (Belo) for which and from which Mark wrote, as we can see from the still simple though richer terminology of the early chapters of Acts. Later evangelists would, in their gospels, quite naturally use the later titles of Christ that were current in their own day, even when describing the life and times of Jesus, just as they would 'smooth out' what they regarded as careless theological statements made by Mark. Their usage may be slightly anachronistic, but it is very natural. There is therefore no problem here, nor any reason to criticize Mark on the grounds of a supposed 'limited Christology'.

If Mark speaks less directly of the Holy Spirit in personal terms than other gospels do, particularly in reference to the life of the disciples, it is because Mark's Gospel, in material if not in date of writing, is clearly 'pre-Pentecostal' as surely as John's

Gospel is 'post-Pentecostal'. Again, this is not to say that the later evangelists invented sayings about the Spirit that were of a 'post-Pentecostal' nature, and inserted them in their Gospels, in contrast to Mark. But it may well be that, in the light of Pentecost, later evangelists both understood and explained old sayings in post-Pentecostal language, so as to bring out their full meaning. There were doubtless many utterances of Jesus about the Spirit, the true meaning of which could be recognized only after Pentecost (cf. Jn. 7:39, and, in a different context, Jn. 12:16). Mark is certainly not culpable here; he is merely acting as a faithful transmitter of early material. After all, apart from John, none of the evangelists have much to say of the Spirit: the watershed in New Testament theology is Acts chapter 2, after which a rich vocabulary is developed, especially in the Pauline Epistles.

If the 'apocalypse' of Mark chapter 13 is general in expression and couched entirely in the language of Old Testament apocalyptic, that may well be because the material was originally handed down either in written form (cf. 13:14) or orally, in this format, a generation before its partial fulfilment in the Jewish War of AD 65–70.If this is so, it is reasonable to believe that it preserves the original discourse format used by Jesus (so originally Beasley-Murray, although Beasley-Murray has now modified his position considerably: see NTS, 29, July 1983, pp. 414–420, 'Second thoughts on the composition of Mark 13'). If Luke chapter 21 interprets the same symbolism in terms of Roman armies attacking Jerusalem, the reason may lie in Luke's desire to explain the meaning more clearly to the reader after the event (but see Morris). This probably springs from Luke's concern to set events in their historical context, not a major interest in Mark. If we like, we can assume that Jesus gave an 'inner explanation' of the apocalypse to the apostles either at the time or later, just as He gave an explanation of the parable of the sower to the disciples (4:10–20), although it is not necessary to assume this. In any case, it is certainly not fair to blame Mark for giving an 'attenuated version' of the apocalypse if his is in fact an accurate account of Jesus' actual teaching on the occasion.

Seen therefore in the light of Mark's concept of what a gospel was, most of the supposed difficulties disappear, especially if we allow that Mark was reproducing his material in its original form, not as interpreted by later and fuller Christian knowledge, and choosing his material selectively, to fit his particular restricted concerns.

V. ARAMAISMS OF MARK

In this context, 'Aramaisms' refers not to points of style or even possible ambiguities of translation, but the actual preservation in the Greek text of Mark's Gospel of Aramaic words and phrases such as *talitha cumi* (5:41), *ephphatha* (7:34), *rabbi* (9:5 NIV), *rabboni* (10:5 RV), *abba* (14:36), and the cry from the cross, *Eloi, Eloi, lama sabachthāni* (15:34). If Mark's is a missionary gospel written for Gentiles, circulating in some Gentile church centre such as Rome, is not this preservation of Aramaic words a contradiction in terms, even allowing that the words are also translated in every case? Of course, if we accept a direct Petrine source for Mark, we can argue that these words were vivid Petrine memories, carried over from the original Aramaic tradition into the later gospel in Greek. But even without this possible assumption, their preservation is explicable in terms of unself-conscious reproduction of words which already were 'fossilized' in the Greek tradition as it came to Mark. The evangelist, even if writing for Gentiles, was not at the stage of sophistication where he would have felt it necessary to remove uncouth 'foreign' words, as later evangelists might do, while he might well think it necessary to translate them. 'Foreign' they certainly might be to most of his readers, but not to him, and assuredly not to the first generation of Jewish Christians who had handed down the tradition to him. Some Hebrew or Aramaic words or phrases actually became so embedded in the substratum of the gospel that they passed into the ordinary vocabulary of worship of Gentile Christianity, as witness our use in worship of 'hallelujah' and 'amen' and 'hosanna' even today. Paul shows that 'abba' and 'maranatha' were equally familiar to Gentile Christians in his day (Rom. 8:15; 1 Cor. 16:22, see footnote in Bible text).

Mark's retention of these Aramaisms is therefore neither a contradiction in terms nor a conscious attempt to retain an archaic flavour (as perhaps it might have been had it appeared in Luke) but an unself-conscious retention of a genuinely early feature, whether derived directly from Peter himself or indirectly through the general tradition. It is therefore in this sense not incongruous with the whole nature of his gospel, but thoroughly consistent with it. It in no sense supports the theory, however, that an earlier draft of Mark's Gospel was written in Aramaic, although it is reasonable to suppose that much, if not all, of Jesus' teaching had been given originally in Aramaic, and that there had at least been cycles of Aramaic oral tradition in Palestine itself, certainly in Galilee and perhaps in Jerusalem. If Mark had been a 'translated gospel', then these phrases too would surely have been translated initially into Greek, like all the rest, for (with the possible exception of the cry from the cross) they have no special theological importance or interest. In fact, it is hard to see any logical reason why they were specially preserved in Aramaic rather than a dozen other sayings, delivered in similar circumstances; but, as has been said, the indiscriminate (almost chance) nature of the memories is typical of genuine oral tradition in all languages. Once again, the very conservatism and simplicity of Mark's Gospel is the strongest guarantee of the early nature of its material, and therefore presumably of its early date of writing.

VI. WHO WAS JESUS, ACCORDING TO MARK?

For the purpose of this discussion, we shall simply take the gospel at its face value, as it lies before us, as indeed all its early readers would have had to do, without going behind the text, and without the benefit of later theological definition.

Let us suppose that we are the first readers of Mark, and that we have no other written sources of Christian knowledge about Jesus open to us apart from perhaps a passion story and possibly a few collections of sayings or miracles. Our church might possibly have received an early Pauline epistle, but that is not likely, and, even if we had, it would have told us very little of the earthly life of Jesus. To restrict ourselves to the gospel alone may well be an unfair limitation, for we would first have come into contact with a community of believers in Jesus. Otherwise we would scarcely have been reading the gospel in the first place, or, more probably, hearing it read to us, for 'private copies' would have existed only for very wealthy people (Lk. 1:3). Most Christians would have to depend upon a 'church copy'. Indeed, it is most likely that some other Christian would have introduced the gospel to us (*cf.* Lk. 1:3–4). So in fact we would be reading the gospel within the broad continuum of early Christian tradition, which is for us today contained in writing in the New Testament. Obviously, not all of this additional material would be available to the first-century enquirer, but parts of it would be known, whether orally or in writing. Admittedly, several of the Pauline epistles, and perhaps the Book of Acts already existed, but it is unlikely that they circulated widely so early. Let us therefore approach the question on the basis of Mark's Gospel alone, as his first readers probably did. The answer will be both interesting and revealing, if we still think that Mark's Gospel contains a 'minimal' presentation of Christianity. Theological definition may well be lacking as yet, but all the raw bones of Christology are present already, as we can see by examining even the limited number of titles which Mark applies to Jesus in the gospel.

Mark begins by describing his book as 'the Good News about Jesus *Christ*, the *Son of God*' (1:1). We may therefore take '*Christ*' or '*Messiah*' as the first title for examination. Although '*Christ*' does not have the definite article before it here, nevertheless in spite of that, it does not yet seem to have become merely a personal name or surname (as it virtually becomes in the Epistles). It is therefore still a title, and so, even without the article, equivalent to the Hebrew 'Messiah', 'God's Anointed', whether or not Mark's Gentile readers understood the full meaning of this word. Indeed, it was probably an early Gentile failure to understand the distinctively Jewish meaning of the title 'Christ' that led to its later use as a virtual synonym (if not an honorific) for 'Jesus'. It is true that Jesus is never called 'Christ' during the main narrative of Mark, a fact that has led to the hypothesis of the 'messianic secret', whether in its extreme form (as that of Wrede) or in more moderate modern forms. It seems as if Jesus, before passion week, deliberately avoided using this title of

61

Himself or allowing others to use it of Him. Nevertheless, Jesus accepts the title of Christ-Messiah when Peter gives it to Him (8:29), even if He immediately orders His disciples not to tell others. So Jesus in Mark is the Messiah, however this term is to be understood. Mark's Gospel certainly suggests that 'Messiah' is to be understood in a very different sense from the popular 'triumphalist' view of nationalistic Judaism, a view which has been recently challenged, but on seemingly inadequate grounds. Jesus, in fact, was not to be a political Messiah at all, though a claim to be 'the Messiah' was one of the incriminating semi-political charges brought forward at the trial of Jesus by the high priest (14:61). The title 'Son of David' may also imply messiahship (10:47), as mentioned below, although not necessarily or universally so. Although Jesus does not actually say that the Messiah must suffer, yet, as soon as Jesus is hailed by Peter as the Christ (8:29), He immediately tells His disciples of His coming rejection, death and rising again (8:31), using the term 'Son of Man' (not Messiah) to describe Himself in this context. But this Messiah is also 'the Son of the Blessed One' (14:61) and 'the King of Israel' (15:32), possessed of supernatural powers (see 13:21–22), for whose coming at the end of time all wait (13:5–6, 21–22), so there is always a certain ambiguity in this title, between suffering and glory.

The phrase '*Son of God*' is omitted by some manuscripts in 1:1, but, even if it ought to be omitted here, it makes little difference, for the title is given to Jesus later in the gospel (*e.g.* 5:7, and *cf.* 1:24 'God's Holy One'), culminating in the declaration by the Gentile centurion at the cross (15:39), in many ways the 'high point' of this 'gospel for the Gentiles'. Whatever the centurion himself meant by this confession, it is clear that Mark understood it in the fullest theological sense. 'Son of God' is the title conferred on Jesus by the voice from heaven, both at baptism (1:11) and at transfiguration (9:7). It is also the title uttered by the demon-possessed (3:11), who recognize the true nature of the Messiah, even if they are forbidden by Jesus to reveal it (3:12). It is the title put forward as a theological trap by the high priest at the trial of Jesus (14:61), and accepted by Jesus as true (14:62), though He must have known that such acceptance would bring an instant charge of blasphemy (14:64), as indeed it did. Also, while in 13:32 Jesus confesses His own ignorance of the exact time of the end of the age, yet the clear juxtaposition in this verse of the words 'the Son' and 'the Father' points to this same unique relationship of sonship with God. No Jew would ever have understood 'Son of God' in the loose Hellenistic sense of 'semi-divine human' (*theios anēr*), as sometimes claimed. A Jew might have thought of the term as applying to Israel (Ex. 4:22), or to Israel's king (Ps. 2:7), or to angelic beings (Jb. 1:6), but, as applied to Jesus, in Mark's Gospel, it is obvious that the title goes far beyond this, and conveys full divine status. Judaism did not apparently use 'Son of God' as a title for the Messiah: this is a distinctively Christian usage (see Morris, *New Testament Theology*, page 101).

Son of man: This is not the place to enter into lengthy discussions about the antecedents of this term, for which Cullmann and others may be consulted. Initially we may note, with many commentators, that there seem to be three distinct usages known to the early Christians, whatever their origins. The first is that of an apocalyptic figure, returning at the end of time: the second is a suffering figure: the third is purely descriptive of Jesus Himself. Some scholars have tried to separate these figures, especially the first, from the historic figure of Jesus. Here we are concerned with the narrower question of actual usage within the gospel, and what impression a reader or hearer would gain from that alone, since in Mark, 'Son of man' is the only title that Jesus actually employs of Himself. It is therefore all the more reasonable (and doubtless historically correct) that there is no reference to anybody else using it of Him in the gospels (see, however, Acts 7:56). But this very usage of 'Son of man' by Jesus as a self-description poses a difficulty for us. When Jesus says that 'the Son of man' must suffer, die and be raised from the dead (8:31 *etc.*), does He mean that death and resurrection are inherent in the actual concept of 'Son of man', or simply that He, Jesus, who calls Himself the Son of man, must die and rise? As there is no hint in the Jewish background that a 'Son of man' was ever previously thought of in terms of suffering, the second alternative must be correct. In that case, we must assume that the thought of suffering and subsequent vindication springs rather from the 'suffering Servant' concept, which will be treated separately. When Jesus speaks of the Son of man as having power to forgive sins on earth (2:10) or as being Lord of the Sabbath (2:28), the assumption is therefore that He possesses these powers in His own person, rather than as Son of man, since again there is no Jewish evidence that the Son of man was ever regarded as having such powers.

There is of course the possibility that 'Son of man' simply means 'human' in general, and that Jesus is a representative human, as though He said 'humanity has power to forgive sins', and 'humanity is master of the Sabbath'. This, however, seems banal, unless the reference is again strictly to Himself, as humanity's unique representative. Admittedly, this understanding of the phrase would do more justice to its Semitic background, which seems to support the general meaning rather than a specific one.

There remains a whole class of passages in Mark where the Son of man is portrayed as coming with power and glory, to be God's agent in judging the earth. This is clearly derived directly from Daniel 7:13, quite irrespective of any further inter-testamental developments of thought on the subject. 'Son of man' here denotes a supernatural and mysterious figure (whether individual or collective), in special relationship to God, whose agent He is. Whatever of Daniel or other literature, there is no hint in Mark that the phrase 'Son of man' is a collective term, rather than an individual figure. But it is this Son of man, coming with the angels and in all the Father's glory, who will be ashamed on the last day to acknowledge those who were ashamed of Jesus in this life (8:38). It seems therefore perverse, in such a close-knit context, to attempt to separate the two figures of 'Jesus' and 'Son of man' here, especially as elsewhere in Mark 'Son of man' is such a consistently self-chosen title for Jesus. If Jesus is the 'Son of man' who will rise from the dead (9:9), then He must also be the 'Son of man' who will come in glory in the clouds, in all the terrors of the last day (13:26), where the resemblance to Daniel is particularly close, and whose angels will gather His chosen people from the four quarters. In view of the direct personal reference by Jesus in 13:6 to those who will come 'using my name', any separation into two separate figures is again perverse. It is this Son of man whom the corrupt high priests will see enthroned and vindicated at God's right hand (14:62). This is a highly significant passage, for 'Son of man' is set in the context of the two other titles 'Messiah' and 'Son of God'. Therefore we are justified in seeing in this title 'Son of man' a supernatural connotation, firmly predicated of Jesus by Mark. While we cannot claim a specifically divine sense for the title in itself, yet this 'Son of man' stands in a peculiarly close relationship to the 'Ancient One' (Dn. 7:13) in Daniel, and therefore presumably in Mark too.

Son of David: to the Jews, this seems to have been in the main a Messianic title, though not necessarily involving more than earthly kingship. When a blind beggar uses it of Jesus in Mark's Gospel, we cannot be sure of its force for the beggar, but we can be sure of its force for Mark (10:47). If the crowds used it at the triumphal entry (11:9), it certainly has its full sense, for the Messiah was specifically connected, in Hebrew thought, with the introduction of God's kingdom, which was to be a restored Davidic kingdom. But although Matthew has 'Son of David' here (Mt. 21:9), Mark does not actually make the attribution directly (11:10). The Jews may have thought only of an earthly and human Son of David, but, to Jesus, the position as 'Son of David' clearly involved supernatural status, as we can see from the famous controversy story (12:35–37), and was specifically equated by Him with that of Messiah. This evidence is all the more compelling, since the subject was deliberately introduced by Jesus on this occasion: it did not simply arise in controversy, nor was it introduced as a 'trick question' by His enemies. It was therefore a point of importance which He wished to make, to correct their limited and humanistic understanding of the title 'Son of David'.

Servant: while in Mark's Gospel Jesus does not ever actually call Himself 'the Servant' in the exact sense of Isaiah 52:13, He does say that the Son of man has come to serve, and to give up His life as a ransom for many (10:45). This is clearly a double self-identification with the Servant of the servant songs, as portrayed in Isaiah 53:10–11 (verse 10, the reference to giving of life for others: verse 11, references to both the 'servant' and the 'many'). While the Servant is a mysterious figure, and certainly

65

a divine agent, there is no suggestion in Isaiah of the divinity of the Servant himself, nor indeed is it always clear whether the Servant is seen as an individual or as a collective figure. Since in Mark, however, Jesus takes the suffering and triumphs predicted of the Servant in Isaiah, and uses them to explain the work of the Messiah (8:31), whom He certainly sees as a divine individual (12:37), and since He accepts this title for Himself, the gap is bridged.

This brief study of the titles of Jesus in Mark leaves us with a clear picture of Jesus as a supernatural figure, although Mark is not interested in how such a figure came into our world, nor does Mark speculate about any pre-existence. This depiction as supernatural is all the more remarkable in view of Mark's simultaneous picture of Jesus as an intensely human figure, with fully human emotions (*e.g.* 14:33–34). If John the Baptist is seen by Mark to be the messenger and forerunner prophesied by Isaiah (Mk. 1:2–3), then Jesus must be directly equated with God, for what was originally described by Isaiah as the coming of Yahweh is in Mark transferred to the coming of Jesus. In conformity with this, John describes Jesus as 'one more powerful than I' (1:7), and claims, prophet though he is, to be unworthy to do Him even the slave's service of undoing His sandals. While not necessarily indicating divine status, this certainly points to it. The so-called 'nature miracles', such as the calming of the storm (4:41) and the walking on the water (6:48), confirm this divine status, since they show Jesus acting as the Creator-God. Perhaps the same could be said of the feeding of the five thousand (6:30–44) and of the four thousand (8:1–10), for it was God's task (not that of Moses), to feed His people with bread in the desert (Ps. 78:20). As far as His enemies were concerned, Jesus' claim to forgive sins (2:7), to override the Sabbath (2:28; 3:4), and to be the Messiah and God's Son (14:61–62) were quite sufficient to indicate that Jesus claimed to be divine. The fact that they rejected these claims so vehemently is the strongest proof that they actually involved a claim to deity. They would never have dared to invent such a 'blasphemous' claim, though they were ready enough to seize on it and use it for their own purposes.

In no sense therefore can Mark be accused of holding a defective Christology, although it may well still be an unreflective

Christology. Perhaps deep theological reflection would come only with Paul or John. Mark's theology may have been influenced by Paul (although this is disputed), who was writing within twenty years of the crucifixion, and therefore presumably before Mark, but Mark's 'raw material' certainly was not influenced, and he was preserving it faithfully.

VII. WHAT WAS THE GOOD NEWS OF THE KINGDOM?

John the Baptist, whose witness is recorded briefly in Mark's Gospel, sees the work of Jesus as springing directly from His person and position (1:7) and defines it as the giving of the Spirit, which is described under the metaphor of a 'baptism' (1:8). It seems perverse to understand (with Brown) this 'baptism with the Spirit' as referring to Jesus' works of love and power towards the needy, although of course they (like all his words and works), were done in the power of the Spirit. Since this metaphor of 'baptizing with the Spirit' is used in the context of John's baptism, which accompanied the preaching of repentance with a view to forgiveness (1:4), Jesus' work must also have been seen in a similar context of repentance and forgiveness of sins. In Mark, this phrase 'baptism with the Spirit' is not used to describe any higher level of spiritual life, but the commencement of spiritual life in reality, as opposed to the symbolism of John's baptism. Certainly both these aspects are mentioned repeatedly elsewhere in Mark as part of the message of Jesus (1:15 and 2:5).

The major task of Jesus, and indeed His self-declared calling, was to proclaim the good news of the near approach (some would say: the arrival), of God's rule (1:14–15, 38), a concept which is not further defined in Mark, presumably because its content was already familiar from the Old Testament to all his original hearers. The response demanded on the part of all was repentance and belief in the good news (1:15), which meant belief in Jesus, and a following of Him (1:17). He taught with a ring of authority (1:22); He expelled demons at a word (1:27); He healed the sick (1:31); He cleansed the leper (1:42); He raised the dead (5:42), all as signs of the coming of the kingdom and the defeat of Satan (3:27). To the horror of the orthodox, Jesus forgave sins (2:7), indeed He maintained that he had come to call sinners, not the righteous (2:17). Presumably, this is all part of the 'good news' of the kingdom that He proclaimed. He proclaimed that to do God's will created the closest possible of relationships, far surpassing ties of family and blood (3:35). He therefore summoned all people to do this will of God, as subjects of God's kingdom. Although this 'rule of God' is nowhere defined in Mark, it is described in metaphors. The kingdom grows slowly, silently, imperceptibly, as a crop grows in a field, until the harvest is ready for reaping (4:26–29). It seems from the context that the task of Jesus, in preaching the kingdom, is only to sow the seed (4:14). It will be for God to reap the harvest at the end of all time (4:29). For Mark, therefore, this rule of God is at one and the same time already present in Jesus and in those who respond to Him, and yet in another sense it is still future, to be brought in by God. To that extent, the kingdom is eschatological and apocalyptic (as in Revelation): it will never be fully realized in this world, although some of its fruits and signs may be seen and enjoyed already. All this is part of the good news of the kingdom.

There is, however, a cost involved for Jesus, in order to make the good news of the kingdom available to all. When Peter greets Him as Messiah (8:29), a title which Jesus accepts, He at once begins to tell His disciples of the divine inevitability of His rejection, death and rising from the dead (8:31). This is clearly shown in Mark to be God's path for Jesus, for although the exact reason for it is not made plain here, a hint will be given in the ransom metaphor used later (10:45), for Christ's death is the ransom price to redeem God's people. That it is not an easy path for Him to tread is shown by His words to James and John (10:38) and by His prayer in Gethsemane (14:36). But it is only in the context of this prophecy of His death and rising again (8:31) that He tells his followers of the coming of God's kingdom 'with power' (9:1). Therefore it is not unfair to say that, in Mark, the purpose of the death of Jesus is to introduce God's rule 'with power', and that this reign can be introduced only by the path to the cross.

It is hard to see how this thought of the coming kingdom can

be separated from the thought of the covenant that will introduce the kingdom. We may therefore compare 14:24, where
Jesus, at the last supper, equates His coming death with the
sealing of this covenant (whether or not the manuscripts read
'new' makes little difference), by the usual covenant sacrifice
with its sacrificial blood. This connection is confirmed by the
reference to the drinking of wine in God's coming kingdom
(14:25), and may also link with the bitter play on the words
'King of the Jews' (15:2, 18 and 26). 'King of the Jews' itself is of
course a Gentile and political term. Jews themselves, even if
they rejected the claim in the case of Jesus, would use the
religious term instead, 'King of Israel' (15:32). The death of Jesus
on the cross must therefore be the way in which he is to 'give his
life a ransom for many' (10:45), since at the last supper (14:24)
Jesus describes his blood as 'shed for many', which is yet
another reference to the task of the servant in Isaiah (53:11–12).
However little of this argument a Gentile would understand, the
connection between forgiveness of sins and the death of Jesus is
clear. As goal of the good news, Jesus in Mark talks of 'entering
into life' (9:43): he equates this with 'entering into the kingdom
of God' (9:47). This is in contradistinction to 'entering Gehenna'
(9:43), with its vivid picture of the traditional rubbish dump of
Jerusalem (9:44), an interpretation which, although recently
challenged, still seems valid. This 'life' of which Jesus here
speaks, must be, from the context, the life of the coming age; it
is the 'eternal life' which the rich man is seeking in vain (10:17).
He goes away sadly from Jesus (10:22) and so goes away from
eternal life, for he has failed to enter the kingdom of God, and is
an instance of the difficulty that a rich man has in entering the
kingdom (10:23, 25). But the disciples who obey Jesus, and leave
all for His sake, will have 'treasure in heaven' (10:21) and 'eternal
life' (10:30). Jesus therefore came to bring eternal life, the life of
the age to come. This life is obtained by repentance, obedience
and belief in Him, though the exact nature of the connection
between this belief and the death of Jesus is not made explicit in
detail by Mark. That, after all, is not his immediate aim as an
evangelist.

This is the 'good news' of a missionary gospel, as preached to
early Gentile listeners: it will be left to Paul and a later Christian

generation to theologize and explain it. For an evangelist, it is sufficient that he proclaims the gospel message, and sees the response.

PREACHING THE GOOD NEWS

We have seen that Mark calls his book 'Jesus' good news' (1:1), which can mean both 'the good news about Jesus' (or 'consisting of Jesus'), and 'the good news preached by Jesus'. In a sense therefore the whole gospel is a preaching of this good news by word and deed. The task of Jesus as already mentioned was to proclaim this good news (1:14), and to call men and women to repentance and belief in it, which involves also belief in Him (1:15). He must preach the good news as widely as possible (1:38); indeed, that was His expressed aim and whole purpose. Jesus will heal, exorcize, feed, as signs of the kingdom and proofs of authority, but also He will teach and preach this message (2:2). We have seen that it is a message concerned with the forgiveness of sins (2:5); it is addressed to confessedly sinful, not self-righteous, people (2:17); and it issues in a call to repent and follow Jesus (2:14). But it is not Jesus alone who preaches this message. He appoints the twelve specifically to do the same task (3:14). Like Him, they are to expel demons and to heal sickness as well as preaching (3:15). Their preaching, like His, was therefore to have the ring of authority (1:27), an authority coming, in their case, from their calling by Christ (3:14–15), just as Christ's authority comes from God's appointment of Him (implicit in 11:30). As to the scope of the good news, Jesus initially restricts the scope of preaching to Israel, God's children (7:27), but He does not on that account refuse to meet the need of a Gentile woman (7:30). Others besides His own disciples may show the powers of the kingdom in their proclamation of the name of Jesus (9:38); they must not be hindered or stopped (9:39). To leave everything for Jesus' sake is also to leave it for the sake of the good news, so closely are Christ and the gospel connected (10:29). The spreading of the good news demands costly sacrifice, calling for the abandonment of one's nearest and dearest (10:29), but this sacrifice will be rewarded abundantly even in this present age, and in the age to come it will be requited with eternal life (10:30). Whoever loses life, for the sake of Jesus and for the sake of the good news (again, the two concepts are inextricably bound together), will 'save' it (8:35). At the very heart of Mark's Gospel therefore stands the proclamation of the good news. There is no more important or more urgent task; and it warrants any sacrifice on our part, as it warranted any sacrifice on the part of Christ. The cross, after all, was the price of preaching the gospel for him: the price will not be any less for us (10:39).

The appointment of the twelve to preach the good news is in 3:13–15: later in Mark, the specifics of their mission are set out in more detail (6:7–13). They are to preach a change of heart, revulsion from sin, and turning to God (6:12), all topics that are familiar from the prophetic message of the Old Testament. They, like Jesus, will show outward signs of the powers of the kingdom by exorcising and healing (6:13). So weighty is their good news that rejection of it is to be marked by the semi-sacramental act of shaking off the dust of the unrepentant place (6:11). This means that the proclaimer of the good news is no longer responsible for the coming judgment which repentance and response would have averted. Rejection of the good news is therefore in itself a self-condemnation, for it is a rejection of Christ Himself, by the rejection of His messengers (9:37).

There is, however, clearly envisaged by Jesus a time when the good news must be proclaimed, not merely to Israel but also to 'all the nations' (13:10). This too will cost the disciples dearly (13:9–13) with flogging, persecution and arrest. But this preaching will be done in the power of the Spirit (13:11), and it will be one of the signs of the last days, before the coming of the Son of man (13:26). Not only so, but, wherever the good news is proclaimed in all the world, the sacrificial gift of the woman of Bethany will be remembered (14:9). As this act of hers is seen as a symbolic pre-enactment of the anointing and burial of the body of Jesus (14:8), it is clear that the good news must involve at its heart the story of the death of Jesus. But there is another integral part of the good news, mentioned in all three passion predictions (8:31, 9:31 and 10:34), although Mark's Gospel contains no actual accounts of its fulfilment. It is the news of the

71

rising of Jesus from the dead, to which an angel bears witness
(16:4–6), with the promise of a meeting with the risen Lord in
Galilee. This is the good news which the women are bidden to
carry to Peter and the others (16:7), although Mark, in his
typically blunt, truthful way, shows that they failed to do so
initially through fear or awe (16:8). There is therefore no need
for Mark's Gospel to include a separate account of a final 'great
commission' delivered by Jesus to the disciples as a culmination
of the gospel, as in Matthew (Mt. 28:18–19), although such a
commission may possibly have formed part of a now lost
original ending, and was soon added to Mark by an early editor
(16:15). The command to preach the gospel in all the world is
implicit in the whole theology of Mark and has indeed already
been made abundantly explicit (13:10, 14:9). That is why Mark is
first and foremost a missionary gospel, with a message for us
today: to him, Christianity is above all the good news about
Jesus Christ, which must be shared with all.

VIII. IS ROME THE BACKGROUND?

It is necessary to ask this question, because many modern commentaries, ranging from the scholarly to the popular, explain
detailed points in the gospel with reference to the presumed
'real life' situation in Rome and the Roman church, in the first
half of the first Christian centuries (see Lane and Minear). Some
commentators, with less likelihood, had seen this background
as being in Galilee (Marxsen), Antioch, Alexandria or elsewhere. Sometimes these explanations are helpful; always they
are interesting; but is the basic assumption well founded? And is
it necessary to prove this or any other theory to produce satisfactory exegesis? Can the same results be obtained by a more
general hypothesis, or do they stand or fall with one particular
hypothesis? The question has become much more important for
us than for our predecessors, in that every incident and each
gospel is now seen against its assumed 'real life situation', in
which and for which it was first preserved and told (or even
created, in the views of extreme liberal scholarship). This 'real
life situation' is then, in its turn, often invoked as the reason for

presumed changes in the form or content of the event or saying, as the case may be. If this is legitimate (for it may be only a circular argument), to establish the original situation is all-important: but can we really do it with any certainty? In the case of a New Testament letter, we have some hope, for we have clues, if not direct attribution. What of a gospel, particularly if it is a 'first gospel', and we have therefore no earlier material with which to compare it?

At first sight, however strange it seems, this task looks more promising in the case of Mark than of the other gospels. Tradition is consistent that the gospel was produced 'in the area of Italy', usually specified as Rome, for we have seen that the variant tradition of Alexandria as background is later, and has a ready explanation. Mark's Gospel certainly must have been adopted at an early stage by some 'great church' or it would neither have survived nor become the basis for other gospels, as it evidently did. As to apostolic source, tradition, if it speaks at all, mentions Peter. We may feel that there is inadequate solid evidence to support this tradition, but, if we take it at its face value, it is at least highly probable that Peter was at Rome towards the end of his life (1 Pet. 5:13) and, from the same verse almost certain that John Mark was there also (*cf.* 2 Tim. 4:11). Of course there is even better evidence for Peter being at Jerusalem (Acts chs'. 1–6) and Antioch (Gal. 2:11), also 'great churches'. We have seen that two reiterated themes of Mark's Gospel, that of the persecution of Christians and that of betrayal of the Lord (whether repented of later, as in the case of Peter, or final, as that of Judas), would suit this particular Roman background. Wherever else in the Empire there was or was not persecution, there was sure to be persecution at Rome, since the church was directly under the eye of the emperor, and also was of such a size as to attract attention.

Linguistically, all we can say is that the Greek of Mark does contain some Latinisms but, in the judgment of most competent scholars, these are no more than might appear in the 'legionary Greek' anywhere in the Roman Empire, particularly in the great cities of its western or Mediterranean half (Funk). Arguments as to whether certain Roman coins (like the *kodrantes* of 12:42) ever circulated or were known in the eastern part of the Empire are not really compelling in themselves. For a full study of the so called 'Latinisms' of Mark, see Lane, or any other of the longer commentaries.

At this point, frustratingly, the trail ends; and, if we are honest, we shall have to say that while the road may lead to Rome, again it may not. All we can safely say is that the gospel was produced in some such place as Rome, and therefore presumably with the needs of some such place in mind. After all, others, on exactly the same biblical evidence, can argue just as strongly for Galilee as the gospel's place of origin; if such divergent views are possible, then the evidence may not be as compelling as we think. True, Mark translates any Aramaic phrases which he preserves, and explains any Jewish customs: but this indicates only a Gentile, not necessarily a Roman, audience.

Externally, if Peter was a source (even indirectly) then he was a well-known gospel preacher. Rome was certainly a major centre of such evangelistic outreach, as well as being the place where Peter traditionally spent his latter years. If Mark was writing a missionary gospel for Gentiles, he could hardly have written it in a more suitable place. But once again we must leave the question of place of origin as 'not proven', attractive though the hypothesis of a Roman background is: we must not make our exegesis in any way dependent on it, while we may cautiously use it for illustration.

IX. THE STATUS OF WOMEN

Since the position of women in the New Testament is coming under close scrutiny today, we should examine the evidence of Mark, the earliest Christian gospel. His evidence will be all the more valuable, since it is not a question to which he expressly addressed himself, so that the evidence is not contrived or forced. What then does Jesus say about women, as recorded in Mark, for we are not merely interested in Mark's views on the subject?

Although Mark has no account of the annunciation, the virgin birth, or the infancy stories, and therefore says next to nothing about Mary, the Lord's mother, who is indeed named only once in the gospel (6:3), and although he does not show Luke's deep concern for women, that is not to say that women play a small part in the gospel. For instance, the gospel begins with an account of the healing of Simon Peter's mother-in-law (1:31), while it ends with the appearance to a group of women of the angel telling of the resurrection of Jesus (16:6), and there are numerous incidents recorded in between where women play a major role.

There is therefore a naturalness and 'mutuality' in the relationship between the sexes as depicted in Mark that goes far beyond both the problems and solutions of our self-conscious modern world. For example, in Mark, Jesus admittedly chose twelve named men as His associates (3:14), but he also had a group of close women followers, several of whom are named in Mark – Mary Magdalene, Mary, mother of James and Joses, and Salome, for instance (15:40; 15:47; 16:1). Even this inclusion of women was unusual in the ancient world, not to mention first-century Judaism. True, Jesus in Mark rejected a claim made on Him by Mary because it was based purely on their natural relationship (3:33), but He also proclaimed that those who did God's will were as mother and sister and brother to Him (3:35), where the different words are equally chosen to denote, by metaphor, the closest of relationships.

It was for a young girl, daughter of Jairus, that Jesus performed His first recorded miracle of raising from the dead (5:23): it was on the way to the house of Jairus to perform it that He healed another woman of a long-standing haemorrhage (5:29). This whole passage is full of a delicacy fully equal to that of Luke: the embarrassed woman is addressed as 'daughter' (5:34), the girl as 'talitha', 'child' (5:41). The sick woman's saving faith is singled out by Jesus for praise (5:34): the girl's mother is specifically mentioned by Mark as being called in, along with the father Jairus, to witness the resurrection of her daughter (5:40). This too shows a thoughtfulness and consideration for women rarely seen in the ancient world, although Mark typically does not comment on it, but merely records it.

Jesus is, with complete naturalness, identified by the unbelieving Galileans as 'Mary's son'. There is no need to assume a sneering reference here to the virgin birth: if anything, it probably refers only to her position as a widowed mother. It is noted equally naturally that His sisters, like His brothers, are still living nearby (6:3). True, two women, Herodias and her daughter, are recorded in Mark as being the direct cause of John the Baptist's death (6:24), yet the same Mark also records that it was a Phoenician woman who won the Lord's special commendation for her humility and faith in seeking healing for her daughter (7:29).This is typical of Mark: he suppresses neither good nor bad side, in an attempt to make a point, as we might be tempted to do in such circumstances.

No-one ever spoke more strongly of the divine permanence of the marriage bond than Jesus did: He saw woman, equally with man, as being God's creation (10:6), and demanded that women, just as much as men, should be protected in marriage, disagreeing with the current interpretation of the law of Moses (10:11), whereby many rabbis allowed a husband to divorce his wife on the most trivial of pretexts. True, on the same theological grounds, He also forbade divorce and remarriage as sternly to women as to men (10:11–12): men, like women, were to be protected. That, after all, is the other side of 'mutuality'. Some commentators (see Anderson) claim that women did not have this assumed legal right to divorce their husbands under Jewish law at the time, but they certainly had it under Graeco-Roman law, and some may well have used it. Mark, after all, was writing a gospel for Gentile converts, and Jesus was teaching in a Palestine where not all were orthodox Jews, especially in Galilee, with its many Gentile inhabitants.

Jesus was indignant when the disciples began to rebuke and drive away the mothers who brought their children to Him for blessing (10:14). He could fully understand the desire of mothers to obtain blessing for their children, even if to the apostles the whole thing seemed a waste of the Lord's time on those whom they felt to be unimportant.

With true insight, Jesus saw the giving up of sisters, mother or wife as being as great a sacrifice for the kingdom as giving up brothers or father (10:29): neither is put at a higher level than the others. When the Sadducees came to Jesus with their coarse illustration about the woman married seven times, a story designed to pour scorn on the doctrine of the resurrection, the Lord brushed it away in one quiet sentence (12:25) which did not degrade women in the process.

Mark records that the chief crime of the hypocritical scribes, according to Jesus, was to cheat widows of their livelihood (12:40), while a poverty-stricken widow's gift to the temple treasure was made by Him a lesson to all (12:43). Jesus had a special and typical concern for those mothers with young children who would be living in the days of the eschatological woes (13:17), a fact which Mark takes the trouble to make clear.

It was a woman who anointed Jesus' head with costly ointment at the meal held in Simon the leper's house (14:3), a sacrifice for which, though criticized by others, she was defended by Christ (14:6). It was therefore a woman, more than any other, who understood the secret of His coming death and burial (14:8); and so it was a woman who would be remembered for her insight of love wherever in later days the gospel was preached throughout the world (14:9).

When all Christ's other followers had fled from the cross, Mark makes plain that women disciples still stood watching, even if it was at a distance, as Asian culture demanded (15:40). These included not only the small 'named group' of close women disciples (15:40), but the far larger 'anonymous group' who had also followed Jesus from Galilee. Indeed, it is from this passage in Mark that we learn that this group had actually supported Jesus and His apostles, doubtless financially as well as otherwise (15:41). Women disciples were therefore to be among the witnesses of the death of Christ (15:40), and of His entombment (15:47): notice that, as Jewish law demanded, there were at least two witnesses recorded in either case, even if Jewish law would not accept the evidence of women.

So, fittingly, on the resurrection morning, as already mentioned, it was to a group of women bringing spices to the tomb (16:1) that the angel appeared, bringing the first news of the resurrection of Jesus (16:6). It was therefore to these same women that the first preaching of the resurrection message was entrusted (16:7), although Mark's Gospel breaks off tantalizingly, if honestly, with the words 'they said nothing to anyone, for they were afraid' (16:8). But even if they were afraid, and unable to grasp and share the good news at first, that is after all just what their brothers were to do initially, as recorded in the other gospels (Luke 24:41).

Herein is the whole strength of Mark, where women take their natural place as followers of Jesus alongside men, with no special comment, in this the first story of Jesus and His earliest disciples. Mark is sometimes described as a 'primitive' gospel, but this attitude shows true Christian maturity and naturalness of approach, to which it is hard to feel that we have attained today, in spite of all our artificial striving for it. Perhaps the simplicity of the Spirit brings more balance than all the complicated theological argument on either side, with their 'special pleading', that we so often hear today.

X. SIGNS AND WONDERS

In view of present interest in 'signs and wonders', often seen today as an essential ongoing feature of the life of the Spirit within the church, and a particular interest in the place of such manifestations in evangelism, whether New Testament or modern, it may be relevant to study the part played by signs and wonders in the ministry of Jesus as recorded in Mark's Gospel. Having done that, some tentative conclusions will emerge, though it should be emphasized that they will be valid only for Mark's Gospel, not necessarily for the rest of the New Testament or for us today. Unfortunately this is not a topic to which any of the biblical commentators have as yet seriously addressed themselves: more popular studies will be found in Wimber and Brown, not of course dealing exclusively with Mark.

It is probably unfair to adduce as 'signs' in this sense either the baptismal experiences of Jesus (the dove and the voice, 1:10–11) or the ministry to Jesus by angels in the desert during His temptations (1:13), since, however real as signs, they seem to have been personal and private experiences, either totally unwitnessed by others, in the case of the temptations, or only witnessed by John, in the case of the baptism. The experience of vision and voice at the transfiguration (9:4–7) is clearly different, in that it was witnessed by the three apostles as well: but they were strictly forbidden to speak of it until after Christ's resurrection (9:9). Already, some reserve in the use of signs appears.

But the expulsion of the evil spirit in 1:26 was witnessed by a whole synagogue, and became the subject of widespread comment (1:27), so it clearly falls into a different category, that of open signs. It is important to note that, in this initial case, teaching by Jesus occurred before the miracle was performed (1:21) and this was recognized as being teaching delivered with a new note of authority (1:22). Indeed, the actual miracle itself seems to be mainly regarded as an outward sign and proof of the authority of his teaching (1:27). This may represent a general principle, and indeed account for the common use of the word 'sign' to describe such deeds. The 'miracles' therefore do not stand in isolation or in their own right; they are not unexplained magical acts, for they always point beyond themselves to Jesus.

The healing of Simon's mother-in-law (1:13) is a miracle done for those who were already believers in Jesus and in response to a request. The evening healings (1:32–34) are on a far wider scale, while we have not enough material to answer questions as to whether they were in response to faith: but, without faith, would the people have come for healing at all? All we are told is that Jesus would not accept evidence as to His divine nature given by demonic sources during exorcisms (1:34), and that He retreated afterwards to prayer (1:35). Indeed He retreated at once to other parts of Galilee (1:38), when Peter told Him that everybody was looking for Him, presumably because of His new-found fame as a 'spiritual healer' (1:37).

Certainly we can say on the basis of this early passage that, while Jesus undoubtedly had the power to heal and exorcise, as even His enemies admitted (3:22), and while (so far as we know) He never turned away any who came to Him for healing, He did not wish to be widely known as a mere healer. Indeed, He regarded widespread preaching (1:38), presumably preaching the good news of the kingdom of God (1:14), as His real mission. This is borne out by the later pattern, when He preaches in all the Galilean synagogues (1:39), though He also expels demons there. Indeed, He also heals a leper (1:41), but He cautions him to tell nobody of the healing (1:44), a caution which is immediately disregarded (1:45), with the predictable results. This now becomes part of a later widespread pattern, by which Jesus forbids the healed to tell others of their healing (5:43), as earlier He had forbidden demons to speak (1:34). Contradictions to this rule are so rare as to be specially mentioned in the text (5:19) and must therefore have special reasons.

Perhaps then another reason (apart from the priority of His main aim of gospel preaching) for the reluctance of Jesus to heal widely was the inevitable consequent gathering of crowds, whether curious or needy, making any such preaching or teaching almost impossible (2:2). Jesus never sought fame or notoriety, nor did He try to convince the unbelieving by signs and wonders (8:11–12), even when asked for them as a proof of His claims.

Yet, even so, He did not refuse to heal a paralysed man in answer to the faith of his friends (2:5), although the prior necessary 'healing' in this case was apparently in the heart of the man himself ('your sins are forgiven', 2:5). Indeed, the actual physical healing is specifically said to be a 'sign' that Jesus has this far greater power to forgive sins, which He has already exercised (2:10). Presumably, this prior and deeper 'spiritual healing' was always true in cases of demon expulsion. Whether it was also true in cases of 'physical healing' we cannot say, but certainly some of those healed are specifically recorded as becoming followers of Jesus (5:18; 10:52).

So far then, Mark has clearly shown us a Jesus who possesses and uses supernatural powers both of healing and of expelling demons. In most cases (perhaps in all), these acts are done in response to faith, either faith on the part of the person concerned, or on the part of others. Whether this is simply faith in Christ as a healer (as often in younger churches today), or faith at a deeper level, there is not evidence enough to say. But these healings are set mostly in the context of Jesus' preaching or teaching, to which they are adjuncts and subordinate. They are seen as confirmation of the authority of His teaching (1:27), and they lead to the glory of God (2:12).

Apparently the ability of Jesus to do such miracles was never questioned, whether by friend or foe. The sole question raised by His enemies was as to the source of the power by which He did them (3:22), just as they would later question Him as to the

source of the authority with which He acted in other areas
(11:28). The question as to the source of His power always
aroused Jesus' anger, as we can see from 3:29, because the
answer was already self-evident to those not wilfully blind.

Chapter 3 contains the story of the healing of the man with a
withered hand, but again it is not merely a healing miracle, but a
'sign' to illustrate the right use of the Sabbath (3:4), a fact which
the Pharisees fully realized (3:5) – hence their violent reaction
(3:6).

The 'healing campaign' which followed (3:10–11) seems
involuntary and in no sense sought by Christ Himself. Indeed, it
would be true to say that in Mark, Jesus is never shown as
initiating a healing mission, although He responds when people
come in need. This time, it was the result of the coming of
crowds who had heard of His earlier healings (3:8). The consequences were the same as before; first, withdrawal by Jesus to
a small ship (probably in order to preach to the crowd, 3:9), and
then to a mountain, presumably to pray (3:13 *cf.* 1:35). The next
step is to choose the twelve (3:14), to share Christ's work. A
fuller account of their activities is given in 6:9–12, but essentially
the picture is the same as here.

The terms of their appointment are clear: apart from accompanying Christ, they too are to preach, to heal and to expel
demons (3:14–15). We should note two things: their task of
preaching is put first and mentioned separately from the other
two, and is therefore presumably their primary task, whatever
the place of the others. Secondly, there is no hint in Mark that
these powers of healing and of expulsion of demons were given
at this particular time to any other than the twelve, and it is
reasonable therefore to suppose that they were given only to the
twelve as guarantees of their particular status as Christ's special
emissaries. That would be a strict parallel to the way in which
the Lord's miracles are equally regarded as confirming the
authority with which He Himself spoke (1:27). Mark has no
account of a wider choice of 'seventy' with whom these powers
were shared, as Luke has (Lk. 10:1–11), who could perhaps be
regarded because of their number as symbolic representatives of
the whole body. It is true that elsewhere in the gospel we read
of a person expelling demons in the name of Jesus, yet who is

not one of the twelve, nor even one of the wider group of professed followers (9:38), and of approval by Jesus of the act. This, however, seems to be an isolated case, since it is used by Jesus as a teaching model (9:40).

Of healings or exorcisms performed by disciples outside the twelve, we read nothing in Mark, and we are warned by 9:28 that attempts by the twelve were not automatically or invariably successful. The surprise at their failure on this particular occasion, however, seems to show that it was an unusual experience.

When the Jerusalem scribes accused Jesus of expelling demons by the use of the very powers of darkness itself, we learn from Jesus' rebuke to them the deepest purpose of His expulsion of demons: it shows the downfall of Satan's kingdom (3:27). In that sense, every demonic expulsion, like every healing, is a 'sign', even if Jesus refuses to accept the verbal witness to Himself that accompanies it (3:11–12).

While powers of healing and expulsion of demons were shared by Christ with the twelve, it is significant that He does not share the power to work so-called 'nature miracles' with them in this way. Only Jesus, not the twelve, can calm the wind and the sea (4:39 and 6:51). This is a distinction which the twelve, who are with Him in the ship at the time, are quick to see, (4:41). In Mark, only Jesus walks upon the sea (6:49). Only Jesus Himself multiplies bread for the crowds (6:41–43, 8:6–8), although the twelve may share in the miracle by handing the food around (6:41). Only Jesus, never the twelve, is recorded in Mark as raising the dead (5:42 etc.). Only Jesus can curse a fig-tree and see it wither (11:21), although the context certainly suggests that equally great powers, whether literal or meta-phorical, are open to His followers (11:23). Finally, only Jesus Himself rises from the dead (16:6); no apostle can raise himself.

There is therefore a very clear distinction in kind, not just in degree, between the powers committed to the twelve by Jesus, and the powers that were His inherently and by right. There is no hint in Mark that these powers, at either level, were to be extended to a wider group than the twelve, either at the time or later, which does at first sight present us with a problem when we consider the evidence of Acts and the apostolic letters.

Our explanation of the reason for this particular doctrinal 'omission' will depend on our views as to whether Mark has or has not a 'truncated ending' at 16:8. If we regard the present truncated ending as a mere textual accident, we can always say that some such promise of extension of spiritual powers was contained in the lost original ending as is now found in the so-called but later 'longer ending' (16:9–20). If we believe that the present 'shorter' ending of Mark was deliberate and original, we are certainly left with a problem, but perhaps no greater problem than that posed by the lack of record in the gospel of any of the resurrection appearances of Jesus. Of course Mark must have known of these resurrection appearances (16:7), as of course he must have known of the miracles recorded in the early chapters of Acts, although, curiously enough, these are recorded there as having been performed only by the eleven themselves or by other 'apostolic persons' – Stephen, Philip, Paul and the like – as distinct from other New Testament evidence of performance by a wider group (e.g. 1 Cor. ch. 12). If Mark had been in contact with Paul, he must have known of this wider diffusion of spiritual gifts, although Paul himself can speak of miracles as 'signs of a true apostle' (2 Cor. 12:12 RSV). Mark must therefore, as before, be restricting his account to what was actually true at the time, without any reference to later developments.

Both of these points (the absence in Mark of references to resurrection appearances of Jesus, and the absence of reference to a wide performance of 'signs and wonders' in the Christian church) were just as great problems to the early church as they are to us. This is shown by the early editorial additions or 'longer endings' appended to Mark's Gospel, of which the best known is 16:9–20, to fill these gaps. This 'longer ending' is not part of the text of Scripture, however, and we must be careful not to treat it as such, although much of the detail can be paralleled from elsewhere in the New Testament, and therefore stands independently. Here we find explicit reference to signs that 'will accompany those who believe' (16:17), in a passage which seems mainly to be made up of instances recorded in Acts and presumably therefore already known to the early church. True, we know of only one biblical instance where a disciple did 'pick up serpents' unharmed (16:18), in the experience of Paul at Malta (Acts 28:3), but even this, to a Semitic mind, would justify the vague generalization 'they will' of the text. We have no biblical instance of the drinking of poison without harm being caused (16:18), but there is one such case mentioned in tradition (see Commentary); otherwise it would hardly have been included in this early list.

We have, however, no warrant to 'generalize' from these two particular cases, and, in point of fact, only a few isolated Christian sects have ever done so. The other 'signs' mentioned here do appear frequently elsewhere in the New Testament (e.g. Acts, Corinthians, etc.), though again whether we should 'generalize' their occurrence as possible for all Christians at all times is a disputed point. The wording seems descriptive, not mandatory, in the context, and as a description of what happened (and may still happen), it is perfectly true. It is interesting that there is no reference in this Marcan list to the raising of the dead, although both Peter (Acts 9:41) and Paul (Acts 20:10), who are 'apostles' in the wider sense, are recorded as having performed this particular miracle. This probably means that no other instances were known to the early editor, and that he did not therefore regard it as a generalized or even widespread gift.

But we should notice two things. The first is that, even within this later 'longer ending', such miraculous activity has been set firmly in the context of a 'great commission' to preach the gospel (16:15), which, although not found in the canonical text of Mark has apparently been supplied by our author. The second is that the 'signs' are set in the context of an existing Christian faith (16:17). Indeed, such 'signs', whether performed widely or by selected individuals like the apostles, are seen as confirmation, illustration and vindication of the preached word (16:20), and not seen in isolation. Whatever else we may think of this early editor, he was at least a good theologian, for we have seen this to be the very emphasis of Mark himself in the gospel.

Once again, we must remind ourselves that Mark is a 'pre-Pentecostal' gospel, in material if not in date, and Mark is being strictly faithful to his early material. It was only after the outpouring of the Spirit at Pentecost that spiritual gifts were 'generalized' (Eph. 4:8), although not even then 'generalized' in

the sense that every gift was given to every Christian (Eph.
4:11). Mark therefore (if we reject the longer ending), cannot
help us with the question as to whether such 'signs' were
intended by God to be performed regularly or universally at a
later date. To find an answer to that, we must turn to the Acts
and apostolic letters. All we can say is that the picture given
here of the accompaniment of the preached and believed word
by 'signs' is consistent with what we read of the activity of Jesus
and the twelve in Mark; the picture of the performance of 'signs'
in isolation or as an end in themselves is to be found neither in
the gospel nor in the longer ending.

XI. THE STRUCTURE OF MARK'S GOSPEL

It has been said of all the gospels that each is basically a passion
story with an extended introduction, and, while this is of course
an over simplification, there is certainly some truth in it.
Nowhere can the situation which led to this statement be seen
more clearly than in Mark's Gospel, where the passion narrative
occupies one third of the book, and can be readily divided into
four sections (the journey to Jerusalem, 8:30 – chapter 10; the
ministry there, chapters 11–13; the passion, chapters 14–15; the
resurrection, chapter 16), and gives every impression of being
carefully constructed. By comparison, the first part of Mark's
Gospel seems at first sight to be loosely constructed, and is far
less easy to analyse. Some have suggested, somewhat unkindly,
that the reason for this difference is that Mark found the passion
story already constructed, while the first part of the gospel was
entirely his own composition from whatever material, oral or
written, which was available for him to use.

Against this it should be said first that, even if a written
passion narrative already existed, nobody seriously suggests
that Mark simply reproduced it word for word. The actual style
in the second part of the gospel is the same as that in the first
part, suggesting that Mark dealt with his raw material in both
parts in exactly the same way. Secondly, we do well to remember that even in the first part, Mark was dealing with material
that was already highly traditional in the main (witness the

'smooth stone' effect of some of the stories, doubtless because used often for teaching long before). While Mark undoubtedly selected and arranged his material, he may not have felt at liberty to omit traditionally known stories and sayings, even if not directly relevant to his purpose. Thirdly, there is a plan and purpose to be seen in the first part of the gospel too, although, because of the complexity of the theme and the number of separate issues involved, it may not be as clear as in the second half of the gospel. It is therefore easier to take the second half of the gospel and work backwards from there, if we wish to see the plan: perhaps that is indeed how Mark wrote it.

The clearest statement on what we may call the 'external structure' is to be found in Nineham, who points out that there is a clear break in the gospel after 8:26. Up till then, there have been numerous miracle stories recorded: indeed, it has been reckoned that a third of the gospel is taken up with them, an equivalent length to the whole passion story. The action is largely set in Galilee. There is frequent reference to Jesus' teaching, but is usually directed to the crowds, couched in parabolic form, and mainly concerned with the coming of God's kingdom. In this section, Jesus never claims to be Messiah, and discourages demonic witness to His position: the reason for this will be discussed under the heading of 'The Secrecy Motif'. He seems at times to disengage Himself from the crowds who come for healing by deliberate withdrawal: He does not apparently want to be known merely as a miracle worker.

But from 8:31 onwards, there is a complete change in Mark's presentation of the teaching of Jesus. The action now moves largely out of Galilee to either Gentile areas or to largely hostile Judea: hardly any miracles are recorded and, instead of teaching the crowds, Jesus seems basically occupied with the teaching of His disciples. Commentators of a more critical frame of mind may see this as a pattern imposed by Mark on his material: a more obvious and satisfactory view is to say that it corresponds, at least in broad outline, to the plan adopted by Jesus Himself. In that case, the structure of Mark's Gospel would be dictated in general terms, as in the case of the passion narrative, by the material itself. Mark is only following the 'flow'.

In between these two clearly defined sections, as the

watershed of the whole gospel, is 8:27–30, the confession by Simon Peter of the Messiahship of Jesus. Now, while it is true that Mark nowhere directly says that this was the first recognition by His disciples of the true nature of Jesus (John for example seems to place the recognition far earlier), yet it is certainly the most obvious interpretation of the verses. In any case, once Jesus has been recognized as Messiah, there comes intensive teaching as to the true nature of that Messiahship, particularly as involving rejection, suffering, death, apparent failure and ultimate vindication by God in resurrection. Mark records this as being three times reiterated by Jesus to His disciples. There is no need to perform miracles now: the lesson as to His person has been already learned. What is now needed is intensive teaching of the disciples who have recognized Him as Messiah as the pace quickens on the road to the cross, and opposition heightens all the way. Whether therefore this was or was not the first occasion upon which Jesus was recognized voluntarily as Messiah (as distinct from the involuntary confession wrung from the lips of demoniacs), the point is equally clear in either case. From the moment that He is so recognized, all is different. All teaching is 'inward' now, instead of 'outward', as it had been before. The important thing now is to understand both what Messiahship already means for Jesus, and what this path will therefore mean for those who follow Him as disciples. Now the true meaning of the parables and the true nature of the kingdom of God will be apparent in a way that they could not be before, although, even before this, Mark lays stress on the fact that the disciples had 'inside knowledge' (4:11) given by Jesus.

But all this, though true, deals basically with the second part of Mark, where the structure is already fairly clear, and with the 'fulcrum' that leads from the first part to the second part: what of the first part itself? Clearly, in Mark's mind, the whole of the first part is a 'lead in' to this strategic declaration by Peter. His gospel therefore begins, almost defiantly, with a proclamation of the true nature of Jesus (1:1), which will take even His disciples, slow and stupid as they appear in Mark, so long to learn, and which will remain to the last a mystery for most, even to the crowds whom He has fed and healed. The motif of John the

Baptist is introduced early (1:4), not only to link the mission of Jesus with God's plan outlined in the Old Testament (1:2–3), but also because John is in many ways a 'prototype' of Jesus: rejection, suffering and death were to be his path, as they were to be the path of the Messiah. In that sense, John is not only a forerunner of the Messiah, but also a pattern disciple.

That this is not to be the path for Jesus alone is shown by the way in which immediately He catches up others into the same vocation (1:16–20). At once (typically Marcan), Jesus teaches in the synagogue, and His authority impresses them (1:22). The same authority is shown in exorcism and healing (1:27): Jesus' true nature is showing through. This indeed seems to be the purpose of the miracles of Jesus, as recorded in the early part of Mark. They are not only acts of compassion: they are also to display His divine person, and nowhere is this made more clear than in His claim to forgive sins (2:10). Opposition grows steadily (2:16): this new wine cannot be contained in the old wineskins of ceremonial Judaism (2:22). Once this is clearly realized by the religious authorities, the cross is inevitable. Demons will recognize and perforce confess him, but they will be muzzled (3:12): the healed will be warned not to speak of their healing (1:44). Even His friends think Him mad (3:21): the Jerusalem scribes say that He is demon possessed (3:22): but the inner ring of those disciples who understand are to Him as brother, sister, mother (3:35).

All the basic themes of the gospel have appeared already: the hiddenness of the Messiahship of Jesus, except to the eye of faith: the path of suffering that both He and His disciples must tread: the slowness of all to apprehend it: the true person of Jesus, as Son of God (5:7). His disciples may not realize it fully as yet, but after the calming of the storm, at last even they realized something of His supernatural nature (4:41). Signs Jesus has given in plenty in the feeding of the five thousand (6:44) and of the four thousand (8:9), but the disciples still failed to understand (8:21), and the Pharisees, in unbelief, refused to accept (8:11). Finally, Jesus heals a blind man (8:25): and it cannot be an accident that in Mark's arrangement the next incident recorded is Peter's confession (8:29). The blind disciples have received their sight at last, but, like the blind man in the story (8:24), they do not see perfectly as yet. The verses that immediately follow are the beginning of the teaching process that will bring full spiritual vision to them, as Jesus brought it to the blind man.

Seen in this light, the first part of Mark's Gospel is an integral part of the whole, and a necessary introduction to the second part. Here we have no haphazard collection of anecdotes, but a carefully constructed preparation for what follows. That will become even more abundantly clear when we consider some of the typical emphases of Mark, which reinforce and bind together the main themes of what proves to be a closely knit book, although not perhaps in our modern mathematical sense.

XII. CHIEF MOTIFS

Telford (IOM) well summarizes these under seven heads (although perhaps some could have been subsumed under others) as: the secrecy motif, Mark's interest in Jesus' passion, the kingdom of God and the return of the Son of man, his interest in Galilee, his use of the word *euangelion*, 'gospel', his interest in the Gentile mission and his interest in persecution and suffering as the true path of discipleship. Perhaps we might add to this his interest in the failure of both disciples and crowds to understand, and indeed the plain spiritual stupidity displayed by the disciples, even by the greatest of them. While there is no space in a brief introduction to examine all of these in detail, a cursory glance at a few of the main headings will be helpful.

A. THE SECRECY MOTIF

This is more often phrased as 'the Messianic secret', referring to the way in which Jesus neither Himself proclaimed His Messiahship nor accepted the attribution of it to Himself by others, in the first half of Mark's Gospel. This is of course in marked contrast to the second half of Mark, where Jesus accepts and acknowledges such a confession from Peter (8:29), and henceforward devotes much of His time to explaining to His disciples the nature of this Messiahship. It is no longer a secret: it has been revealed to the few, even if the many are still blind to it. In one sentence, this explains both the apparent stupidity of His followers, who are so slow to see it, and the unremitting hostility of His enemies, who are wilfully blind to it. These two motifs are subsumed under the secrecy motif. Just as Peter's declaration is the watershed of the gospel, so, in a sense, the declaration by the Gentile centurion at the cross is its culmination: 'truly this man was the Son of God' (15:39).

Some biblical critics have viewed the whole 'Messianic secret' as a creation of Mark to explain why it was that Jesus during most of His lifetime did not apparently claim to be the Messiah, but was universally hailed as such by the church after His death and resurrection. But this is perverse, ignoring not only the clear testimony of Mark, but of all the other evangelists, including John. Besides, it seems to have been the deliberate purpose of Jesus to lead on His disciples step by step by what He did and by what He said, so that finally they came to the point when, with blinding clarity, they realized at last who He was. The traditional reason given for this still seems the best explanation: Jewish concepts of Messiahship were so triumphalistic and 'this worldly' that for Jesus to simply accept the title of Messiah without also explaining the nature of His Messiahship would only have misled people into nationalist dreams, not revealed God's plan. Even after Peter's declaration, much care was needed to explain this to the disciples. Indeed their behaviour during passion week suggests that it was only after the resurrection that they truly understood the meaning of Messiahship for Jesus.

A further proof of its genuiness is that this secrecy motif, or the hiddenness of the gospel, reappears again and again in other contexts in Mark: it is not an isolated phenomenon, found only in the context of Jesus' Messiahship. It corresponds to the 'hiddenness' of the teaching of Jesus by parable (chapter 4). It corresponds also to the hiddenness of the kingdom of God, which, at this stage, can only be described allusively, presumably for the same reason of probable popular misunderstanding. King, kingdom and Messiah were all alike explosive words at the time, full of political overtones alien to the mission and work of Jesus. Even His own self-chosen title Son of man, with its deliberate ambiguity, and depths of meaning open only to the eye of faith, is another example of 'hiddenness', one day to be open to all.

So it is only after the confession of Jesus as Messiah that there can come the glory of the transfiguration, when Jesus is seen in His true splendour (8:2), and only then seen by disciples who have already made the transforming discovery by faith. If, as is likely, 9:1 refers in Mark's mind directly to the transfiguration, then the true nature of the kingdom is only then apparent. No more will Jesus use parables: He will speak openly to those who understand.

In another sense, the kingdom already present in Jesus and His followers, will be ushered in by God in all its fulness, at the last day: that is the message of chapter 13. This aspect of the truth accounts for Mark's interest in the Son of man as bringing in God's kingdom (8:38) as God's agent: it is again the fulfilment of the pattern of concealment finally becoming revelation (4:22), which is basic to the pattern of Mark because he sees it as basic to the plan of God. Jesus, the humble and despised earthly Son of man in this life (for it is as Son of man rather than as Messiah that Jesus says that He must suffer, 8:31), must yet return as the triumphant and transcendent Son of man that all may see and believe.

Is Mark also thinking of the small and doubtless despised Christian church of his day at Rome? Is this 'hiddenness' to remind them that ultimately they too will triumph in glory, as God's chosen vessel?

B. SUFFERING IN MARK

This subject is closely connected with the previous topic, since the suffering, rejection and death of Jesus are all part of the 'hiddenness' that characterizes His whole mission. The threefold prediction of the passion by Jesus (8:31; 9:31; 10:33), tells, with rising intensity and greater and greater detail, that this suffering is not accidental but a divine necessity, inevitable to His calling. Scholars of a more critical frame of mind maintain that there is no direct connection made in Mark between this suffering and the forgiveness of sins, as there certainly is in Paul and elsewhere in the New Testament. But 10:45 clearly says that the whole purpose of the coming of the Son of man was 'to give his life as a ransom for many,' while in 14:24, Jesus describes His death ('my blood of the covenant') as being 'poured out for many'. In view of these passages, and the numerous references to, and reminiscences of Isaiah chapter 53 which they contain, it is not enough to say that there is at most a vague and unspecified connection in Mark's mind between the death of Jesus and the forgiveness of sins. It is clearly through the suffering and death of the 'servant of the Lord' in Isaiah that forgiveness is achieved for 'the many' (Is. 53:11–12), and, if Jesus applied this picture to His death, then the same must be true of that death too. Mark's interest in the suffering of Jesus is therefore his interest in the gospel, for the two are inseparable. Likewise, he must end his gospel with an announcement of the resurrection even if, as we have it at least, the gospel contains no account of a resurrection appearance, but only a promise of one to come (16:7). Without the vindication and ultimate glorification of the servant, not only would the 'hiddenness' still remain, but the pattern of Isaiah chapter 53 would also remain unfulfilled.

So much for the suffering of the servant, and it is obvious why it is a point of central interest to Mark, since it is so central to the gospel. But Mark is also concerned to show how Jesus, from the very start, showed His followers that the path of discipleship must also be that of suffering. Already, in the parable of the sower, Jesus had warned of the 'tribulation or persecution' that would test the Christian (4:17). The death of John the Baptist was another warning (6:27), for, if John was not technically a follower of Jesus, he was certainly a witness to Him (1:7). After Peter's declaration, when Jesus has explained that the Son of man must suffer (8:31), He goes straight on to explain that any follower of His must also 'deny himself and take up his cross' (8:34). Peter's outburst of expostulation (8:32) shows how uncongenial this doctrine was to natural humanity, even in the shape of a committed disciple, but Jesus reiterates the unwelcome message again and again. True, those who leave to follow Him (as the rich man was unwilling to do, 10:22), will 'receive a hundredfold', but it will be 'with persecutions' (10:30). James and John, in spite of their misplaced ambition, will drink, says Jesus, 'the cup that I drink' (10:39), if they too are followers of the 'suffering servant'. But it is in chapter 13 that we come to the clearest teaching on the subject: from verses 9 to 13, the inevitability for the Christian of persecution, suffering and even death, is pointed out. The only reason given is that it will be 'for my name's sake' (13:13): to follow Jesus of necessity means to tread the way that He trod, for that is the whole meaning of following.

But why does Mark stress the inevitability of suffering for the Christian and why is it such an interest through the gospel? Basically no doubt it is because Jesus had stressed it: perhaps also it is because of the natural human reaction against such an uncongenial doctrine, and therefore there is the need to reiterate it. Yet surely another reason was the local situation of Mark's own church, harried and persecuted at every turn, and doubtless wondering why this should be so. If, as suggested, Mark was writing in and for the Roman church, this would have been particularly appropriate. No church had suffered more from sporadic bursts of cruel persecution, culminating in AD 64, under Nero's reign, when, after the great fire at Rome, Nero was seeking for scapegoats. Here was reassurance of the strongest and most bracing kind: this was the path which their Lord had taken, and this was their Christian calling. Mark may not say of suffering as bluntly as Peter 'for to this you have been called' (1 Pet. 2:21), but he puts it just as clearly in other words.

C. MARK'S INTEREST IN GALILEE AND GENTILE MISSION

If Cranfield is right in seeing Mark's two special purposes in writing for the Roman church as being to 'support its faith in face of the threat of martyrdom and to provide material for missionary preachers', then the teaching of Jesus on suffering, as recorded by Mark, certainly met the first need. This section shows how Mark attempted to meet the second of these needs, for Galilee, by its very position, surrounded as it was by Gentiles, unlike Judea, forced the missionary issue. It also, for another reason, emphasized that the call of Jesus was to the poor and despised of this world.

But having said this, it is important to realize several points. The first is that Mark did not create his material. Jesus may have been born at Bethlehem (a fact unrecorded by Mark), but He comes to be baptized from Nazareth of Galilee (1:9): His first recorded preaching was in Galilee, not Judea (1:14): His first disciples were called in Galilee (1:16). Here we are dealing with historic facts: Jesus is known, even by His enemies, as 'the Nazarene' (14:67), and Peter is recognized at once as a follower of His for, as the bystanders say, 'you are a Galilean' (14:70). This is not a mere idiosyncrasy of Mark. Acts 1:11 has an angel addressing the apostles as 'men of Galilee', while Acts 2:7 says, presumably of the whole of the early Christian body (1:15), before the 'mass conversions' in Jerusalem at Pentecost: 'Are not all these who are speaking Galileans?' There is some evidence from Zealot sources that 'Galileans' was one probably contemptuous name for the disciples in early days, before the wits of Antioch coined the name of 'Christians' (Acts 11:26). Obviously Jesus must have had a large number of followers in Galilee if these things were so, and, equally obviously, that implies a considerable ministry there, thus confirming the Marcan picture. To judge from the Johannine picture, Mark may well have arranged all the Galilean material in the first part of his gospel and put most of the material with a Judean background in the second part. If this is so, we should recognize that it is purely a matter either of editorial convenience or of theology, for John certainly suggests earlier Jerusalem visits by Jesus, as indeed we would expect if the public ministry of Jesus extended over three years. But Mark is not incorrect in recording a Galilean ministry of Jesus, for it was certainly a historical fact, and undoubtedly he would have found it in his sources, particularly if they were Galilean, if not Petrine.

Why, however, did he emphasize it so? It was not as if Mark wished to contrast a supposed 'Galilean springtime' of acceptance and success with the increasingly bitter opposition and outward failing that awaited Jesus at Jerusalem. Scribes and Pharisees had opposed Jesus in Galilee as well as in Judea (2:7, 16, 18, 24). Indeed, it was in Galilee that His death was first determined (3:6). True, sometimes this criticism came from 'the scribes who came down from Jerusalem' (3:22), but this seems to be at a later date. Even 'in his own country' (6:1, probably Nazareth), Mark says that 'they took offence at him' (6:3). Mark paints no unreal rosy pictures of Galilee.

But has Mark any other reason for giving it such prominence, other than the fact that Galilee undoubtedly held a large place in the ministry of Jesus? In 14:28, Mark records Jesus as promising His disciples that, after His resurrection, He will precede them to Galilee: in 16:7 an angel reiterates this promise, all the more remarkable since the other gospels do not record a specific resurrection appearance in Galilee (though see Mt. 28:16). Apart from these two occurrences, Lightfoot points out that Galilee is mentioned nine times in Mark, four of these being in the first twenty five verses, a very remarkable initial emphasis on Galilee.

Marxsen and those who follow him see a highly symbolic use of the word 'Galilee' in Mark. To them, 'Galilee' stands as a symbol for the wider Gentile Christian world, just as 'Judea' or 'Jerusalem' stands for the Jewish world. This links with Marxsen's somewhat fanciful view that Mark's Gospel was an exhortation to Jerusalem Christians to flee to Galilee in AD 70, or that it was written to meet the contemporary situation of the church in Galilee, as it was awaiting and expecting Christ's parousia or second coming. Galilee therefore stands for Gentile mission, and what we have here is an encouragement of the largely Gentile church of Rome to engage in it. Does Jerusalem and official Judaism reject the Messiah and indeed reject Christianity? It should be no surprise: this is what they have always done. The earthly Jesus began His mission in Galilee: His first disciples were all Galileans, not Judeans. Finally, it is at the last in Galilee that He promises to manifest Himself after His resurrection, for it is most unlikely that this refers to His second advent. As Lightfoot rightly says, 'The reader's thought is turned to the story of the ministry in the early chapters of the book', where Galilee was equally the focus of attention.

Now, it is true that Galilee was called 'Galilee of the Gentiles', but this seems to have been more because it was physically ringed by Gentile peoples than because of the nature of its population. No part of Palestine was more fiercely nationalistic than Galilee, as its long record in the Roman wars showed, although historically a large proportion of its population might be descended from the non-Jewish tribe of the Ituraeans, forcibly Judaized in the aftermath of the Maccabean wars. It is true that Galileans were despised by the inhabitants of Jerusalem, but that seems to have been because of their alleged simplicity and uncouthness rather than their supposedly Gentile racial origins (*e.g.* Jn. 1:46; 7:52). So, in itself, a ministry in Galilee cannot encourage a church to Gentile mission, but it can reinforce the message of Jesus as being to the poor, the downtrodden, and the despised, to tax collectors and to sinners (2:16). The proud scribes of Jerusalem considered themselves as 'those who are well' and 'the righteous': they felt 'no need of a physician' (2:17), so could not receive the good news. Moreover, the centre of Galilean religious life was the synagogue, rather than the temple which dominated Jerusalem: in this at least, it was more akin to overseas Judaism of the dispersion. The synagogue had sometimes welcomed Jesus: the entrenched temple never did. Perhaps this thought also was in Mark's mind as he wrote the gospel: perhaps too, the comparative receptiveness shown by Galilee compared with the stony indifference shown by Jerusalem is another aspect of the 'hiddenness' of the gospel (*cf.* Lk. 10:21).

But the second aspect of Galilee certainly does speak of the Gentile mission. Surrounded by Gentiles as it was, contact with Gentiles was inevitable there. It is probably false exegesis to see the two feeding miracles recorded in Mark (chapters 6 and 8 respectively) as being one feeding of Gentiles and one of Jews, but, in the great crowds that gathered to hear Jesus (4:1; 6:56; *etc.*), it is hard to believe that no Gentiles were present. The healed demoniac of the Gerasenes may have been a Jew, although the title 'Son of the Most High God' has a Gentile ring (5:7). But certainly the population of the Decapolis, where he was commanded by Jesus to preach (5:19–20), had a strong Gentile component. Some have seen significance in the choice of Caesarea Philippi as the place of Peter's confession (8:27), for the rabbis saw this city as the very boundary between Jew and Gentile. In 7:24, Jesus deliberately enters the territory of Tyre and Sidon, where He heals a Gentile child.

It is, however, typical of Mark that he does not distort the tradition, even in favour of his beloved Gentile mission. He records Jesus as saying 'let the children first be fed' (7:27): the time was not yet ripe for the Gentile mission. But in 11:17, it is the fact that mercenary trading, occupying the court of the Gentiles, has made it impossible for the temple to be as intended by God 'a house of prayer for all the nations', which particularly raised the anger of Jesus. So God's vineyard will be given to others (12:9): these can hardly be other than the Gentile Christian church. Best of all, in the so-called 'little apocalypse' of chapter 13, Jesus tells His followers that 'the gospel must first be preached to all nations' (13:10): that is to be one of the signs, ushering in the end. If the cup at the last supper represented covenant blood 'poured out for many' (14:24), it is hard to believe that this in Mark's mind was restricted to those within Judaism, especially in view of the context of Isaiah chapter 53. Finally, corresponding to the great confession by Peter the Jew in 8:29, comes the equally great confession by the Gentile centurion at the cross 'Truly this man was the Son of God' (15:39): this is the fruit and goal of all Gentile mission.

Even if the so-called 'longer ending' did not come from the pen of Mark, yet it certainly expresses the mind of Christ and the messsage of the gospel when it records the risen Lord as giving the order, 'Go into all the world and preach the gospel to the whole creation' (16:15), a saying to which Mark must have set his amen. If the Gentile Christian church could find no stimulus to Gentile mission here, there was no more that could be said.

D. SUMMARY OF MAIN MOTIFS

Before we begin the study of the gospel in detail, it will be helpful for us to remind ourselves of the chief motifs observable in Mark, so that we can look out for them in the text. They are well summarized in Telford (IOM) as:

1. The *secrecy* motif and the writer's interest in the true but hidden *identity* of Jesus;
2. An interest in the *passion* of Jesus (His suffering, death and resurrection) and its significance for Christology;
3. An interest in the nature and coming of the *Kingdom of God* and in the question of Jesus' return as *Son of man*;
4. An interest in *Galilee*;
5. His use of the term *'gospel'* (*euangelion*);
6. An interest in *Gentiles* and the Gentile mission;
7. An interest in *persecution, suffering* and *martyrdom* and the true nature of *discipleship*;
8. His stern treatment of the *Jewish leadership groups*, Jesus' *family* and especially His original *disciples*.

Of course, as to the interpretation of these, scholars may differ, but as to their presence, there is no doubt; rightly seen, they only reinforce the message of the gospel.

ANALYSIS

I. PREPARE THE WAY: THE PREPARATION FOR THE EVANGEL (1:1–13)
A. THE TITLE OF THE BOOK (1:1)
B. THE FORERUNNER (1:2–8)
C. THE BAPTISM OF JESUS (1:9–11)
D. THE TEMPTATION (1:12–13)

II. HIS OWN DID NOT RECEIVE HIM: THE EARLY GALILEAN MINISTRY (1:14 – 3:6)
A. THE KINGDOM OF GOD IN GALILEE (1:14–45)
   i.   *The first Galilean preaching (1:14–15)*
   ii. *The call of the disciples (1:16–20)*
   iii. *Jesus at Capernaum (1:21–28)*
   iv. *Peter's mother-in-law (1:29–31)*
   v.   *The evening healings (1:32–34)*
   vi. *From Capernaum to Galilee (1:35–39)*
   vii. *The cleansing of the leper (1:40–45)*

B. THE BEGINNING OF CONFLICT (2:1 – 3:6)
   i.   *The healing of the paralysed man (2:1 – 12)*
   ii. *The ministry of Jesus (2:13)*
   iii. *The call of Levi (2:14–17)*
   iv. *Controversy about fasting (2:18–22)*
   v.   *Controversy about the sabbath (2:23–28)*
   vi. *The man with the withered hand (3:1–6)*

iii. *The cross* (15:22–32)
iv. *The death* (15:33–41)
v. *The burial* (15:42–47)

VII. THE THIRD DAY: THE RISEN LORD (16:1–20)
A. THE RESURRECTION (16:1–8)

B. THE LONGER ENDING (16:9–20)

COMMENTARY

I. PREPARE THE WAY: THE PREPARATION FOR THE EVANGEL (1:1–13)[1]

A. THE TITLE OF THE BOOK (1:1)

'The beginning': as in Genesis, God is about to begin a new creative work (Minear). The first clause, as well as being the title of the book (which, it should be noted, is *the gospel of Jesus Christ*, not 'the Gospel of Mark', as we tend to say), is also a summary of its contents. The gospel is the 'news' or the 'tidings'. How far the first-century reader was conscious of the meaning 'good' as being involved in the Greek word *euangelion*, is uncertain. There is some Old Testament evidence to suggest that the word ought usually to be translated 'reward for bringing good tidings' at an earlier date. But, in any case, from the very nature of its content, the gospel soon took on this meaning of 'good news', an example of how the early church moulded its own vocabulary to express new concepts.[2]

The subject of this good news is a person named Jesus, a common enough name both in its Hebrew form of Joshua, in

[1] For 1–13, as being Mark's 'introduction' to his gospel, see Lightfoot: Westcott and Hort see the introduction as 1–8, while Dodd regards it as 1–15. But Lightfoot is right in seeing 14–15 as a summary of Christ's preaching, and comparing it with Luke's account of the sermon at Nazareth (Lk. 4:18–21).

[2] For the various meanings of the word *euangelion*, 'gospel', both in Mark and the rest of the New Testament, see Kertelge (in IOM). From being oral and missionary preaching it becomes a book. For Mark as the first written gospel, and its literary form and models, see Perrin (IOM). Schulz, in the same volume, points out the great difference here between Mark and the apocryphal and heretical so-called 'gospels'.

Old Testament days, and in this Hellenized form, derived from the Aramaic *Jeshua*, in the New Testament world.[1] Both by common etymology and by historic precedent, the name meant 'Yahweh is salvation', the name given to the divinely-appointed leader, sent to save God's people in their hour of need (Jos. 1:1–2). What Moses could not do, Joshua would accomplish: that would make the name 'Jesus' even more appropriate for the coming saviour.

Not alone, however, is Jesus to be Saviour; He is also to be God's appointed agent upon earth. This singling out for a particular task is described in terms of being 'anointed', as any king or priest of Old Testament days would have been. Both the concept and the word are very common in the New Testament, occasionally in the Semitic form of *Messiah*, but more commonly as *Christ*, or 'the Christ', using a word derived from the Greek root *chriō* which has the same meaning as the Hebrew root *māshaḥ*, 'to anoint'.

Whether or not in this verse the clause *the son of God* should be included is doubtful; the manuscript evidence is inconclusive.[2] But in any case, it is a title of Jesus that has abundant testimony elsewhere in Mark (*e.g.* 3:11), and was indeed the very claim for which Jesus was condemned to death by the Sanhedrin (14:61–62). This Sonship, to the early Christians, was no spiritualized metaphor, nor did it simply mean the adoption of a mortal man into the Godhead. A fitting expression, though not the origin, of divine sonship is to be found in the account of the virgin birth of

[1] Schweizer points out how little the evangelists were interested in the personal details of the man Jesus of Nazareth. There is no description of His appearance till the days of the apocryphal gospels: they do not even point out that He was unmarried (as He clearly was), though this feature was most unusual in Judaism. It is nonsense to see in the account of the wedding at Cana (Jn. ch 2) any contradiction of this.

[2] Since RSV, NEB, JB, and NIV in their translation, have included the clause 'Son of God' here, to weigh the evidence may be of interest. Against its inclusion are the great uncials Sinaiticus (in its original, not corrected, reading) and Koridethi; 28, and a few other minuscules; some oriental versions, and the bulk of early patristic evidence. Supporting the clause (either with or without the definite article) are the uncials Alexandrinus, Vaticanus, Beza, and Freer, in addition to several important families of minuscules. This makes a strange problem, in view of the patristic silence; but it is easier to see why such a clause should be added later (from other New Testament contexts), than to see why it should be omitted by the Fathers, if known to them. It may perhaps be considered an early addition here, in spite of its theological truth, although Tasker (*Greek New Testament*) accepts it as part of the text.

Jesus, though this is not specifically mentioned by Mark. It may be that this was a doctrine taken for granted by Mark rather than something explicitly propounded. It is not likely that he was ignorant of it, but he may well not have considered it as fundamental to primary gospel preaching.

Another notable gap in Mark is the absence of any statement of the pre-existence of Jesus (Anderson); but a clear statement of this doctrine will not come until John (Jn. 1:1). Again, it was perhaps assumed by Mark rather than stated. 'Abstract' questions of this nature do not seem to have exercised the mind of the earliest Christians as greatly as did God's manifest activity in Jesus. If Mark is primarily an evangelist, concerned with the Gentile mission of the church, such an omission is even more understandable: except perhaps when dealing with Moslems, the pre-existence of Christ is not usually an element in primary evangelism even today.

B. THE FORERUNNER (1:2-8)

2-3. Furthermore, this good news stands in direct relation to God's whole revelation to His people in the past. The New Testament is to Mark not a breach with the Old Testament, but a fulfilment of it (2), although he does not quote the Old Testament as frequently as other evangelists do. This may be because, probably unlike Matthew, he was not writing for a Christian group who had a Jewish background.

Yet, strangely enough, the scriptural prophecy quoted here[1] to provide the necessary 'link' has primary reference not to Jesus, but to John the Baptist. It is as if Mark wants us to realize that the gospel era was ushered in by John. Mark does not have as full an account of the Baptist as that contained in the other

---

[1]The prophecy, loosely quoted here with a reference to Isaiah, is in fact a combination of Malachi 3:1 and Isaiah 40:3, perhaps coming from some early Jewish collection of texts relating to the Messiah. Such combinations are not uncommon elsewhere in the New Testament, and were a regular feature of Jewish exegesis. Schweizer (in IOM) well points out the significance of this Old Testament quotation, since Mark, by contrast with Matthew, rarely refers back to the Old Testament. This is not of course to deny that Old Testament thought underlies Mark's whole theology, especially his understanding of Christ: indeed, as Schweizer (GNM) points out, this prophecy introduces the entire book.

gospels, but John's importance is equally clear, as this verse makes plain. The Baptist is God's messenger and the Messiah's forerunner; his status, unrecognized by Jewish officialdom, is unequivocally stated here. His task is to make a road for God, and his method is by preaching; the content of his preaching is a stern uncompromising call to all to prepare themselves for the divine coming by turning from their evil ways and turning back to God.

4. John's baptism was not in the name of Jesus, nor was it directly associated with the gift of the Holy Spirit (8), as baptism by the Messiah was to be. Disciples of John are therefore re-baptized by Paul, as being ignorant of the coming of the Spirit, and as not having been baptized 'in the name' of Jesus. (Acts 19:5). But note that there is no evidence in Mark for the re-baptism of those disciples of Jesus who had previously been John's disciples, and who may thus be presumed to have received John's baptism already. John's baptism was therefore only one of the initiatory and purificatory rites of later Judaism, and was an outward sign and symbol of the message that he preached. He called his hearers to a change of heart and purpose, which would result in a forgiveness of their sins by God; and it is clear from the common gospel tradition that John also demanded a changed life as proof of this truly changed heart. So far, there was little new in his preaching, powerful though it was.

5-8. The initial response to John's message showed him to be in the true Old Testament prophetic succession; he was recognized at once as bringing a word from the Lord. Dress and food[1] and living-place alike marked him out as being in the rugged tradition of Elijah and the other desert prophets (*cf.* 2 Ki. 1:8), as did his eschatological and 'forward-looking' preaching. But in John's case there was an urgency and imminence about the messianic preaching that had been lacking of old; God's intervention, which all the prophets had promised and which was to result in the establishment of His rule upon earth, was now at

---

[1]John's is the ordinary food of the desert nomad, not of the later monastic ascetic, as Schweizer points out. The nomadic period had often been seen as Israel's 'honeymoon' period with God (Je. 2:2) and the diet reminds us of the coming messianic age (Is. 7:15).

the very doors. All this was accompanied in John by an over-whelming consciousness of the relative unimportance of his own work and ministry, compared with that of the 'Coming One' of whom he spoke.

C. THE BAPTISM OF JESUS (1:9-11)

9. Jesus came to receive John's baptism: Mark does not give the reason for this act on the part of Jesus. It was not, of course, through any consciousness of sin (a difficulty seen by the her-etical 'Gospel of the Hebrews'), but according to Matthew, through a desire to 'fulfil all righteousness' (Mt. 3:15), *i.e.* to fulfil every ordinance of God for His people. That John himself protested against any idea that Jesus had need of such baptism of repentance is also made clear from the previous verse in Matthew's account. Both of these explanations, however, are omitted from Mark's more clipped version: such theological misunderstandings had perhaps not yet arisen. Jesus' accep-tance of baptism may well have been part of His total identifica-tion with humanity, but, if so, Mark does not make a point of it: he simply records the bare fact without explanation, as his custom is. Kline thinks the baptism was an 'ordeal sign': in that case, the baptism of Jesus would be an acceptance by Him of God's general judgment on human sin. This is possible, but there is no hint of it in the context.

10-11. This is one of the great 'trinitarian' passages of the New Testament. Here the Spirit and the Father both bear witness to the Son. As in the book of Genesis God created by His word and through the Spirit (Gen. 1:2-3), so it was fitting that, at the very commencement of God's new work of re-creation, there would be the same operation of the whole Godhead. Here, on Jordan's banks, God speaks His word again, and again the Spirit is brooding over the waters,[1] as in Genesis (Gn. 1:2). Mark does

---

[1]Lightfoot sees a parallel between the *heavens opened* here, and the great curtain of the temple being *torn in two* at the crucifixion: the same Greek verb is used. To him, the descent upon Jesus of the divine presence like a dove is Mark's description of the incarnation: but

not say that the Spirit descended on Jesus only at His baptism, however, still less that He only then became the Son of God. Mark is clear that Jesus is already Messiah and God's Son (1:1): what he is describing here is a vision that either Jesus or John had, after the baptism, as a sign confirming the existing reality of the person and status of Jesus.

The *voice from heaven* (11) is a combination of Psalm 2:7, which deals with the Messiah, and Isaiah 42:1, which deals with the suffering Servant. This creative fusion of two concepts is a perfect expression of the double nature of the work of Jesus. The Greek word *agapētos*, translated *beloved*, has also the nuance of 'only' when applied to a child, and so was particularly appropriate here. The other word for *son* in Greek, *pais*, can mean both *son* and 'servant', so would have been doubly appropriate when describing Jesus, but although used of Jesus in Matthew (12:18) and Acts (3:13), Mark does not use the word at all, for whatever reason.

Anderson well says, with Lightfoot, that the text does not invite us to a clinical or psychological investigation, either of the phenomena described or of the inner mental processes of Jesus: these are strictly modern interests. Mark is solely concerned with the reality of what happened at the baptism, and the witness borne to Jesus there, a witness the truth of which will be gradually confirmed in subsequent chapters.

D. THE TEMPTATION (1:12–13)

12. *The Spirit* is seen here in two lights. He is the gentle 'dove' (10) hovering over the waters of baptism, as Noah's dove had hovered over the ark of salvation and the waters of judgment (Gn. 8:8ff.)[1]; but He is also the mighty Spirit of creation, hovering over the baptismal waters, out of which God will call His new creation, in terms of new-made men and women

---

that would favour 'adoptionist' theology, unless it is seen as pure symbolism. Mark has the 'beginning' of the gospel before the baptism (Anderson).

[1]Schweizer rightly rejects the suggested misunderstanding of a supposed Hebrew original of *like a dove*, *shekeyōnāh* as though it were *shekinah*, 'the presence of God'. Such ingenuity is misplaced, and the interpretation is fanciful.

(2 Cor. 5:17). It is this Spirit of power who irresistibly impels Jesus *into the wilderness*, the place where so many of the Old Testament prophets received their initial commission and revelation, far from human habitation. For an Australian, 'the bush' would have the same connotation today. For Mark's hearers, in the midst of persecution, the sequence of baptism, Spirit, and immediate testing would have relevance to their own case, as often for converts today.

13. In the loneliness of the *wilderness*, Jesus remained for *forty days*, the length probably corresponding to the forty years of testing that Israel, God's child, also endured in the wilderness (Ps. 95:10). The *wilderness* was, to the Hebrew, a gloomy place of terror, the abode of devils and unclean beasts. To be *with the wild beasts* had therefore no such romantic associations for Mark's hearers as it has for a world of jaded city dwellers today. There may be the further thought here of divine protection; as God shut the lion's mouth to save His servant Daniel (Dn. 6:22), so He would preserve His servant Jesus from the wild beasts. Again, like Israel in the desert (especially to the eyes of late Jewish orthodoxy), *the angels ministered to him*.[1] In the fuller account of the temptation in the other gospels (Mt. ch. 4 and Lk. ch. 4), it is made clear that the purpose of this wilderness period was that Jesus might face and conquer the peculiar temptations involved in His calling as Messiah before commencing His task. Again, Mark is clipped and direct. He records the bare fact of the temptation itself, without any comment or explanation of its content, but it is certainly not true (with Lightfoot), to say that Mark's account is 'so brief as to be barely intelligible'. The meaning is quite clear, especially from the narrative which follows: while Israel, God's child, had failed in the desert, Jesus, God's Son, triumphed. That Mark knew the basic content of the temptations seems clear (8:33).

---

[1] Nineham and Schweizer are probably right in seeing the 'ministry' as referring to the supply of food, as in the case of Elijah (1 Ki. 19:4–8). But this is no reason to deny the earlier 'fasting', mentioned in other gospels, if not in Mark. Schweizer also points out that peace will reign in the animal world when Messiah comes (Is. 11:6). Is the thought that a 'new Adam' stands among the animals of paradise, but this time with angels serving Him, not driving Him from the garden (Gn. 3:24)?

II. HIS OWN DID NOT RECEIVE HIM: THE EARLY GALILEAN MINISTRY (1:14 – 3:6)

A. THE KINGDOM OF GOD IN GALILEE (1:14–45)

i. The first Galilean preaching (1:14–15)

At this point, Mark merely refers in passing to the whole story of John's denunciation of Herod for immorality, and John's consequent imprisonment and death (for full account, see 6:14–29). The incident serves here only as a date-line, for from this moment began the preaching of the good news by Jesus. That the initial point of preaching was hard-pressed, stubbornly nationalistic *Galilee*, surrounded by Gentiles, always first target for any invader from the north, is seen by Matthew to be no accident (Mt. 4:12–16). As in the words of the prophet, so in the earthly ministry of Jesus, Galilee appropriately symbolizes God's people in bondage, to whom the light of salvation would first come (Is. 9:1–2).[1] Nevertheless, this does not justify us in downgrading (with Marxsen) the geographic reality of the location of the mission in favour of theological symbolism.

14. *The gospel of God*: there is a variant reading 'gospel of the kingdom', which is certainly the sense of verse 15.

15. The news which Jesus now heralded in Galilee was that God's hour had struck, the time to which all the Old Testament had looked forward. God's reign upon earth, a concept familiar from the prophets, was about to begin (*is at hand*). All were therefore called to a change of heart (*repent*) and to a belief in this good news, for which John had already prepared the way. This is the only instance in Mark where *pisteuo en*, *believe in*, is used: see BAGD p.660, where 'put one's trust in' seems a better

[1]It has often been noted that the gospel can be roughly divided into two parts: an early 'Galilean' or 'receptionist' period, contrasted with a later 'Judean' or 'rejectionist' period at Jerusalem. This is of course not an absolute distinction: Nazareth would reject Jesus (6:3), while the pilgrim crowds at Jerusalem would welcome Him (11:9). This is no basis, however, on which to claim some figurative or 'theological' use of 'Galilee', as distinct from a literal meaning: half Gentile and therefore religiously suspect, Galilee was probably always more open to new ideas than rigidly orthodox Jerusalem.

translation than 'believe on the basis of the gospel'. What all had yet to learn, and what proved to be the hardest lesson for the disciples of Jesus to learn, was that the reign of God was not to be a cataclysmic external triumph in the here and now by an earthly Messiah, but a peaceful rule over the hearts of those who responded to the message, although no reader of the Old Testament could think of it as purely an internal matter. True, the gospel involves the kingdom: but it also alters all contemporary concepts of the kingdom (see Schweizer). *Is at hand*: this might possibly be translated, following the sense of the presumed Semitic original, 'has come'. In one sense the kingdom had already come in the person of Jesus, who was fulfilling God's will perfectly. In another sense, it was gradually coming, in lives surrendered to God. In a third sense, God would introduce it universally at the 'last day'.

ii. The call of the disciples (1:16-20)

Jesus called Simon and Andrew to be *fishers of men* (17), and while the use of the metaphor in their particular case may have been suggested by their occupation at the time, yet this is a universal calling for every disciple of Jesus.[1] Fisherman, farmer, builder, reaper, shepherd, steward, servant: all are examples of the homely metaphors used by Jesus in the gospels, each describing a different aspect of our common Christian obligations to our Lord and to our fellows.

Both pairs of brothers found that obedience to the call of Jesus was costly; it meant abandonment of all that they held dear, and all earthly security, in simple committal to Jesus. Nor can we say that those who left father and hired servants and boat left more than those who left their nets alone,[2] since both left all that they had; that is always the minimum requirement for the Christian

[1]It has been noted (*e.g.* by Cranfield and Nineham), that, while this is a common Old Testament metaphor, it is used in a bad sense only: but in Jeremiah 16:16 the fishers are at least sent forth by God, and so find a place in His purpose for Israel. In the present context, a 'good' sense seems obvious.

[2]Although Schweizer may be over-exegeting when he tries to prove that Simon and Andrew were poor, because they were only using a casting net here. Other gospels mention Simon's boat (Lk. 5:3), which implies some capital at least. Fishing was a prosperous business in Galilee, and the lake a rich fishing ground.

(8:34). *Left* and *followed* (18) correspond to the double call of Jesus in verse 15 'repent and believe' (Minear).

It has been well pointed out by scholars that to the ancient world, unaccustomed to walking abreast on a wide path as modern pedestrians would naturally do, the word *followed* meant to 'walk with', in modern idiom. To walk with Jesus as Enoch had walked with God (Gn. 5:22), these fishermen gave up all earthly prospects. Nevertheless it is true that, by New Testament times, the verb 'to follow' had added to its meaning an ethical aspect, for it is always the teacher who walks ahead, and the student who follows: therefore, at the least, a rabbi-disciple relationship is implied.

iii. Jesus at Capernaum (1:21–28)

It was the consistent practice of Jesus to attend both temple and synagogue; but, unlike any other teacher whom his audience had heard hitherto, He neither quoted nor relied on any great rabbinic names as precedent for His teaching. His hearers were amazed, not only at the content of His teaching, but also at the assumption of personal authority[1] displayed in the manner of its presentation. This was in direct contrast to the caution and pettifogging of the scribes, to whom the new handling of law and tradition by Jesus must have seemed cavalier, to say the least. Anderson well points out the stress given in Mark to the teaching programme of Jesus, although the content of His teaching is not detailed.

23–26. The immediate result of the preaching of Jesus was not harmony, but division and strife, exactly as He later warned (Mt. 10:34). This strife might lie concealed in the minds of the congregation, but it was made plain in the outcry of the demoniac. He, at least, bears unwilling witness to the person and work of Jesus, though he recoils instinctively from His purity, realizing that here is a preacher with whom he had

---

[1] In Mark's Gospel at least, it seems as if the chief function of the miraculous was to assert the authority of Jesus to teach and act as He did (27). This is of course not to deny that such miracles were not also works of love and mercy (41) and signs of the coming of the kingdom (3:26).

nothing in common, crying *what have you to do with us?* (24).[1] Capernaum, the scene of the miracle, was a proud city of unbelief, compared with which Tyre and Sidon would fare better in the day of judgment (Mt. 11:23–24). It is a strange commentary on the spiritual situation in Capernaum that a demoniac could worship in the synagogue with no sense of incongruity, until confronted by Jesus, and indeed apparently with no initial desire to be delivered from his affliction. The instant response of Jesus was to muzzle this involuntary demon-testimony and free the man from the incubus. The Greek word *phimōthēti, be silent* (25), is better translated as 'be muzzled': it is both strong and blunt, like 'shut up' in modern colloquial English. The main emphasis is on the silencing of the demon, to maintain the so called 'messianic secret'. See the Introduction (p.89f.): Jesus will not accept compulsory witness to His godhead, when given by the powers of evil.

27–28. This exhibition of power only confirmed the impression left in the minds of His hearers, that here was one invested with authority. But, though it often led to wonder, a miracle did not lead necessarily to belief. This seems to be one of the reasons why Jesus performed healing miracles so sparingly and selectively, and seemingly only for those in whom faith already existed, no matter in how small a degree (9:24). Of course, in the case of a demoniac, it would be useless to seek for such faith before liberation. Faith, in any case, if produced merely by the spectacular and the abnormal would be inadequate (Minear and Schweizer).[2]

[1]Best well points out (IOM) that 'God's Holy One' is not, according to Mark, the usual phrase on the lips of the demonized, but 'God's Son'. As there is no special reason in the context for this change, we can only conclude that we have here the preservation of an original tradition. Nineham sees it as a messianic title, though unparalleled in the N.T. Robinson correctly sees Mark as the history of a cosmic struggle between God and the Spirit, on one hand, and Satan on the other. The coming of Jesus marks the overthrow of Satan: this is shown by the expulsion of evil spirits. He is misleading, however, when this correct interpretation leads him to underplay the basic historicity of the account in Mark's Gospel.

[2]In view of revived modern interest in the miraculous, attempts have often been made today to draw up a statistical assessment of the place of miracles in Mark's Gospel. Statistics are notoriously unreliable, but Kertelge (in IOM) points out that the bulk of Mark is narrative material, not sayings, and that, in this narrative material, the miracle stories occupy 156 verses, as against 119 verses of passion narrative. In view of Kähler's famous definition of

iv. Peter's mother-in-law (1:29-31)

This 'domestic miracle' gives us one of the rare glimpses into the home lives of the apostles. Simon's wife may even have accompanied her husband on his missionary travels later, as she is mentioned specifically by Paul in 1 Corinthians 9:5.[1] This incident is often claimed as a 'Petrine touch': certainly, of the apostles, only Peter, James and John were present (and Andrew?).

As so often in the gospel narrative, the touch of Jesus brought instant healing (31); and the consciousness of healing brought grateful devotion to Him, expressed in the way in which she *served* or 'waited at table'. It is incorrect, with Schweizer (quoted in Anderson), to compare 15:41, and to see this service as being the model of discipleship for a woman. Humble service like this is the model for every disciple of Jesus alike (10:43-45), but a strict rabbi would have forbidden a woman even to serve at table.

v. The evening healings (1:32-34)

The miracle in the synagogue and the miracle in the home are the natural preludes to the general healing described in these verses. The two isolated miracles had actually taken place on the sabbath; now, after sunset, with the sabbath over and the first day of the week begun, crowds assembled to seek healing. The evangelist may have intended us to see that it was appropriate for such general healing and blessing to be on what was to the church 'the Lord's day'. The question of healing by Jesus on the sabbath does not seem to have yet arisen as a controversial point. Presumably this was so because the healing of the demoniac was involuntary, and the healing of Peter's mother-in-law took place inside a private house, and would therefore be unseen by and unknown to the orthodox. Orthodox Judaism

Mark as 'a passion narrative with an extended introduction', this is interesting. Wimber's different statistics are capable of several interpretations, but he maintains that a far higher percentage of the verses of the gospel are concerned with miracle stories. Schweizer rightly says that miracles, when taken alone, are 'something very ambiguous'.

[1] Although the Greek verb used in 1 Cor. 9:5, *periagein*, 'to lead about', may be weaker in meaning, and simply refer to Peter's married state, not to accompaniment by his wife when on his travels, as RSV takes it.

permitted healing on the sabbath only when life was in danger, and there is no evidence that such was the case here. As the Pharisees do not appear on the scene till 2:16, however, their absence may have also been the reason for the absence of controversy as yet. For a rigid Jew, breach of the sabbath was punishable by death (Nu. 15:35).

34. Once again, the Lord refuses to accept demoniac testimony to His Godhead. All such testimony is non-voluntary, an unwilling recognition by the powers of darkness of an empirical fact, and therefore it corresponds to no morally or spiritually transforming discovery. Jesus is prepared to await the revelation to be made by God Himself that alone will enable every disciple to say with Peter, 'You are the Christ' (8:29). James 2:19 shows that such grudging acceptance of God by the demons as an unwelcome reality is far apart from true Christian faith: though demons may well admit, they do not trust[1], but only 'shudder'. That is not the biblical 'fear of the Lord' (Ps. 19:9).

vi. From Capernaum to Galilee (1:35–39)

All the varied healings mentioned here must have taken a considerable time. We know that on some occasions at least, the miracle was accompanied by a conscious flow of healing power from Jesus (5:30). Healing may therefore have been an exhausting experience to Him, although this is not actually stated in Scripture. If so, it would have been another reason for the frequent withdrawal of Jesus after such occasions, as now.

It was after a busy sabbath of worship and ministry in the synagogue, at a time when others might seek rest and relaxation, that Jesus sought God in private prayer (35). In this way

---

[1]The refusal of Jesus to accept demonic testimony, however, is only one part of His general reluctance to allow Himself to be known at this stage (see Kertelge in IOM). This is the so-called 'messianic secret', familiar in Mark's Gospel, sometimes called 'the tension between hiddenness and revelation'. But there is no need to assume that this is a framework imposed on his material by the evangelist, still less that it is an artificial creation: it is consistent with the whole pattern of the life and teaching of Jesus, as recorded in Mark. The clash of Jesus with demonic powers was not incidental but integral to His ministry as Messiah, and as introducing the kingdom of God: but that did not mean that He was bound to accept their demonic witness to Him.

He was accustomed to spend His 'preacher's Monday morning'. The earliness of the hour and the pains taken to secure a quiet place for uninterrupted prayer left a lasting impression on the disciples. Simon and the others seem to have thoroughly disapproved of this 'unrealistic' strategy in withdrawing from the bustle and opportunity of Capernaum to the silence of a lonely spot (37). They must have been still more puzzled when Jesus saw, in this heightened local interest roused by His healing work, the signal to move on, and to preach in other villages (38). This, He explains, was in fulfilment of His mission, which now became a general preaching and healing mission of a peripatetic nature, based on the synagogues of Galilee. Lightfoot notes that, in Mark, there are three specific references to Jesus at prayer (1:35; 6:46; 14:32). All are at night, and all at times of tension: but surely this early rising for prayer shows a general pattern.

vii. The cleansing of the leper (1:40-45)

This account of the healing of the leper is only one example of a type of incident that must have been repeated many times in the unrecorded ministry of Jesus, which obviously (3:8-12) was much more extensive than our scanty records show. In this miracle, told by Mark in his usual laconic way, there are only two characters involved. The first character is an untouchable, conscious of his own state, earnestly desiring to be cleansed, humble enough to ask for cleansing and believing that Jesus had the power to heal him. The other figure is the compassionate Jesus,[1] who does not shrink from laying His hand even on the loathsomeness of leprosy. Wherever the compassionate Christ and the yearning sinner meet, there then comes instantaneous and complete cleansing. In the antiseptic cleanliness of modern hospitals, we lose sight of the wonder of the parable of Jesus in all His purity stooping to touch the ugliness and stench of our sin to bring healing and forgiveness. In the ancient world, the

[1]But, as Anderson reminds us, a few manuscripts have 'moved wih anger' instead of 'moved with pity'. If this is the true reading, then Wimber thinks the Lord is angered by Satan's act in causing this man's leprosy: Anderson thinks that He is angered by the Jewish attitude to leprosy and the helplessness of the Jewish law in face of it.

attitude towards leprosy was not unlike the popular attitude to suspected sufferers from AIDS today. To the pious Jew, conscious of the ritual uncleanness of the leper (Lv. 13:3), the wonder became even more staggering: Jesus was willing to incur defilement (as they saw it), so that the defiled leper might be made clean. The whole of the gospel is here in a nutshell: Christ redeems us from the curse by becoming under a curse for our sake (Gal. 3:13).

43-44. Once again, the commands of Jesus run counter to all natural human thought.[1] To the healed leper, the most natural thing in the world, the spontaneous expression of gratitude, would have been to tell others. This, in his case, was forbidden in the most explicit terms, which was surely because Jesus never desired people to be drawn to follow Him simply in hopes of material benefits to be obtained from Him. Unwise publicity by witness to physical healing might attract others from wrong motives. This is one of the paradoxes of the ministry of Jesus. He sees the hungry crowd, has pity on them and feeds them; and yet He rebukes crowds who come to Him solely for feeding (Jn. 6:26), and disciples who fail to learn the lesson from it (8:17). He has compassion on the sick, and does not turn them away when they come for healing; but He makes no attempt to seek out the sick to heal them. Rather, He withdraws Himself when the crowds seeking healing become too great, for this makes His teaching ministry, which is alone able to interpret His healing ministry, impossible (38). His primary purpose was 'preaching the gospel of God' (14). Jesus certainly performed miracles and healed the sick, but to say, with some, that He banished sickness and death from Israel for three years, goes far beyond Scripture, and ignores His purpose.

For the healed person to show himself to the priest, on the other hand, and to make the necessary offerings, was both a fitting expression of gratitude to God for his healing, and also an obligation to a law which was at once the medical and hygienic, as well as the ceremonial, code of Israel (cf. Dt. 24:8, reinforcing

---

[1]Schweizer rightly points out how strong is the word used in the command, although it certainly did not carry its original meaning of 'snorting' (as of a horse) at this stage. Nevertheless, just as strong a word is used of the anger of God in the Old Testament.

the injunctions of Lv. 14:2). It was a *proof* that he had been healed. It was also a *proof* to the priest of the healing power of Jesus (1:44): but no danger of wide publication was involved here.

45. Disobedience to the express command of Jesus, even if undertaken from the best possible motives, could lead only to a hampering and hindering of His work. Perhaps that was why Jesus had warned him so strongly against it in verse 43, but all in vain.

B. THE BEGINNING OF CONFLICT (2:1 – 3:6)

i. *The healing of the paralysed man (2:1–12)*[1]

Whenever Jesus entered a house, the verdict of the gospels is that the fact could not be concealed (7:24), so pervasive was His presence. Soon the crowds gathered again in Capernaum, which, after the move from Nazareth, now became His home (for the move, see Lk. 4:31). But this time the crowds came, not merely to be healed of bodily illnesses or afflictions, but to hear the word of God (verse 2). The temporary withdrawal by Jesus in 1:38, and the Galilean preaching tour of 1:39, had served their purpose; the wheat had been separated from the chaff, among the hearers of Jesus.

Nevertheless, because the needs of those in Capernaum were many and varied, and because Jesus would meet all those needs, however diverse, there was still healing: and healing, after all, was another messianic sign (Lk. 7:22). The crowds that milled about the door of the house, whether it was Mary's new home or the house of Simon's mother-in-law, or the house of some other unknown friend of Jesus, were hungry to hear the word of God; and so the poor had the gospel preached to them (Mt. 11:5), the last great messianic sign.

3–5. *Their faith.* The four who came in faith were anxious to obtain physical healing for their friend; it was granted. The

[1] Anderson prefers to entitle this section 'The Bringer of divine Forgiveness'. But he seems

paralysed man himself, to judge from Jesus' dealing with him, was not so much conscious of his physical need as he was of his spiritual burden; so Jesus granted to him forgiveness as well as healing. Only the scribes, arrogantly self-satisfied, and therefore conscious of no need, received nothing. Verse 17 is the later comment by Jesus, not without wry humour, on this seeming anomaly.

As usual, Jesus healed in response to faith. Here Scripture does not make clear the attitude of the sick man himself. He, too, may well have had faith, but it may be that he was too conscious of his own sin to have any confidence in approaching Jesus. It is simplest to assume that Jesus worked the miracle in response to the active faith of the four others, who brought a helpless friend and laid him at Jesus' feet. Their faith showed its reality by its obstinacy and stubbornness in refusing to give up hope. This could be a veritable sermon on the text of James 2:26, illustrating the truth that faith, unless it shows its reality by action, is unreal and self-deceptive, and therefore cannot be expected to achieve results.

6-7. These *scribes* (NIV 'teachers of the law', which is loose, but correctly defines their status) were men of theological acumen. They were not the local synagogue officials of provincial Capernaum, but a fact-finding commission of the type that had already minutely cross-questioned John the Baptist (Jn. 1:19; Lk. 5:17). They saw at once down to the theological roots of the matter. Of course, none but God could forgive sin; how dare a mere human like Jesus claim such authority? Again and again during the life of Jesus the same dilemma was to re-appear. If He were not divine, then He was indeed a blasphemer: for He must be 'either God, or mad, or bad', as the old saying runs. There could be no other possible explanation. If the scribes did not accept Him, then they must condemn Him. At least some of them would see the logic of this (3:6) and so they would begin to plot His death in cold blood. Already, the path to the cross was determined.

mistaken in saying that Jesus does this 'only as God's representative'. The angry reaction of the scribes shows that they understood it as forgiveness given directly in the person of Jesus, and so involving a claim to deity by Him.

8–9. Nevertheless, in the case of some of the scribes, the bewilderment may have been genuine enough, as it surely was in the case of the honest scribe of 12:34. To help such bewildered people to make the staggering equation between the human Jesus and Godhead, Jesus gave them an unasked sign of His divine power, by healing the paralytic before their eyes. Of course it was equally easy to utter the two phrases in the text, and equally easy for divine power to vindicate the note of authority in either phrase. But there is no outward sign by which the inward reality of the forgiveness of sins can be tested, while it is at once clear to all whether a lame man actually walks or not. In other words, in this physical sphere it could most readily be seen whether the assumption of authority by Jesus was justified or unjustified. So, as often, Jesus took His enemies on their own terms and refuted them; verse 8 shows that He acted in full knowledge of their thought processes. It was, in point of fact, a much easier thing to heal the body than to restore the soul, for even a prophet might heal, while no mere prophet could ever forgive sins; but the scribes, with their incessant demands for visible signs, were unlikely to see this (see 8:11). In any case, Jesus both healed and forgave on this occasion, leaving them speechless. If they had eyes to see it, here was the very sign they had wanted; but none are so blind as those who refuse to see.

10–11. 'The Son of man has authority on earth to forgive sins –'. There are two ways of understanding this passage; both lines of exegesis are fruitful, and, if pursued far enough, ultimately merge into one. The first interpretation is, in paraphrase, 'You say that only God can forgive sins? but I will show you that here is a *human* who has the same power', so leading the thoughtful hearer to the equation of the human Jesus with God. This would involve understanding the phrase *Son of man* as being merely the common Semitic paraphrase for 'mortal' (Ezk. 2:1, *etc.*). The second interpretation would take *Son of man*, in this instance, as Jesus' own self-chosen title for Himself, as it must be in 8:31, *etc.*[1] If it is taken in this way, then we should paraphrase 'to

---

[1] *Son of man* as a title seems derived primarily from the use in Dn. 7:13, with further development during the intertestamental period. This title of the Messiah speaks of Him in His capacity as 'representative man', the human agent of God, especially as finally vin-

show you that I in person have this power to forgive sins . . .' In either case, the miracle has evidential value to prove the divine authority of Jesus. Most, if not all, of the healing miracles recorded in the gospel seem to have had this aim as well as the exhibition of divine love; they certainly produced this result to those who were not wilfully blind.

12. Once again, the word of Jesus proved to be effectual, a word of power and authority. As in Genesis God had created from nothing by a word (Heb. 11:3), so, at a word, God's Son could bring strength out of weakness, so that something which was impossible by nature became possible, and a paralysed man walked home, carrying his mattress. The natural reaction of the unbiased section of the crowd was to praise God who had committed such authority to humans (*cf.* Mt. 9:8), so vindicating Jesus' reason for performing the miracle. The crowd at least realized that an entirely new factor had now entered the situation; this was the 'finger of God' (*cf.* Ex. 8:19). But they were as yet content to wonder at such authority committed to a human, without asking the further question as to who this human was. The full answer to that was not to come till Caesarea Philippi (8:27–30), and it was a question for which not even the closest disciples of Jesus were as yet ready.

ii. *The ministry of Jesus (2:13)*

Jesus is frequently described as engaged in open-air preaching, especially beside the Sea of Galilee, where many villages were clustered round the shore of the lake in thickly populated Galilee (see Josephus). One reason for this choice may have been that the sloping shore provided a convenient amphitheatre for a large audience, especially if Jesus preached from a boat moored just offshore in shallow water (as apparently in 4:1). Perhaps the same practical reason, as well as the geography of Galilee,

dicated by God and returning in judgment. In Mt. 26:63–64, the title is linked specifically with 'the Christ, the Son of God'. This identification of 'son of man' with 'God's Son' was the ultimate blasphemy for which Jesus was condemned to die by the Sanhedrin (14:61–64). The title will occur frequently, but this is its first use in Mark (Anderson), which, in the context, may be significant.

influenced the Lord's fondness for teaching on hillsides. He had grown up in hilly Nazareth (1:9), where His (presumably married) sisters apparently still continued to live (6:3), even after His own move down to the lake (Lk. 4:31). See the comment on 2:1 for Capernaum as becoming His home in later years. Several of His disciples are specifically mentioned as coming from the shores of the lake (1:16–19). As far as the three active years of His ministry go, the area immediately around the Sea of Galilee was therefore His home base, rather than the hills of central Galilee, although the 'sermon on the mount' may well represent a summary of His teaching in these central highlands (Mt. chs. 5–7). As Luke chapter 6 contains an account of a very similar 'sermon on the plain' instead, it is reasonable to suppose that this represents a summary of the main teaching of Jesus given on the level land by the lake. Alternatively, 'plain' may refer to a level plateau in the mountains of Galilee, as Blomberg suggests (in Carson and Woodbridge, *Hermeneutics, Authority and Canon*, p. 147). In that case, the teaching here mentioned, but not particularized by Mark, may have been part of this Lucan outline, for we may assume a generally similar pattern of teaching throughout the Galilean ministry.

The ministry of Jesus is explained in various Greek terms. He 'heralds' the news (1:14); He 'teaches' (1:21); He 'speaks' the word (2:2). Perhaps we may see here a rough division into evangelism, systematic instruction and informal teaching, all given in turn by Jesus; we have examples of all three types recorded in the gospels, although least material is recorded in Mark on systematic instruction.

iii. The call of Levi (2:14–17)

Levi, usually equated with Matthew (Mt. 9:9), was a tax-collector and, since he was working in Galilee, doubtless an agent of the hated half-Edomite Herod (*cf.* Lk. 23:6–7).[1] This made him as much an outcast from orthodox Jewish society as the leper of 1:40 had been. Such tax-collectors were often, if not always,

---

[1]Schweizer well says that the picture of Levi is introduced 'with the conciseness of a woodcut'; but that is typical of Mark, who draws a character with a few strokes of the pen.

rapacious and immoral, apart altogether from the nationalistic prejudice against them, since they were working directly for the Romans or the Herods. Yet, as Jesus had laid His hand on the leper and cleansed him, so He called Levi to be one of the apostles, one of the foundation members of His new society (cf. Rev. 21:14 with Eph. 2:20), one of the twelve 'new patriarchs', heads of His new Israel (cf. Lk. 22:30). Levi cannot be said to have been a likely choice for an apostle, but then neither had his ancestor been a likely choice (Gn. 49:5), before God changed him (Dt. 33:8-11), as Jesus would change this Levi now.

15. It seems that this meal was in the nature of a reception given by Levi to his old business acquaintances, to enable them to meet his new-found master. This verse, and the biting criticism of the Pharisees in verse 16, seem to prove that the Lord already numbered many such tax-collectors among His followers.[1] The meal with Levi was therefore not an isolated instance, but chosen by Mark as a typical example of the mission of Jesus.

16. Jesus never excused or condoned sin; no scribe or Pharisee ever condemned it in stronger terms than He did. But this criticism of Jesus by the Phraisees was ill-based for several reasons. First, when a man or woman became a friend or a follower of Jesus, then he or she ceased to be a sinner, but was changed. Secondly, the reason that Jesus mixed so freely with people of this sort was just because their need was so great, and because they, unlike the 'religious', were conscious of their need and therefore responsive to His message. It was apparently a common complaint that Jesus was not sufficiently particular in choosing His friends, unlike other rabbis. Jesus Himself must have known that the common Pharisaic view of Him was as a greedy and hard-drinking person, and as a friend of tax-collectors and sinners (see Mt. 11:19). Nevertheless, in spite of all this criticism, it is probable that the main objection of the Pharisees to social intercourse (whether by themselves or by

---

[1]Cranfield prefers to take the *many* as simply introducing somewhat awkwardly a reference to the numbers of the Lord's disciples in general, and not tax collectors in particular; but syntactically the traditional interpretation seems preferable.

Jesus), with such strata of society was not a truly moral scruple, but merely a fear lest they themselves should contract ceremonial defilement by contact with those who were ritually unclean (cf. Jn. 18:28). So Jesus would willingly touch the leper (1:41), but the priest and Levite, because of their office, dared not help even an injured and bleeding man at the roadside (Lk. 10:31–32), for fear of incurring ceremonial defilement. (On the question of the 'table fellowship' of Jesus, see Joel B. Green, *How to Read the Gospels and Acts*, pages 48–57. It is possible that the early church saw in this passage a reference to the Lord's Supper.)

17. Jesus not only refused to deny the imputation; He claimed that to act in this fashion, by deliberately seeking out the sinful, was the whole purpose of His mission, and indeed an irrefutable proof of His messiahship. As in the case of Zacchaeus, the Son of man came specially to seek and to save the lost ones (see Lk. 19:10). His whole mission was directed towards the sinful, or *those who are sick*, to use the imagery of the present passage. He did not mean that any were in truth *righteous* or *well* and thus without need of spiritual healing. The point is that, without the primary pre-requisite of a sense of need, there could be no healing for them, for they were unwilling to come to Him, the sole source of healing, to seek it (cf. Jn. 5:40).

iv. Controversy about fasting (2:18–22)

John's disciples, and so, we may infer, John himself, were meticulous in keeping the ceremonial law. This orthodoxy of John the Pharisees grudgingly admitted, even in their criticism of Jesus. John was therefore no heresiarch, but a bastion of orthodox Judaism, although as caustic in his remarks on the priesthood as many a prophet before him had been. Since several at least of the disciples of Jesus had been John's followers before the Baptist's testimony sent them away from him to follow Jesus (Jn. 1:35–37), this strictly orthodox background of the apostles is important. Both to the Pharisees, and to John himself at times, it must have looked suspiciously as though these disciples had chosen an easier way in following Jesus. Although regular weekly fasting was not part of the law of

Moses, by the first century such fasting had become an important part of the practice of Judaism, from which it passed into
early Christianity, with only a change in the actual days
involved.[1] To the orthodox Jew this one minor point of fasting
raised the whole question of the attitude of Jesus to the whole
ceremonial law. He had already healed on the sabbath (1:31),
though this had not yet become an issue; His disciples ate food
without the prior ceremonial hand-washing customary in
Judaism (7:2), and they even husked corn on the sabbath day
(2:23). Taken together, this was highly suspicious: did this rabbi
reject the traditions?

19-22. As often, Jesus answered the Pharisaic criticism at two
levels. First, He replied on the superficial level at which these
carping questions were usually asked. Then, having already
demolished the objection of the Pharisees on their own premises, He proceeded to deal with the question at a far deeper
theological level. Here one might paraphrase the question as, 'in
a time of joyous fellowship, who thinks of fasting?'[2] Fasting is,
in the Bible, a sign of disaster, or penitence or mourning, or
voluntary abasement of spirit. The grief which finds expression
in this fasting will come soon enough of its own accord, when
the fellowship of the disciples with Jesus is broken[3]; the
disciples will have sorrow then, at His departure to the Father
(Jn. 16:20). To apply the analogy, which so obviously fits human
affairs, it might be said that the time when Jesus was with His
disciples on earth was in many ways an interim period and not
normative for the church. No generalization can therefore be

---

[1]See Didache 8:1 for some curiously naïve reasoning here. Paul's words in Rom. 14:5 may
refer to this custom, especially as the context treats of fasting: but it may equally well refer to
sabbath observance by converted Jews.

[2]Of course, as Minear points out, the Pharisees too believed in a 'wedding feast', a time
when there would be no more fasting. But to them, it was the messianic banquet, in the
distant future: they could not realize that joy had come here and now, with Jesus. For the
importance in Hebrew culture of a wedding feast, see Schweizer: a rabbi would even leave
his teaching post to join the celebrations. The argument of Jesus, if accepted, was therefore
unanswerable.

[3]See Cranfield for the very plausible view that John's disciples were probably even then
fasting in mourning for the martyrdom of their rabbi: this, taken with the *aparthē*, 'is
(violently) taken away', gives the whole saying a grim point, and makes it indeed a passion
prediction.

drawn from the practice of His disciples at that time, without careful comparison with the subsequent practice of the New Testament church, after Jesus had ascended into heaven and the Holy Spirit had been outpoured.

But there was a far deeper question, which not even the disciples saw until their forcible expulsion from the ranks of orthodox Judaism in the days of the Acts. Was the whole structure of Jewish ceremonial, fasting naturally included, really consonant with the new spirit of the followers of the Messiah? A new spirit must find new forms of expression; that is the lesson of the parable. Indeed, the book of Acts shows with increasing clarity the utter impossibility of containing this new Christianity as a mere 'Reformed Sect' within Judaism, although fasting is known in Acts even in largely Gentile churches (Acts 13:1-3). It was no accident that not only the Judaizers but even the non-heretical Jewish-Christian churches known to Eusebius (both of whom continued to observe the law), died out in later centuries: they had tried in vain to put *new wine* into *old wineskins*. Whenever the fresh life of the Spirit breathes in the church, the same problem arises, as the church seeks for appropriate forms in which to contain and express the new life, without losing continuity with the old. Yet Christianity, for all its outward differences, was not a breach with Judaism, but its fulfilment (see on 1:2).

v. Controversy about the sabbath (2:23-28)

Neither to the 'temporary' nor to the 'essential' reason for the failure of the disciples to fast did the Pharisees give any reply; indeed, it is hard to see what they could have said. None the less, the two incidents with which this chapter closes, and with which the next chapter begins, show further clashes on two other points of ceremonial observance, so it is obvious that, on the wider issue, the orthodox Pharisees were still far from satisfied. Here it was the behaviour of the disciples, not Jesus Himself, with which they found fault. It is very noticeable that the religious leaders were not able to bring anything against Jesus personally, not even the most trivial charge of breach of the ceremonial law. The sole proven charge against Him was that of healing on the sabbath. That this charge would not stand in the religious court of the Sanhedrin as a true case of sabbath-breaking is shown by their failure to bring it forward at the trial of Jesus, when they were catching at any straw of evidence against Him as a make-weight. Like Pilate, try as they might, they could find no fault in Jesus (Jn. 19:4): their only way to achieve their goal was to use 'false witnesses' (14:57).

The disciples were charged with 'working' on the sabbath, probably on several grounds. Pulling ears of corn was 'reaping', and that was one of the thirty-nine activities specifically forbidden on the sabbath (Anderson). Schweizer also points out that even 'walking' was a breach of sabbath law, unless the distance was strictly limited. One wonders what the Pharisees were doing in the cornfields themselves: their sole purpose may have been to criticise the disciples of Jesus. In addition to 'reaping', the disciples not only pulled the ripe ears, but also husked them between their palms, according to Luke (Lk. 6:1). The actual eating itself was of course not culpable, even in Pharisaic eyes. The disciples seemed to have acted in the matter quite unselfconsciously, and so not for the first time, we may be sure. But then, they had not been trained in the niceties of the rabbinic schools. We know how bitterly the Pharisees despised the 'am hā-āretz, the 'people of the land', the common people, ignorant of the law, and therefore considered accursed (Jn. 7:49). Even the Lord was regarded with great suspicion as an unlettered rabbi (Jn. 7:15), that is, one without formal training in the law at the feet of some recognized religious teacher. Such culpable ignorance displayed by His disciples with regard to subtle legal points would but condemn their master further in rabbinic eyes. It was, in the last resort, the professional jealousy of the theologians of Israel that hounded Jesus to death. None were so blind as those who boasted themselves of their theological insight.

Again, the answer of Jesus was twofold. First, He showed them that there was biblical evidence for the law of need taking precedence over the law of ceremonial,[1] and instanced this is the case of no less a personage than David himself. Further, he

---

[1] With deference to those commentators who disagree, this seems the plain meaning of the text before us. David had been in need, and so were the disciples of Jesus. To argue that

showed that in David's case this was not the mere question of picking and husking corn, but the much more serious charge of eating the *bread of the Presence*, which, after its solemn presentation to God, was hallowed from secular uses, and might be eaten only by the priests.

This action of David, though the Pharisees must of course admit it as an historic fact (whether or not it took place *when Abiathar was high priest*[1]), and also must admit that it stood unreproved in Scripture, they might nevertheless have deprecated, and regarded as at best a poor palliative of the offence of the disciples of Jesus, strict parallel though it was. Jesus must go further than this, to justify their action.

27. So Jesus now makes a far deeper claim. He claims that the Pharisees, with all their hedging restrictions, originally designed to avoid any possibility of infringing the sabbath, had ended by making the sabbath an intolerable burden (*cf.* Mt. 23:4). They had by now quite forgotten that in origin the sabbath was God's merciful provision for His creatures. Humanity was certainly not created simply to exemplify and observe an immutable theological principle of sabbath-keeping, as some rabbinic extremists were quite ready to uphold. To do them justice, the same extremists were quite prepared to be slaughtered rather than to resist their enemies on the sabbath (Schweizer), and so they were at least consistent. But at the last, it was this stubborn 'consistency' that kept them from response to Jesus: they lived in a sealed world of spiritual blindness and hardness of heart.

28. Even this principle, that the sabbath was made for humanity, some Pharisees might accept, but Jesus goes further.

---

the disciples were not dying of hunger is beside the point: neither was David, so far as we know.

[1]There is a well-known crux here, in that Abiathar became priest (the title 'high priest' does not seem to have been used in his day) only after the slaughter by Saul of Abimelech his father because of this deed of David's. Many MSS omit the clause in whole or in part, almost certainly because of the difficulty. We may cut the knot with the stout-hearted Jerome, by arguing that our concern is not with names and such like (*cf.* 1:2, where the citation from *Isaiah the prophet* actually covers Malachi as well), or else say that *epi* should be translated as 'in the passage dealing with'; *cf. epi tou batou* (12:26), 'in the story of the bush'. On the whole question of Abiathar, see Blomberg, in Carson and Woodbridge, *Hermeneutics, Authority and Canon*, pp. 147–148.

If the sabbath was truly made for our spiritual and physical good, and not vice versa, then *the Son of man* is master of the sabbath, and can interpret its regulations as He sees fit to do. This, in fact, was what the rabbis had been trying to do themselves, though in a wrong-headed way. Once again, if Jesus is using *Son of man* as a personal title for Himself at this point, and if His opponents understood His use of it so (neither point is certain), then the claim becomes even more pungent. It would mean that, instead of denying the charge, He freely admits it, but claims to have the absolute right to overrule the sabbath, because of His person and work as God's representative. Such a claim leads naturally enough to the major clash over sabbath healing at the beginning of chapter 3. It is at last dawning on them that His sabbath healings (1:25 and 1:31) were no mere accidents, but undertaken intentionally because He regarded the sabbath as His by right. So they resolve to lay a trap for Him, by making a deliberate test case; but as so often in the New Testament, the issue, when forced, moves them from the judge's bench into the prisoner's dock.

The other possibility is that Jesus here uses 'Son of man' merely as a synonym for 'mortal man'. The meaning would then be 'humans have precedence over the sabbath': but this is less likely.

vi. The man with the withered hand (3:1–6)

There is no evidence as to which particular *synagogue* this was, except that it was in Galilee. The likelihood is that it was in Capernaum, since the theological delegation from Jerusalem still apparently held its watching brief. This miracle concerned a man powerless to work until he received the healing touch of Jesus. One interesting early tradition[1] says that he was a plasterer, to whom naturally the use of both hands was particularly important. Some of these extra-canonical details preserved in such sources may perhaps be true; it is hard to see why they should have been invented, if they prove no theological truth.

[1] The 'Gospel of the Hebrews', quoted in Jerome's commentary on Matthew 12:13. See Anderson for a translation of the verses in question.

Much oral material about Jesus must have lingered on in Palestine, at least until the disaster of AD 70 broke the living lines of tradition, as the exile had in 597 BC. This detail, however, sounds more like a later 'preacher's amplification' of the text than a genuine memory.

2. The condemnation of the Pharisees is that they utterly failed to see in this man a case of need. All they saw was a possible ground of accusation against Jesus if He took advantage of this sabbath encounter to heal. By such moral blindness, they stood self-condemned, even before a word was spoken.

3. If the man truly desired healing, he must be willing to confess his need and to show his faith in the power of Jesus by standing up in the face of the whole congregation and displaying his need. To a sensitive person, such public display of a maimed limb would be a cup of shame, bitter to drink; but this costly confession of need Jesus often demanded (cf. the woman with the 'flow of blood' or haemorrhage in 5:33). In Israel, even an animal, if for presentation to the Lord, must be perfect, without a blemish: the blind or disabled were not acceptable (Lv. 22:22). No maimed Israelite could act as a priest of the Lord (Lv. 21:18).

4. The query of Jesus on this occasion, like the question about the source of John's baptism in 11:30, was one which the Pharisees could not answer honestly and directly without at once abandoning their own theological position. Matthew 12:11, with the homely parable of the animal which falls into a pit and is at once retrieved by his owner, sabbath or no sabbath, makes the same point even more obviously. The Galilean farmers would have chuckled at that: it was after all an appeal to the common-sense of the ordinary man or woman, as was the question of Jesus here. Frequently, by Semitic idiom *to do good or to do harm* can simply mean 'to do anything', but here each part obviously has its full sense, for the two halves are strongly contrasted,[1] as

---

[1] It is possible that the second clause, 'or to do evil', may merely be a typically stylistic addition, to balance the first clause. The meaning of the whole phrase would then be the same as the simple 'to do good'. But the exegesis in the commentary seems more natural

to save life or to kill. Yet everyone, by admitting the justice of
Jesus' question, admitted that it was therefore lawful to do good
on the sabbath day; for to heal a helpless cripple was unquestionably *to do good.* Further, to abandon the helpless man would
be to cause him to remain crippled; this would clearly be *to do
harm.* Whatever course of action was chosen, something must be
done on the sabbath day. The only freedom of choice was as to
whether to do *good* or *harm, to save life* (better 'heal') *or to kill.*
Technically speaking, on their own terms, a wrong deed would
be a far greater 'profanation' of the sabbath than the good deed
which they were scrupulously refusing to do. Mark does not
here record the conclusion to be found in Matthew 12:12 'so it is
lawful to do good on the sabbath', but this is clearly the meaning
of Jesus, whether stated or not. Mark usually leaves his readers
to draw such conclusions for themselves.

5. This is the first reference in Mark to that *hardness of heart* or
'refusal to respond' experienced by Jesus, not only among Pharisees, as here and 10:5, but also among the common people (Jn.
12:37–40), and even among His own disciples (6:52). Such 'hardness of heart' angered Him when found among His enemies; it
grieved and amazed Him when among His disciples. 'Hard-
hearted' to us usually means callous or cruel, but to the Hebrew
it meant a stubborn resistance to the purpose of God, the very
opposite of that humility and gentle teachableness which God
requires. It is a form of pride and, like unbelief, it is in part at
least an attitude of the will. So, if wilfully sustained, it can end
by becoming the unforgivable sin against the Holy Spirit (3:29).
It should be noted that this is a sin to which, to judge from
Scripture, the theologian and the religiously-minded are more
exposed than are the publican and sinner: and if any of us fears
this sin, it is proof that we have not committed it. 'Heart' in
Hebrew comes close to 'mind' in English: it is not primarily
concerned with the emotions but with the thoughts and the will.

and satisfactory, since it gives an appropriateness to both halves of the clause. Alternatively, we may take 'to do good or ill' as being the common Semitic idiom meaning 'to act'
in general, or 'to do anything', since all possibilities are included here. In either case the
problem is more linguistic than theological; the lesson is the same.

6. The result of the man's faith and obedience (if the two concepts can be distinguished) was complete healing (5). Mark, alone of the gospel writers, tells us that from this moment onwards the Pharisees and Herodians[1] began to plot the death of Jesus. That was equally the result of the same miracle; for grace can either soften or harden the heart, but it was not leave it untouched.

The Pharisees were outraged at what they regarded as a clear and deliberate breach of the law. But it is hard to believe that in their plot to kill Jesus they had already secured the backing of the high priestly authorities at Jerusalem, to whom as yet Jesus cannot have appeared a very formidable antagonist. Why *the Herodians* were involved in the plot is not so clear; whoever they were (see the preceding note), they can scarcely have been zealous for the law. Their anxiety, to judge from their name, may have been purely political.

III. ALL WHO RECEIVED HIM: THE CALL AND TRAINING OF THE DISCIPLES (3:7 – 8:26)

A. THE CONFLICT INCREASES (3:7–35)

i. The breach with the religious leaders (3:7–12)

These verses seem to mark the first decisive breach between Jesus and organized Judaism. If this is correct, it took place near the start of the ministry of Jesus, and is quite as marked and

---

[1]The exact identity of the Herodians is disputed. Mark mentions them certainly in 3:6 and 12:13, and possibly in 8:15 (a variant reading) as opposing Jesus, along with the Pharisees. With the exception of Mt. 22:16, the other gospels do not mention them at all, in most cases linking the Sadducees with the Pharisees instead. Because of this, some commentators have doubted their very existence, or even identified them with the Sadducees, but this is hypercritical. Mark knows of Sadducees also (12:18) and introduces them alongside Herodians and Pharisees. Herodians, however, are not mentioned outside the New Testament and literature dependent on it.

The term probably therefore describes those Jews who saw in Herod Antipas and the Herodian dynasty the hope of Israel (so Bickerman and, in general, Knox). Blood-stained tyrant though Antipas was, he was at least a native ruler, and had saved half the land from coming under the direct rule of Rome, as Judea had come. They may possibly have been largely members of the priestly aristocracy, numbering Sadducees within their ranks. The Pharisees, previously bitter enemies of the House of Herod (see Josephus), had by now reached an uneasy understanding: but a Pharisee could scarcely be called a Herodian.

decisive in the synoptic gospels as it is in John. Jesus now moved away from those who had become His enemies, by a deliberate act of separation, and His disciples accepted the consequences of this separation by following Him (7). Not only so, but big crowds poured down, not merely from Galilee now; from Edom in the south to Tyre in the north and Transjordan in the east (so possibly including Gentiles), they gathered to Him, eager to be healed. It is as if the sabbath healing by Jesus in the synagogue was being vindicated by the common people, though official Judaism repudiated it. It is a marked biblical stress that in spiritual matters the plain judgment of the simple heart is a truer guide than the wrangling of the learned. What is hidden from the wise is revealed to mere babies (Mt. 11:25–26). For the generally favourable attitude to Jesus of the *ochlos*, the 'crowd', in Mark, see Minear. Yet, at the last, in Jerusalem, this very 'crowd' seems to have turned against Him, when 'stirred up' by the chief priests (15:11).

9–10. There are several other references in the gospels to Jesus' practice of sitting in a ship moored offshore, and preaching to the crowds on the beach, when ordinary means of reaching such large numbers had failed. It was only one of the instances in which it was proved that the prior life and training of His fisherfolk disciples was by no means wasted, though they had forsaken it to follow Him. Frequently Jesus used their skill and strength to cross the sea by boat, although they had to learn that, even in the sphere where they felt most at home, Jesus was still Lord (*cf.* 4:41). There is at least one gospel reference to Peter being commanded by Jesus to 'cast a hook' and fish (Mt. 17:27), and one of the resurrection stories finds the disciples fishing under the direction of Jesus, this time using their nets (Jn. 21:3). It is therefore reasonable to suppose that the skill of the disciples may often have supplied them all with a meal. God does not always meet our needs by supernatural miracles: that is the exception, not the rule. To sit in the boat on this occasion was a good idea, but it was not a miracle, and the boat itself was not miraculous but provided by a disciple, in a perfectly 'natural' way. Yet there were miracles in plenty in the context, in healings and exorcisms by Jesus, and indeed it was the crowds resulting from these miracles that led to the need for the boat.

11-12. Note the steady refusal of Jesus to accept demonic testimony to His person or work, though such testimony would have been irrefutable.[1] The reason for this refusal is not given by Mark, but it seems reasonable to suppose that Jesus wanted others to find out who He was by listening to His words and by watching His deeds. This is made clear in His reply to the puzzled disciples of the imprisoned John, who were sent to ask bluntly whether Jesus was the Christ or not. 'Go and tell John what you have seen and heard' (Lk. 7:22). Here were messianic signs in plenty; but it needed the eye of faith to interpret them.

But the scribes and Pharisees, who, of all others ought to have known from their close study of the Old Testament how to recognize the Messiah when He came, not only watched His mighty deeds unmoved; they actually attributed His expulsion of demons to demonic power (3:22). This was a deliberate distortion of the truth which called forth from Jesus the solemn warning as to the danger of such sin against the Holy Spirit, which, by its very nature, is unforgivable (3:29), since it has rejected in advance the only path to forgiveness provided by God.

ii. The call of the twelve (3:13-19)

Following this breach with the church of Israel, Jesus began to constitute His own church. He retired from the lakeside into the hill country of central Galilee (this is more probably the meaning of the Greek *oros*, rather than some one particular *mountain* near Capernaum),[2] and spent a whole night in prayer (Lk. 6:12) before selecting for special teaching and training twelve from out of the general company of His followers.[3] Johnson acutely

[1]Of course, as Anderson notes, the demon's declaration is not a dogmatic or doctrinal confession. It is wrung unwillingly from the demons as they bow before God's superior power, at work in Jesus.

[2]To biblical writers 'the highlands' means either the hilly country of central Galilee, or else the mountainous plateau of Judah, with 'lowlands' elsewhere, especially along the seashore or lakeside. But perhaps the word only reflects Aramaic *tūrā*, 'open country' (Black, quoted in Anderson), and has no reference to the height of the area.

[3]Just as the old Israel had twelve 'founding fathers', so had the new; even some of the names of the founders are the same. In both old and new, there is a Simeon and a Levi, as well as a Judah. Other correspondences unknown to us may well exist, for Andrew and

points out that Mark is not particularly concerned with church order, or with the later status of apostles: to Mark, the twelve are pattern disciples, to spread the good news.

14-15. The primary purpose of the appointment of the twelve was so that they should be continually in the company of their 'rabbi', who was at once teacher and leader of the group. They would thus receive both formal and informal instruction, and treasure and lay to heart His casual sayings, in the manner familiar from the disciples of Socrates and Confucius as well as from the common rabbinic practice of the time of Jesus and later. The secondary purpose was so that He might send them out as His own personal representatives, on missions for Him. At this stage, their mission was defined as that of being heralds of the news of the establishment of God's rule. By virtue of this, they had an authority, delegated to them by Jesus, to expel from human lives the demon forces that had hitherto ruled them (15).[1]

16-19. Mark's list of the apostles contains more of the personal nicknames, naturally Aramaic,[2] than do any of the lists in

---

Philip almost certainly had a Hebrew 'name in religion' as well as their Greek names (see Cranfield). As there had been of old a beloved tribe, Benjamin, so there was now a beloved disciple, John; and, in the new Israel, all are both priestly and royal (Rev. 1:6), as ideally in the old Israel (Ex. 19:6).

[1]The question now arises as to what extent the driving out of demons still forms part of the ordinary Christian's calling today. Exorcism was clearly a spiritual gift committed by Jesus to the apostles: it is mentioned in the 'longer ending' of Mark 16:17, although not in the 'great commission' of 16:15: it also appears in Acts 5:16, etc. Nowadays, with the re-emergence of the concept of a 'deliverance ministry' within the church, this debate has once again become a burning issue. While not in any way minimizing the reality or possibility then or now of partial or total possession by demonic power, it should be noted that the gospels use this concept and the consequent phraseology more freely than in Acts, and that the Epistles, while mentioning opposition by Satan, do not mention exorcism at all as a spiritual gift or task, suggesting that the question is more linguistic than theological. Of all the gospels, Mark is closest to the Hebrew usage, by which many types of ill health were ascribed directly to the devil, without mentioning any 'secondary causes'. This should warn us against the generalization on too wide a scale of the concept of 'demonization', and lead us to be cautious both in our perception of the need for exorcism and in its application, except in very clearly marked cases.

[2]There can be little serious doubt that Jesus and His disciples habitually used Aramaic both in conversation between themselves, and in conversing with others, in Galilee at least, although there is much dispute over the exact dialect and vocalization. Matthew Black is still the safest guide. Few now would hold with Torrey's extreme views, for which see Albright.

the other gospels. If, as suggested in the Introduction, even if his gospel is not directly Petrine, Mark depends directly upon early Palestinian tradition, this is very understandable. *Simon* (16) is to be *Peter*, or *Cephas* in Aramaic, 'the rock'[1]. *James* and *John* (17) are a hot-tempered pair; they are to be called *Boanerges*, translated by Mark as *sons of thunder*. *Thaddaeus* (18) is probably to be equated with the Lebbaeus of other lists, an equation specifically made in some manuscripts. It is in either case probably to be translated as 'big-hearted', though, if it is a nickname, the exact point made by the name (courage? intelligence?) is uncertain. Some, however, had equated this apostle with 'Levi', as Origen seems to have done, presumably on the basis of the similarity between 'Levi' and 'Lebbaeus': but this may be simply an attempt to settle the identity of the twelfth apostle. All lists are agreed on eleven of the names, though additional names are to be found in apocryphal and Jewish sources (Schweizer). *Simon the Cananaean* (18) would be better translated as 'the Zealot' (see BAGD) or 'the activist', following Luke 6:15. This also is more likely to be a nickname than to denote actual membership of the later Zealot party. If we translate the name as 'the keen', we can recapture some of the original pun as well as the sense of the word. Perhaps *Cananaean* is not so much a mistranslation of the presumed Aramaic original form *qan'ān* as a deliberate precaution against possible suspicions of treason. Mark's Gospel was written early, and there was no certainty that it would not fall into the wrong hands. Other instances of similar caution in Mark's wording will be mentioned below, in chapters 13–14. Likewise *Iscariot* (19) is at least as likely to mean 'the dagger man' (the ancient equivalent of the modern 'gunman') coming from the mixed Graeco-Latin word *sikarios*, as it is to mean 'the man from Qeriyōth' (meaning either 'villages' in

---

Written Aramaic sources for the gospels (as distinct from oral Aramaic sources) become progressively less and less likely in view of the almost total dearth of Aramaic literature in this period, apart from certain of the Dead Sea Scrolls. The fact that spoken Aramaic was very much alive, however, is shown especially by Mark, as is very natural, if he has a Palestinian source or sources. See also 5:41 and 7:34, for entire 'fossilized phrases' of Aramaic.

[1]Nineham points out that, from now on in the gospel, the old name 'Simon' is dropped (except in 14:37) in favour of 'Peter', the Greek for 'Cephas'. Compare the way in which the old name 'Saul' is dropped in Acts in favour of the Roman name 'Paul' after the commencement of the Gentile mission (Acts 13:9).

general, or one specific place-name). Even if translated 'knife-man', it could be either a pure nickname, or a hint of direct political associations with the various extremist parties loosely grouped together under that name. For the suggestion that the name was *sheqarya*, 'deceivers', see under 14:10. Whether Thomas ('The Twin': see Jn. 11:16) is a nickname or not, is quite uncertain: he may well have been so named from the circumstances of his birth.

Even if these last few instances are indeed to be understood as nicknames, however, there is no direct evidence that they were names conferred by Jesus, as the names 'Peter' and 'Boanerges' certainly were, according to Mark (verses 16 and 17), but there can be no doubt that they were the names used within the group, to judge from their later familiarity in the church. The Talmud contains many examples of what we would call today 'surnames' or 'nicknames', used to distinguish various rabbis who shared a common name. A 'trade-name' is for instance frequent (*cf.* 6:3 'the carpenter', of Jesus), or a 'place of origin' (14:67 'the Nazarene'), or a parent's name (6:3, 'the son of Mary'): Jesus, after all, was a widely used name (see on 15:7), and even 'Jesus, son of Joseph' was not uncommon as a combination, even being found on a tomb.

In the choice of the disciples, there is an example of what can only be a mystery to the modern mind. Jesus chose at His own sovereign will, and those whom He chose responded to His call (13), so much is clear from Mark. But why choose this particular twelve? Or has this question any meaning when applied to God's sovereign grace? It would be easy to say that Jesus chose those who had already proved themselves most responsive to His teaching, since He chose the twelve from among the larger number of those who were already His followers, and had therefore been to some extent already sifted and tested. It may even be said cautiously that the parable of the talents would tend to support this general line of argument. But this cannot totally plumb the mystery, for perfect divine foreknowledge (Jn. 2:24-25) still chose Judas among the others (19). Perhaps it was because Jesus saw capacity even in Judas for response to divine truth, or perhaps the choice of Judas was like the handing to Judas of the morsel at the Last Supper, a token of love (although some would dispute this meaning: see Morris, NICNT, *John*, p. 627, note 27), that would either win him over or else condemn him. In his usual way, however, Mark does not concern himself with the abstract problem: he simply records the incontrovertible fact of the choice of these twelve by Jesus, stumbling-block though it may have been to the early church in certain instances. Indeed, so far from avoiding the difficulty, Mark underlines it: Judas Iscariot is described as *who betrayed him*. Mark does not mention the handing of the 'sop' to Judas at the supper, though he can hardly have been ignorant of it: it is his way to understate rather than overstate.

iii. *Mounting opposition: the Beelzebul controversy (3:20–30)*

21. The consequence for Jesus of sonship of His heavenly Father was misunderstanding by His nearest and dearest upon earth: *his family* went out to seize Him, believing Him mad (verse 21). His own brothers apparently did not believe in Him during this earthly ministry (Jn. 7:5), although Acts 1:14 shows that afterwards some at least were numbered among the church, and Galatians 1:19 refers specifically to James, the brother of Jesus, as occupying high position at Jerusalem.

In 3:31, 'his mother and his brothers' seem to have tried to presume upon their 'natural' family relationship, and to have received a gentle rebuke from Jesus.[1] When He said 'a man's foes will be those of his own household' (see Mt. 10:36), he may well have been speaking from bitter experience. Why should His friends or relatives say (21), doubtless with rough kindness in spite of their obvious irritation, that he was *beside himself (i.e.* 'out of his wits')?[2] What had made those who knew Him best so convinced that He was mad, that they were even prepared if necessary to detain Him by force, for His own protection? It was

[1]The unreformed churches of the world, with their exaltation of Mary, have not always realized the consequence of this principle, that a temporary physical relationship to the incarnate Lord gives no special claim on Him. 2 Cor. 5:16 is a wider extension still, applying to the whole incarnate life of Jesus.

[2]It is, however, quite possible that *elegon* should be translated with RSV in the vague sense of *people were saying*, or 'it was rumoured'. The subject would then be the people in general, and not specifically the relatives of Jesus. The action of his family would then be taken in response to a widespread rumour which had reached them, and would not be the result of a considered judgment on their part: but the net result was the same.

was not, apparently, because of the content of His preaching, but because of its unexpected results; such numbers had come to hear or to be healed that set mealtimes were impossible (20). This, to them, was the last straw; like Peter when he heard of the cost to Jesus of the road to Jerusalem (8:32), they decided that they must save Him from the consequences of His own vocation. Again, like Peter, they thought that they acted as His friends: but such friends were more dangerous to Him than enemies. Like the disciples at the well of Samaria, they had no concept of the true food that sustained Jesus, the moment-by-moment obedience to the Father's will (Jn. 4:32–34).

22. Relatives and close friends might misunderstand Jesus; even His followers might be puzzled by Him. But it was left to the theological commission of enquiry to misinterpret Him deliberately.[1] There is a calculated bitterness in their terse judgment which is lacking even in the rough words of His friends or relatives: there is a great difference between *he is beside himself* (21) and *he is possessed by Beelzebul* (the original form of the Hebrew ba'alzᵉbûb ['Lord of the flies'] probably a mocking alteration of ba'alzᵉbûl, meaning 'Prince Baal'). The theological commission was less concerned with speaking the truth than with speaking cutting words. We may compare 'He has a demon, and he is mad' (Jn. 10:20).

It is a strange paradox that in any times of religious revival or obvious working of God's Spirit, it is often the religious leaders who oppose the work of God most strenuously, and seem to misunderstand it most wilfully. This is because every person's danger of spiritual 'stumbling' over Christ comes through that which they take to be their strong point, in which they pride themselves. God, says Paul, traps the wise by their own wisdom (1 Cor. 1:19–21). The *scribes* in this passage are a living illustra-

[1]This charge against Jesus of being in league with demons is reiterated in the Tannaitic formulation, which may stem from official Sanhedrin records (Stauffer, quoted in Lane). Certainly, the charge of sorcery is made in the Talmud. But, if so, it is remarkable that no charge of sorcery was made against Jesus at His trial (Lane), unless it was in the bungled charge about the promised rebuilding of the temple. It has often been noted that the core of the hostility to Jesus comes from the Jerusalem religious authorities (Schweizer), and this is another example.

tion of this truth: their venomous remark was not a sudden outburst of anger, but a sustained attitude. These Jewish ecclesiastics could not deny that Jesus had indeed expelled demons. Yet, running counter to all common sense, as Jesus Himself pointed out by a simple illustration (23-25), they attributed this good work to an evil agency. This would assume a dichotomy of evil, a civil war within the kingdom of darkness itself, which would not only be a practical impossibility, but also a theological absurdity (26). Prejudice, in its full sense of a prior conceived judgment, had blinded their eyes to what was at once obvious to simple souls.

23-26. Nevertheless, Jesus dealt graciously with them, in spite of their stubborn blindness. He first shows by parables the patent absurdity of their position in this assumption of a fatal division within the realm of evil, which would be tantamount to the suicide of Satan.[1] The other two synoptists add that He also asked the relevant question as to what power was used by confessedly orthodox Jewish exorcists in performing a similar task with similar results; was that demonic power also? (See Mt. 12:27; Lk. 11:19.) We may note the casual reference in Mark to the one casting out demons in the name of Jesus, who was not a regular 'follower' of His (9:38), and the story of the sons of Sceva, the exorcists of Acts 19:14, as illustrations of the widespread nature of exorcism in first-century Judaism. Exorcism was by no means such a new or isolated phenomenon in Judaism that the scribes should misunderstand it so. What may have been new was the universal success with which Jesus employed it, in contrast to the occasional failure even of His own disciples (9:28),[2] and of Sceva's sons in Acts.

[1]Lane may possibly be right in seeing here a side reference to the family of Jesus itself in the simile of the *house divided against itself*.

[2]Those who live or work among the younger churches will recognize the reality of this phenomenon as an empirical fact of Christian experience and in the life of the church, while perhaps adopting a reverent agnosticism as to its explanation. Even in cynical Europe, two world wars have unleased such demonic powers that western Christendom is now more inclined to accept demon possession as a sobering fact, even if the outward forms are different. Psychological explanations are merely explanations of the mechanism involved, and are no doubt valid as far as they go; but they cannot exhaust the meaning, for they leave unsolved the nature of the driving force under and behind such cases. The Bible never encourages idle speculation on these matters; our thought and speculation is to be Christocentric, not demonocentric. Certainly it seems that in the days of Christ there was a great

27. There was only one possible deduction; if Jesus did expel demons, it could only be because He was in possession of a power and authority stronger than that of Satan. So great a power, to any Jew, could only be the power of God (Lk. 11:20). This in turn meant that Satan's reign of sin and death was over, and that God's reign had already begun, in the hearts and minds of men whom Jesus had ransomed and redeemed from Satan's power. Nor is there to be any triumphal return for Satan; the strong man has already been bound, as these exorcisms show.

28–30. This leads to one of the most solemn pronouncements and warnings in the whole of the New Testament, coupled, as often, with one of the greatest promises. There is forgiveness with God for every sin and blasphemy except one, which may be the deadly sin of which John speaks so cautiously in 1 John 5:16. This is the sin of the wilfully blind, who persistently refuse the illumination of the Spirit, oppose the Spirit's work, and justify themselves in doing so by deliberately misrepresenting Him. For such, there can be no forgiveness, for they have refused the only way of forgiveness that God has provided: indeed, they have slammed the door (verse 30). Anderson notes that the adjective 'holy' very rarely occurs as qualification of 'Spirit' in the sayings of Jesus as recorded in Mark, so that we may possibly have the vocabulary of a slightly later period being used here by Mark. But this is no proof that Jesus did not sometimes use it: otherwise, its later almost universal use would be quite inexplicable. Further, the usage is already found in the Old Testament: see Psalm 51:11. The question is purely linguistic, not theological.

---

outburst of Satanic activity. just as there was an outpouring of the Holy Spirit's power, manifested in miracles of healing.

Whether the same is true today or not, and whether the outpouring of the Spirit witnessed in many parts of the world is accompanied by consequently increased demonic activity, is another question, to which not every Christian would give the same answer. Whatever the answer, the modern Christian over-interest in the demonic and demon-possession does not seem to be either biblical or healthy, while a recognition of the spiritual nature of the warfare in which we are engaged is both of these (Eph. 6:12).

iv. The true relatives of Jesus (3:31-35)

Presumably this arrival of His mother and brothers is still to be seen in the context of verse 21, where *his family* was ready to restrain Him by force, through a misunderstanding of the nature of His ministry. A similar total misunderstanding underlay the reaction of Peter in 8:32 to the news that the path of messiahship involved suffering and death. The reason for the misunderstanding was the same in both cases: God's thoughts and plans run contrary to all natural human inclinations (8:33).

There are still crowds coming to Jesus and He is still teaching them, in a systematic fashion, to judge from the verb *sitting* in verses 32 and 34, which to a Hebrew mind would imply a teaching relationship. Compare 4:1, where Jesus sits, as a rabbi might do, in a boat to teach the crowds. Preaching, on the other hand, seems usually to have been done while standing, to judge from the prophetic pattern of the Old Testament. It was the work of a herald, and the messages were usually much terser.

32. *Your mother.* Those who brought the message through the crowd to Jesus obviously felt that an external family relationship such as that of mother or brother constituted a valid prior claim on Jesus.[1] There is even a note of mild rebuke in their words, a certainty that as soon as Jesus knows the true facts of the case, He will at once acknowledge the justice of the claim and interrupt His teaching to come out to them. But of such a claim, based on such a physical and natural relationship, the biblical Jesus shows Himself utterly unaware. Even to Mary, this son of hers was a stranger, until she learned the nature of the new relationship which must now bind her to Him. For, having first destroyed the initial false confidence with which His mother and brothers came, Jesus shows that there is indeed, in the

[1]Minear is correct when he points out how revolutionary the teaching of Jesus is here, especially in a Jewish context where a primary obligation was to one's own family, and where respect of parents was enforced by the law (Ex. 20:12). The same would be true in any 'old fashioned' part of the third world today. Schweizer is probably going too far, however, when he says that this teaching is designed to forbid a later 'caliphate' in the church of Jerusalem. True, James, the Lord's brother was an early leader there (Gal. 1:19), and Eusebius says that other relatives of Jesus were leaders later (Schweizer), but there is no evidence that they were universally accepted.

doing of the will of God, a new and deeper confidence with which they may come, and which does allow such a claim to relationship (35). This new relationship is, however, spiritual and inward, not outward and 'natural', as was generally assumed by Israel in the time of Jesus, when they assumed that the Messiah belonged to them by right. The attitude of Mary and the brothers of Jesus is therefore only typical of the attitude of the whole nation: they confidently claimed a prior right to the kingdom of God because of their physical descent from Abraham (Mt. 3:9; Jn. 8:39). To find that this is not so will be the great stumbling-block of the gospel.

But it cannot have been easy for one as loving as Jesus to say such stern words: they can be understood only in the light of the searching demands of the gospel (10:29), overriding all natural human relationships, however close.

35. There is only one condition for admission to this position of peculiar intimacy with Jesus; we must know and participate, as He did, in doing *the will of God*. It is a constant New Testament stress that mere knowledge of doctrine, even with intellectual assent and appraisal of its truth, is inadequate without acting on it (Jas. 1:22). To that extent, the modern phrase 'doing theology' (rather than 'studying theology') contains a biblical truth: 'good soil' is that which produces a crop (4:8). Mere intellectual assent ultimately leads to our self-deception and downfall.

B. PARABLES OF THE KINGDOM (4:1–34)

i. The parable of the sower, and the reason for the use of parables (4:1–25)

If we are to stress the Greek word *palin, again,* 'a second time', in this verse, it would mean, as in 3:7, a determined turning of His back by Jesus on those who misunderstood Him, and so a fresh acceptance of His divine vocation.[1] But while in 3:7 those on

---

[1] It is only fair to say that most modern editors (*e.g.* Cranfield), take the following block of material as composite. But this, even if true, does not weaken the force of the argument:

whom He turned His back then had been His enemies, here they were His own relatives and friends. The path of Jesus was to be a lonely path, as Hebrews 13:11–13 makes plain. He must suffer 'outside the camp' and be rejected by His society: but, as in Hebrews, so here, there were others who were prepared to risk the wrath of official Judaism and go out to Him outside the camp, bearing His reproach.

Indeed, so great was the response that Jesus was forced to resort to what apparently became for Him now a common mode of teaching.[1] He taught, as we have seen, sitting in a boat, probably anchored in shallow water, while the listening crowds sat on the foreshore all around. He taught by using *parables*, or as we might say, 'illustrations', a system of instruction specifically designed to sift the wheat from the chaff among His hearers. Other teachers might rejoice when great crowds followed them, but not so Jesus; for He knew only too well the mixed motives of the human heart (Jn. 2:25). Here is an unusual teacher; His parables are designed to test rather than to illuminate, and to test, not the intelligence, but the spiritual responsiveness of His hearers. Further, there is a sort of arithmetical progression in things spiritual. To one who already has something, more will be given (25), since spiritual insight into the meaning of one parable will lead to further insight into the meaning of other parables (13). Contrariwise, failure to understand will lead us further and further into the fog, until we are completely mystified (12). In this, as in all other spiritual matters, either we *hear* or we do not hear (verse 9). To see the spiritual truth (to *hear*) is the proof that we have received the illumination of that Holy Spirit who alone can open our spiritual eyes, blind by nature, to the truth of God.

2. The parable of the sower is not the first of the 'illustrations' used by Jesus as recounted in this gospel. The reply given to

Jesus turns from His fleshly kin to His spiritual kin, and teaches them. This chapter, with 13, is the only long continuous section of teaching preserved in Mark's Gospel (Lightfoot).

[1]Schweizer (IOM) points out that while Mark uses *kerussein*, 'to proclaim' of Jesus, he also uses it of the Baptist and the twelve. But *didaskein*, 'to teach' (with its cognate noun), occurs twenty times, always of Jesus. 'Teaching' is therefore seen by Mark as typical of and central to the mission of Jesus, even if little detailed teaching is recorded in the gospel itself.

His critics in the Beelzebul controversy was specifically stated to be parabolic (3:23), and the reference to members of a bridal party, and to new wine in old bottles, had been equally obviously so (2:19–22). But this is the first sustained parable of which we have a full explanation given by Jesus Himself to the disciples. It stands, in all three synoptic gospels, at the head of a series of parables, apparently corresponding to a definite pattern of teaching which Jesus used. Further, in a sense this parable is the key to all the other parables, for it deals with our reception of all of His teaching (4:13). There was of course nothing strange to the Hebrew mind in this method of instruction: the Old Testament contains examples of similar parables used for instruction (cf. Jdg. 9:8–15). In fact this seems to have been one of the favourite forms in which the rabbis couched their teaching, to judge from the Palestinian Talmud.[1] A good general rule of interpretation is to remember that a parable is normally designed to convey one central truth only. We should therefore not try to find a spiritual meaning in every fine point, recognizing that some details are only the 'background' of the parable. Otherwise, it would become an allegory, not a parable, and allegory has little place in the New Testament, and none at all in the teaching of Jesus.

3. It is very possible that the subject of this parable was suggested by the sight of an actual sower at work on the hillside above the lake. There is, however, no hint in the context as to the season of the year (compare the obvious connection between the injunction to look at the fields in John 4:35 with what the open-air congregation could actually see at the moment). Jesus taught, not in some cloistered rabbinic school, but in familiar everyday surroundings: and for this teaching, He used homely illustrations drawn directly from that life, for teaching divorced from daily life has no support in the example or word of Jesus. As Anderson points out, parables are not allegories: the story is always a possible true life situation. Obviously, this is why the crowds loved to listen to Jesus.

[1] It has been well pointed out that *māshāl*, *parable*, to the Hebrew had a far wider range of meaning than the Greek *parabolē* (see BDB and KB under the Hebrew word). It has, however, been less commonly recognized that, in biblical Greek, *parabolē* gradually

4–8. This parable deals with the problem that is greatest of all to the thoughtful mind: how is it that scribes and Pharisees can so misrepresent Jesus? And how is it that even His kindred and disciples can so totally fail to comprehend Him? Why does not the hearing of the doctrine produce the same result in every heart? The answer, as given by Jesus Himself, is that the operation of the divine word on the human heart is not automatic, and that, while the doctrine is unvarying, the nature of the response is dictated by the nature of the heart that receives it.

It is sometimes fashionable today for exegetes to blame the sower in the story for the poor harvest, and to point to the indiscriminate nature of the sowing as the reason; but to adopt this attitude is to misunderstand the whole purpose of the parable as well as to ignore a great theological truth. God sends rain on just and unjust alike (Mt. 5:45), and sends His word to all, whether they will hear or whether they will not hear (Ezk. 2:5). We are not called to praise or blame the sower for the choice of methods: the parable is concerned with the empiric fact of the seed falling on different sorts of ground. The hard heart, the shallow heart, the overcluttered heart, and the good heart, all are in fact present, whenever the word of God is preached. This does not merely refer to the initial preaching of the gospel or the initial response of faith, but to all subsequent preaching too. The whole of the Christian life is one of continual and progressive response to fresh spiritual revelation. This illustrates how appropriate it is that the parable of the sower should stand as the introduction to a long teaching passage, itself largely consisting of parables.

9. *Let him hear*: this cryptic phrase is a warning to the hearers that the parable requires thought and action in response, lest we dismiss it lightly without applying its truth to our own hearts. After all, that is what three groups of those described in the parable had done, and doubtless what the majority of the hearers of Jesus on this occasion would also do.

---

extended its sphere of meaning to cover the wider range of the Hebrew word that it was translating. In classical Greek, its meaning had been much more restricted.

10. Simple the parable may be when the explanation is known, but it puzzled the disciples enough for them to seize the first opportunity, when they were alone with Jesus, to ask its meaning. Matthew 13:10 adds that they enquired wonderingly as to why He used the parabolic method of teaching at all. Mark does not record the question, but He records the answer in verse 12. It is plain that even the disciples found this parabolic method taxing. Yet only by the use of parables could there be that process of spiritual sifting that would be either eternally rewarding or eternally baffling, according to whether those who listened had *ears to hear* or not, that is to say, whether or not they earnestly desired to understand God's ways. If their will was rightly directed, then intellect would present no problem (Jn. 7:17).

11. The answer is given in solemn words, designed to make them realize how privileged was their position as disciples of Jesus, and it introduces some of the deepest theological mysteries of the whole New Testament. God had been pleased to reveal to this little group the 'mystery of the kingdom' still hidden from others. They alone could talk with Jesus face to face, and ask for explanations of what puzzled them, whereas to those *outside*, the only explanation would be by another parable, which will test them afresh. The judgment is written plain for those who hear and yet fail to appropriate: their capacity for apprehension and appropriation of spiritual truth steadily dwindles until it disappears. Contrariwise, the more of God's revealed truth that we assimilate, the more our capacity for assimilating further truth will grow. Further, spiritual perception of God's truth is perilous: it only condemns us unless we act upon it. Increased knowledge merely brings increased responsibility (Lk. 12:48). God's solemn choice of us is very far from favouritism, as indeed the history of Israel in the Old Testament makes plain.

12. Because spiritual truth is not a set of isolated intellectual propositions to be mastered, but a whole to be comprehended by that sudden flash of spiritual insight which is the revelation of the true nature of Jesus made to us by God (8:29), so, to those outside, all must be in parable, because it would be useless to teach them deep spiritual truths until they had mastered the elementary level. But in any parable there was enough to lead the thoughtful, questing soul on: as Jesus says in verse 20, those sown on the *good soil* would hear and receive the word, and would transmute that truth into life. In terms of the parable, they will bear a crop, although in varying degrees.

So that: there are several ways of explaining this verse. One way is by saying that in the Greek of the New Testament the particle *hina*, which should grammatically mean 'in order that' and should therefore express purpose, sometimes at least means 'so that' and merely expresses consequence.[1] To translate in this way would remove a possible theological problem altogether. The second is to see the strong antithesis as an idiomatic but typical Hebraism, deliberately stating the position in a more extreme form than it really means: this would come to the same result as the grammatical solution suggested above. The third possibility is to see these stern words in their Old Testament context of Isaiah 6:9–10, where it is plain that it is Israel herself who has obstinately shut her eyes and ears against God's pleading. Israel's blind condition is therefore culpable and a judgment which they have brought upon themselves; and so it is inevitable that they should fail to understand. This is probably the best solution to adopt. We can add to this the theological truth that God has willed that those who so refuse to accept His truth shall remain blind: in this sense, it is all within His purpose, and we can justify the *so that*. The fourth possible explanation, which carries the third suggestion even further, is to take a strong theological position, and to say that God has been pleased to reveal His Son to some and not to others, and that what is revelation to some is therefore merely baffling to others. This introduces again the mystery of God's choice, to which Jesus refers in verse 11. As usual, Mark does not attempt to explain the mystery: he merely records it.

13. Jesus gives warning that this parable is, as it were, a 'parable of the parables', for it describes in vivid picture

---

[1] See BAGD, under this word: the explanation probably lies in Semitic idiom, and in the

language the reaction of His hearers to the whole system of parabolic teaching. It is not only the simplest of the parables; it is therefore the key to them all, as this verse says.

14. The parable of the sower owes its peculiar appropriateness to the fact that, at the very moment when He was telling the parable, Jesus was Himself sowing the good seed of the word, and so, by telling the parable, He was actually exemplifying it, quite irrespective of whether a farmer sowing the fields was at the moment visible to the hearers or not, as some commentators assume.

15–20. There is another question to ask: are people really themselves to blame for the state of their own hearts? This is often denied today. But have they themselves, by multiple prior choices, determined whether their hearts are by now hard, or shallow, or overcrowded with cares and pleasures, or, instead, are 'good soil'? This problem Scripture does not answer: the sole point made in the parable is that our hearts do in fact vary like this, and that this variation governs our response to the preached word. Although we are not specifically told to copy the seed sown on *good soil*, this is the obvious lesson, just as verse 9 is an invocation to us to *hear*.

21–25. It is probable that, in this particular instance, the primary lesson of the parable is not that stated elsewhere, as in 'let your light so shine before men' (Mt. 5:16). Perhaps the disciples felt as puzzled as any modern reader by His use of parables, and asked Him, 'Is this teaching in parables a deliberate obscuration of the truth to those outside?' No, says Jesus, answering as usual on their level: who would light a lamp and then deliberately hide it? If truth is temporarily hidden in the parables, it is only so that it may be later revealed: the ultimate purpose of a parable is therefore not to conceal truth but to reveal it. It is because of this that we must *take heed what you hear*, remembering the double law of 'spiritual wastage' and 'spiritual

---

underlying Aramaic saying (Schweizer). Although old, however, the principles of Moulton's *Prolegomena* (vol. 1 of Moulton and Howard's Grammar of the Greek New Testament), should also be weighed here.

growth' according to whether we respond or not. To those who learn, and then pass on to others what they have learned, more will be given (verses 24 and 25). This argument from 'minor' to 'major' is a favourite with the Jewish rabbis: if even we humans would not act so foolishly with a lamp which we have lit, how much less so would God?[1] The same paradox is seen in the case of Jesus: God is at one and the same time both veiled in Him, and revealed in Him,[2] but the ultimate purpose is that He may be revealed to all (13:26). The 'messianic secret' is only temporary.

ii. Two more parables of growth (4:26–32)

The first (26–29), which has no parallel in the other gospels (Schweizer), is a further explanation of the parable of the sower, being at once an amplification of the law of spiritual growth, and also a parable in its own right. As such, it illustrates the nature of the reign of God in the human heart: it suggests the Christian doctrine of 'growth in grace' (2 Pet. 3:18); and it inculcates a continued trust in God, who will give a harvest in due time (Gal. 6:9 and Phil. 1:6). The sower's daily sleeping and rising, and his ignorance as to how the seed grows, is only a part of the human 'back-cloth' of the parable and need not be spiritualized.[3] The process of spiritual growth is spontaneous within the kingdom of God, but it remains a total mystery to natural humanity. For the parable of 'fruitbearing' compare John 15 (frequently), Luke 6:43-45 and Galatians 5:22–23, where in every case the spontaneity of the process, given the necessary spiritual conditions, is stressed. The last sentence (verse 29) seems to be a warning of the coming end of the age. When the time is ripe, God will intervene decisively in the affairs of humanity (Joel 3:13) and

---

[1] Minear gives this a slightly different twist: even if outsiders seem deaf, we should not cut down our preaching of the word to them, for the only purpose of the lit lamp is to shine.

[2] Cranfield discusses this gospel paradox at length, and suggests a reason for it.

[3] This illustrates Anderson's point that a parable is not an all-encompassing allegory. Belo makes a great theological point of this mention of 'ignorance', as though it meant that even Jesus Himself was ignorant of what form the kingdom would take ultimately. But this is clearly an over-exegesis of the text, even if the theology expressed had been consistent with the rest of Scripture. Anderson is closer to the point when he says that the phrase describes a daily miracle that happens in the earth, quite independent of humans.

establish His rule, so that all may see. The metaphor of reaping, with its inevitable separation of wheat from weeds (Mt. 13:30), or grain from husks (Mt. 3:12), is a common picture in the Old Testament of the end of the age. It always involves the concept of judgment as well as salvation: chaff and weeds are burnt, wheat is saved. This is to be the final realization of the rule of God, which has begun already in Jesus.

30–32. The concept of the reign of God was still not clear to the disciples, who seem to have consistently looked for an establishment of the messianic kingdom in their lifetime; witness the selfish request of James and John (10:35), and the eager question asked of Jesus by the disciples even after the resurrection, as to whether now was to be the time for introducing the kingdom (Acts 1:6). The small beginnings and slow pervasive growth of the kingdom were beyond either the patience or the understanding of the disciples, but both were well illustrated by the growth of the tiny mustard seed known to them all. It is quite beside the point to quibble, and to say that ultimately the mustard seed produces only a large bush and not a tree: the point is that, from being a tiny seed, it grows until it far outstrips other similar plants. All Scripture must be read sensibly, and such quibbling would be rejected at once in the case of any other secular book.

The exact point of the reference to *the birds of the air* (32) is not clear: the words may be merely indicative of the size of the mustard plant, for small birds could indeed perch in such a bush[1]: but this need not exhaust the meaning. Some commentators have seen in it a reference to the mixed nature of the church, but this seems to be over-exegesis, though 'birds of the air' does sometimes have a sinister meaning in the Bible. It is best to see the explanation as lying in the Old Testament passage from which this is a quotation (Dn. 4:14). There, the birds in the branches, like the animals below the boughs, are part of the 'back-cloth' of the vision seen by the prophet, and simply

---

[1]See BAGD under the word *kataskēnoō*: esxpecially in view of Dn. 4:21, their translation of 'nest' seems preferable to the usual 'perch'. But in this particular case, perhaps the birds would be eating the seeds, as some commentators point out, rather than 'nesting' in the bush.

indicate the size and importance of the tree in question. Those who prefer to see a derogatory connotation in the word 'birds' will lean heavily on passages like Genesis 40:19, Joseph's interpretation of the dream of the royal baker, but these are birds of prey, as specifically mentioned in the context. On the size of the mustard bush, see Schweizer for the story of the rabbi who climbed up a mustard bush in his garden, but this must have been exceptional.

iii. The summing up of the parables (4:33-34)

Mark has given the above specimens of the parabolic teaching of Jesus (obviously not an exhaustive account), and he now suggests both a reason for the employment of parables, and also for the careful gradation in their use, in the words *as they were able to hear it*, or 'to understand'. In the school of Christ, none may move to advanced lessons till they mastered the elementary studies. To the outsider there was always the stumbling-block of the form of the parable to be penetrated: only for His own disciples were there private explanations (verse 34), as Mark makes clear on several occasions.

C. MINISTRY ROUND THE LAKE OF GALILEE (4:35 – 7:23)

i. Jesus calms the storm (4:35-41)

With the series of parables closed, we enter a new section: here Jesus will be shown as Lord of nature. This is a new revelation in Mark, yet a very necessary one, if Jesus is God: for, both in the Law and in the Prophets, God is seen as Controller of the natural world and natural phenomena. The God who blew with an east wind and dried up the waters of the Red Sea before Israel His people (Ex. 14:21), is now about to make a path over the wind and waves of Gennesaret for the disciples, the new 'people of God'. Already, Mark has shown Jesus as one who sees heaven opened, one upon whom the Spirit rests, who is responsive to the Spirit's guidance, who enjoys angelic ministry, and who receives the testimony of demons to His divine nature. Jesus in Mark preaches and teaches with a new ring of authority: He heals the sick, expels demons and forgives sins. Now, only the one who had initially created the wind and sea in the first place would dare to rebuke them so (verse 39): their instant obedience shows His full deity as Creator as well as Redeemer. The wondering question of His disciples in verse 41 shows that they realized in part at least the implications of His action here. It is significant that no 'nature miracles' are recorded in Mark as having been performed by the apostles, although (as Anderson well points out), Mark would not have distinguished nature miracles sharply from healings and exorcisms, as we might do today. Apart from calming storms (here and 6:51), Mark records Jesus as multiplying loaves (6:41 and 8:6) and withering a fig tree (11:20): he therefore accepts completely the power of Jesus over the natural world, as Son of God.

36. Mark is the only gospel that tells us of the *other boats* being with Jesus here: the calming of the storm therefore becomes a miracle of mercy on a wider scale than the mere saving from drowning of a boatload of frightened disciples. We may perhaps compare the closing words of Jonah, 'and also much cattle' (Jon. 4:11), with its undertone of the infinite mercy of God. Of course, the detail of the other boats may simply be a small irrelevant reminiscence included by the matter-of-fact Mark, which assures us of the historicity of the event.

37–39. The voyage across the lake had been undertaken at the express suggestion of Jesus, in unquestioning faith and obedience. This, for the disciples, made the coming of the storm all the harder to understand, and the relaxed attitude of Jesus quite inexplicable to them. There is more than a hint of reproach in their words, *Teacher, do you not care if we perish?* (38).[1] Why had He allowed them to enter such a situation? Jonah's storm, after

---

[1] It is quite unnecessary to see with Weeden (IOM) the derogatory way in which the disciples are painted in Mark as part of a 'polemic'. The explanation of accurate reporting by Mark of facts well known to all, before these 'Christian patriarchs' were idealized, is both far more likely and far more satisfying theologically. Tannehill (also in IOM), approaching from a 'literary' angle, has a healthier approach. He sees it as a 'paraenetic' method adopted by Mark, attempting to make us identify ourselves with the erring disciples, and so come to a better frame of mind: Mark by this 'encourages the reader to associate . . . with the disciples.'

all, had been a punishment for disobedience (Jon. 1:4), but they had been obedient: no wonder that they felt aggrieved at what had happened to them. The Lord's sleep did not only show His very natural weariness: it also showed His tranquil faith (verse 38). Faith and fear are mutual exclusives in the Bible: it was because of lack of faith that the disciples feared that they were about to drown (verse 40), and so it was for lack of faith that they were rebuked. No command is more often reiterated in the Bible than the simple 'Do not fear' (see Ex. 14:13; 20:20, *etc.*).

40–41. In spite of their lack of faith, Jesus calmed the storm with a word. But the disciples, inconsequentially, still feared[1]; a friendly, familiar, human Jesus they wanted, but not a supernatural Son of God. Their reaction at the mount of transfiguration (9:6), and even at the resurrection (16:8), was to be the same: compare Revelation 1:17.

ii. The Gadarene demoniac (5:1–20)

After the section of teaching in parables, there follow some miracles of healing, of which the first is the healing of the 'demonized' man in the territory of Gerasa, or Gergesa or Gadara, with other MSS. The difficulty is that Gerasa was forty miles from the lake, and Gadara was only six miles away, but with a deep gorge in between. Mark does not say that the miracle took place in any of these towns, however, but only in the general area where they were situated. The manuscripts are confused as to the place name, but this is no reason to accuse Mark himself of lack of knowledge of Palestinian geography (Schweizer), just because his copyists were ignorant of it. Jesus had expelled demons often before: there had been a first specific instance already mentioned (1:26) followed by a general campaign (1:32), and expulsion of demons was a general power entrusted to the apostles (3:15), as surely as was the task of heralding the news.

[1] It is possible, however, that this is an indefinite idiomatic use of the third person plural, corresponding to the indefinite *on* in French: see Moule, p. 180. The reference would then be general, not specifically referring to the disciples, and would refer to the widespread reaction to the revelation of the Godhead of Jesus which had just been made.

But this particular demon-expulsion has several peculiar features, which merit its inclusion here. For this was a man long 'under treatment' (like the woman suffering from a haemorrhage, mentioned in verse 25). It was in the failure of all human methods that Jesus acted decisively. The medical treatment given to this man was that commonly still used in many parts of the world today: he was loaded with chains, in a vain attempt to curb his inner turmoil by outward restraint. Not surprisingly, this proved quite futile (4). It was also probably part of his 'treatment' to drive him away from inhabited areas, to find in graveyards on desolate hillsides his 'isolation block'. But isolation, whether self-chosen or enforced by others (as in the case of lepers), meant only that the destructive force of evil, instead of turning outwards in outbreaks of violence, vented itself on the patient, in acts of senseless self-torture, as stated here (5).

6–8. It is strange that the insight of evil into the nature of Jesus should be so clear and instantaneous, while ordinary people were so slow to see His godhead.[1] Such truths, as James tells us, 'even the demons believe – and shudder' (Jas. 2:19), because for them these truths are not merely abstract principles, but forces with which to reckon. The demons knew Jesus at once, for fear, as well as love, sharpens the eyes. They acknowledged the status of Jesus all unwillingly, confessing at once the vast gulf that existed between them, and showing the searing effect that good has on evil. A better reply to the Pharisaical accusation that the Holy Spirit, which rested on Jesus, and the spirit of evil were fundamentally one spirit (3:22, a view not unknown in some Eastern religions), could hardly be found: here was evil itself refusing to acknowledge Jesus as in any way akin to itself. It is interesting how often in the gospels the demons themselves take the initiative and react violently to the very presence of Jesus, even before He says a word of rebuke or exorcism.

9–10. In this case, apparently Jesus had already spoken a word of authority (8) which was perhaps what provoked this

---

[1]Demons often recognize Jesus as 'Son of God' (3:11). 'Most high God', the title used here, is a Gentile title, suited to a Gentile area (Anderson).

demonic outburst (7).[1] Next, Jesus asks the man his *name* (9), to make his need apparent to all around, and perhaps to bring home to the man's own clouded mind the awful situation in which he was. In the Bible, *name* stands for 'nature': so the man was virtually asked to confess the nature of the evil by which he was enslaved. His reply is at once a confession of human impotence, and also vivid expression of the might and destructive force of the demonic powers by which he was gripped. It was a veritable 'army' of evil[2] which controlled him: no wonder that 'no one had the strength to subdue him' (verse 4).

11–13. There are several puzzles here: why did Jesus allow the demons in this particular case to vent their destructive force on the herd of pigs? Sometimes in the gospels the expelled demon spent his force in a last attack on the patient (*e.g.* 9:26, the epileptic boy); sometimes we have no record of any special manifestation on exit. We know so little in this realm that we do well to tread reverently: it may be that such an outward sign was required in this case to convince bystanders of the reality of the expulsion. The size of the herd of pigs would in turn make plain to all, by symbol, that the man had been tortured by countless conflicting evil impulses: he was not even 'integrated' in his evil. It may well be that, in some way that we cannot grasp, this was some sort of spiritual 'safety valve' to avert violence from the patient. It is sometimes half-humorously suggested that, if the owners of the pigs were Jewish, presumably engaged in selling what was to them ceremonially unclean pork to the Gentiles of the district, then this was a punishment to them as well. But it seems unlikely that Jesus would take such pains to punish a breach of ceremonial law, when He Himself constantly faced the

---

[1]Schweizer notes that, in dealing with demons, Jesus does not call on God to act, as He sometimes does in healing miracles: He acts directly on His own authority.

[2]There is certainly no hint here of the idea, common among pagan and Jewish exorcists of the day, that it was necessary to know the name of a demon in order to gain power over it and so exorcize it. Such an idea is foreign to the Bible (no examples can be found in Scripture), and belongs more to the area of magic and spells. Jesus addressed His question directly to the man, not to any demon: otherwise, the text would have said 'it', not 'him' in 9, since *pneuma, spirit,* is neuter in Greek. We are probably therefore dealing only with a nickname for the man here. In Acts 16:16, where some translations have 'Pytho', the RSV is correct in translating as *spirit of divination*; no name of a specific demon is implied, but purely the nature of the outworking of evil.

charge of breaking it (7:5). Even today in Israel, it is not unknown for a 'kibbutz' to rear pigs, in spite of all the outcry from the orthodox, although, in deference to scruples, they will be called *ḥaberim*, 'comrades', instead of *ḥazirim*, 'pigs'.

Note that the Bible clearly differentiates between various degrees of demonization. Usually the account only mentions 'a demon'; 'seven demons' is a stage worse, seen in Mary Magdalene's case history (16:9). But this man is, by contrast, filled by a veritable army of militant demons. No-one familiar with the biblical use of symbolism would press the numbers literally. Seven is continually used in the Bible as a metaphor and symbol, not so much of 'divine perfection', as is often said, but of completion and totality (*e.g.* Gn. 41:2).[1] Yet the inference is quite plain: there are varying degrees of control of humans by Satan, just as there are varying degrees of their control by the Holy Spirit. This man of Gerasa was completely bound by Satan as he had never been by the chains and fetters imposed by humans. So, at his healing, equally drastic manifestations of divine power are not to be wondered at. It is worth mentioning that the Bible never uses the term 'possession' by demons: humans may be 'troubled' by demons, or may be 'in the power of a demon', or 'demonized' (Wimber's good translation). If the participle is used, RSV as here paraphrases as *the demoniac*, but this has lost its force in modern English. Note also that Mark distinguishes very clearly between the sick and the demonized (*e.g.* 3:10 – 11): they are not the same.

14-17. The immediate reaction of the *herdsmen*, at this very obvious exhibition of supernatural power, was fear (*cf.* 4:41, for the similar reaction of the disciples at the stilling of the storm by Jesus). They seem to have scattered in their flight: both city and country nearby heard the news, and came to see for themselves. As soon as the local people were convinced that the demoniac

---

[1]This therefore does not support the theory that we should try to discover the number of demons 'resident' in a particular case, and expel them one at a time. The Bible only mentions in the singular 'an evil spirit', or 'seven evil spirits', or 'an army brigade', as here; there is no mention in other places of two, three, four, or five, as one would expect if this were a strictly numerical count. Of course, if we choose to use 'demon' simply as a metaphor to describe some particular weakness or temptation, we can begin a numerical count, but that is not a biblical usage.

had been truly healed, they shared in the same fear. When they had heard from eyewitnesses (16) *what had happened to the demoniac and to the swine* (a vivid detail which Mark adds, alone of the evangelists), they begged Jesus to leave their area. To their terror was now added the thought of the financial loss, possibly mixed with uneasy consciences, if they really were Jewish pig-breeders. The saddest thing in the whole story is that Jesus granted their request, and left them. There are times when the worst possible thing for us is that the Lord should grant our prayer (Ps. 106:15, 'He gave what they asked'). The Gerasenes wanted only to be left alone by this frightening supernatural Jesus. It was to be their judgment that Jesus did leave them, to return no more, for there is no evidence, in Mark at least, for any later ministry by Jesus in this area.

18–19. There is a striking and deliberate contrast here between the attitude of the inhabitants of Gerasa and the attitude of the healed demoniac. The Gerasenes begged Jesus to go, and He granted the request. The healed man begged to stay in the company of Jesus, but his request was refused. There is another paradox: the healed leper (1:44) had been strictly forbidden to tell anybody about his healing, but this healed demoniac was ordered to return home and bear witness to what God had done for him (19). There are good reasons for what might at first seem arbitrary and inconsistent. For Jesus Himself to continue preaching in the Gerasene country was clearly now impossible: therefore, in refusing the man's request to leave with Him, Jesus was ensuring a continuity of witness in a needy area.[1] When the leper of 1:44 had been healed, there were already unmanageable crowds milling about Jesus for healing; there was no need to spread the news any further, especially as the main task of Jesus was not to heal but to preach the kingdom (1:38).

20. This healed man was called to a peculiarly lonely and difficult task, which he fulfilled faithfully and with success, as can be seen from the summary account given here. We might

[1]Cranfield further points out that Decapolis was a largely Gentile area, where there was the less need to suppress news of a miracle, in that there was the less danger of misunderstanding the Messiah in terms of Hebrew nationalism.

have thought that his understanding of the gospel was inadequate: but he had recognized who Jesus was (even if it was initially through a demonic confession), and had experienced His saving and cleansing work. He had made the equation between God ('how much the Lord has done for you', 19) and Jesus (*how much Jesus had done for him*, 20) and knew himself to be the recipient of God's saving mercy (19). No-one could make such an equation except by the revelation of the Holy Spirit (1 Cor. 12:3) and therefore, he was truly a disciple, even if not permitted to follow Jesus literally.

iii. Two more healing miracles (5:21–43)

The next two miracles continue with the theme of human despair and helplessness meeting with the power of God in Jesus.

22. *Jairus by name*: there is no conceivable reason for the name to appear here in Mark, unless because it was firmly embedded in the tradition. It therefore shows the conservative way in which Mark handled his sources. 'Jair' was of course a familiar name from the Old Testament (Nu. 32:41) meaning 'He (*i.e.* God) gives light'. We may like to see a spiritual appropriateness in its use here, but there is no evidence that Mark did, let alone his Gentile public, ignorant of Hebrew as they would be.

25–29. The woman suffering from haemorrhage is the centre of a minor miracle 'bracketed', in Mark's fashion, in the context of the healing of Jairus' daughter. Mark makes plain in the bluntest language, which is somewhat softened down by Luke, the doctor (*cf.* Lk. 8:43), that earthly doctors and treatment were powerless to aid her.[1] A doctor, like a fisherman, must learn that without Jesus he can do nothing. It is easy to trust God at our 'weak points' when we have no other hope; we must learn

---

[1] The Talmud says 'the best among doctors is worthy of Gehenna' (Anderson), doubtless reflecting the lack of skill in early days, and consequent popular distrust of doctors. See the words of Ecclesiasticus 38:15, also somewhat ambiguous. No-one in the apostolic group, however, seems to have thought ill of Luke (Col. 4:14).

that we have equal need to depend on God, at what we consider our 'strong points'.

The woman heard of Jesus (27) and acted on what she had heard, by coming to Him. She showed the greatness of her faith, not merely in that she believed that Jesus could heal her, but in that she asked for so little contact: merely to grasp His robe would be sufficient. Such faith on the woman's part was at once rewarded by a healing of which she was instantly conscious (29). But Jesus makes plain, in His reply, that it was her faith which had healed her, not the mere touching of His robe. Otherwise it would have been either superstition or magic (with Schweizer). See Acts 19:12 (Paul's handkerchiefs) and Acts 5:15 (Peter's shadow) for similar instances, doubtless with a similar explanation: the sick were healed by their faith in Christ, however this faith was shown. We may dismiss later tradition that the woman was Bernice, a princess from Edessa, though there were Christians (and Jews) numbered among the Edessan royal family from very early times.

30. This is an interesting verse, in that it shows that Jesus was at least sometimes conscious of the flow of healing power from Himself to the sick individual. It may have been that such healings cost Him much spiritual energy, for we read of Him escaping for times of recuperation and prayer (6:32 etc.). Mark, unlike Matthew (Mt. 8:17) or Luke (Lk. 4:18) gives no theological reason for the healing miracles of Jesus, other than that they were signs of authority (1:27), and that Jesus was moved with compassion (1:41). That was sufficient for the practical Mark; that was all that was necessary for the Gentile mission.

31-33. Here is yet another instance of the disciples' expostulation with Jesus for what they regarded as His unreasonableness: compare 6:37 with its indignant 'shall we go and buy ... and give it to them to eat?' But Jesus ignored the expostulation in both cases: for the meaning of His question was at once apparent to one hearer at least, the woman herself (33). It was not enough to believe in her heart: she must as well confess with her mouth (Rom. 10:9). In front of all the crowd, she must confess, first her great need of healing, and then, the glad fact of her salvation.[1] That is was a costly confession, we can tell from the words *in fear and trembling* (33). For a woman to speak in public before an Asian crowd, and above all to speak of such personal matters, would be very humbling for her, but humility is an essential within the kingdom of God.

34. She had been already healed by her faith, but open confession brought her a word of confirmation from Jesus, and so a fuller understanding of her own recent experience. This in turn brought a realization of the means by which she had entered into this experience (*your faith* . . .), the promise of God's peace, and a sense of security for the future. Confession therefore brought to her, not healing, but assurance. This woman's bodily healing is a good picture of healing of the soul.[2] She suffered from a disease which, to Judaism, made her ceremonially unclean (like leprosy) and which, again like leprosy, barred her from access to God in His temple and from fellowship with God's congregation in worship. Conscious of her need, she had made many costly attempts to remedy it: but the human help, sought by her and given to her in all sincerity, was all in vain – indeed, it only worsened her situation. Her sense of need, coupled with the glad news of Jesus (for both factors must have been present), led her to come, although at first only as a nameless member of the crowd. Her faith was at once exercised and displayed in the contact with Jesus. The exact nature of the contact was, it seems, unimportant: it is the greatness or littleness of faith that dictates the mode. Little faith (like that of Naaman in 2 Ki. 5:11, or Thomas in Jn. 20:25) would have insisted on a close personal contact, but the greatness of this woman's faith lay precisely in the fact that she asked for so little

[1]For 'salvation' and 'healing' are the one word in Greek: as Anderson says, she has been brought into a close personal relationship with Jesus, shown by the use of the word *daughter*. So, for her, physical healing has passed already into spiritual salvation.

[2]All of the miracles of Jesus may be seen in this light: that is why John has singled out seven of them, and called them 'signs'. But Belo is quite right when he says that the church, in so doing, has often forgotten that the miracles were in origin physical acts of compassion performed for the sick and the poor. Indeed (though he does not say it), this is the reason why they can become 'signs'. In Mark's Gospel, however, one basic function of such miracles, apart from showing the love of Christ, it to establish His status and authority as proclaimer of God's message. They are therefore an adjunct to His preaching of the gospel, and do not stand independently by themselves.

contact. She would have been willing to slip away in the crowd, with her immediate physical need met: but Jesus had something greater in store for her, which could only come by open confession.

35. This verse brings us back again to Jairus, whose story had begun in verse 22. He also is a man in need, unashamed to make that need known publicly ('he fell at his feet', 22). His faith may not have been as great as that of the woman with the haemorrhage, but yet it was saving faith. If Jesus only came and laid His hands on the girl, Jairus believed that all would be well, though she might be at death's door already. There was a purpose in the delay caused by the slow push through the crowds, which must have irked Jairus sorely; and there was a purpose in the turning aside to heal one woman in the middle of a crowd, which must have tried the patience of Jairus still further. Verse 35 seems to show that such impatience was justified. In this time so spent, the opportunity of healing seemed to have gone, the girl was dead, and there was therefore no need to worry the Rabbi further, they said. But human despair was God's opportunity. Jesus had already been shown as Lord of nature; it was necessary that He here be shown as Lord of life and death. This was an important proof of Godhead, for it was supremely fitting that He, who had created life even before sin and death entered the world, should show Himself Master of death and the grave. More, this was an important piece of preliminary evidence for His own resurrection: He who had already conquered death for others would one day burst its bonds Himself. The central miracle of the Bible is therefore the resurrection of Jesus, because it is the central fact of all Christian experience, here and now as well as later. That is why the resurrection is never a matter of indifference in the gospels and why, even in the 'shorter' form, Mark's Gospel ends with a proclamation of it (16:6), even if no resurrection appearances are described.

36. And so to Jairus as well as to the disciples comes the command to abstain from fear and, instead, to *only believe*. The one condition of God's working is that we trust Him: this is not an arbitrary demand, but a demand necessarily springing from the very nature of the relation between Godhead and humanity. We are called to trusting, dependent love and obedience, for this is the biblical meaning of faith, not merely intellectual assent. Such faith is the only fitting expression of our helplessness, and the only fitting acknowledgement of God's power; and so it is an essential to salvation, though it is only the means of God's working, and not the source. This is what distinguishes the miracles of Jesus from so-called 'faith healings' brought about by mechanical psychological means alone: this is also what distinguishes them from mere magic, with no moral or religious content.

37. Peter and James and John (rarely Andrew also, but see 13:3 for an exception), were singled out to receive further revelation on this and other occasions, as at the transfiguration (9:2). It may have been because of their responsiveness to what they had already received that they were trusted with more. This certainly is a principle of God's spiritual dealing, already laid down in 4:25. It is therefore all the more remarkable that Mark records the selfish request of James and John (10:37), along with John's narrow-mindedness (9:38), as well as Peter's denial (14:72). Yet, in spite of weakness, all three appear as leaders of the church in Acts (*e.g.* 3:1). Of James we hear least of all in later days, but that may be due to his early death (Acts 12:2), at the hands of Herod, which meant that his place was apparently taken by James, the brother of the Lord (Gal. 1:19; 2:9).

38-40. The *weeping and wailing* (38) may not have necessarily been entirely that of hired mourners, though it certainly would have included them: such an influential man would have many friends who would come to share his grief.[1] But the scornful laughter (40) with which they greeted the words of Jesus seems to show that there was little real sorrow there, in all the noise. This unbelief (for such it was) excluded them from seeing the miracle to which the parents were admitted. The pity of it was that it was their superior 'knowledge' which excluded them (*cf.*

---

[1] Although Anderson quotes the Talmud to show that 'even the poorest in Israel should hire not less than two flutes and one wailing woman', thereby illustrating a Palestinian custom, to which Josephus also refers.

Luke 8:53, which adds 'knowing that she was dead'). In point of fact, the girl was indeed dead, by our earthly standards: but Jesus, knowing that He would raise her from the dead, rightly described her condition as a 'sleep', because from sleep comes wakening.[1] So, too, the early church described the dead as 'those who have fallen asleep' (1 Thes. 4:14), for the same reason. Mark does not use the verb *koimaō* here for 'sleep' (which also gives our modern English 'cemetery'), but the verb *katheudei*, however, the meaning is exactly the same.

41. *Taking her by the hand*: Jesus never hesitated to contract ritual defilement by touching a leaper, or blood, or the dead, precisely because His touch at once cleansed and revived, and thus, as a Jew would say, removed the 'mother of defilement', their term for the source of pollution. In the Old Testament, ritual 'holiness' as well as ritual 'defilement' could be transmitted, as being contagious: in the same way, others 'contracted' life and purity from Jesus, and not He the impurity from them. This too explains His readiness to eat and drink with 'tax collectors and sinners', the morally defiled (2:15).

His words to the girl, *Talitha cumi*, in her own Aramaic mother tongue (some MSS read *cum*, which would be the more likely vocalization), are preserved in Mark alone. If, as tradition has it and internal evidence may in part at least support, Peter was Mark's informant, then the scene must have made such an impression upon the three apostles present that the actual words of Jesus were remembered long after. Mark, as usual, explains the Aramaic phrase in Greek for the sake of his Gentile reading public.

Space does not permit here a full discussion on the assumed linguistic situation in Palestine at the time. Everywhere, Greek would seem to have been understood, but Aramaic seems to have been the usual speech of the Jewish home, especially in Galilee. Greek was certainly the literary and cultural language, even if Hebrew was the religious language of all Jews. Spoken

[1]It is not correct to say (with Schweizer), that it was easier for Mark's contemporaries to believe this miracle than it is for us to believe it: raising from the dead (like cleansing a leper) was regarded by rabbis as impossible. But he is right to say that resuscitation of a corpse is not the same as resurrection to a new kind of life.

Hebrew may well have lingered on around Jerusalem, as a semi-artificial religious or nationalistic survival: it was certainly so used, in a corrupt form, by the Zealots at a later date. Every appearance is that Jesus and His disciples were bilingual, though, as coming from strongly nationalist Galilee, surrounded by the Gentiles of Decapolis and Syrophoenicia, their mother tongue was probably Galilean Aramaic. Proofs are to be found in the nicknames like 'Cephas' and 'Boanerges', specifically stated by Mark to have been given by Jesus Himself, both being Aramaic in form.[1] Other fossilized pieces of Aramaic preserved in this gospel are the command *'ephphatha'* given to the dumb man (7:34) and the cry *'Eloi, Eloi, lama sabachthani'* uttered on the cross (15:34). *'Abba'*, as an address to the Father, is common to both gospel and epistles (14:36 and Rom. 8:15). Whether Jesus ever delivered His teaching in Greek is doubtful, though it was a view held by earlier scholars which has recently been revived. Even if He did so at times, there would be a special appropriateness in using her own mother tongue in talking to the girl, just as the risen Lord apparently spoke to Mary in her own tongue (Jn. 20:16), for she certainly so replied. Perhaps the mention of the fact that Aramaic was used on these particular occasions suggests that it was not always so used. Those brought up in bilingual areas will appreciate to the full the emotive value of such a use of the hearer's mother tongue, even if another language is just as well understood.

42–43. At once Jesus proved Himself stronger than death. Other similar miracles involved the son of the widow of Nain (Lk. 7:15) and Lazarus of Bethany (Jn. 11:44), although neither is recorded in Mark. The loving care of Jesus is shown in His command to give the girl something to eat. His usual concern lest idle sightseers flock to Him as a miracle worker is shown

[1] It is not clear whether the Semitic nickname 'Thomas', *didymos* in Greek, ('the Twin') was given to Thomas by Jesus or already borne by the apostle, of whose personal name we are uncertain: to judge from the Syriac, it may have been Judas. But in any case, this surname or nickname was Aramaic, again denoting the mother language of the apostolic group. Attempts have been made to link the nickname 'Twin' with the fact that Jesus sent out his apostles two by two (6:7): but this is far fetched. Alternatively, there is the possible suggestion that, when twins were born in the ancient world, the first to arrive was given a name, while the second was merely called 'Twin'. This did not happen in Old Testament days, however, for example Gn. 25:25, 26.

again by His strict command to the parents to tell nobody of the miracle: compare His similar words to the healed leper of 1:44, on a like occasion, when the crowds were also gathering round Him, as now (verse 31).

iv. His own city rejects Him (6:1–6)[1]

Jairus had been a synagogue elder in one of the small lakeside towns of the western shore, to judge from the various topographical details. Now Jesus and His disciples seem to have moved inland from the lake to the highlands of Galilee, for He is found teaching, apparently in the synagogue of Nazareth (although unnamed by Mark), which is always *his own country*, the town of His boyhood, though He may later live and work in Capernaum (Mt. 4:13). To the last He is 'the Nazarene, Jesus' (14:67), in spite of His birth in Bethlehem and base in Capernaum. Moreover it is Matthew, not Mark, who sees a prophetic appropriateness in this (Mt. 2:23).

2. Even in Nazareth, the effect of His teaching was startling: no-one who heard it could deny the *wisdom* displayed in it. Nor did they attempt to deny that He had already done miracles elsewhere, but instead of laying either of these things to heart, they were simply concerned as to their source. They were in fact much more concerned with the mechanical question 'how' than the theological question 'why'. Yet the question in itself was a good one. It was indeed the question that was to exercise the scribes and Pharisees later (11:28): what was the source of the authority of Jesus? Like John's baptism, His authority could only be 'from heaven or from men'. For, although the scribes suggested a third possible demonic source, it is doubtful, from the sternness of the reply of Jesus, if even they took this bitter suggestion seriously. So the question of the synagogue congregation at Nazareth was well directed, had they only been ready to accept the obvious answer. From 1:22 onwards, the fact of the authority of Jesus has been obvious to all those not already self-blinded by their own theological prejudice: it only remained

[1] Lightfoot, quoted in Johnson, points out that this is the beginning of the process of rejection that leads to the death of Jesus in Jerusalem.

to recognize its source, and that would be declared unequivocally by Peter in 8:29.

3. They were right in rejecting the earthly background or relationships of Jesus as being the source of His power. It was not as Mary's son, nor as eldest brother of Joseph's family, that He did such things: nor was it as the village *carpenter*[1], as they would have considered Him to be. One can sense their slow bewilderment in the listing of His brothers by name. But, having rightly rejected any human source, they boggled at attributing both the wisdom and the miracles to a divine source. They were staggered by such an equation; they *took offence* or 'stumbled' at Him, as the Bible says. The people of Nazareth 'knew all the answers' about Jesus: they were not prepared for any fresh revelation. Familiarity, to quote the English proverb, had bred contempt, as apparently it also had among His own brothers (see on 3:31). Jesus Himself will sadly quote a similar Semitic proverb in verse 4: the only place where the prophet of Nazareth (Mt. 21:11) was not acclaimed was Nazareth itself.

4–6. So it was that, in the very place where Jesus had been brought up as a boy, the only exhibition of divine power that He was able to give was to heal a few sick folk who were humbled enough by pain and need to believe in Him (5). He who was to rejoice at the faith of the Syrophoenician woman (7:29) marvelled at the lengths to which unbelief could go in His own townspeople (6). They might be staggered at Him: but here Mark says that he was staggered at them.[2]

v. The sending out of the twelve (6:7–13).

The earthly ministry of Jesus seems to be roughly divisible into periods of intensive localized teaching and periods of more

---

[1]The task of 'carpenter' of course included that of 'builder' in those days. Jesus rarely uses metaphors derived from carpentry (but see Mt. 11:29), while He often used those drawn from building (see Rawlinson, quoted in Anderson, for the 'builder' translation). It is only in this passage, with the parallel in Matthew, that Jesus' occupation is mentioned.

[2]Cranfield here points out that these are indeed the only two places where the verb *thaumazō*, 'wonder', 'marvel', is used with Jesus as subject. But there are other places in Mark where Jesus reacts to human unbelief with grief, or even anger (3:5).

general peripatetic evangelism. The sending out of the twelve was a logical extension of His own ministry of evangelism. It was indeed part of the very purpose for which He had initially called them (3:14), for this was both that they should stay in His presence (intensive teaching) and that He might then send them out (extensive evangelism).

Both in this case and elsewhere (*e.g.* 11:1), Jesus never seems to have sent out a disciple alone: they normally went in groups of two.[1] Perhaps this constant association of disciples in small groups may account for the set patterns in which the lists of names of the disciples have come down to us, apart altogether from the convenience in the teaching needs of the church. The twelve were given authority over demons (7), so they expelled demons: they 'preached that men should repent' (12): they 'anointed' the sick with oil, and healed them (13). All three functions are illustrated 'in action' in these verses[2], and all three were associated with the proclamation of the kingdom of God, which had come in the person of Jesus.

8-9. It may be that here we have a programme of 'village evangelism' (see verse 6) after the larger population centres of Galilee had decisively rejected Jesus. This task demanded a scattering of personnel, a wandering ministry, and a deliberate renunciation, a studied simplicity of lifestyle, designed both to encourage and to demonstrate trust in God. This simple explanation serves better than to attempt to find subtle meaning in the renunciation of each particular article: besides, the lists

---

[1]Minear may well be right in seeing this as in obedience to the law of Moses and its stipulations, where 'two witnesses' were always required (Dt. 17:6). They were to witness to the nearness of the kingdom in this case: they were also to be witnesses of condemnation, if the message of the kingdom was rejected (6:11).

[2]One of the questions today is how far these gifts were generalized among the disciples, for, in the gospels, they seem to be restricted to the twelve and the seventy, unless these are to be simply seen as representatives of the whole. After Pentecost, true, the gifts seem widespread, although even in Acts they seem to be restricted in their exercise to the wider 'apostolic' or 'pioneer missionary' group (including Stephen, Philip, Paul, and Barnabas). The division of opinion occurs between those scholars who believe that such gifts ended with the apostolic age or shortly after (on the grounds that there was no further need), and those who see them as intended to be continued in the life of the church today, and indeed as an essential part of the gospel. Mark cannot help us here, unless we regard the so called 'longer ending' (16:9-20) as canonical Scripture.

given seem to vary in different accounts. The point therefore lies in the renunciation, not its details nor its purpose or its extent. The Bible never sees renunciation as a good thing in itself, but only as a necessity in some circumstances. We have no reason to suppose that this particular type of renunciation was intended to be a universal rule, binding on all disciples at all times, while such a simple faith as theirs is indeed the universal rule, in whatever way it is expressed. Later, in Gethsemane, Jesus, having first ascertained that His disciples had thoroughly learned this lesson of not trusting to material helps, told them to take with them all the helps that they had: purse, bag, even sword (Lk. 22:36). This shows no lack of faith, for they have already learned that none of these things is necessary for the one who goes in simple trust, obedient to the Lord's command, and looking to God to supply all needs.[1] Poverty is never an ideal in the Bible, although, if need be, it must be gladly embraced in God's service and for Christ's sake.

10–11. The mission of the disciples was to be marked by a humble persistence: they were to try to get a hearing by all means, but never to force themselves on those unwilling to hear them. Such a rejection they were, however, not to treat lightly, knowing the condemnation that comes to those who refuse the gospel. To preach the gospel is therefore always a joyous task, but never a task to be entered upon light-heartedly, in view of the eternal issues with which such teaching is concerned. The latter part of verse 11 ('more tolerable for Sodom and Gomorrah') is omitted here by both RSV and NEB, following the principal uncial MSS. It was no doubt added here from Matthew 10:15, where it certainly belongs to the text; it rings true to the teaching style of Jesus nevertheless. Orthodox Jews 'shook off the dust' when they returned to the Holy Land from Gentile regions (Anderson). Those who reject the message of Jesus, brought by His servants, are not 'God's people', but have similarly made themselves 'Gentiles' as far as the kingdom of God is concerned, in front of the 'two witnesses' demanded by the Law (Dt. 17:6).

---

[1] This seems more likely than to explain it, with T. W. Manson, by the rabbinic prohibition of carrying staff, sandal and wallet on the temple mount. The Talmudic passage in question is quoted in Cranfield.

12-13. Often we speak of 'spiritual' and 'healing' work as though they were two distinct avenues of Christian witness. It is very doubtful if the early church made such a distinction, the more so as they saw most if not all disease as a manifestation of Satan's power, though not necessarily connected directly with sin on the part of the individual (contrast 2:5 with Jn. 9:3). Anointing with oil was not in this case a medical treatment but a spiritual symbol, though it appears to be used medically in the case of the good Samaritan (Lk. 10:34), who poured 'oil and wine' on wounds. The anointing by the disciples practised here seems to be the matter-of-fact anointing of James 5:14, which, accompanied by prayer, can heal the sick. Oil is a biblical symbol of the Holy Spirit's presence (1 Ki. 1:39), and so the very anointing is itself an 'acted parable' of divine healing by the Spirit's power. It seems in the New Testament as if there are two sorts of healing practised. The first is the dramatic use of healing as a 'sign', often giving an opening for evangelism: the second is unspectacular pastoral healing, as in the letter of James, a healing which seems to find a place quite naturally in the ongoing 'body life' of the church alongside many other activities of the Spirit.

vi. Herod's estimate of Jesus (6:14-16)

This preaching tour in Galilee brought Jesus for the first time to the notice of Herod, in whose jurisdiction Galilee lay at the time (Lk. 23:7). The last mention of John the Baptist had been a brief note (1:14) of his imprisonment, as marking the end of his preaching ministry, and the beginning of that of Jesus. Verses 17-29 will give, in a parenthesis, the reason for John's arrest and subsequent execution: but at this point, his death is simply assumed.[1] (Schweizer and Anderson both note that this is the only story in the whole gospel which is not centred on Jesus.) The chief interest, and indeed the reason for its introduction

[1]Mark 'sandwiches' the story of the martyrdom of John between the sending out of the twelve (7-13) and the account of their return (30), as noted by Anderson. Is this Mark's way of warning of the cost of discipleship? He likewise 'sandwiches' the story of the cleansing of the temple between the two halves of the cursing of the fig tree, to make the application of the 'sign' plain: it is therefore a feature typical of his style.

here, lies in the instant guilty reaction of Herod to the news about Jesus. True, he had killed John, but that he had not silenced his own conscience is clear from his equation of Jesus with a John 'returned', raised from the dead. It is true that some manuscripts have suggested that this was a widespread view: but that does not alter the fact that Herod himself believed it. It is strange that, though John in his lifetime had done no miracles of any kind (Jn. 10:41), yet Herod showed no surprise at the thought of this greatest of all miracles, a rising from the dead, taking place in John's case. Even Herod had theological insight enough to see that, if John had truly risen from the dead, then other miracles, like those reported of Jesus, were not only possible but logical. Compare the way in which Jesus persistently refused to give any 'evidential' miracle to His foes except to foretell the greatest possible sign of all, that of His resurrection (8:31). Apparently from this time onwards Herod wanted to see Jesus, hoping to watch Him perform a miracle (Lk. 23:8), but what may in origin have been genuine religious feeling on the part of Herod had dwindled into a mere craving for the sensational and the spectacular. This craving God never creates, and so He does not satisfy it, though it is at times a dangerous temptation to the church. Spiritual life cannot be nurtured on thrills alone; any more than faith, in the true sense, can be created by signs.

15–16. As later, when Jesus questioned His own disciples at Caesarea Philippi (8:28), there were already various popular interpretations of Jesus' nature and work: until Casearea Philippi, none saw the full truth. But Herod clung sombrely to the view suggested by his own uneasy conscience, and the very starkness of the words *whom I beheaded* (16) emphasizes his self-torture. The house of Herod was, true, a strange mixture of cold cruelty and religious fanaticism. The family was by background Edomite, not Israelite, but the Herodian masonry of the great enclosure at Hebron surrounding Abraham's tomb was intended to show to all that Abraham was their ancestor too. In truth, Herod seems to have been superstitious rather than religious at heart, and his reaction to the news about Jesus makes this plain.

vii. The martyrdom of John the Baptist (6:17–29)

This uneasy speculation about Jesus was on a par with Herod's moral perception throughout. The Herods (*cf.* Agrippa in Acts 26:3) were religious dilettantes, and the tetrarch had recognized well enough the spiritual stature of John (20) and had been afraid of his moral greatness. He not only gladly heard him preaching, but paid attention to what John said. *He was much perplexed*, the best reading in verse 20, suggests that John's preaching put Herod into a tight corner, and so he evaded the issue by doing nothing. But inexorably he was pushed to a decision, first to imprison John, then to execute him. The less likely reading in verse 20, 'he did many things', would make Herod actually respond to John's teaching: but there is no evidence of that. Similarly, Pontius Pilate would be gradually pushed, against his will, to take a decision about Jesus (15:1–15), which led to the crucifixion. RSV in verse 20, with *kept him safe*, is banal.

18–22. John's condemnation of Herod's incest brought imprisonment by the tetrarch, who could hardly tolerate such open criticism of himself in his own domain : but it also brought something far more dangerous, in the undying hate of Herodias. Even while John was in gaol, he was probably in no great danger of his life, as far as Herod was concerned: that is clear from verse 20. Herod wished only to stop John's mouth. A humiliating defeat by Aretas, the father of his rejected first wife, was doubtless punishment enough for adultery as far as he was concerned, without John's condemnation. But with Herodias, it was a different matter: she was only waiting her time to kill John. She would have killed him at once, but there had been no opportunity (19); and now the opportunity had come, in the birthday feast of Antipas, as this member of the house of Herod is usually called. A glance at the family tree of the house will show the succession of murders and incest that it contained: one more murder was not surprising.[1]

[1]See Johnson: even Salome, the girl in question, was married to her uncle at the time. She was the daughter of Herodias' first husband.

22–25. It was Herod's infatuation with Herodias that had led him to imprison John: and so even devotion to partners can lead astray. Such is the human distortion of values that his courtiers saw Herod's rash promise to a dancing-girl as generosity, and his compliance with a wrong demand as faithfulness to his word. Even the obedience of a daughter to her mother becomes in this case a sin: and so, outside Christ, even 'natural' virtues can become distorted into vices. Jezebel, in the Old Testament (1 Ki. 21:7), is another example of one who was bitterly opposed to a servant of God, and through devotion to whom a marriage partner becomes equally guilty. Similarly, in Acts, Ananias seems to have led his wife Sapphira into the sin of lying to the Holy Spirit (Acts 5:2). The kingdom of God demands a deeper loyalty, overriding the closest of earthly ties (10:29).

26–28. Unquestionably, Herod's grief at this request was real (26); but he had already been trapped, and he knew it. It had been wrong to bind himself to such a rash promise. It was doubly wrong to keep it; but if he did not keep it, he would 'lose face' before his own nobles, who had heard the royal oath. So John died alone in the grim dungeon of Machaerus, by the shores of the Dead Sea. One wonders whether even Herod's callous courtiers were not shocked by such a banquet dish as this (verse 28). But Mark does not point the moral: he simply leaves the tragic story to speak for itself. John's career ends with his body lovingly laid in a tomb by his disciples (verse 29). Does Mark see a parallel in the action of Joseph of Arimathea in 15:46?

29. Within Palestine, this seems to mark the end of 'John's disciples' as a coherent group, whose ritual practices can be quoted against those of the disciples of Jesus (2:18). Ever since early days, the disciples of John had been gradually leaving him, according to John's Gospel, and following Jesus: and John was content that it should be so (Jn. 3:30). Now, when John was dead and they came to bury him, Matthew 14:12 adds a further significant clause, saying that 'they went and told Jesus', which probably points to a further amalgamation, although Mark tells us nothing of this. Outside of Palestine, however, John's disciples still persisted as a separate group, as can be seen from

Acts 18:25 and 19:3, where they are still a 'sect' waiting for the coming of the Messiah. John's disciples were therefore fully orthodox Jews (2:18), who had a messianic expectation, but little more. Those of them who were not absorbed into the growing Christian church may have slipped back into the pre-Christian Essene movement, to which they had many similarities, or heretical groups like the Mandaeans, in whose writings John the Baptist has a prominent place.

viii. The feeding of the five thousand (6:30–44)

There is a delightful naivety in the account of the apostles' reporting to Jesus, not only what they have done, but also what they have said. This was true wisdom on the part of Jesus in allowing them time to unburden themselves to Him, before even suggesting a time of rest. After the weariness and rush and strange faces of the mission, the disciples craved solitude and rest in the company of Jesus. While He did not care that He Himself had no time to eat (*cf.* 3:20), yet He would not ask the same sacrifice of His weary disciples. There had been a similar preaching tour in Galilee before (1:39), but that had been undertaken in the company of Jesus; this was the first time that the twelve had gone out alone, relying solely upon His word.

33. The short lake voyage, back to the old familiar surroundings of the sea, after tramping the dusty roads, must in itself have been a rest and relaxation for the Galilean fishermen. But the small size of the Sea of Galilee made it quite possible for the crowds, travelling along the shore, to outdistance the little ship, which probably had no favourable wind. Many a modern deepwater harbour is bigger than the whole Sea of Galilee, and the average harbour ferry boat of today far bigger than the ship used on this occasion.[1] There is no biblical reason to hold that 'big is beautiful': God works often in the small and despised. To small groups of Christians, dwarfed by the scale of Rome or Antioch, this was all-important.

[1]Nowhere is this better shown than in the many excellent photographs of the lake in Grollenberg.

34. It is easy to imagine the groan of despair that must have gone up from the exhausted disciples, when they saw, long before they had reached the other shore, that the inevitable curious crowd had forestalled them. It is probable that this natural weariness accounts for the note of irritation in their question to Jesus in verse 37, as well as their obvious hint in verse 36 that the crowds had had more than enough teaching already. But Jesus, just as weary as the disciples and seeing the same crowds as they, *had compassion on them* (34)[1] Note that He did the preaching to the crowds Himself; He did not call upon His disciples to join in the task now. Compare His anxiety to secure proper rest for them after their wearisome preaching tour, careless though He might be for Himself.

35. The objections raised by the disciples were all very reasonable. It was indeed *late*, and the place was in truth *lonely*. If bread must be given to the crowds, it would have to be brought in from a distance; and it certainly would have cost, at the most conservative estimate, two hundred denarii to feed them all. Their calculations were therefore quite correct; but they had omitted from their calculations Jesus, the incalculable factor. At the seeming 'unreasonableness' shown by Jesus their suppressed irritation grows, for God's way is always foolishness to 'natural' humans (1 Cor. 1:18). This miracle is therefore an illustration of the central stumbling-block of Christianity: all alike stand condemned with the disciples here, an example of Mark's 'paraenetic' used of his material, a use all the more remarkable in that he never draws attention to it.

36-38. The sequence here is interesting. Once the disciples have seen the need of the crowd (35-36), then Jesus lays upon

---

[1]Note how many of the miracles of Jesus are mentioned as springing initially from love and compassion towards physical needs, whatever theological objectives they might also have. This is yet another link between the miracles of Jesus and the miracles of prophets of the Old Testament, like Elijah and Elisha. These 'prophetic miracles', and not the reported wonders performed by Hellenistic *theioi andres* ('divine men'), are the spiritual ancestors of Jesus' works. It is only fair to say that the very existence of such a Hellenistic group has recently been challenged: see Craig Blomberg, *The Historical Reliability of the Gospels* (IVP), 1987), pp. 81ff.; also Kee, *IDBS*, under 'Divine Man'. Kee rightly says 'Firm documentation of the concept in Christian or pagan literature of the first century AD is lacking.' He

them the task of meeting that need (37). Half angered, and half humiliated, they confess their own utter inadequacy to do so. Then Jesus reminds them that they can meet any emergency which is not of their own making (for we may not 'test' God, Mt. 4:7), by the use of what they have, though it is totally inadequate, if only it is first offered in its totality to Jesus to be used by Him. God does not usually lead us to see a need, unless it is in His mind to meet that need, often through us, unwilling though we may be.

39–40. The disciples must have faith that Jesus could and would use their inadequacy, and this faith must be shown by making the crowd sit down in ordered expectancy, *by hundreds and by fifties.* Perhaps it is not unfair, too, to see a hint in this detail, that God is a God of order, One who at the dawn of time brought order out of chaos (Gn. 1:2), and who loves order even in worship (1 Cor. 14:40), instead of the disorder that could so easily arise from the unrestricted use of spiritual freedom, as may have been a danger at Rome as well as Corinth.[1] But it is not enough for disciples to have faith: the faith must be exhibited in some action that, as it were, implicates them. The disciples would indeed look foolish now, in the eyes of the expectant crowd, if no miracle of feeding took place; but this is the risk which faith must take, if it is to be truly faith. 'No risk, no faith' is a good rule of thumb, if over simple.

41. The loaves were taken up, blessed[2] and broken by Jesus and finally given to the disciples to distribute to the crowds. By this the disciples were themselves, almost unwillingly, pulled into participation in the miracle. So, too, at a deeper level, Jesus Himself had already taken up and blessed a human body at His

---

therefore sees the miracles of Jesus in Mark, in line with Jewish apocalyptic expectations, as signs of the coming of the kingdom.

[1] As the early church, rightly or wrongly, often saw these feeding miracles as an anticipation of the eucharist, this aspect would not have passed unnoticed by it, and the exegesis is not as far-fetched as it might seem at first sight. But it is possibly only another vivid eyewitness detail, assuring us of the veracity of the account.

[2] While it is true (with Cranfield) that the *berākāh*, 'blessing', had primarily God as object, not the loaves, yet, to the Jew, the broken bread was held to be hallowed by the hallowing of the divine Name through it. This illuminates many New Testament passages: perhaps the 'bread of the presence' (2:26) would be a parallel.

incarnation, though Mark does not actually mention this in his gospel. But Mark's readers would remember how, at the last supper, Jesus had taken bread, given thanks, and broken it, before giving it to the disciples to eat, saying 'This is my body' (14:22). So too, He can take, bless and use our lives, once given to Him, to bring blessing to the crowds hungry for God in the world around us.[1] Yet in all of this legitimate spiritualization we must not forget what actually happened on that day so long ago: five thousand hungry people had been fed, as Belo would insist. It is true that they were hungry because of long hours listening to God's Word, but that does not lessen the deed.

42-44. It is a mark of God's provision that it is always enough and more than enough for all our needs: and yet it is also typical of God's economy that there should be no waste (43), and that we should learn to be good stewards of God's bounty. Of the twelve, each disciple had presumably gathered a basketful of pieces, and we may be sure that this was to be their food in the days to come. They could not simply throw away the bread already provided and expect Jesus to work a special miracle like this every day, exciting though that would have been. Note that God guarantees to supply all our needs, but not necessarily all our foolish desires: the meal by the lake was satisfying, but the food was simple. There will always be those who grumble at what God supplies. Israel in the desert soon tired of 'the bread of the angels' (Ps. 78:25) and begged for more earthy sustenance (Nu. 11:6). No doubt many a disciple was tempted to similar thoughts as he chewed dried up fish and stale crusts on the next day, or the day after. But, in God's economy, that which we call the supernatural shades into the natural; He meets our needs through both alike, so that ultimately there is no distinction between the two, as far as His provision is concerned.

[1]At a later date, Mark's readers probably saw eucharistic significance in this miracle, as in the feeding of the four thousand: John certainly seems to have done so (Jn. 6). This is the sort of interpretation that rouses the ire of modern commentators like Belo, who see it as an evasion of the challenge to feed the hungry. Nineham sees in the miracle a clear reference to the messianic banquet, as well as to the miraculous feeding of Israel with manna in the desert: again, John makes this explicit. The early Eucharist was also an *Agape*.

ix. The walking on the water (6:45–52)

A further touch of the understanding love on the part of Jesus was to send His overtaxed disciples on in advance, while He dismissed the crowd, perhaps giving them farewell counsel. Yet even after that, He went, not to rest, but to prayer on the hillside: indeed, it was only the sight of the storm-tossed disciples that brought Jesus from prayer to their rescue (48). No supernatural vision is necessarily implied here, although it is possible. The boat could have been clearly visible from the spot where Jesus was praying high up on the hillside above, especially if there was moonlight at the time. The supernatural element will enter later, with the words *walking on the sea* (49).[1] The author remembers watching such boats on the Sea of Galilee after dark, clearly outlined in black against the silvery water.

This whole episode is a good illustration of the life of discipleship, seen as a constant experience of testing and deliverance; for it was again (*cf.* 4:35) not through stubborn self-will, but through direct obedience to the command of Jesus, that the disciples found themselves in this danger. The storm did not show that they had deviated from the path of God's will: instead, God's path for them lay through the storm, to the other shore of the lake. Moreover, it again appeared as if Jesus had forgotten them; they were alone, at night, and making heavy weather with the rowing. This storm, however, was no sudden squall such as had preceded the earlier calming of the waves (4:37), but a tiring, continuous head wind, necessitating steady, back-breaking rowing. Then, at the darkest hour of the night, in their time of greatest need, and in a totally unexpected way, Jesus came to their rescue. In both of the storms at sea (*cf.* chapter 4) it must have seemed to the disciples at first as if Jesus

[1] It is sheer exegetical nonsense in this context to talk of 'shallow water', or even 'sandbanks', or (still worse), to translate the phrase *walking on the sea* as 'walking by the lake'. None of these happenings would have terrified, or even surprised, seasoned Galilean fishermen. Whether we like it or not, this is portrayed as another 'nature miracle', bearing witness to the divinity of Jesus (*cf. the wind ceased* in 51). In the gospels, no disciple ever walks on the water, except Peter, at Christ's direct invitation (Mt. 14:29), and even he fails. Jesus delegated certain powers to His apostles (*e.g.* healing and exorcism), but not those powers inherent in His own person as God (th so called nature miracles). In Job 9:8 God Himself is described as walking on the waters (Schweizer): in Gn. 1:2, the Spirit of God moves over the face of the waters.

was irrelevant: on the first occasion, He was asleep in the stern of the boat, and on the second occasion, absent at prayer on the mountain. On both occasions it must have seemed as if He was careless of their danger, and yet the result showed that nothing could be further from the truth. Why does Mark say that Jesus *meant to pass by them* (48)? Perhaps it was a test of their faith, just as His sleeping in the stern of the ship had been on the previous occasion (4:38). If they had sufficient faith, they would be content even without His presence with them. Perhaps Jesus, on the other hand, wanted His disciples to recognize to the full their need of Him before He came to their help: Mark does not tell us which it was.

49. The cry of the disciples was merely one of fear, and not even necessarily a cry of prayer, let alone a cry of faith directed to Jesus; but it was enough to ensure His instant response. God's willingness to answer is not limited by the poverty of our asking, and Jesus was often contented with an initial response of what we would consider a totally inadequate nature (9:24).

50. As so often, the exhibition of miraculous power by Jesus merely threw the disciples into fresh fear and confusion. So the initial entry of Jesus into their situation was marked by an increase in the tempo of the strife (*cf.* 9:26, the healing of the demoniac boy), although that would soon pass into tranquility. Minear points out that, in answering with the words *It is I*, Jesus may have been deliberately using the name of God (Ex. 3:14). This would only have increased the awe of the disciples, although it could also have given them a clue as to the true nature of Jesus, if their hearts had not been hardened (verse 52).

51–52. As before, at the previous storm on the lake (*cf.* chapter 4), the presence of Jesus brought peace and calm to the disciples. But their fear and their amazement alike are traced by the evangelist to their failure to learn the previous lesson of the feeding of the five thousand. Smallness of faith and hardness of heart are two constant sins even of the disciples in Mark. Hardness of heart is that lack of spiritual perceptivity, that lack of readiness to learn, for which we are ultimately blameworthy ourselves, and which, in the extreme case of the scribes, can lead at last to the sin against the Holy Spirit. Smallness of faith is a failure to remember God's working in the past and to apply that knowledge of His nature to our present problems. If the early Christians, especially in centres like Rome, saw these storms as pictures of persecutions through which they must go, then this was an important lesson to learn.

x. Healings at Gennesaret (6:53–56)

This brief account in Mark is a summary of what must have happened on many similar occasions: the spontaneous spreading of the good news under the stimulus of the presence of the healing Jesus. This is what has led many Christians today to claim that physical healing is either an integral and inseparable part of the gospel itself (which seems to go beyond Scripture) or at least an important adjunct to it.[1] There was on the part of the crowds a recognition of Jesus, a realization of their own need, a belief that Jesus could meet that need, and a determination to grasp the opportunity afforded by His presence: all these are factors in every case of healing of the soul or body. The reaction of the crowd was both spontaneous and unselfish. There must have been many a patient carried in on a mat by friends (verse 55), and the faith of the patients in asking only to clutch at the fringe of His clothing, reminds us of the faith of the woman with the haemorrhage (cf. 5:28). Again, as in her case, it was not the magical touch of a garment which healed them, but their faith in the one who wore that garment.

xi. A further clash with Judaism (7:1–23)

The Pharisees and scribes described here are presumably another official fact-finding commission of theologians from Jerusalem (verse 1), sent to investigate a campaign of healing and preaching that by now must have caused some stir. Even

---

[1]Since, in the New Testament, the verb sōzō means equally 'to heal' and 'to save' (as does the underlying Semitic verb), this is an easy biblical correlation, where the spiritual sense is a metaphor from the physical meaning. But spiritual salvation is always assured for those who trust in Christ: physical healing is not, for it depends on God's sovereign will.

the secular ruler Herod knew of Jesus (6:14), let alone the religious authorities. Such a commission had come before, as the incidental reference in 3:22 shows. There, the bitter words about the casting out of devils through the power of Beelzebub had been spoken by the scribes from Jerusalem. That being so, it is probable that the carping criticism with regard to sabbath observance came from the same source. A previous commission had similarly examined John as to his right to preach and baptize (Jn. 1:19, 25), to which Jesus may refer in 11:30. It thus comes as no surprise that the theological commission in this chapter is biased and suspicious from the start. This is apparent in their niggling, fault-finding attitude. They attacked Jesus, not personally, but through His disciples (verse 5), just as in 2:24 they had attacked His disciples for picking corn on the sabbath, and in 2:18 they had criticized the failure of His disciples to fast. They here attacked the disciples again on a point of ritual, not of faith, and a point of ritual drawn not directly from the law, but from the body of explanatory tradition that was growing up round the law, later codified to form the Mishnah and Gemara, the modern Jewish Talmud. Of course, if the disciples were found to be ignorant of the 'oral tradition', the inference as to the ignorance of their rabbi would be obvious. Mark thinks it necessary to explain the whole system of ritual washing to His Gentile readers (verses 3-4), though the sabbath, He assumes, will be familiar to them already.[1] The Pharisees themselves, in so asking, betrayed their own position, for their indignant question was confined to a breach of the *tradition of the elders* (5), not a breach of the Mosaic law itself. So Saul the Pharisee could describe himself as being 'extremely zealous for the traditions' (Gal. 1:14) before his conversion.

6-8. No-one ever disputed the earnestness of the Pharisees in keeping these traditional observances, nor disputed that such

---

[1] This is one of several passages which can be adduced to prove that Mark's Gospel, whatever its source, is a 'Gentile gospel', in the sense that it was, unlike Matthew, addressed to largely Gentile readers. See Johnson for a comment on this ritual washing. It was a Pharisaic custom, going far beyond the law (where only priests were required to do so), but adopted generally on the principle of 'setting a fence about the law', *i.e.* safeguarding it by further regulations.

customs were genuine historical traditions, nor denied that they were originally aimed at the honouring of God, as being extensions, perhaps legitimate, of biblical principles already given by revelation. Why then is the strong word *hypocrites* or 'those acting a part' (6), used by Jesus here, with reference to scribes and Pharisees?[1] He sees, in their hollow, insincere attitude, a fulfilment of biblical prophecy, and therefore a vindication of the authority of the very Scripture upon which they claim to lean, but for which they actually substitute their own traditions (verse 7). It is noteworthy that Jesus here not only quotes Scripture but also adds to it in verse 8, thereby interpreting it. Indeed, the whole of the New Testament is a wider illustration of this, for the words of Jesus always stand on a par with any 'thus says the Lord' found in the Old Testament, and so the early church treated them. In the first place, then, Jesus sees the Pharisees as those who act a false part, who pretend to be other than they are. They indisputably display an outward honour to God, but this is directly and totally contradicted by the Pharisaic attitude of mind. Their outward show of reverence does not correspond to any of that inward reality of which it should only be an outward expression and sign: compare the prophetic attack on much of the meaningless and hollow religious ritual of the days of the kings of Israel.

That is the first 'prong' of the attack by Jesus. But the second, in verse 7, is more serious still. Even if the Pharisees had been earnest in heart, yet their whole position is vitiated by the fact that what they teach depends entirely on human, not divine, authority. Nor is that all, though it is bad enough in all conscience: this clinging to human traditions makes them actually neglect the plain command of God. Once again, note how Jesus answers on two levels those who criticize Him. First, He answers on their level, using their premises: then, having thus demolished their position, He takes the argument to a far deeper level.

[1]This phrase is probably a figure of speech, and should be translated 'the scribes belonging to the Pharisaic party', rather than as referring to two quite different groups. More striking is the fact that Jesus apparently regards both 'Pharisees and Sadducees', the strictly orthodox and the anti-supernaturalist, as being equally guilty. They certainly are two different groups, coming under equal condemnation, although, so far as we know, the Sadducees are not in Mark's Gospel accused by Jesus of hypocrisy but of unbelief and failure to grasp the Scriptures (12:24, contrasted with 7:6 of the Pharisees).

The latter part of verse 8 is not found in the best MSS. It may have been included, as an explanation of *tradition of men,* following Mark's own earlier explanation for Gentile readers in verse 4. It is, in any case, a fair summary of the position.

9-13. Such outspoken criticism may well have caused a murmur, so Jesus at once gives an instance of how obedience to a rabbinic tradition means breaking God's command. This, however, is only one instance chosen out of many, as He reminds them (13). At the very heart of the law, honour to parents is commanded, but, by a typically rabbinic twist of values, it was possible to vow to the temple all the money that would normally have been expended in the future on the maintenance of parents, and so avoid the plain demands of duty, obvious enough to the pagan outside.[1] This is a wise warning that the reference to leaving parents for the sake of Jesus (10:29) must be seen to be in the context of genuine family love as a Christian duty: natural ties are not abrogated, though they may be overruled by Jesus. Perhaps, when biblical scholars today are tempted to use distorted exegesis of the New Testament to prove a pet theory which is the very opposite of the plain sense of a passage, we are guilty of exactly the same sin as the rabbis blamed here.

14. This rebuke by Jesus seems to have silenced the scribes for the time being, but the major principle of the validity of the ritual law was still at stake. The disciples of Jesus had, in point of fact, eaten with unwashed hands, and therefore still stood condemned, if the traditional law on this point was valid. The discomfiture of the Pharisees in the last argument did not therefore necessarily mean the acquittal of the disciples, unless the whole principle behind this piece of oral tradition was to be overturned: and so it was, in this miniature parable. It must have seemed to many Pharisees in early days that Jesus came dangerously near to espousing the Sadducean cause, with His

---

[1]For a discussion of the whole *corban,* question, see Anderson. Later and more lenient rabbis would have agreed with Jesus here, but obviously some did not at the time. The legal question was that of the sanctity of oaths.

firm rejection of the 'tradition of the fathers'. Of course, no Sadducee would agree with that estimate: the championing by Jesus of the doctrine of the resurrection made Him an enemy as far as they were concerned (12:24).[1] What Jesus had to say next was too important to be restricted to scribes or Pharisees alone, so He deliberately called the crowd together before He spoke, to enunciate a new principle.

15. This bold statement by Jesus ran contrary to all the rabbinic teaching. To them, for any defilement to occur, there must be a 'mother of defilement', an external source, by physical contact with which the uncleanness was contracted. They, in other words, assumed an initially pure state: not so Jesus. For Him, the source of defilement was not external, but within, and already existent. There is a world of difference between these two theologies, as there is between the two views of sin.[2] To the Pharisees, lack of ceremonial purity, as in the case of the disciples of Jesus, was undoubtedly sin: whereas the list of sins given by Jesus here is restricted to moral failures, whether in thought or act.

Verse 16 is omitted by RSV and NEB following the best MSS, but it may well be genuine, for it is the usual injunction to 'listen', commonly appended by Jesus to His parables (cf. 4:9).

17. There must have been many other such occasions when we owe the explanation of a parable presented in the gospel to

---

[1]The whole tragedy of the battle between Pharisees and Sadducees is that each group was anxious to claim that God was on their side: the thought that both of them might be equally wrong, in the spiritual sense, never entered their heads. So their only real interest in Jesus was to find out on which side He was (like Joshua, when faced by the angel in Jos. 5:13). When they found out that He did not support their party, they lost interest at once, or regarded Him as a dangerous enemy to be removed. That is why they both stand under equal condemnation in the New Testament: neither of them had time or place for Christ. Note that Jesus refuted both groups, but did not 'play off' one group against the other, as he could have done. Even Paul did this in Acts 23:6, an action which he later regretted (Acts 24:21).

[2]Cranfield points out the fatal flaw. Instead of accepting the law's verdict on them as sinners, the rabbis, as Paul says in Rom. 10:1-3, were anxious to use the law to prove their own righteousness: and, to do this, they must always substitute human legalism for divine law. But the root cause is a reluctance to accept the initial and basic sinfulness of humanity. It is not only Confucianism which teaches that all enter this world sinless by nature, and are

the inability of the disciples to see its relevance and application in the first place, and to their consequent coming to Jesus to ask for an explanation later. The classic instance is the full explanation given of the parable of the sower in chapter 4. Naturally, if not understood, an unexplained and meaningless parable would be of no value in the teaching programme of the early church, and so would not be included in the gospel. Therefore, even if we fail to understand a parable, we are not justified in saying that the early church likewise failed to do so: if so, it would not have been preserved. If there is no explanation asked or given, then the disciples (and therefore the early church) must have understood the parable immediately. Of course, there were some sayings of Jesus which the disciples understood fully only after the resurrection of Jesus (cf. 9:10).

18. The unbelief of the disciples grieves Jesus. Their spiritual dullness amazes Him even more (16:14), for this is the quality that also distresses Him in the Pharisees (3:5). The chief thing obvious to a modern reader is the utter failure of the disciples to understand even His simplest utterances. They consistently and crassly misinterpreted Him, taking His words in the most crudely literal sense (cf. 8:16). Admittedly, all this was before the coming of the Spirit, the great Interpreter (Jn. 14:26): and the same blindness is, according to Paul, still seen in 'natural' unconverted people (2 Cor. 3:14).

19. The outspoken words of Jesus might be paraphrased as saying that 'the mind and not the body is the danger-point for man'. The last clause of this verse, *he declared all foods clean*, is best taken as an explanatory comment on the words of Jesus by the evangelist: we could paraphrase it as 'by saying this, He was abolishing all distinction between ceremonially clean and unclean foods.'[1] This generalized interpretation is born out by the additional negative clause in Matthew 15:20 which does not appear in Mark: 'but to eat with unwashed hands does not defile

---

only later corrupted by their environment: it is a universal belief of 'natural religions', and creeps readily even into 'revealed religion'.

[1] If Mark's Gospel was indeed produced for Gentile Christians at Rome, this clause would have great practical value, as Minear points out.

a man'. If we see the interpretative comment in Mark as coming from the preaching of Peter, then it takes a new meaning in view of Peter's vision before the visit to Cornelius (Acts 11:5ff.). God had taught Peter that Gentiles, who did not keep the ceremonial law, were still to be acceptable in God's sight (Acts 10:35), and were therefore 'clean'. Even if this did not come through the Petrine tradition, its relevance to the Roman church and the Gentile mission is obvious.

20–23. Jesus here (as more explicitly in Mt. 5:28) makes no distinction between sins of thought and sins of deed, unlike the law of Moses, which, like any other law codes, can take cognizance only of outward acts, not the mental attitudes which ultimately find expression in such acts. The one possible exception is the tenth commandment, which forbids coveting. Of course, in view of the fact that the central principle of the Mosaic law was love (Ex. 20:6 'those who love me'), ultimately the law was basically concerned with attitudes as well. See 12:28–31 for the summary of the law given by Jesus in terms of love towards God and love towards neighbour.

D. MINISTRY IN NORTHERN PALESTINE: RETURN TO GALILEE
(7:24 – 8:26)

i. The Syrophoenician woman[1] (7:24–30)

The previous activity of Jesus had been on the lake shore of Galilee: now He withdrew further north and west to the territory of Phoenicia, on the Mediterranean coast. Possibly it was for a time of rest and preparation, for He wanted His presence kept secret (24), although this proved impossible. Crowds even from this area had already come to Him for healing (3:8): it would be interesting to know if any of them had been Gentiles.

25. The story of the healing of the Syrophoenician woman's daughter recorded here reminds us that Elijah the prophet had,

---

[1]This is of course to distinguish her as a 'Phoenician of Syria' from the other groups of Phoenicians known to both the Jews and the Greeks, that is to say, the western Phoenicians

in roughly the same territory, worked a miracle for another, presumably also heathen, widow (1 Ki. 17:9ff.). It may be a recollection of this Elijah incident that prompted Matthew to add 'and Sidon' after 'Tyre' (Mt. 15:21) in his geographic note,[1] from which it has entered the text here in some MSS. The two towns of 'Tyre and Sidon' are often loosely linked together in the New Testament (compare 3:8). This story shows that Jesus was known at least to the Jews settled in those parts, since it must have been in the home of some Jewish disciple or friend that He was now staying incognito. That this miracle of Elijah was already in the mind of Jesus is shown by Luke's account in 4:25-26, where, after His rejection at Nazareth, Jesus gives clear warning of a coming mission to the Gentiles, using the widow of Zarephath as an illustration. It is in the light of this background that we must read the initial response of Jesus to the woman, for, although Mark does not mention the widow of Zarephath as Luke does, she cannot have been far from his thoughts as he recorded this story.

26. This woman was *a Greek,* that is a Gentile, as the woman of Zarephath of 1 Kings 17:9 had almost certainly been (*cf.* the wording of 1 Ki. 17:12, 'as the Lord your God lives'). We are not told that this particular woman was a widow, but as no husband is mentioned, it is likely: and, like the widow of Zarephath, it was the great need of her child that brought her to God. It was fitting that both widows should receive help from a God who cares specially for widows and orphans (Dt. 10:18; Ps. 146:9, *etc.*

27. First, it is important to remember that Jesus is here probably only quoting a popular proverb on the appropriateness of an action. Secondly, His quotation of the abusive term *dogs* occasionally used for 'Gentiles' (*kynaria, puppies,* the diminutive form found here, is not in any sense affectionate, nor does it

---

of Carthage and her colonies. In either case, though perhaps Greek in language at this stage, although Semitic by background, they were non-Jewish in religion.

[1]Here, many MSS omit *Sidon* in verse 25, although Alexandrinus, A, B, and other good MSS contain it. It may have crept in by later assimilation to verse 31, or because of the parallel Matthew passage. But 'Tyre and Sidon' is a phrase that seems to have been used loosely for the whole area, in popular speech at least.

lessen the blow[1]) did not mean that He recognized this description as in any sense accurate. He may have wanted to see
whether the woman was ready to take such a lowly position in
order to win healing. True, Matthew stresses that Jesus had a
strong consciousness that, in His earthly lifetime, His immediate mission was restricted to Israel (Mt. 15:24), so that he
actually forbade His disciples, at this stage, to preach to Gentiles
or Samaritans (Mt. 10:5). Mark contains no such direct statements, but certainly the words of Jesus here, with their sharp
contrast between *children* and *dogs* infers it, and it is clear that
the woman understood it so (28). After the cross and resurrection, it would be a different matter: then, the gospel must be
preached 'to all nations' (13:10). It is not surprising that Mark,
with his interest in Gentile mission, does not mention these
early restrictions on Gentile evangelism, particularly since they
were removed later: but his recording of this incident shows that
he knew of them. At this stage therefore, a Gentile woman had
no claim, as a Jewish woman would have had. She must realize
that her only hope lay in the uncovenanted mercies of God.
Unless she was prepared to approach the Jewish Messiah in the
knowledge that she was still a Gentile, outside the old covenant,
then her day of healing had not yet come. After the cross, when
the 'dividing wall' had been broken down, it would be another
world (Eph. 2:14), with Jew and Gentile made one in Christ.

28-30. The Syrophoenician woman gladly accepted this
humble position as an 'outsider', and showed that, even on
such terms, she still claimed healing for her daughter. God's
abundance for His children was so rich that even the total
outsider could share in it. It was a great Old Testament truth
that in Abraham, and therefore in Israel, all nations would be
blessed ultimately (Gn. 22:18): she claimed this. In an attempt
to avoid the difficulty, some commentators say that the *dogs* are

---

[1]See BAGD for this point, the last entry under the word. Compare the common linguistic
phenomenon of the 'deterioration of diminutives' in the New Testament and Hellenistic
texts generally: instances can easily be found in any collection of *koinē* texts like that of
Wikgren. Johnson, who finds this saying 'abrupt', suggests a 'development of Jesus'
understanding of his mission': but, in Mark, this self understanding of Jesus is clear cut
from the start (1:14).

simply part of the 'stage scenery' of the parable, since the whole stress is on the children of the house, whose the food is by right: but this, while true, only highlights the plight of those who have no such rights, not being 'children'. It is true that in most parables there is a certain amount of 'back-cloth' which is incapable of exegesis, but to explain in this way would ignore the express statement that she was a Gentile (26). Other more shallow exegesis would make the healing a mere reward from Jesus, delighted by her quick wit, but there is no hint of this in Mark. To Jesus her reply demonstrated not her wit but the depth of her faith (Mt. 15:28). As often in the Old Testament, what would pass today as a witticism had a solemn religious meaning then. All that really matters to Mark and his readers is that the woman's daughter was healed (30). As she was a Gentile, this clearly has relevance for the Gentile mission of the church of Mark's day.

ii. The deaf and dumb man (7:31-37)

Decapolis, though again largely a Gentile area, had considerable resident Jewish colonies, and was indeed the very region where the healed demoniac had already witnessed so faithfully to what Jesus had done for him (5:20). Even in early days, numbers of Jews had come across from this area to hear the preaching of Jesus (3:8). There is therefore no need to assume necessarily that this man was a Gentile, the more so as Jesus spoke the word of power to him in Aramaic.[1] Of course, throughout Syria many of the Gentile population were Aramaic-speaking, under a superficial layer of Hellenism; there cannot have been many Greeks by blood in these country areas, although the frequent use of 'Greek' in the New Testament, as the opposite of 'Jew', suggests at least a veneer of Greek speech (7:26). Even today, however, Orthodox Jews continue to use 'Greeks' in this way, to describe 'Gentiles'. To Mark's Gentile readers, the healing of a man from

---

[1]See comment on v. 41 above. Here, however (since the man was still deaf at the time), the usage might show only that Aramaic was the mother tongue of Jesus, not necessarily that of the patient. Some editors hold that the stern form of the command suggests that this healing too was the expulsion of a demon, but this does not seem to be a necessary interpretation.

a predominantly Gentile area may well have been a sign of what was to come, irrespective of whether the man himself was Jew or Gentile. But it is probably over-exegesis to see the feeding of the four thousand in chapter 8 as being a feeding of Decapolis 'Gentile' crowds, as opposed to the 'Jewish' crowds fed in chapter 6, even if chapter 8 is still set in the Decapolis area.

32–35. Here, too, it was the faith of friends that brought the deaf mute to Jesus at first: but, as in the case of the paralytic (2:3–5), Jesus seems to have looked for at least some response in the man himself as well. All the actions of verses 33 and 34 were miming the man's present need, the process of healing, and the source from which such healing alone could come, in a way which even a deaf mute could understand (the blocked ears opened, the symbolic removal of the speech impediment from the tongue by spitting, the upward glance and sigh of prayer). So there is no need to assume purely vicarious faith here, any more than there is in the case of the paralytic of 2:3. Saving faith, however small, must be exhibited by the subject of salvation: but it is not irrelevant to point out that the faith of his friends came first. For comments on the use of the Aramaic *Ephphatha* (34), see the discussion on 5:41. Some have felt that the abrupt form of the command indicates an exorcism by Jesus (Anderson): but no mention is made of a demon here, so this is unlikely.

36. Presumably, Jesus, in issuing this command for silence, had no wish to be known as a mere miracle-worker, like some of the early rabbis of the Talmud: wonder-working in itself had no necessary moral or spiritual connotation, any more than magic would. That the result was unwelcome publication of the news and notoriety, contrary to the command and expressed wish of Jesus (*the more ... the more ...*), is only an illustration of the strange perversity of human nature of which Paul speaks (Rom. 7:8), and which Augustine feelingly confirms from his own experience. It certainly does not prove, as is sometimes suggested, that Jesus had this very result in mind when He forbade any telling of the incident. Such cheap-jack psychology is utterly inconsistent with the Jesus of Mark's Gospel, and would defeat the whole purpose of the 'Messianic secret'.

37. The parallelism between the words of the crowd and Genesis 1:31 may have been unnoticed by the original speakers, but can hardly have escaped unseen by the early church. All God's creative works are perfect, and so is the manifestation of His Son's power. Not only God saw that His work was good (Gn. 1:4), but even, on this occasion, humans also. Nevertheless, while it amazed them, it did not enable them to make the equation between Jesus and God: only revelation and faith could do that.

iii. The feeding of the four thousand (8:1–9)

By no process of the imagination can the feeding of the four thousand be regarded as a mere 'doublet',[1] or a variant account of the feeding of the five thousand. There are too many differences of detail in the stories for this view to be maintained: and both Matthew and Mark contain separate accounts of the two miracles close to each other, which shows that the early church had no such doubts. See on 7:31 for the suggestion that one was a 'Gentile' and the other a 'Jewish' feeding: but this is most unlikely, and there is certainly no hint in the context of Mark that this is so. A little reflection will show that, in oral tradition, it is far more likely that two originally different accounts should be later assimilated, rather than that two parallel accounts of the same event should be later 'dissimilated'. Further reflection will show that if we find two stories of generally similar miracles, there is no need to assume that they are necessarily variant

---

[1]In one sense, this is part of the wider question of the occurrence in Mark of accounts, often very similar, of 'parallel' incidents, a feature which is so frequent as to be almost a point of his style. But it is also far-fetched to claim, on geographic grounds, that one feeding was of Gentiles and one of Jews, so proving the 'ecumenical' nature of the Lord's mission (a patristic view). At this stage, there is no sign of a deliberate outreach by Jesus to Gentiles at all. Nor can we dismiss the second account by saying that the attitude of the disciples would be 'inconceivable' (Anderson), if they had already witnessed the first miracle. Their attitude is on a par with that recorded of them throughout the gospel – consistent obtuseness and failure to understand.

accounts of the same miracle. Jesus performed many unrecorded miracles, as the early church knew well (Jn. 21:25). There must have been several similar original incidents in many cases, of which one would live on in one line of tradition and one in another. It is interesting to note that one theory of textual criticism (the multiple source theory) broadly agrees with this: it postulates multiple early variant sources, only later to be 'ironed out' into the great major traditions of later days.

2-3. There is a tendency today to spiritualize the miracles so much that we lose sight of their primary meaning, which is that, when Jesus saw anyone cold, hungry, ill or in distress, His heart went out to them in love and pity (verse 2).[1] In other words, although the miracles of Jesus were certainly used as 'signs' to point a spiritual message, the recipient was not made merely a spiritual 'stalking-horse'. The root of all ministry, whether physical or spiritual, is this genuine inner constraint, which the New Testament writers unanimously see as the love of Christ, at work in us (2 Cor. 5:14).[2] But Jesus did not attempt miraculously to heal every sick person in Israel, nor to feed all the hungry: there was a curious 'selectiveness' in His ministry which is explained by pointing to Old Testament examples, to show its consistency with God's plan. Nevertheless, this particular group in verse 1 had a special claim on His gracious provision for their needs, in that they had not merely sought Him for the food that He would give, as those of John 6:26 had. This audience had proved their sense of spiritual values by three days of eager listening to the preaching of Jesus first (verse 2). It was not merely that they were hungry, but that they had become hungry in God's service, and so theirs was to be an experience of 'seek first his kingdom . . . and all these things shall be yours as well' (Mt. 6:33). Like Jesus in His ministry (3:20), in their hunger to know and do God's will, they had scarcely been conscious of their own physical hunger up to this moment. For such people,

[1]This, as mentioned, is the great theme of Belo's commentary, although he takes it to such an extreme as virtually to deny altogether the spiritual meaning of the gospel.
[2]See Cranfield on 6:34: he sees in this yearning of Jesus over the multitude the key to the understanding of His mission. For a rabbinic definition of this sort of love, see *Pirqe Aboth* 5:19 (Singer, p. 206).

Jesus would work a miracle, and give them the food that they had not sought first.

4-7. This time, the disciples' question as to the source of the supply (4) was one of sheer bewilderment. Their own resources were so small that they had never even thought of them as a possibility; and once again they had not taken Jesus into account. So little had they learned from the feeding of the five thousand; equally little were they to learn from this new miracle, as we see from verse 21 of this same chapter. This failure to learn from the second miracle is the strongest possible confirmation of the truth of the statement that the first miracle had left no impression on them: their attitude was constant throughout. There is still a puzzle, it is true; but it becomes now the puzzle as to the reason for such continual failure to understand that the paucity of their own resources was irrelevant. Modesty and self-distrust, even a shrinking from the task, is an essential preliminary to all Christian service: but, once we are convinced of God's call, to persist in such an attitude betrays lack of faith in God's power, and is therefore culpable (Ex. 4:14). The siting of the feeding *in the desert* may be highly significant, as Minear points out. Israel had been fed by God with manna in the desert, and, in the messianic age, the desert was to blossom (Is. 35:1-10).

8-9. It has often been pointed out that the *spuris*, the word used for *basket* here, is quite different from the *kophinos*, or travelling basket, used to store the fragments in the former miracle (6:43). In fact, the *spuris* seems to have been a flexible bag rather than stiff wickerwork (see Morris on 'John', NICNT, p.345, note 25). These little differences of vocabulary must go back to the original tradition; otherwise it is hard to account for the fixity of the vocabulary in either case. The *kophinos* was essentially a Jewish 'travelling-bag' as we can see from Roman accounts, commonly used by travelling salesmen, or 'bagmen' in the ancient world. Luggage made of wickerwork is still standard in many parts of the third world today for its cheapness and lightness.

There is no need to see any spiritual symbolism in the

numbers. The twelve 'vendor's baskets' would doubtless be those regularly carried by the twelve apostles, hence the number. The seven baskets now borrowed (it is unlikely that peripatetic preachers carried such things around with them) simply pin the story to history as surely as does the number 'four thousand' for the crowd. Such a figure as this could in no sense be used either symbolically or metaphorically for a large number, as five or ten thousand could perhaps have been.

iv. The Pharisees demand a sign (8:10–13)

This is an account of a mission to *Dalmanutha* (or Magadan, Mt. 15:39) apparently on the opposite shore of the lake (10). It might have been as spiritually fruitful as any other place, but seems to have failed to achieve any spiritual results, because it was met from the outset by a stubbornly 'theological' opposition on the part of the argumentative and unbelieving Pharisees. We may compare the attitude in Nazareth, where little exercise of the miraculous power of Jesus was possible because of stubborn unbelief (6:5–6). It is striking that in both cases the stumbling-block to faith was self-important knowledge, whether theological knowledge here, or knowledge of the local origin of Jesus in the case of the people of Nazareth. Knowledge is not of course wrong, but, as Paul says, it can 'puff up' (1 Cor. 8:1) and create pride, which is a spiritual obstacle: it is love that 'builds up'.

11–13. This demand by the Pharisees for a sign is so significant that it is recorded in all four gospels. The reaction of Jesus (*he sighed deeply in his spirit,* 12) may be impatience which He always showed towards lack of faith in those who might be expected to possess it. Compare His reaction towards the faithless and powerless disciples, at the foot of the mountain of transfiguration (9:19). It is clear that unbelief lay at the root of the Pharisaic attitude too. To those in such a state of unbelief, even a sign if given would not convince, for these Pharisees must surely have already heard of some at least of the many miracles which had already taken place in Galilee, such as the feeding of the four thousand just before. John's Gospel rightly says that the difficulty lies in the will, not the intellect, as far as

acceptance of the 'signs' of Jesus is concerned (Jn. 7:17).[1]
But even apart from the impossibility of convincing people
against their will by mere signs, such an attitude of sign-seeking
strikes at the root of the biblical concept of the nature of faith. It
might be theoretically possible to base a belief upon signs and
wonders, but this sort of 'belief' would not be 'faith', but only a
logical conclusion (Schweizer). Perhaps this is yet another
reason why Jesus used His undoubted miraculous powers so
sparingly, and only in response to already existent faith. So
Jesus refused the request of the Pharisees of Dalmanutha, and
left the place (verse 13).

By contrast, to the Christian, 'believing is seeing'. Hebrews
11:1 presses this still further: the eye of faith sees here and now
what actually has yet to be realized in the future, and so obtains
strength to endure.[2] This was the faith which Peter was soon to
express, in 8:29, in defiance of all outward appearances.

v. The danger of yeast (8:14–21)

In this section, again, the lack of spiritual perception of the
disciples is brought out, although the rebuke loses some of its
sting, when we realize that the story owes its very preservation
and recording to the recollections of one at least of this very
group. Hence we have not merely a condemnation of the
disciples by Jesus, but a condemnation of the disciples by themselves as they remembered. There is no need (with Nineham) to
see this episode as a deliberate creation by Mark: as usual, he is
bluntly telling the truth, and showing the disciples exactly as
they were, faults and all.

14. It does not appear that Jesus was greatly concerned as to
whether they had brought bread or not: He had already shown

[1]Many modern editors have pointed out that the Johannine use of *sēmeion*, *sign*, is
different from the usage of the synoptists. The key surely is that in John *sēmeion* is a sign
granted by God to belief, while in the synoptists, as here, it is a sign demanded by
unbelievers.
[2]This is the sense in which John uses 'signs' to describe the seven miracles which he
selects from the life of Jesus. They are 'signs' because, to the eye of faith, they reveal to us
what God is like. We might go further and say that all miracles are transparent to the eye of
faith, and so become 'signs'. To the unbelieving, the miracle will never be a 'sign': it will

that He could meet their needs. But the disciples certainly were worried about it, and probably they had a guilty conscience about their oversight. This can be seen both from the use of the words *had forgotten* (14), and from the way in which, as soon as Jesus mentioned *leaven* (15), their minds at once flew to this point. Psychologically, this is very true to life: they expected to be blamed for their culpable lack of foresight, and so they saw reproof where none was intended. They were not blamed by Jesus for their lack of foresight, but for their lack of faith. We look for good business men in His disciples, but God looks for saints, in whom businesslike qualities are of course encouraged (Rom. 12:11; 1 Cor. 14:40).

15. Jesus, by His use of the word *leaven* here, was using a pithy one-word parable for unseen pervasive influence. This influence was something that unfitted for the service of God, if we are to judge from the analogy of the use of unleavened bread in Old Testament religious festivals (see Lv. 2:4, *etc.*) and Paul's 'cleanse out the old leaven' (1 Cor. 5:7), referring to the well-known Hebrew custom in both biblical and modern times of clearing the home of yeast, before Passover is celebrated. Yeast is in this context clearly a biblical symbol of sin: but the clarity with which it bears that meaning here is due to the direct association with 'Pharisees' and 'Herod'. In itself, the symbolism of 'yeast' is merely that of unseen pervasive spreading, as in the parable of the kingdom (Mt. 13:33). Admittedly some exegetes have been forced, by a false ideal of consistency, to see the picture even here as one of the spreading of evil within the church: but the more natural meaning would seem to be simply the gradual spread of the church within the world.[1]

What then was the insidious danger that lay before the little band of disciples, the proto-church at that time? It was the

---

prove nothing. Indeed, he or she will not even believe it, for seeing is not necessarily believing. There will always be an alternative explanation, for faith is a system of interpretation of facts, which, by definition, must always be capable of other interpretations.

[1] It is, however, true that this is the only New Testament context (with synoptic parallel in Luke) where *leaven* has a good sense (Cranfield). This is probably because, in the Old Testament, *leaven* or 'yeast', like fermentation in wine, was regarded as a type of corruption, and so could not be offered to God. To the rabbis, yeast was always a symbol of evil (Schweizer).

danger of allowing their thinking to be approximated and assimilated to that of the world around them, the world of the Pharisees and Herodians, two religious and political circles respectively of their day.[1] In the Old Testament, Israel had been warned of the gulf between God's thinking and its own (Is. 55:8), and Jesus' words of rebuke to Peter would underline this in the New Testament (8:33). The *leaven of the Pharisees* was hypocrisy (7:6), while *the leaven of Herod* (a variant reading has *Herodians*) may have been that procrastinating time-serving which had led Herod first to imprison John the Baptist, then to execute him, though fighting his own conscience all the time (6:14-29). Matthew 16:6 has 'Sadducees' in place of *Herod* or *Herodians* here: they were the shrewd, wealthy, priestly aristocracy, with a worldly leavening influence at least as dangerous as that of the hard religious formalism of the Pharisees. But at each stage of the history of the church, the exact source and nature of the danger changes, while the danger itself remains. Vigilance is always necessary (14:38).

16. The Greek *hoti*, untranslated in RSV, (AV, *because*) may be used here merely as a particle to introduce a direct quotation. A lively translation would then be: 'They reasoned "But we have no bread at all!".' NIV paraphrases more tamely as ' "It is because we have no bread." '

17. '*Why do you discuss?*' The Greek word *dialogizomai* represents a mental activity which often has a bad sense in the gospels, like *meteōrizomai*, 'to be doubtful', or *tarassomai*, 'to be troubled'. It is not their discussion which is being condemned, but the lack both of faith and of spiritual perceptiveness which had given rise to the discussion in the first place. They are still as blind and spiritually obtuse as ever: this is what grieves Jesus. Even the experience of God's provision of their physical needs during their preaching trip of chapter 6 (note especially v. 8 *no bread*), had left no mark on them.

---

[1]The specific sin of the Pharisees here was the demand for a sign from heaven (11). If this unbelieving spirit spread to the group of disciples, and pervaded it, it would destroy all spiritual life, as surely as leaven would spread through dough.

18–21. The disciples credited Jesus with spiritual insight, and did see in His previous remark supernatural perception, but limited that perception to material objects: they thought that He was referring to their lack of bread. They were so blinded by their immediate bodily needs that they had again forgotten to seek first God's kingdom, with the faith that, as they did this, their bodily needs would be met, as those of the hungry crowds had been met twice already (verses 19 and 20). As Jesus said, they still did not understand (verse 21): see again 6:8, where Jesus had forbidden them to make provision for their own needs, and yet those needs had obviously been met by God (Lk. 22:35).

vi. The blind man of Bethsaida (8:22–26)

The disciples had been blinded to spiritual truths by their constant preoccupation with their own immediate bodily needs. It was only fitting therefore that the next miracle should be the opening of the eyes of the physically blind man of Bethsaida, as a picture of what God would yet do for them. It is also fitting that 8:29, immediately below, should contain the account of the opening of the eyes of Peter to the messiahship of Jesus, and that chapter 9 should contain the story of the transfiguration. Of course, we are specifically told that Jesus healed many blind in the course of His ministry (Lk. 7:21), but this particular miracle is recorded only in Mark, naturally enough, if it occurred in Bethsaida, the home town of Peter (Jn. 1:44), and if Mark, even indirectly, depends on Petrine tradition. No name is recorded: with the exception of Bartimaeus (10:46), such people are usually nameless in the gospels, particularly in Mark.

22. It is clear from the words *brought* and *begged* in this verse that, as in other miracles, the faith of others besides the afflicted man was also involved. Here is the great gospel warrant for intercessory prayer to God on behalf of others, both on behalf of the physically sick and of the spiritually blind.

23. The taking *by the hand* is an eyewitness touch, particularly appropriate in the case of a blind man, as is the leading *out of the* *village* of the sightless man, bewildered by the noise of the crowd, to a place of quiet, where he can hear and understand Jesus whom he cannot yet see. The saliva applied by Jesus to the man's eyes is unlikely to have been used for its supposed therapeutic effect. It was simply an acted parable, to draw the man's attention to what Jesus was about to do. The laying on of hands by Jesus would have the same effect; touch means more than sound to a blind man, and only by touch could the meaning of Jesus be conveyed. There must be an understanding by him of the act of Jesus before that act could become revelation. Unexplained miracle, unrelated to God's loving purpose, is too close to magic, and of magic we have no instance in the Bible, except outside a Christian context, where it is strictly condemned (Acts 19:19-20).

24. The point of the man's reply seems to be that he could and did see, but indistinctly. There are non-biblical parallels to this sort of phrase (see BAGD), but the contrast with the adverb *tēlaugōs, clearly*, in verse 25, makes the meaning abundantly plain in any case. We must not blame the excited man for inaccurate description: after all, he had seen neither people nor trees before until that moment, though he was doubtless familiar with both by touch. The English use of the word 'trunk' for the body of both tree and human does denote a basic visual similarity between the two. The unusual nature of the reply (one would expect 'yes' or 'no'), and its vivid detail assures us that we are dealing with a well-remembered tradition.

25. Scripture does not make plain why two applications of the hands of Jesus were necessary here: was it a lack of faith on the recipient's part? Nowhere else is such twofold healing action recorded of Jesus.[1] But the important theological point is not how difficult the healing was, nor what the peculiar nature of

---

[1] This in itself is proof positive of the genuineness of the story: such an unusual detail would never have been invented (Taylor, in Cranfield), for it might be seen as a criticism of the ability of Jesus to heal. The passage is sometimes seen nowadays as an encouragement to persistence in prayer for healing, even if the Lord has not completely granted it on the first occasion of asking. Minear sees a symbolism of two stages of spiritual healing, but this seems fanciful.

MARK 8:26–33

the difficulty was, but that Jesus did not desist till the man was completely healed (cf. Paul's confidence, expressed in Phil. 1:6). The very fact that Jesus, after laying His hands on him, asked the man whether he could 'see anything' (23) suggests that He was conscious of some lack of faith in the blind man. There was no need to ask such a question of others, for they were completely healed. At Nazareth, Jesus had not been able to do many miracles, because of their unbelief (6:5–6): perhaps this is a similar instance of little faith.

26. Jesus does not want to be known as a miracle-worker; and so (as in 7:36) he forbids the man to tell others. He is to go straight to his home: he is not to go even into his own village first, for fear the news spreads. In a village, there are no secrets: the alternative manuscript reading, warning him not to speak about it to anyone in the village, therefore comes to the same thing. Whether the man obeyed or disobeyed, we do not know: but certainly the story of the healing made a great impression on the disciples, and found its way into the tradition, perhaps because of the incident which followed.

IV. HE FIRMLY SET HIS FACE: THE ROAD TO JERUSALEM (8:27 – 10:52)

A. CONFESSION AND TRANSFIGURATION (8:27 – 9:10)

i. Peter's confession: the first passion prediction (8:27–33)

Now comes the great confession of the Messiahship of Jesus by Peter on the road to 'Philip's Caesarea',[1] and the first clear prediction by Jesus to the disciples of His coming death. It is of course no accident that these two are joined. If the disciples see Jesus as the Messiah, it is essential that they see Him as God's Christ and not a human Christ, and that they understand the path of Messiahship which has been ordained by God. The

[1] To distinguish it from other towns also named 'Caesarea', in honour of the emperor. Only Mark mentions the location of Peter's confession as being here. Schweizer sees the place as appropriate, since the rabbis considered it as the boundary of the Holy Land with Gentile territory.

natural mind never objects to the concept of a Messiah, provided that he is to be a Messiah who commends himself to the
natural mind. This careful explanation by Jesus was doubly
important, not only so that the disciples might be kept from
nationalistic or other misconceptions of Messiahship, but also
because Christ's path would determine theirs, as Jesus would
soon explain to James and John (10:39). It was a prophetic word
when the light-hearted city wits of Antioch called the 'followers
of the Way' by the coined name 'Christians', that is, 'the messianic people' (Acts 11:26), since they must walk the same path
as He did. It is also appropriate that such a revelation should
now be brought to the spiritually blinded disciples by the one
who had so recently proved His power to open the eyes of the
physically blind.

28. It is always easy to answer in the third person, and give
the views of others as to the nature of Jesus. We have seen that
Herod saw Jesus as a 'John returned' (6:16), and it seems from
this passage that Herod was not alone in this belief. Others saw
Him as 'Elijah returned', a common Jewish concept of the day,
derived from Malachi 4:5, and endorsed by Jesus as having
reference to John the Baptist (9:12; Mt. 17:13). The interesting
thing is that both Elijah and John were, as all recognized, only
forerunners of the Christ, and not the Christ Himself. So none
of the outside world had as yet guessed the true nature of Jesus
as Messiah. Others could not make as definite an identification
as Herod did, but agreed that clearly Jesus was a prophet. The
Emmaus Road conversation witnesses to the persistence of this
'minimal' view of His Person and nature, even among Christians (Lk. 24:19); and the *nabi Isa*, 'prophet Jesus', of the *Qur'an*
bears witness to its survival in Mohammed's days among the
decayed Christian churches of Arabia. A shallow Christology
like this will ultimately lead to even grosser heresy: for it
inevitably makes Jesus Himself only a forerunner and not God's
last word to rebellious humanity. It is interesting to speculate
what spiritual qualities, seen and noted in Jesus by outside
observers, led them to make these identifications. Every
prophet spoke with authority, in God's name, bringing the
word of the Lord, and vindicating that word with signs: John is

the stern eschatological prophet of doom; Elijah is the fearless wonder-worker, appearing and disappearing from the desert, the great example to New Testament saints of the power of prayer (Jas. 5:16–18). All of these prophets differed individually, yet each found a place in the portrait of Jesus. As often, if we want to understand His person and work, we must draw into one the several threads of Old Testament revelation, for all lines of revelation meet in Him. So, while they were inadequate, these views expressed above were not entirely wrong. Indeed, Lightfoot is correct in saying that their error lay in the fact that all these were roles of preparation, not fulfilment and consummation.

29. But now, as it continually comes to us, comes the personal question that transfers theology from an armchair discussion to an uncomfortable dialogue between God and us. Are His own disciples still as blind as the others? The rest may be, but not Peter: at once, the answer was made, 'You are the Christ', that is, 'the Anointed', or 'the Messiah'. The weight of MS evidence here seems to point to this wording as being the full Marcan statement: the addition of 'the Son of the living God', with poorer MS evidence, is almost certainly an assimilation to the text of Matthew 16:16, where it properly belongs.[1] Simon Peter's similar declaration in John 6:69, should be compared, although this seems to be on a different occasion. Here was the identification of Jesus with the Christ that shows a Christian, for no-one could make such an equation without the inner illumination of the Spirit. Matthew 16:17–19, at this point, continues with the blessing of Peter, the declaration that this is none other than the Spirit's revelation, and the subsequent promises to Peter: none of these are recorded in Mark, although he must surely have known of them, particularly if Peter was among his informants. It would seem commonsense to say that Peter suppressed them out of modesty, while still retaining the rebuke that followed. If

---

[1] In whatever form, this declaration has long been realized as the 'watershed' of the gospel. It is a parallel to the confession by the Gentile centurion at the cross on 15:39 (Kertelge, in IOM). This is a fair observation: but whether we are justified in seeing the centurion's confession as a 'foil' to Peter's denial (14:68), is quite another question. Nevertheless, in this instance, His own reject Him, while the Gentile world acclaims Him.

Mark omitted them, it was because he did not consider them relevant here. If Mark was indeed the gospel of the early Roman church (as seems likely), then this omission must be significant. If we want to find the Petrine promises, we must turn to the Palestinian tradition underlying Matthew's Gospel: the one place where they were not proclaimed was at Rome. Mark is concerned here only with the revelation of the messianic secret, for that alone is relevant to his purpose at the moment.

30. Why were the disciples forbidden to tell others of the Messiahship of Jesus? Presumably because at this stage none of them (not even Peter: see verse 32) really understood what was involved in Messiahship, and so those outside could not fail to misunderstand such a claim. Even the fact of His Messiahship was a discovery which each disciple must make individually, as Peter had done, although in every case, as for Peter, this must come as the Spirit's revelation. But the nature of the Messiahship of Jesus is an even deeper revelation which is still to come to them. Here, in a nutshell, is the mystery of the gospel: we are very conscious of our human part in the process of discovery at the moment of conversion, and yet, from the other side, we learn in reverent wonder that all was God's work in revelation (Jn. 15:16),

31. This is the first of the three occasions on which Jesus carefully explained to the twelve the cost and meaning of Messiahship:[1] compare 9:31 and 10:33, which gradually give a fuller picture, presumably as the disciples were better able to bear it. This in itself shows that none of the later Jerusalem happenings took Jesus by surprise.[2] Indeed, as soon as He had accepted the

---

[1] Although it is striking that Jesus does not say here 'the Messiah must suffer', but *the Son of man must suffer, i.e.* probably, 'I must suffer'. For a summary of views on the meaning of this self-chosen title, see Cranfield, pp. 272-277. See also Perrin (IOM); the titles of 'Christ' and 'Son of God' are given a new 'conceptual content' by the use of 'Son of man' here, for the 'Son of man' can be explained as 'suffering', while the thought was not inherent in either of the other titles. This is of course distinct from the two other uses of 'Son of man', whether as a 'charismatic' present figure, or an 'eschatological' future figure: see Tanner (IOM). All of these different aspects unite in the historical figure of Jesus.

[2] This is of course a great stumbling-block to liberal scholars, who find it hard to admit that Jesus foresaw His own death, still less that He prophesied it three times in detail. Such scholars regard the three prophecies as artificial creations by the disciples after Christ's

vocation to Messiahship, He had thereby accepted the vocation to suffering. To 'suffer', when applied to the Messiah in the New Testament, is a 'theological shorthand' for His death upon the cross (Acts 3:18, etc.). But to *suffer many things*, as here, doubtless includes far more than His actual death, for Hebrews 5:8 makes clear that the cross was the culmination and supreme point of a life of suffering for Jesus. It is only after we understand the person of Christ that we can appreciate His work: that is the great theological lesson, and explains why Jesus made no attempt to tell of the cross until now. *Apodokimasthēnai, be rejected* (31), is an interesting word: it means literally 'fail to pass the scrutiny'. The thought is that the Sanhedrin, the priestly court of Israel, will scrutinize the claims of Jesus, and then deliberately reject Him. But the true danger for all is that of failing to pass the scrutiny of God, as Paul saw (1 Cor. 9:27, where a word from the same root is used). The meaning of *rise again* is apparently incomprehensible to the disciples as yet, for much later they are still puzzled by it (9:10).[1] Perhaps, like Martha (Jn. 11:24), their trouble was that they balked at a resurrection here and now, while accepting one 'at the last day' quite happily. Within Judaism, only Sadducees rejected the whole concept of resurrection: but that was on a par with their general anti-supernatural bias (Acts 23:8), which was not shared by the theologically orthodox Pharisees or the great mass of Israel.

32. *Began to rebuke him.* Typically, Mark simply records the fact: he refrains from quoting the terms of Peter's remonstrance to Christ as Matthew does (see Mt. 16:22). It was enough for Mark to show that Peter had failed to understand the necessity of the cross: he understood only too clearly the meaning of the words of Jesus (Minear).

All the apostles seem to have been present on this occasion, and each would have had his own recollections of it, some fuller

---

death. But if we allow prophets of Old Testament and New Testament alike knowledge of their future fate, why not the Son of God? (*cf.* Acts 20:23.)

[1] See Lane for the addition, in a few manuscripts, of the phrase 'and then he will speak the word openly'. However true this may be, it reads suspiciously like a late explanation of what actually happened.

than others. 'Turning and seeing his disciples' (33) suggests that all would share in Peter's rebuke (Anderson).

33. No sterner rebuke ever fell on any Pharisee than fell on this disciple of Jesus, this proto-Christian. In speaking as he did, Peter was voicing, not the mind of God revealed by His Spirit, but that 'natural' mind which is the mind of the enemy: and so Peter could be addressed by Jesus directly as *Satan*.[1] The avoidance of the cross had been a temptation faced and overcome by Jesus in the wilderness, to judge from the fuller account of the temptations contained in the other synoptists (*e.g.* Lk. 4:1–13). For Peter to suggest it was therefore to think in human terms, and not in divine terms. The Aramaic form *Sātānâ* suggests that here we have a relic of another original Aramaic saying of Jesus (*cf.* 4:15). Otherwise, the Greek *diabolos*, 'devil', might have been used as elsewhere (*cf.* Jn. 6:70). It is unlikely that there was any gradation in meaning between the two words, which seem to be mere synonyms in the two different languages. Note that Satan's suggestion is not blasphemous or obviously evil: it is smooth, attractive and 'natural', appealing to all 'natural' human instincts. That is why it is so dangerous.

ii. The cost of discipleship (8:34–38)

Now we see why it was so essential that Peter should grasp the conditions of Messiahship for Jesus: otherwise, Peter could not grasp the conditions of discipleship for himself. This correspondence between the path of master and servant was fulfilled very literally, if we accept the universal tradition as to the manner of Peter's death at Rome by crucifixion. For archaeological evidence for Peter's Roman martyrdom, see Kirschbaum and Guarducci. The place of his death has of course nothing to do with subsequent claims as to Peter's position, a fact seemingly forgotten by protagonists and opponents alike.

So the Lord warns all the crowd, not just His professed

---

[1]Holl, quoted in Anderson, aptly says 'Who from the primitive community would have dared to call the revered Cephas "Satan"?' This is a clear proof that Jesus actually said these words, though whether it is proof that Peter and not another preserved them is another matter.

disciples, that to follow Him means to deny all natural inclinations[1] and to 'shoulder one's stake'. 'Stake' in modern English, preserves the association of shameful death better than
cross does. Compare 10:39 for the equally solemn words of Jesus
to James and John as to the cost of discipleship. The thought is
plain to every child playing the game of 'follow my leader', in
which there is only one rule, that no follower shirks going to any
place where the leader has first gone. Ultimately, to the Christian, this following of Jesus becomes the hope of heaven, since
our leader has already gone there (Heb. 6:19-20): but first comes
the cross. 'No cross, no crown' is a pithy piece of theology
which must have been ever-present in the minds of the early
Christians at Rome and other centres of persecution.

35. The one who tries to live this life 'for self', who hoards it
jealously and selfishly, will lose it. This is true, not only finally
in the death that all must face, but moment by moment, for such
selfish life is no true life, but only animal existence. Life, like
sand, trickles between our fingers whether we will or no, and to
grasp it the more tightly means only that it flows the faster from
us. So a refusal to accept this 'death to self', which is the bearing
of Christ's cross and following Him, is a spiritual death;
whereas, by a divine paradox, spiritual life is to be found only
by dying to self (Gal. 2:20).

The additional clause, which only Mark preserves, *and the
gospel's* makes plain the exact way in which life is to be 'lost' for
Christ. It is to be spent in His service, in the spreading abroad of
the good news. The Christian therefore has not two goals, but
one: Christ and His gospel are ultimately one (see 10:29 for a
similar link). Schweizer well compares Luke 18:29, where 'for
the sake of the kingdom of God' is similarly used.

36-37. The metaphor in *profit*, *gain*, and *forfeit* is commercial
rather than judicial. As usual, Jesus is meeting or anticipating

---

[1]This is why the cult of 'selfism' (self fulfilment, and the like), much favoured by the so
called 'me generation', is utterly foreign to the gospels, and, in particular to the teachings of
Jesus, as recorded in Mark. See on 12:31, where there is no commendation of self love, but
only a realistic recognition that we do in fact always desire to promote our own good
(Anderson).

objections at our own level, appealing to the shrewd commercial instincts of these Galilean tradesfolk, as He appealed elsewhere to the common sense of fisherfolk (Mt. 13:48) or farmer (Lk. 13:15). The kingdom was a good 'buy' at any price, if only these hard-headed businessfolk could see it.

38. But then, as usual, when we have been defeated at our own lowly level of thinking, Jesus takes the argument to a deeper level, this time with an eschatological reference. *Son of man* He has used as a self-chosen title before (*e.g.* verse 31), but now, through the Petrine declaration, 'Son of Man' has been definitely equated with 'Messiah'. Jesus has shown that the biblical interpretation of the anointed one is not, initially at least, the conquering king eagerly awaited by the Jews, but the rejected suffering Servant (Is. 53:1–12). Yet, in spite of all this, as 'Son of man' He was still to be God's chosen instrument of judgment at His coming-again (*cf.* Dn. 7:13). The biggest difficulty for the disciples must have been the problem of how to join all these different concepts in one and to relate them to the Jesus before them. The humble Christ of history is always humanity's great stumbling-block, not only to His own generation but to ours also.[1] God is revealed in Christ, but only to the eye of faith: to others, God is hidden in Christ, and they cannot see Him. This is the great 'messianic secret'. It is no accident that, in Mark, the story of the transfiguration directly follows, for, in it, something of the true glory of Christ is revealed to those who have already recognized Jesus as Christ in His lowliness.

iii. The transfiguration (9:1–10)

To what does the prophecy in verse 1 refer? That depends on our understanding of the exact moment when the disciples were to see *the kingdom of God has come with power.* There are two distinct

[1]That is, if *genea* is to be interpreted *generation*, as seems probable in view of its similar meaning in other contexts in Mark (e.g. 8:12). See BAGD's discussion of the word, paragraph 2. The later Jewish use of *dōr*, 'generation' in *e.g. dōr hammabbūl*, 'the generation that lived at the time of the flood', is in point here. Less probably, *genea* could mean the Jewish 'people, nation': but the main message would still be the same. Schweizer points out that the words 'this generation' are often found in the immediate context of the words 'Son of man' (*e.g.* 13:26–30).

questions involved here: the first question is, what did the disciples initially think the meaning to be? The second and more important is, what did Jesus Himself mean by the saying? As regards the first, we know that many in the early church expected the Lord's second coming to be within the lifetime of the first generation of apostolic witnesses. The first apostolic generation may well, then, have thought that this saying of Jesus was a direct reference to His *parousia*, the second coming of Christ for judgment and establishment of His reign. This view could of course nowadays be maintained only if we understand *will not taste death* in a mystical sense as 'will not perish eternally', which is possible, but unlikely. In Semitic idiom, *taste death* is simply poetic for the blunt 'die', and so the apostles themselves would presumably have interpreted it. But the supposed views of the first generation have for us now only a past historical interest. By the date of the writing of the Gospel of Mark, even Peter had probably passed away, so this literal interpretation, with reference to the second coming, would have been no longer possible. Now, Mark certainly would not have recorded a saying which was meaningless to him and also useless to the church. The verse must, therefore, refer either to the transfiguration which follows immediately after, which seems reasonable; or to later events, still within a human lifespan, such as Christ's triumph on the cross, confirmed by the resurrection (Col. 2:15); or to the coming of the Spirit; or to the later extension of the blessings of the kingdom to the Gentiles as outlined in the book of Acts. Of these, perhaps the combined event of cross and resurrection is the best interpretation, if we reject the transfiguration as the meaning. But perhaps we do wrong to associate the prophecy exclusively with any one isolated point of time in our human sense of the word: R. T. France (in *Matthew*) sees it as a general reference to the vindication of Jesus. In any case, the transfiguration is a foretaste of the final triumph of Jesus, whether it is seen in itself as a fulfilment of this prophecy or promise of Jesus.

2. There may be no theological reason for the *six days* of Mark, though attempts have been made to connect them with the 'six days' of God's working in Genesis, followed by His sabbath rest. It may simply be one of the irrelevancies of the memory of

an eyewitness, assuring us that the story is firmly set in place and time, though we may not always be able to reconstruct either from the scanty data given. Mark, as noted, has little interest in recording exact time or date or geographic location. In Exodus 24:16, Moses is shown as waiting 'six days' for a revelation (Anderson), which may be a parallel, but both Mark, with *six days*, and Luke, with 'eight days' (Lk. 9:28), may be giving only an approximate number of days, meaning 'about a week', as we would say today.[1] Only in the passion story is there a similar note of time (Schweizer). Again, as often, Jesus took with Him *Peter, and James, and John*: for His possible reasons for this choice, see the comment under the story of Jairus, in chapter 5. The way in which the story is told by Mark recalls the leading of Joshua up the mount of revelation by Moses (Ex. 24:13), and the way in which Moses was unwittingly transfigured by the glory of God while on top of the mountain (Ex. 34:29), although Moses had only a fading and reflected glory, as the Bible makes plain (2 Cor. 3:7, 13). In contrast, Christ's glory on the mountain was His own: He was but reassuming that divine glory which was His with the Father before the world began (Jn. 17:5). In a sense, we are wrong to call this 'the transfiguration', as though it was unique: the true great transfiguration, the *metamorphōsis*, had already taken place at Bethlehem when God took human form, as Philippians shows (Phil. 2:6–7). On the mount of transfiguration Jesus was but re-assuming His own true form, even if only temporarily: faith had momentarily passed into sight, for the three disciples.

3. The lasting impression left by the vision was one of unearthly purity. So, too, when any in the Scriptures see God's spiritual ministrants, they appear to them as wearing white robes (16:5). In spite of modern Bible illustrations, white was not a common colour for working clothes in biblical days: it soiled too easily in a workaday world. If it had not been unusual for people to wear gleaming white garments, the

[1]Although Cranfield may be right in seeing such precise dating as proof that Mark at least saw in the transfiguration the fulfilment of the promise of Jesus in 8:38, Jesus has already been shown to the three apostles (the 'some', 9:1) in His Father's glory, as foretold.

detail would not have been recorded here, for the Bible, like most other ancient documents, makes very few references to colour.

4. We often loosely take the appearance of *Elijah with Moses* with Jesus on the mountain as the witness of Law and Prophets to Christ; and so it is, but it is more. Moses had himself spoken of Christ prophetically[1] (Jn. 1:45; Lk. 24:27), and scribe and Pharisee alike looked for Elijah to come as Messiah's forerunner (9:11), on the authority of Malachi (Mal. 4:5). True, as Jesus hinted, there had already been a fulfilment of this prophecy at one level in the coming of John the Baptist (9:13), but nevertheless there was a special appropriateness in the presence of Elijah in person here. Anderson notes that Elijah had been translated directly to heaven, while nobody knew where Moses was buried: is there a hint that Jesus too was to be taken up to heaven? This, however, seems far-fetched.

5-6. Luke adds the detail (9:32) that the disciples had been asleep, as in Gethsemane, which suggests that the transfiguration took place by night. The briefer account of Mark mentions none of these things, but they would fit with his story. Peter, suddenly awakened from sleep in time to see the glory, was talkative in his terror, as some are. Now that they had seen the shekinah-glory that had once covered Israel's meeting-tent of old (Ex. 40:35), Peter thought that another such tent, or even three such tents, was appropriate now (5). Peter did not realize that the shekinah-glory, the manifestation of God's presence, was already 'living in a tent' on earth, in the body of Christ (Jn. 1:14). Anderson sees a reference to the Hebrew 'feast of booths' in the suggestion (Lev. 23:34). The use of *rabbi* by Peter here is another interesting touch, which may be original. Matthew (17:4) has the usual polite *Kyrie*, 'Lord', or 'sir', and Luke (9:33) has the Gentile title *epistata*, 'master' or 'overseer'; but Mark keeps the original Semitic word, used by Peter, the usual title for their teacher used by the apostolic band.

---

[1] Is there a hint therefore of the promised coming of 'the prophet like Moses' at the end time, along with Elijah, who was to introduce the final age? So Schweizer suggests.

211

7–8. *Cloud,* or light, had been the sign of God's presence in the wilderness (Ex. 40:38); and, in true Old Testament style, on this occasion too there came a voice from the cloud (*cf.* Ex. 24:16). It is at least a striking coincidence that it was also after 'six days' that Yahweh's voice came from the cloud of Sinai.[1] This time, however, it strikes less terror into the hearts of the hearers than it did then (*cf.* Ex. 19:16). Once again, as at the baptism, God the Father was bearing witness from heaven to His Son (*cf.* 1:11). The Greek *agapētos, beloved,* almost certainly has the connotation of 'only' Son here, as at the baptism.

9. The full meaning of this vision would be apparent only after the resurrection,[2] and so they were forbidden to tell others of it until then. Perhaps this forbade a sharing of it even with their fellow disciples. Anderson points out that this is the only place in Mark where a definite limit is set after which the 'Messianic secret' can be freely proclaimed. It is, however, a commonplace of the gospels that only after the resurrection could many sayings of Jesus be understood (*e.g.* Jn. 12:16).

10. This is an interesting incidental confirmation that the disciples never really understood the words of Jesus about His coming resurrection, so that naturally they were amazed by the event when it occurred (16:8). The strange thing is that, on so many other occasions, they did the very opposite, and misunderstood His words by taking them with the crassest literalism (compare 8:16). The only answer to this problem is that given earlier: they lacked the key of faith (8:17–18). Of course, as orthodox Jews, resurrection at the last day was no problem to

---

[1]Oepke, quoted by Cranfield, has the interesting suggestion that *episkiazein* means 'conceal' rather than *overshadow.* When Moses ascended Sinai, he was lost to Israel's sight in the cloud (Ex. 24:18). Even at the moment of revelation, there was to be concealment (Ex. 19:21). This however seems too complicated a concept to be deliberately intended by Mark, although it could perhaps be linked with the so called 'messianic secret'.

[2]It is always in the gospels 'the Son of man' who will rise from the dead: Perrin (IOM) points out that neither 'Christ' nor 'Son of God' are very frequent in Mark, though both terms are highly significant theologically when they do occur. 'Son of man' on the other hand occurs very frequently (14 times in all). This particular title does not, however, seem to have survived the move from a Jewish to a Gentile environment later, for it hardly occurs outside the gospels (though see Acts 7:56): perhaps its distinctively Semitic ring was the reason.

them (Jn. 11:24): but clearly the words of Jesus here referred to some other earlier event, and this puzzled them greatly, as the words of Jesus puzzled Martha in John's Gospel. There had of course been resuscitations from death recorded in the Old Testament (*e.g.* 2 Ki. 4:36), but for some reason they cannot have considered them applicable to Jesus.

B. THE PASSION FORETOLD AGAIN (9:11–50)

i. 'Elijah returned' (9:11–13)

The appearance of Elijah upon the mountain had raised another question in their minds. Was not Elijah still to appear, not merely in a vision, but in bodily form, to usher in the messianic age? As they descended the mountain, they put this question to Jesus. This at least proves that all of them now believed in His Messiahship, however they understood it. Otherwise the question, as to whether or not the teachers of the law were correct in their exegesis, would have had no meaning.

12–13. Jesus not only agreed with this scribal interpretation of Malachi 4:5 pronouncing its fulfilment in John the Baptist, but also showed the parallelism between John's and His own case. The problem now was not whether 'Elijah' would come again or not (for he had come already), but why the Son of man (for whom 'Elijah' had prepared the way) should be rejected. In rejecting John, Pharisees and scribes had rejected God's counsel for them (Lk. 7:30) and made it all the more sure that they would reject the Messiah when He came. None of this took God by surprise, for all was as it had been written (vv. 12–13). This must mean that Jesus linked both the 'Son of Man' and 'Elijah Returned' with the 'suffering Servant' of Isaiah 53:3. As John's coming was a heralding of the Messiah's coming, so John's rejection was a heralding of the rejection of the Messiah: and both alike were in fulfilment of Scripture. It is standard exegesis to say that in Mark there are three passion predictions by Jesus to His disciples, for so there are. But this is a fourth, usually unrecognized, for it is made only to the 'inner ring' of the three: doubtless there were others too.

213

ii. The epileptic boy (9:14–29)

But sterner work than abstract theological discussion awaited the little group at the foot of the mountain, where spiritual failure had shamed the other nine apostles, and drawn a crowd, as failure will do as surely as success. As usual, those theological critics, the scribes, were at the forefront, doubtless, in the face of this failure, questioning once again the theological credentials of the disciples or their rabbi. One wonders why these same scribes, instead of embarrassing the crestfallen disciples before the crowd, did not set about exorcising the demon themselves, as a proof of their orthodoxy. Some orthodox Jews acted as exorcists, presumably in the name of Yahweh: indeed, Jesus elsewhere appeals to this to justify His own activity (Mt. 12:27). Others, including Sceva's sons (Acts 19:14) seem to have been unsuccessful, unorthodox frauds: yet others expelled demons legitimately in the name of Jesus, without actually following Jesus (verse 38). The practice seems therefore to have been relatively common in the first century.

16. The first questioning words of Jesus do not necessarily show ignorance; they seem designed to draw the attention of the crowd away from the humiliated disciples, and to direct it to Himself, as verse 19 makes explicit. Nor was this done just to spare the feelings of the disciples; it corresponds to a deep spiritual principle. First, those in need must confess their own inadequacy, and then they must be brought to see the power of Jesus to meet that need. To concentrate on the person of His servants is irrelevant, as John the Baptist had enunciated in 1:7–8. For a similar question by Jesus, asked perhaps for a similar reason, see Luke 24:17, on the road to Emmaus.

17–18. The outward symptoms of the boy are certainly those of epilepsy, but we should always observe a reverent agnosticism on matters of demonization.[1] The very outspokenness of

[1] To add to what has been already said on this subject, it may be noted that Mark has numerous references to the expulsion of demons both by Jesus Himself and, by delegated authority, through His apostles (e.g. 1:25 and 3:15). But by no, means all sickness is attributed in the gospels to demons (e.g. 1:40 and 2:3 for 'ordinary' sickness), nor is sickness

the man's answer emphasizes his weary despair. The father had brought the lad to the disciples, hoping for healing, but *they were not able*, lit. 'were not strong enough' to do it.

19. The reaction of Jesus is a half quotation from Psalm 95:10, referring to God's patient endurance of the faithlessness of the Israelite 'generation of the wandering' in days of old, a generation which finally came under God's judgment. It gains in poignancy when we realize that the generation of the ministry of Jesus was also to be a generation of God's judgment, which would descend upon the land some thirty five years after the crucifixion of Jesus (13:2). There is a great reluctance in modern days to see God's judgment in historical or sociological events, but, while of course we may be incorrect in our interpretations, the principle is clearly biblical. God works through the laws of cause and effect, in the world which He has created, to produce either judgment or blessing in the lives of nations as well as of individuals. By its ambivalence, this is far from a shallow 'prosperity cult'. Indeed, after the fall of Jerusalem, in AD 70, apart from the Christian church which had fled to Pella in Transjordan (*cf.* 13:14),[1] few of the original hearers of Jesus would be left alive: for many, their bodies would fall in the wilderness, as had those of their unbelieving forefathers (Heb. 3:17). The Roman legionaries would be terrible agents of the wrath of God on a stubborn rebellious generation (13:14–20), and civilian casualties would be very heavy.

But whose was the culpable lack of faith on this occasion: was it on the part of the disciples', or the father? It seems from the

---

usually associated with sin on the part of the patient (though see 2:5). Indeed, the concept of 'demon possession' seems to be applied only when the mind of the patient is affected, thus making communion with God impossible. Both Jesus and the apostles have therefore a purely healing ministry in addition to exorcism (1:34 and 6:13). The demonized are usually described as 'in (the power of) an unclean spirit' (*e.g.* 1:23), as later in the New Testament Christians can be described as 'in the (Holy) Spirit' (Rev. 1:10), or, as often 'in Christ' (*e.g.* 2 Cor. 5:17). Although Jesus calls the spirit in this story a *dumb and deaf spirit* (25), this seems purely descriptive of the patient's condition, not of the spirit itself. There is no evidence in Scripture for a multitude of evil spirits, each being responsible for some particular sickness, nor is it anywhere suggested that such spirits have separate personalities: they are simply local manifestations of the power of evil.

[1]Eusebius mentioned that the Christians fled in response to an oracle: was it the words of Jesus in Mark ch. 13 to which he was referring? Or had some Christian prophet like Agabus within the church brought a fresh new warning (*cf.* Acts 21:10.)?

wording of verse 23 that it is the father who is blamed for lack of faith, while the disciples are blamed for lack of prayer (verse 29). But prayer is of course one demonstration of faith, so that ultimately both stand under the same condemnation.

20. The violence of the demonic onset, in the case of the dumb boy, corresponds to the confessional outcry wrung from the lips of the demon-controlled elsewhere (*cf.* 5:7). It was the impotent rage of the defeated enemy, an unwilling acknowledgment of the status and authority of Jesus.

21. Jesus is not merely interested in a 'case history' of the boy. He is helping the father to confess how desperate his need is, and at the same time showing him that he has no other resource but in Jesus.

22. It is a pitiful tale, but the telling of it works the desired purpose; for even though he has so little faith, yet the man who doubts the power of Jesus never questions His compassion. Contrast the robust faith of the leper of 1:40, who said, 'If you will, you can make me clean'. He had no doubt of the power of Jesus; all he doubted was His readiness to help a despised leper like he was.

23. Jesus gently reproves the man's lack of faith. *If you can* might be better paraphrased 'That "if you can" of yours' (where Jesus would be quoting the man's own words): 'Why, everything can be done for one who believes.' This is a statement of the great biblical principle enunciated in 10:27 and 11:24). But we are not called to 'put God to the test' by irresponsible 'believing prayer' for what may well be our human desire but not be His will. We are free to ask what we will, but only if it is what God wills (14:36). This is no mere theological quibble: it is a statement in another form of the need for the 'mind of Christ' in us, given by the Spirit. It is also a warning against taking one statement of Scripture in isolation from others, and basing presumptuous prayer on it.

24. The father cries for help, honestly confessing the poverty of his faith; and Jesus answers, not according to the poverty of the man's faith, but according to the riches of His grace. The man is doing exactly as the Gentile woman of chapter 7 had done: he accepts humbly Jesus' estimate of him, and, even on that basis, pleads for God's mercy, not for his deserts. No better illustration of the doctrine of justification by faith could be found than the father's words here. This is clear from the fact that he used the same verb, *boētheō*, *help*, as he has above (verse 22). He had previously said, 'If you can, *help* me.' Jesus had rebuked this phrase, and so now *with tears* (some MSS) the father said 'Then *help* me just as I am, a doubter.' In other words, the man was not praying that his unbelief might be 'helped' till it came to the point where his faith was worthy of meeting with a response from God. We do not need to ask God to increase our faith until it is deserving of salvation, as a sort of 'congruent faith '. That would still be justification by works, not justification by faith. Instead, the father was asking Jesus for practical help, to be demonstrated in the healing of his son, and confessing, deeply moved, that he had not enough faith to make him worthy of such help. His very coming to Jesus showed faith, and that was enough. This is indeed justification by faith. A parallel would be the so-called 'cry of dereliction' on the cross (15:34). Even at that moment, a cry of seeming despair was in fact in another sense an expression of faith, for it was directed Godwards.

25–27. Jesus never encouraged crowds of idle sightseers, eager for the latest sensation or wonder. He deliberately avoided crowds, when He thought their motives unworthy (*cf*. Jn. 6:26), and he would refuse to perform a miracle for a jaded Herod (Lk. 23:8). Crowds are not necessarily indicative of success in spiritual work. Jesus apparently regarded crowds as a signal to move elsewhere (1:37–38), or to explain more clearly to shallow disciples the true cost of following Him (8:34). For Him, the test of true success was the little group of disciples who followed when the crowds had turned back. When we consider principles of 'church growth', we need to balance them by considering these aspects also. It is noteworthy that miracles, common in the first half of Mark, are relatively rare in the second half: it is as though they have achieved their purpose, once Jesus has been recognized as Messiah. From now, they might only confuse the picture.

28-29. Note that the nine disciples who failed did not include the three who had been with Jesus on the mountain of transfiguration. We may therefore possibly be justified in saying that these nine were less spiritually responsive than the three. But if it was earnest 'prayer' that was lacking, were the three who slept, perhaps on the mount of transfiguration, and certainly in the garden of Gethsemane (14:37), any further advanced than the nine, in spite of all their greater opportunities? There is some good MS evidence for the addition of *and fasting* at this point (29).[1] Scripture does not condemn such voluntary self-discipline as an aid to prayer (1 Cor. 7:5). What Scripture condemns is the outward fast that corresponds to no inward and spiritual reality, and becomes simply an opportunity for pride and self-glorification (Lk. 18:12). Mark has few references to fasting, however, as is perhaps natural in a Gentile church. *Privately*: this word, like *entered the house*, is typical of Mark, who stresses the total lack of understanding of the disciples and their consequent need for private instruction, away from the crowd (Schweizer).

iii. The second passion-prediction (9:30-32)

The plain meaning of verse 30 is that Jesus wished to travel unknown on this Galilean journey, because He wanted to teach His disciples some important truths. It was in fact to be another period of intensive, not extensive, teaching; this distinction has been noted already (see the comment on 6:7). This is an example of how Jesus could neglect one opportunity to take another, without feeling spiritually guilty. He had a quiet purposeful selectiveness, so often lacking in the fevered rush of activism of His followers, which produces nervous breakdowns as part of its bitter fruit. Both Jesus (14:33) and Paul (2 Cor. 1:9) were under tension at times of great stress, but that is not the same thing.

---

[1]Cranfield, however, rules it out, on the grounds that such an addition to the text by the early church was very likely. But to the Jew, fasting was a natural adjunct to prayer: see both Old Testament and rabbinic literature: and *Didache* 8 shows how this passed into Christianity (*see* Lightfoot). Mark, in 2:20, seems to show that Jesus envisaged His disciples as fasting

31. This is commonly called the second prediction of the passion, and is to be found in all the synoptic gospels. In point of fact, as already mentioned, a second 'private' prediction had already been given on the path down from the mountain of transfiguration, in answer to the question of the three apostles about Elijah's return (see verse 12), while yet another 'private' prediction will be made to James and John in 10:38, whether understood or not. This, then, would be the third such prediction, but only the second given to the whole body of the disciples. The use here of the passive *delivered* implies in Semitic idiom that God is seen as active in the event (Schweizer).

32. What did the disciples fail to understand? Jesus own self-chosen title 'Son of man' was by now familiar to them; 'betrayal' and 'death' were hard to accept, perhaps, but easy to understand as concepts. It must have been His reference to a resurrection *after three days* that baffled them, as apparently it had baffled them in verse 10 above. It is true that, by Semitic idiom, 'the third day' could be used vaguely and metaphorically for 'subsequently' so that they are not to be blamed for failure to take it in a literal sense. The Old Testament text (Ho. 6:2) would not help here in its original sense,[1] although the Christian church may have later seen it as a prophetic foreshadowing of the resurrection. When Jesus specifically used the analogy of Jonah, then the meaning would be clearer (Mt. 12:40), for He there stated that the nature of the sign would be in the reappearance of the Son of man from underground after three days: but Mark does not record this particular saying of Jesus.

iv. The greatest in the kingdom (9:33–37)

This sense of awe, induced by the as yet not understood words of Jesus, did not last long. As they walked along, they were

---

after His death, if not in His lifetime: this was certainly true of the disciples in Acts and the epistles (*e.g.* Acts 13:2).

[1] All modern Old Testament scholars would agree with this: the original reference is vague and general, referring to the nation of Israel. But the early Christian church saw such verses as inspired 'reminders' of what God would do one day in Christ. That was what they meant by 'fulfilment', the giving of a new and deeper meaning, that might not have been obvious, or even applicable, at the time of writing. It was their way of underlining both the

strung out in a long line behind their rabbi. No ancient pupil would dare to walk abreast of His teacher, nor indeed would the narrow footpaths of the time allow it. They had been arguing up and down the line as they went (although sometimes *dialogizomai* may be used simply of reasoning in the heart, as in 2:6), and doubtless occasional angry words had reached the ears of Jesus, as He was walking in front (10:32). So His question sounded natural enough, no doubt: but there was already a hint of rebuke in His use of the verb *dialogizomai* (discuss), which often implies argument as well as reasoning. He did not rebuke His disciples in public: they had been already sufficiently humiliated in front of the crowds. Instead, He waited for the privacy of the evening halt, till they were *in the house* (33). Not unnaturally, the disciples were reluctant to answer His question, to which Jesus already knew the answer.

35. *He sat down*: this implies more than a wearied traveller composing himself. It means that the teaching rabbi is once more about to give instruction to his disciples. One interpretation of this next saying of Jesus is the spiritual principle that those who desire or grasp at spiritual position thereby will condemn themselves, as punishment, to the lowest place in the kingdom. This is true; and the song of Mary (Lk. 1:46–55) makes it plain that it is as much part of God's way of working to 'put down the mighty from their thrones' as it is to 'exalt those of low degree'. But Mark's use of the future *estai, he must be*, may reproduce another Semitism from the original tradition, where a future form can also be an imperative or jussive. In that case, the deeper principle will be that, if we desire spiritual greatness, then what we truly desire is the task of service to others, and so we must deliberately choose the lowliest and most humble place. This was the whole key to the life of Jesus, for He came, not to be served, but to be a servant (10:45). Humility, however, is not a 'natural' virtue, and few qualities are more unpopular in our self-assertive world.

---

importance and the divine causation of the final event, along with its continuity with God's previous revelation.

36-37. Another illustration of the same point follows. It is evening, and the meal in the home is over: Jesus calls to Him a child and *taking him in his arms* (Gk. *enagkalisamenos*, lit. 'holding him in the crook of His arm'), begins to teach. The exact connection between this saying (37) and the previous verse 35 is not made clear in Mark. Matthew 18:4, the parallel passage, makes the link clearer by amplifying: 'Whoever humbles himself like this child, he is the greatest in the kingdom of heaven'. This, then, makes the lesson of humility plain: not only is it the law of Christian service, but it is also the law of entrance into the kingdom of heaven (*cf.* 10:15, a very similar instance in Mark). This humility, which is the basic law of the kingdom, demands a complete reversal of our previous scale of values, a reversal which God will one day vindicate (10:31). In this humility, we receive a child as we would the King himself, treating that child as an ambassador of the King (*in my name*), not as we see him or her outwardly.[1] Similarly, even Jesus Himself is to be seen in the light of God, His Sender, and not as He appears outwardly to the false sense of values of this world (37).

v. The man casting out demons (9:38-40)

Next, just as Moses had suffered from the over-zealous partisanship of Joshua (Nu. 11:28), so Jesus was to suffer from the zeal of John, one of the two hot-headed 'sons of thunder' (*cf.* 3:17).[2] It is strange, in view of occurrences like this, to think that one day John would be called the apostle of love. On this occasion, he wanted to forbid exorcisms performed in the name of Jesus but by one who was not a professed disciple, like the twelve. David's sufferings from the misdirected zeal of the sons of Zeruiah are another parallel (2 Sa. 3:39): there was the same

---

[1] There has been much recent discussion on the relevance of the Semitic phrase underlying the *in my name* in this context. Some such idea probably underlies the similar phrase in 2 Cor. 5:20, 'on behalf of Christ', where a comparative study of the rabbinic use of *beshēm*, 'in the name of', would be rewarding.

[2] Anderson points out that only here in the whole gospel is John singled out to play a leading part: but James and John do appear together in 10:35 in an equally discreditable situation. John is still a long way from being the famous 'apostle of love' of later times. Indeed, he is, if anything, to Mark a shadowy figure, even if one of the 'three' chosen by Jesus, of whom only Peter seems to be outstanding.

passionate personal loyalty, combined with the same failure to discern their master's true nature and purpose. The instant reaction of Jesus was to withdraw the prohibition (in which apparently the other disciples had concurred), and give the great 'minimal' test *he that is not against us is for us*. This is reinforced by the commonsense principle that those who do miracles in the name of Jesus are not likely to be foes of His, or to *speak evil* of Him. The whole theology of the Spirit was at stake here: the scribes had seen the work of the Spirit, yet deliberately misinterpreted and opposed it, putting it down to Beelzebub (3:22). But here were His own disciples, seeing and admitting a work of the Spirit, done in the name of Jesus, and still forbidding it, on theological grounds. What is the difference between disciples and scribes, if both alike oppose the Spirit's working, although for very different reasons?

vi. Stumbling-blocks (9:41–48)

If this next saying of Jesus is still in the same context, then there must be a return in thought to the child, standing in front of Jesus; and verse 41 would be the bridge-verse. The link then is the words *you bear the name of Christ* (41). Of course, we could equally well take verse 41 closely with verse 40, and see the gift of a drink of water as being a proof of support of Christ. If this 'belonging to Christ' is such an important bond, then nothing is too precious to sacrifice (not even hand, foot, or eye), in order that we may retain it. In the kingdom, all rules of moral conduct are based on theological principles. Therefore, to trip up or impede one, even the least important outwardly, who enjoys this close relationship to Christ is so terrible a crime and merits such a terrible punishment. The incidental touch of verse 42, *one of these little ones who believe in me*[1] may suggest that Jesus was staying in the house of a disciple and believer at the time. 'Little ones' could perfectly well mean 'lowly disciples', but, in this

---

[1] Of course, 'little ones' need not necessarily be limited to children: it could equally well refer to humble and apparently unimportant members of the Christian community (so Johnson and Anderson). In this context, it seems to be meant literally, although it may move into the other meaning later. Jesus was in the habit of calling His disciples 'children', as Schweizer notes (see 10:24).

context, it is best to take it literally as 'children'. We, too, dare not allow ourselves to be thus tripped: for the consequences for us are so serious. Compared with the attainment of the kingdom of God (47) or of 'life' (43), no sacrifice is too great to make. So hand, foot or eye, the most important members, but also members through which temptation might come, must be sacrificed, if need be, for the good of the whole. As in 8:36-37, Jesus is stressing the infinite value of the soul, compared with which all else is unimportant. Physical self-mutilation, utterly abhorrent to the Jew, is not in question here, though some of the early church Fathers may have taken it so. That would be another example of the crassly literalistic interpretation of the words of Jesus of which disciples are capable (8:16). Nor is it likely that Jesus is referring to the need for exclusion of heretical members of the 'body of Christ', lest the whole church be endangered, as Dr Edward Newing has suggested (in a verbal communication with the author): this is too sophisticated for Mark. What we have is a vivid metaphor, couched in extreme terms that assure us of its dominical nature, for this appears typical.

43, 45, 47. There can be no reasonable doubt that two clear eschatological alternatives are set before us by Jesus here. The one is called *life*, which is therefore not purely a Johannine term for salvation, as sometimes claimed. The other is called here, not 'death' but *hell* or *Gehenna*, and explained as *unquenchable fire* (Gk. *asbestos*), for which Matthew 18:8 uses instead the adjective *aiōnios*, translated *eternal* in the RSV.[1] It is true that the primary thought of *asbestos* is not that of duration; but it does seem to be that of absolute unquenchability, and the two concepts are not far apart. No man ever spoke stronger words about this ultimate alternative than the loving Son of God;[2] but His words on it

[1] It is quite true, and often pointed out, by scholars anxious to minimize the severity of these sayings of Jesus, that *aiōnios* really means 'belonging to the age (to come)', and describes quality, rather than duration. But first, the same adjective is used in John of (eternal) life: the two concepts therefore stand or fall together. Secondly, in the present passage, Jesus also conveys the idea of eternal duration by *asbestos, unquenchable*. But he is not concerned here to develop a doctrine of eternal punishment so much as to emphasize the importance of entering 'life' (Anderson). The negative aspect of the word is brought out more clearly in 3:29, *eternal sin*.

[2] It is true that this passage is cast in a Semitic poetic form, like, *e.g.* much of the sermon on the mount: but Cranfield wisely warns us not on that account to explain it away, although it

were addressed either to His own disciples, as here, or to professed religious leaders (as in Mt. 23:33). We never hear of Him expounding this topic to publicans and sinners, although John the Baptist may have struck this note widely (Mt. 3:7). Jesus therefore spoke of hell to professed saints, and of heaven to acknowledged sinners, unlike many other preachers. Also, when Jesus spoke of judgment, according to Luke, He wept (Lk. 19:41).

48. The Old Testament context (Is. 66:24) helps to explain this solemn imagery. It has reference in Isaiah to 'the dead bodies of the men who have rebelled against me'. Gehenna, the eternally smouldering rubbish-dump outside Jerusalem, is the symbol of the final fate of those who have rebelled against God, amongst whom Jesus warns us that we may find ourselves, unless we enter God's *kingdom* (verse 47), equated with *life* (verse 45). RSV here rightly follows the better MSS is omitting verses 44 and 46 which are identical with verse 48, which is found in all MSS. But this does not lessen the seriousness of the warning; Mark knows nothing of an easy universalism or of a 'second chance' after death, or even of a limited period of punishment, even if such punishment is self-inflicted by refusal to respond to God's grace.

vii. The salt of the earth (9:49–50)

Verse 49 is the bridge-verse, containing, as it does, the thoughts both of *fire* and *salt*: all is to be tested and purified by fire one day (*cf.* 1 Cor. 3:13).[1] The concept of a refiner's fire is found in the Old Testament (Mal. 3:2). It appears, then, that the introduction of the verb *halizomai, to salt,* suggests the further sayings about

---

may well be that not all the poetic details are to be understood in a literal sense. 'Gehenna' ('hell') is a strong word, not like 'Hades', which simply means the place of departed spirits ('Sheol' in Hebrew).

[1]Presumably here, as in Paul, the thought is that the 'fire' of God's holiness will test all on 'the day': for the Christian, whose eternal salvation is already assured, it will only be like the salt added to the Israelite sacrifices (Lv. 2:13). Salt was, after all, one of the signs of Israel's covenant with God. For God's enemies, however, this will be the fire of destruction. There is certainly no thought of a 'purgatory' either here or anywhere else in the New Testament, while suffering in this life is often regarded as being purificatory (Jb. 23:10 *etc.*).

halas, salt. Whether of course these sayings were used at one and the same time by Jesus, or simply strung together later for ease of memory in early teaching patterns, we cannot now say. Early traditions (like those of Papias) certainly suggest this latter explanation as the scheme of construction of Mark's Gospel, rather than the chronological pattern so congenial to the modern western mind.

50. Those who have lived in the third world may not be able to give a chemical explanation, but they will know that salt is often adulterated, as sugar is, and many another commodity, by unscrupulous local retailers. But to enquire what process the adulterated substance goes through, and how it results in final tastelessness, is beside the point, although scientifically interesting. The real point is that such *salt*, salt only in name, is now useless: and if the very thing designed to bring flavour to other substances is itself flavourless, how can its flavour be restored? Here are the very followers of Jesus themselves, quarrelling with one another: how can such be 'a son of peace' (see Lk. 10:6 for this as a Christian term)?[1] Christians are to be the moral preservative of the world; they are to 'salt' life, to purify it, and to stop it becoming utterly corrupt, but how can they do this, if they themselves have lost all Christian distinctiveness? It may be that the use of salt as a covenant-sign in the Old Testament (Lv. 2:13) also underlies the use here. Whether or not this has any special relevance to Mark's 'reading public', whether at Rome or elsewhere, we cannot now say: but Paul's epistles to the Corinthians show us the extent of quarrels in some Gentile churches, and his Epistle to the Romans may show similar dangers.

C. DEPARTURE FROM GALILEE (10:1–34)

i. The local setting (10:1)

Up till now, in chapters 1–9, we have had the record of a

---

[1] Best (IOM) is probably right in seeing the whole reason for the introduction of the saying here as being the final clause *and be at peace with one another*. It was, after all, a quarrel between the disciples which had led to the whole incident, and so to the saying.

basically Galilean ministry of Jesus.[1] Now, from chapters 10 to 15, Mark records a Judean ministry, and the natural assumption would be that this followed immediately afterwards. But, against this view, in between the two, Luke has a great mass of material, covering roughly chapters 9-18 of his gospel, usually called the Lucan travel narrative, which Mark seems to omit altogether. Mark, however, never claims to record 'all that Jesus began to do and to teach', as Luke does (Acts 1:1), and even early Christian tradition recognized that Mark was only a selective account. Probably Mark's arrangement here is theological and abridged, rather than strictly chronological: he hurries on to show at once the resolute turning of Jesus towards Jerusalem that was to lead to the cross. Although Mark is 'historical', we must not think of his gospel as a chronicle in our modern sense: he had a different purpose in view.

The region of *Judea* which Jesus enters now is different in every way from the Galilean highlands in the north.[2] Rugged Galilee, with its simple and strongly nationalistic peasantry, was very different from the sophisticated city dwellers of the south. Galilee was always the most stubborn centre of Jewish revolts, possibly because the 'Circuit of the Gentiles', as its full name means, was surrounded by Gentile and bitterly anti-Jewish populations: even in the AD 70 revolt, Galilee was a hard nut for the Romans to crack, as Josephus shows. Judea was dominated by Jerusalem, and Jerusalem was dominated by the temple, with its Sadducean aristocracy and Sanhedrin: vested religious interests and rigid religious orthodoxy were stronger there than in the north.

ii. The teaching of Jesus on marriage (10:2-12)

What was in the mind of the Pharisees, in asking this question

[1]There is not the slightest doubt that Mark understood the term 'Galilee' here in the usual geographic sense, whatever modern editors may think, and however vague his geography may be at times. It is distorted exegesis to see a theological meaning in its use, except in so far as the Galileans were probably simpler and less 'theologically minded' than their counterparts in the south, who heartily despised them (Jn. 1:46). Mark may well have grouped all the Galilean material together in his gospel, separately from the Judean material, but that is another thing altogether, and purely a matter of arrangement.

[2]As a glance at the excellent physical maps in, for instance, the *Westminster Historical Atlas to the Bible* will show.

about divorce? Their answer to Jesus in verse 4 shows that they were already well conversant with the law upon the score, as was natural enough. From the wording of verse 2, *to test him*, it was obviously only a 'trick question', designed not to obtain guidance, but to make Jesus compromise Himself. If they could trap Him into some rash pronouncement, then He could be accused of having contradicted either the law of Moses or its interpretative tradition.[1] The Sadducean question about the resurrection (12:23) and the Herodian question about the tribute (12:15) are examples of similar smooth-tongued attempts to make Jesus incriminate Himself, all of which failed dismally (12:34). Seen in this light, the wisdom of the answer of Jesus becomes even more apparent. This passage is not therefore the full teaching of Jesus about divorce given 'in the abstract' to His disciples, although, like all His pronouncements, it did become a teaching occasion. It was primarily an answer to a test question, where, whatever He said, some party might seize upon it. It may have been that the Pharisees already suspected this Galilean rabbi, whose disciples regarded sabbath so lightly (2:23), of lax views on sexual relationships, and so asked Him this question with a view to obtaining another handle for attack. John 8:1-11, the record of the forgiveness by Jesus of the adulteress, shows how easily the charge of laxity could be levelled against Him: although this 'pericope' is probably not canonical, the story certainly circulated widely. In addition, the reputation of Jesus for being a friend of tax collectors and immoral people (2:16) and numbering women like Mary Magdalene among His followers (16:9), must have looked suspicious to them. If this was their hope, they were sorely disappointed: Jesus showed no sign of laxity here. Indeed, we can see from verse 10 that His strong views surprised even His own disciples so much that they later in private asked for an explanation. The recording of this private explanation is again typical of Mark (Schweizer). On

[1]They may have had a professional interest because of the well-known difference between the 'stern' school of Shammai, and the 'lax' school of Hillel on this point, as on many others too. But both schools accepted divorce as normal: they only argued on the nature of the necessary justification for it. The Lord's words therefore cut the ground from beneath the feet of both parties. Jesus is not giving a new legal enactment here but declaring God's will and purpose (Anderson). He is not concerned, as the Pharisees were, with our 'rights', and how far we can go (Schweizer).

the other hand, the Pharisees may not have been as surprised as the disciples. They may have already suspected that Jesus was a 'rigorist' on the marriage question, as the Qumran community seem to have been. In that case, they could accuse Him of rejecting the law of Moses on the subject.

3. As usual, Jesus answered the Pharisees first at their own level, by taking then back to Moses, which they doubtless expected: this at once removed any suspicion of heterodoxy, whether in the direction of rigorism or laxity. Jesus thereby made clear that His teaching was designed to give a new depth of meaning to the law, not to dismiss it as superseded (Mt. 5:17).

4. Nevertheless, the Pharisaic group had already been forced to yield ground, if, as is probable, the change from *eneteilato, command* (3), the word used by Jesus in His question, to *epetrepsen, allowed*, the word which they use in their reply, is deliberate. They themselves do not dare to say that divorce had been commanded in the law, even if it was *allowed*, so they have already shown some consciousness of the weakening of their position.

5. Then comes a further blow to the scribes. This law of Moses, said Jesus, was not only as they admitted, permissive, instead of being imperative; it was actually concessive, because of the unresponsiveness of human hearts to God (*hardness of heart*). Better, in the days of the law, we might paraphrase, easy divorce than open adultery and defiance of all marriage codes. It was the lesser of two evils in Israel, but its very existence showed a fatal flaw in humanity, to which Jesus drew attention. Perhaps the toleration of polygamy in Old Testament times is another instance of the outworking of the same principle, as being something permitted in early days, but never praised, and never seen as God's plan for humanity.[1]

6. But now comes, as usual, an attack at a deeper theological level, where Jesus goes beyond the law of Moses, which was

[1] The admission of this 'concession' certainly does not justify Schweizer in saying that

given at a particular point in time, to God's timeless purpose as shown in creation. In appealing to Genesis, He was appealing only to another section of the *torah* or Law, not abandoning it: Paul is equally clear that the Mosaic law was but an 'inset' into God's earlier purpose and covenant of grace, which is eternal (Gal. 3:17). The inviolable sanctity of the marriage tie is not of course merely based by Jesus on the bare words of Genesis 2:24, which are only a description and commentary on the result of God's act, but on God's initial act and purpose itself (Gn. 1:27), in creating two sexes, and so showing that this sexual union was His plan. Jesus assumes of course on the part of the Pharisees a full knowledge of the context of the Genesis passage, explaining why marriage was instituted by God for mutual companionship and support (Gn. 2:18).

7. The natural phenomenon of a person voluntarily leaving the closest social bonding already known (that between parent and child) to form a new and closer bond with a person previously unknown would be utterly inexplicable, unless seen as an instance of the outworking of this purpose of God. As so often, Jesus is appealing to the common sense of ordinary people against the intricacies of the professional theologians (*cf.* 7:15).

8. Marriage is therefore the closest known human bond (*one flesh*), though, being human, it involves a physical bond, and its physical aspect cannot survive death (12:25). So close a bond is it nevertheless, and so deep in the purpose of God, that Paul can use it as a picture of the spiritual union that exists between Christ and His church (Eph. 5:32). Only 'parenthood' can be similarly used as a picture of the union between God and His people (Eph. 3:15).

9. This close bond has been created by God: indeed, it was God's aim in the creation of the two sexes, whereas any divorce

---

'Divorce can be a sign of repentance', although he admittedly says also 'Divorce is only a last resort'. To speak like this would be to overthrow the whole principle established by Jesus, and 'repentance' is not mentioned anywhere in the context.

is purely human. Nothing else needed to be said to the Pharisees. Did they go away crestfallen? Or were there perhaps some who went away thoughtfully, as in 12:32ff.? They cannot have been pleased by the practice of Jesus of going behind the historical law of Moses to God's timeless mind, as expressed in creation, whether it was in connection with marriage, or sabbath, or anything else, but they could not challenge either its legitimacy or His orthodoxy.

10. But we, like the disciples, need more amplification and guidance on the matter, which was denied to these Pharisaic religious strategists, since they did not really want an answer to their question. So Mark says *his disciples asked him again*, when (typically Marcan) *in the house*. The fact that the disciples found it necessary to ask Jesus for further explanation suggests that it was the first occasion upon which He had dealt with the subject, and also that His teaching conflicted, in some respects at least, with generally accepted views shared by the disciples. He who had seemed lax proved to make unbelievably far-reaching demands, based on God's absolute will and purpose.

11–12. This report of the teaching of Jesus on divorce is, again, only of a skeleton nature, and therefore it is by no means a full treatment of a difficult problem. For that, we must turn to the fuller statement in Matthew 5:32, with its so-called 'exceptive clause', however this is interpreted, and to Paul's letters, where the bluntness is somewhat qualified pastorally. But, because of its very bluntness, this is clearly a genuine utterance of Jesus. No early Christian, whether Jewish or Gentile, would have dared to make such a drastic statement, though the Qumran community seem to have appealed to the same biblical principle of strict monogamy (Anderson and Schweizer). Further, Mark's is the downright teaching formula for a Graeco-Roman Gentile church, where immorality was doubtless a grave danger: finer points would be lost on them. Jesus was not creating a new legalism: He was recalling to God's absolute standard and intention. The first century was a time in which divorce was perilously easy and common, whether in Judaism or paganism. Jesus, it is noteworthy, assumes as a matter of course that a divorced party will, in the either case, remarry; it is such remarriage after wilful divorce which is branded as adultery. But, however we explain them, we must not water down the strong words of Jesus, even if they are as unwelcome and unfashionable to us as they were to His disciples when first spoken (see Mt. 19:10).

iii. Let the children come (10:13–16)

We have already seen, from the acted parable of 9:36, that we must not, in the kingdom, despise children: indeed, as we have seen, to welcome children in the name of Jesus is to welcome Jesus Himself. This was an example of the new set of values in the kingdom. Now, we are told that, to enter the kingdom, we must ourselves have childlike qualities (verse 15), though Jesus does not say that all children are, by being children, within God's kingdom already. That is why children must not be hindered from coming to Jesus, for the kingdom is made up of those who share their attitude.[1] The reference may be to the lowliness of a child; but more than lowliness seems to be meant in this context. The wider interpretation is to see a reference here to the trustfulness of a child, the guileless faith placed by a child in one whom it loves.[2]

Apart from this, we may see in the anecdote the faith in Jesus shown by the parents who brought their children to Him to touch (verse 13) in blessing (verse 16). Whether they were actually *paidia*, *children*, (13), or *brephē*, *infants* (as said in Lk. 18:15), is uncertain and indeed immaterial here. There have been those who see something almost superstitious in the action of these parents. But, if it was faith and not superstition to touch the garment of Jesus in hope of healing (5:28), then this is faith

[1]Cranfield refuses to allow this, saying that this would turn faith into a 'work': to him, the weakness and helplessness of the child is the point. No doubt this is involved, but it does not exhaust the likeness to children. It is possible that simplicity is also meant.

[2]This does not however mean, as some in western countries have thought, that children are already 'converted' until and unless they deliberately turn away from God. This view would of course be impossible to hold in the third world, where the children would already belong to non-Christian faiths. We are called here to follow the attitudes of children, not their beliefs. A child has no claim: a child's attitude must be that of total dependence (Minear). Their status, under Jewish law, was that of inferiors: they were 'least', to use a biblical term.

too. It was apparently not uncommon for Jewish rabbis of the time to lay on hands and bless similarly. Unaffected by questions of the age of the children is the brusqueness of the doubtless wearied disciples, shown in rebuking the parents. Perhaps they were jealously trying to guard their rabbi from what they regarded as another unwarranted intrusion upon His time by those whom they still considered unimportant. The disciples certainly made Jesus by no means easy of access: were they perhaps jealously guarding their own privileged position? (*Cf.* 9:38.)

Also unaffected by the age of the children is the indignation of Jesus (14) at this action of His disciples, as showing their utter failure to understand His loving purpose,[1] and, indeed, the whole nature of the kingdom, where none is unimportant in God's eyes. The strong Greek verb *aganakteō*, he *was indignant*, shows how strongly Jesus felt.

iv. The rich man (10:17-31)

The story of the rich man is found in all three synoptics, with individual additions, as the memories of the various narrators recalled different points. From Matthew (Mt. 19:20) we learn of his youth, while the Lucan source records that he was a 'ruler' (Lk. 18:18). His *great possessions* (22), so different from the 'evangelical poverty' in which the disciples lived, deeply impressed the naive Galileans, as did the splendours of Herod's temple later (13:1). He probably belonged to a social group as yet scarcely touched by the gospel, although converted tax collectors like Levi would undoubtedly have been wealthy too (2:14-15), like the rest of the 'sinners', no doubt. From the very start, some women of this circle were numbered among the followers of Jesus (15:41, and *cf.* Lk. 8:3), and used their wealth to further His cause, as indeed Joseph of Arimathea did at the last (15:43). Jesus does not condemn wealth as wrong in itself, but this whole story is a poignant warning of its dangers.

---

[1]Anderson points out that this is the only certain occasion in the gospels where Jesus is said to be *indignant*: to him at least, a fundamental principle of the kingdom was involved in acceptance of the children.

17. The man's eagerness is shown by his running and kneeling in the public highway, if the Greek verb *gonupeteō*, *knelt*, is to be taken literally, and not merely metaphorically as 'begging', which is possible. His spiritual insight is shown by the application of the adjective *good* to Jesus, and his spiritual hunger by his very desire for *eternal life*. His impatient brushing-aside of the expected orthodox Jewish suggestion, that the way to life was by keeping the commandments, shows a spiritual perception far in advance of that displayed by the average scribe (but *cf.* 12:33). But his spiritual insight was not matched by a readiness for committal which would involve sacrifice, and so he went away sadly. In his case, the impediment was his wealth; sooner than give it up, he gave up Jesus. So he becomes a continual warning to all the disciples of Jesus (verse 23) of the dangers of riches.

18. Jesus, as often, tries to draw from the man the full implications of his own words. He had come to a teacher for help and recognized him as *good*: but had he yet realized what was involved at the deepest level in such an attribution? Had he yet made the identification of Jesus with God that would enable him to recognize the true nature of this *good teacher*, as Peter had in 8:29? For only such a divine Messiah could give Him that eternal life which confessedly he desired to have but had not. Schweizer well says that this is not merely the search for a well adjusted happy life, but for something which is far deeper: this man was in earnest, and his quest was right.

But his basic error was far more fundamental than a failure to recognize Jesus as Messiah, although it would have been an error shared by most in Judaism (Schweizer compares Ps.15 and Ps. 24). He still saw salvation as something to be attained by his own efforts. Until he was ready to receive it by faith as something completely undeserved, of which he was not worthy, he could not enjoy it.

The words of Jesus in reply to the man are slightly different in Matthew 19:17, but the main sense remains unaltered, and both could well be loose Greek paraphrases of the same original Aramaic saying. Certainly no Christian would have invented the abrupt form of the saying recorded here in Mark

(Anderson): perhaps then this abruptness was characteristic of Jesus, for we have seen it elsewhere on several occasions. Others, however, would see it as typical of Mark rather than of Jesus.

19. Jesus sums up for the man the commandments of the law that deal with duty to neighbour; He does not as yet introduce the more searching question as to duty to God. If He can induce a sense of inadequacy at this lower level, then so much the better. It was as if Jesus said, in answer to the man's eager question of 'what must I do?' 'Do? if that is to be the way, then you must do all that the Law commands.' It is unlikely that Jesus was endeavouring only to stir the man's conscience by listing these commandments as though, if he really loved his neighbour as himself (12:31), he would already be using his wealth in a different way (verse 21).

20. The man's spiritual experience had not been as deep as that of Paul. He thought only of the outward observances of the law, and not of the inward breach, which Jesus saw as equally important (7:21-22), but he doubtless spoke in all good conscience when he said that he had kept all these commandments externally. Yet at least, even if outwardly self-satisfied, he realized inwardly that he still lacked something. Otherwise, he would not have come to Jesus seeking eternal life, and asked the question which he did.

21. It is clear from the *emblepsas autō* (*looking upon him*, or 'gazing at him') that Jesus saw something attractive at that moment in him.[1] Was it perhaps his spontaneity and earnestness, the qualities that appear in single-minded David, the man whom God described as 'after my heart' (Acts 13:22)? But not even for one whom He loved, and whose discipleship He desired, would Jesus lower the demands of discipleship to make an easy

---

[1]Cranfield does not agree here: to him, the verb *agapaō, loved,* means to display self-giving love, irrespective of the worthiness or unworthiness of the object. But this does not seem capable of linguistic proof in NT Greek: see BAGD under the word. Also, it would evacuate the previous clause of meaning (*Jesus looking upon him loved him*), since it surely implies some particular reason.

convert. This was not an arbitrary decision: whoever wants to follow Jesus must deny self and take up the cross (8:34).

In the verb *hystereō*, *lack*, or 'need', there is a probe at a deeper level. Here was a man who had never physically lacked anything: doubtless this was why he had never been tempted to kill or steal, as a poor man might have been (Pr. 30:9). For such a one, it was easy to observe the commandments outwardly: but he still had an inner lack. Jesus was seeking to bring home to him that the 'poor rich' had a great unseen need too, hidden in his very riches. If he wanted this need met, (*cf.* Rev. 3:17), he had to show his discipleship in a concrete manner (Schweizer), by laying them aside.

This demand for physical renunciation of earthly wealth is made potentially of all disciples, and may be made actually of any at any time or permanently. Jesus demands of all His followers a total initial renunciation (1:18). What He then hands back to us is completely at His disposal: we hold it only as stewards for Him, and it is His to give or take away at will (Job 1:21). But the '*treasure in heaven*' promised by Jesus in return will be ours for evermore, unlike the uncertain treasure of this world, which passes away.

'*Give to the poor*': is this renunciation in favour of the poor the very heart of the injunction? Or is the central point, the command for the giving up by the man, of what has become a spiritual impediment? Older commentaries would stress the second interpretation, most modern commentators the first. Probably there is no contradiction between the two, for, while the New Testament does not say that 'God is on the side of the poor', yet Jesus always showed special concern for the poor. Wealth is not seen as necessarily sinful in the New Testament: it is, however, seen as highly dangerous (23), as well as a great responsibility. Jesus does not accuse this man of acquiring his wealth at the expense of the poor, as a tax collector almost certainly would have done. To the Jew of Old Testament days, honestly gained riches were a sign of God's blessing (Pr. 10:22), but this must not be exaggerated into a 'prosperity cult', for 'the poor' are often equated with 'the righteous'.

22. This is the only man in the whole of the New Testament of whom it is said that he went away *sorrowful* from the presence of

Jesus. Many were sad when they came to Jesus and went away joyful. But, apart from renouncing his wealth, there was no other way by which it was possible for him to be close to Jesus (Schweizer). He could not, by definition, be a disciple (8:34) of Jesus, who had given up his all (2 Cor. 8:9). His reaction shows only too clearly that Jesus had laid His finger on the spot. His wealth was indeed the thing that was holding him back from the kingdom of God, or he would have given it up at once gladly, as the other disciples had done. The apocryphal 'Gospel of the Nazarenes' adds the picturesque touch of the man 'scratching his head' when he heard the words of Jesus, which, however, reads more like a preacher's addition to the text than a genuine piece of early tradition.

23. A literal translation of the words of Jesus would run 'How hard it is for those who have things . . .' (Greek *chrēmata*, translated in RSV *riches*). 'Things' or 'possessions' often occupy first place in the life of the disciple, especially in an age of expensive gadgets and possessions, and can just as easily be barriers against entrance into the kingdom of God. One is tempted to wonder how much of the original sense of *dyskolōs*, ('hardly', or 'with difficulty') is intended to be understood here; how disconsolately, with how ill a grace, do those conscious of being rich approach the kingdom, seeing that for them the cost is so great! This possibility is heightened by the fact that in verse 22 we have a reference to the sorrow of the rich man, expressed by his fallen countenance.

24. The disciples were thunderstruck at what they heard;[1] they had assumed that just as all other things in this world were easier for the rich ('those with advantages', as we sometimes tactfully say), so entry into the kingdom must also be easier for

[1]Although Jesus and his apostles lived in 'evangelical poverty', in the gospels riches are never said to be evil. They are, however, seen as a possible danger or impediment, and the whole story is an illustration of this point. In Mark, Jesus shows both His concern for the poor and His notice of them (12:44); He certainly does not brush them aside as merely an inevitable section of society, if 14:7 is rightly interpreted. But Mark knows nothing of the poor as being a messianic people, nor does he see (in spite of Belo) an opposing and oppressing 'class' in the rich. The concerns of Jesus, as expressed by Mark, go far deeper than that, while not ignoring the question of material poverty and wealth.

them. This is the ordinary viewpoint of 'natural religion'. Apparently it was a view also shared by the disciples, as they looked wonderingly at the receding figure of this man, so obviously ideal in their eyes for the kingdom. But discipleship makes all equal; none start with the balance loaded in their favour, when it comes to entry into the kingdom of God. Only the humble, the 'little ones', find entry to the kingdom congenial: riches can be a stumbling-block, if not a barrier.

But there is a problem at a deeper level, which must have crossed the minds of some at least of the disciples. All of us are 'rich' in something, if not in money: who then can be saved? This is the true puzzle voiced forcefully in verse 26; if it is hard for the rich, then it is hard for all.

Whether or not Jesus actually added the explanatory words *for those who trust in riches*, (the MSS are fairly equally divided), this is obviously the meaning. The shorter and simpler textual reading, *How hard it is to enter the kingdom* makes good sense, for it at once removes the 'rich' from being in a class by themselves. It shows that entry is hard for them, not just because they are rich, but because entry is hard for all. Perhaps such a generalization is not so suitable here, however, for verse 25, immediately following, resumes the 'special' subject of the rich, and the 'general' subject does not reappear till verse 26 and after. The fuller text, then, seems preferable as the sense in verse 24, reading *for those who trust in riches*. Notice again that the 'riches' are not blamed in themselves; it is the trusting in riches that is blamed, just as trusting in anything else would be.

25. It is tempting to read in this vivid saying the like-sounding (in *koinē* Greek) word *kamīlos*, 'rope', for *kamēlos*, camel, but there is no good early MSS evidence for the change. Likewise, it makes somewhat banal what is a palpable folk-proverb of impossibility. The camel was by now the largest animal found in Palestine.[1] There does not seem to be any good early evidence for the view that the phrase *eye of a needle* means a postern-gate in the city wall, with a consequent need for the camel to kneel

[1] True, 'elephant' is humorously used with the same nuance in Strack-Billerbeck's rabbinic saying, quoted by Cranfield; but elephants, known in later ages only by hearsay, had no place in common Jewish folk-proverb, while the camel had, exactly as in Arabic today.

and be unloaded if it is to be pushed through. The ninth century AD is the earliest reference that Schweizer can find for this interpretation: it therefore reads like a pious late fabrication. It is better to see the metaphor as one of sheer impossibility. Is the choice of the camel, traditionally most sulky of all beasts, suggested by the sorrowfulness of the rich man leaving Jesus (22)?

26. The indignant *kai*, 'and', translated here as *then*, at the beginning of the disciples' question almost defies translation. It implies exasperation and indignation and was not by any means the first time that the seeming lack of 'realism' shown by Jesus drew this response from His impatient disciples. *'Saved'* here equals 'enter the kingdom' (Anderson), but it does in addition have a Pauline ring about it.

27. The answer of Jesus contains another divine paradox. It is not merely hard to be saved; it is quite impossible. But God is God of the impossible, and so, for Him, the impossible can become the possible. Unless they believe this, there is no hope of any becoming disciples, least of all the twelve whom Jesus had chosen, and whose weaknesses Mark describes so frankly. Perhaps that is why *Jesus looked at them*: they were living examples of this principle, even if they did not realize it (1 Cor. 1:28).

28. Peter is perhaps slightly jealous of the attention paid to the rich man, and jealous, it may be, not so much for himself alone as for the whole group. Faced with one from a 'higher' economic bracket, there has been an instinctive closing of the disciples' ranks. They cannot forget the ships and nets that they had left behind in Galilee: has their sacrifice really been appreciated? It is a psychological fact that those who have left less are often more conscious of their sacrifice than those who have left more. Yet Peter was not wrong in what he said. Everyone who follows Christ ultimately makes the same sacrifice, for everyone must give all that they have, and Christ does not reckon the sacrifice as great or small by the amount given, but by the amount withheld for self. This will be the lesson of the widow's gift (12:42). So Jesus does not rebuke Peter, for what Peter says is true; at the call of Jesus, the fishermen had indeed left nets and boat and followed Him (1:18-20). It may be that some among them, awed by the wealth of the young man and his refusal to give it up as the price of Christ, were ruefully rethinking their own initial sacrifice, and badly needed this reassurance that Jesus saw and valued it.

29. Here it is Mark among the evangelists who has the fuller text with *for my sake, and for the gospel*, or perhaps 'because of me, and because of the good news'; he thus makes the goal of the sacrifice clearer. The disciple makes the sacrifice for his Master, so that the gospel of his Master may be spread: the possible extent of the sacrifice is given in a solemn rollcall of items involved. Nineham may well be right in seeing the omission here of 'wife' as significant, especially in view of 7 above. Nothing but a martyr's death could break the marriage tie. Peter, for instance, travelled with his wife (Schweizer), if this is indeed the meaning of 1 Corinthians 9:5.

30. To every Christian worker this verse comes with a ring of triumph, but to none more than to the cross-cultural missionary, of whatever race, who finds countless ties of love in the new land of service to take the place of those sundered in the homeland. But there is always the added warning contained in the words *with persecutions*, to remind the disciple that the cross is not only an initial burden, but a constant one. Finally, compensations though there will be in this life, yet fundamentally the disciple's hope must be set on the world to come (*cf.* 1 Cor. 15:19).

31. This may also be a word of reassurance to the disciples that God does not see as we do. The rich man might be 'first' in this world, but the disciples who had given up all to follow Jesus would be *first* in the world to come, where the rich man would be *last*. The widow with her two coins was to give more than any rich man had given (12:43); the disciples, with their nets (1:18), had given all, when the rich man had refused to give anything.

v. The third passion-prediction (10:32–34)

Now comes the third passion-prediction, or the fourth,[1] if we take into account the private words of Jesus to the three disciples on the path down from the mountain of transfiguration. This third saying is the fullest warning yet given; but it is clear from subsequent events in Mark that the disciples still failed to understand, probably, as already mentioned, because of the reference to the resurrection of Jesus. If they did not grasp that, there was no clue to the other enigmas.

32. What was it in the acts or attitude of Jesus on this occasion that filled the disciples with amazement and fear?[2] It cannot have been merely that He was going up to a hostile Jerusalem, for this He had done before; nor was it that He was leading the way for His disciples, though, on less momentous occasions, He might send them ahead of Him (6:6–7). It is unlikely that it was a memory of the two former passion-predictions, for these the disciples had failed to understand or even remember, so that Jesus judged another and clearer reminder necessary here. It must have been either a vague sense of foreboding, or else something in the face and manner of Jesus, that awed the noisy quarrelsome band for once. *Those who followed*: a wider group?

33. The bitterest sting of all was to be not even the rejection of her Messiah by Israel, but the addition in this prediction of the fact that Israel, to reject Him, will betray her Messiah *to the Gentiles*, the outsiders. Rejection and hatred can go no further than this: but this is the pathway to the cross. See Acts 2:23 for another possible reference to this aspect, with 'lawless men' (*i.e.* Gentiles).

34. The preservation of the details of this last passion-prediction may possibly be another piece of Petrine tradition.

---

[1]See comment on 9:31 above: the words on the way down from the mountain were by way of private instruction to the 'inner ring' of the three.
[2]Cranfield tries to distinguish between two groups, the wondering twelve and the fearful 'others': but this distinction seems untenable. The NIV seems to follow it, however, in its translation, and Schweizer supports it.

The patient suffering of his Lord certainly left an indelible impression upon the one who had denied Him (1 Pet. 2:23), and Mark mentions Peter, alone of the apostles, as being present on that occasion (14:54). As Peter saw the horseplay and spitting and flogging, each detail of this passion-prediction may have recalled itself to his mind. If so, it is strange that the final promise, *and after three days he will rise*, seems to have been utterly forgotten by all the disciples in the black days between the death and resurrection of Jesus.

D. THE SONS OF ZEBEDEE (10:35–45)

Although the disciples may have failed to understand the meaning of the passion-prediction, yet something in the manner of Jesus had convinced them that the hour of the establishment of His kingdom was near; perhaps it was this that had already either astonished or frightened them (10:32). But two at least of the twelve disciples are quick to take advantage of it. Ironically, however, although the request of the two 'Thunderers' was wrong-headed, yet at least it denoted faith in the ability of Jesus to establish His kingdom.[1] So Jesus dealt gently with them, more gently than the ten would have dealt, as we can see from verse 41 below. The petty selfishness of His followers at a time like this, when His mind was full of all that lay ahead at Jerusalem, must have cut Jesus to the quick, like their earlier argument as to who was the greatest among them (9:34).

35. They sought from Jesus a monarch's gift, a sort of 'blank cheque' upon His favour. Nevertheless, a wise king would put a top limit on such airy promises; compare wily Herod's restriction of 'even half of my kingdom', in his promise to the dancing girl (6:23), although this was a traditional phrase (*cf.* Esther 5:3). So, no doubt, they would have interpreted the question of Jesus in reply: they would have seen it as natural caution, not spiritual insight.

[1] As Minear says, they comprehend well enough to want special seats at His side. But this very desire shows their total lack of comprehension of the wider issue of the whole nature of the kingdom, as Jesus points out.

36. Jesus, as usual, first allows the brothers to display their own spiritual depth or shallowness by disclosing their aims; for it is by our aims rather than by our achievements that we stand judged. In verse 38 below, Jesus will then show them that, if they had only realized the true meaning of their request, they might have refrained from making it.

37. It was not a desire to be near Jesus at the moment of triumph which moved them to this request; they simply wanted for themselves the highest posts in the new kingdom. It was ambition, not loyalty, that motivated them. James and John were, after all, not only members of the 'twelve', but also members of the 'three' (9:2). Had not King David had his 'three' also who were close to the throne (2 Sa. 23:8)? Moreover, the brothers were known to, and possibly related to, the high priest (Jn. 18:15), so doubtless they were 'well connected', and therefore well fitted (they felt) for such a high office.

38. There was a double irony in their request, in that those actually on the right and left of Jesus at the great moment of His triumph were to be two crucified terrorists (15:27), making plain what in cold reality it meant to share in His *cup* and in His *baptism*. In that sense, the day would come, whether in Jerusalem or on Patmos, that the two brothers would indeed be on Christ's right and left hand.[1] *Cup* had long been an Old Testament symbol for suffering, especially for enduring the wrath of God, as well as for joy (contrast Is. 51:17 with Ps. 23:5). Jesus explicitly used 'cup' in the first sense in the Garden of Gethsemane (14:36). *Baptism* too is an Old Testament picture of undergoing the wrath of God (see Ps. 69:15), which is often seen in terms of flood or sea-waves. We have seen that acceptance by Jesus of John's baptism may have been a symbolic acceptance of this judgment (1:9) on behalf of sinful humanity. Although the

---

[1] It is of course true that, while James died a martyr's death in Jerusalem (Acts 12:2), John, after exile in Patmos (Rev. 1:9) died at peace and in old age at Ephesus, according to tradition anyway. But both had suffered for their faith, and Jesus had not said that both would die. Indeed, the fact that the prophecy is preserved in this form is the surest proof that it is genuine, for it was not altered by the church after the events to fit the circumstances.

New Testament concept of baptism 'into Christ Jesus' is rich and many-sided, it is always baptism 'into his death' (Rom. 6:3). So both baptism and the cup at the Lord's Supper remind forcibly, by their symbolism, of the cost of following Christ; the servant will be like His master in suffering too (45).

39. Whether their brief reply *we are able* (one word in Greek) represents a thoughtless selfconfident spirit, or the quiet answer of a pair suddenly sobered by the words of Jesus, we have no means of telling. Whichever it is, it brings the assurance from Jesus that this price they will in any case pay, for this is not the price of Christian greatness, but the price of following at all. Those who follow Jesus cannot haggle at terms; there are not two levels of Christian discipleship, but only one.

40. This is a reminder that even the Son is in loving submission to His Father; it is not left to Jesus but only to the Father to dispense such honours at will. So, too, the time of the 'last hour' is hidden from Jesus deep in the mind of God (13:32); and yet this is not theological 'subordinationism', for it is voluntary acceptance of this position by the Son. Humility and submission are not popular Christian virtues, but they are basic, for they are founded on the 'servant' example of Jesus Himself (verse 45).

41. *The ten*, in turn, betrayed their spiritual shallowness by being indignant at the ambition and place-seeking of the two, who had so skilfully got in ahead of them. No doubt they felt that they were 'righteously indignant', and indeed, the verb used here, *aganakteō*, is the same as that used in 10:14 to describe the reaction of Jesus to the disciples when they summarily dismissed the mothers of Jerusalem. But our basic character is shown by those things that provoke our strongest reactions, and there is a world of difference between what had stirred the indignation of Jesus and the indignation of the ten. So Jesus justly rebukes both the two and the ten at once, by showing to them their common ignorance of the very nature of Christian leadership (*cf.* 9:35). All such leadership is only humble service, for it takes its colour from the example of Jesus, who is above all, the Servant. Closeness to Him is not therefore something at which to grasp thoughtlessly. Such 'position' is only a prize to be grasped at by those who are ignorant of its nature and cost (verse 38): Christ rejected even such legitimate 'position' for Himself (Phil. 2:6).

42-44. *Lord it over them* is a good translation of the Greek *katakyrieuō*, 'exercise lordship'. But for Christians, such an attitude becomes a contradiction in terms, for our understanding of the verb is derived from the meaning to us of *Kyrios*, 'Lord', the corresponding noun, which is uniquely a title of Christ.[1] Our whole concept of the nature of lordship has therefore changed with the stooping and self-emptying of the Christ, who is Lord of all. The main argument is the same as that of 9:35 above, when the disciples were arguing as to who was the greatest, but the clinching word is yet to come in verse 45.

45. This is an argument of the 'how much more' type, often used by Jesus in the gospels. Even Jesus came not to enjoy the service of others, but to accept a lowly servant's place: how much more His servants! But He also came *to give his life as a ransom for many*. This last saying is rich in meaning: the Son of man concept, found in the Psalms, Ezekiel and Daniel, has been already linked with the servant concept of Isaiah, and both are here linked with the great ransom theme of Old Testament days (Ps. 49:7). Even the wording *for many* is a memory of Isaiah 53:11-12. Jesus gathers into one, as it were, all these different strands of Old Testament thought, and uses them in combination to explain the full meaning of His Messiahship. This ransom-price metaphor was one greatly beloved by the early church, and it is one of the great biblical statements of the purpose and efficacy of the atonement, and of its cost in the death of Christ (1 Pet. 1:18-19). Of course, no single line of explanation is in itself exhaustive, nor can any one metaphor do justice to all the biblical evidence.[2]

---

[1]See the instructive article in BAGD, under this word, with its wide range in meaning. But it is as a title for God in the Old Testament, and of Jesus in the New, that it takes its deepest theological significance.

[2]Schweizer claims that 14:24 is the only other place in Mark where the death of Jesus is described as a *ransom* (although the word is not actually used there): but 1 Tim. 2:6 is an example from elsewhere in the New Testament.

E. BLIND BARTIMAEUS (10:46–52)

46. *Bartimaeus* is a picture of the one in such need that he finds a way to Jesus, even though all the disciples of Jesus try to block the way (*cf.* their obstructive attitude to the mothers bringing children in 10:13, and to the man who was not a disciple and was yet casting out devils, in 9:38). In spite of all such discouragement, Bartimaeus had the grace of perseverance, and his faith was rewarded. But, though he becomes a spiritual illustration, we must not forget that primarily Bartimaeus was a blind man to whom Jesus gave sight in answer to his faith: that was why he followed Jesus on the road afterwards (verse 52).

47–48. There is a world of insight in the use of the one word *heard* of the blind man; he could not see Jesus, but the ears of the blind are necessarily quick. Only this gospel out of the four has preserved the name of the blind man, an interesting eye-witness touch. Even then, he is so unimportant that we know him only by his father's name: but he was important to Jesus. He was healed, and he became a follower.

Jesus of Nazareth is interesting as contemporary evidence for the terminology used to describe Jesus; compare 'the prophet from Nazareth' (Mt. 21:11), 'the carpenter's son' (Mt. 13:55), or even 'Joseph's son' (Lk. 4:22). These last two titles were discarded by the later church, probably as being incorrect and misleading, though the Old Syriac version retains traces of them which need not be heretical, but simply primitive. 'The carpenter' and 'son of Mary' (6:3) are more strictly correct as titles, and are the only two used in Mark, apart from *Jesus of Nazareth*, as here, and 'the Nazarene, Jesus' in 14:67.

Son of David is not so much a name for Jesus as a messianic title[1] (*cf.* for the Old Testament concept, Je. 33:17; and the cry of the pilgrim crowds, Mt. 21:9). The meaning of this title was

[1]This seems abundantly clear, in spite of arguments by some editors that it is here only a polite form of address to one of Davidic descent: but to this usage, 'son (or daughter) of Abraham' would be the only near-parallel. In the full sense, 'David's son' represents the long expected triumphant and kingly Messiah who would bring in the golden age for Israel. There is therefore no hint of suffering or death here. Perhaps that was why Jesus did not use the title of Himself, and indeed, He is not called by this title elsewhere in Mark (Anderson).

shortly to be in dispute between Jesus and the Pharisees (12:35). But at least Bartimaeus, as a Jew, had a right to appeal to the Son of David, whereas a Gentile would have had no such right. To call Jesus by this name was in itself an expression of faith. Further, this blind man begs for pity; he throws himself upon the mercy of Jesus, not claiming anything, except that healing which was associated with the messianic blessings to be brought by David's son in His kingdom.

49. The disciple who impedes the way to the master (as the twelve had done before this), is a contradiction in terms; the disciple is true to his or her calling who says, as here, to the one in need, *Take heart; rise, he is calling you.*

50. Everything here suggests expectant faith on the part of Bartimaeus: the impeding garment is tossed aside, he bounds to his feet. There is a joyous extravagance and recklessness of response, when the soul becomes suddenly responsive to the call of Jesus; Simon and Andrew leave their nets (1:18), James and John leave their boat (1:20), Levi leaves his tax office (2:14).

51. Here is a man who knows what he wants; no wavering in prayer for him (Jas. 1:6). The title which he used for Jesus, *rabbouni*, translated as *Master* here, shows greater respect, if anything, than the common 'rabbi', 'teacher', frequently used of Jesus both by His disciples and others.

52. It was the man's faith, evidenced by his persistence (48) that had saved him, and that same faith made him now a follower of Jesus. The repetition of sibilant consonants in the Greek phrase *hē pistis sou sesōken se, your faith has made you well,* has often been noticed. This, however, probably dates only from the later translation into Greek, with its continuous repetition in teaching, rather than from the original saying, which was almost certainly in Aramaic. If Bartimaeus was Jewish enough to call Jesus 'Son of David', he was most unlikely to converse with Him in Greek. But it is most appropriate that on this note Jesus should commence His

Jerusalem ministry: the Son of David will enter the city of David, and the passion story will begin. In a sense, all that has gone before has been but a preparation for this.

V. ZEAL FOR YOUR HOUSE: THE JERUSALEM MINISTRY (11:1 – 13:37)

A. ENTRY INTO JERUSALEM (11:1–14)

i. The entry (11:1–10)

Now with chapters 11 and 12 begin the Jerusalem days. Mark gives a graphic account of the triumphal entry, the deep impression of which upon the apostolic band may be seen by its recording by all three synoptics, as well as in John (Jn. 12:12– 19).[1] The triumphal entry of the Messiah into His capital city was the fulfilment of many an Old Testament prophecy; here at least was nothing to stumble the disciples. But the mission of the two disciples which preceded it was still a mission of faith, for they went forth into the unknown in trust and obedience to their Master's word. It was, further, like all such missions, one 'through faith for faith' (Rom. 1:17), for naturally their faith for the future would be immeasurably strengthened by finding that every detail was as Jesus had said (4). Jesus always seems to have sent His disciples out in fellowship, as here, even if it was only 'two by two' (6:7). The solitary Christian is never a biblical ideal; it was left to later Christian ages to introduce the *monachos*, the 'on-his-own', or 'monk', and the *erēmitēs*, the 'hermit', that is, the one 'living in the wilderness', where no others live.

2–5. This is only one instance out of several where Jesus shows supernatural knowledge of what will afterwards occur or be afterwards found in another place: compare His words to the two disciples who go to get ready the Passover (14:13). Admittedly, in both cases, the individuals to whom the disciples were

---

[1] Although it is not as obvious here as in the other gospels, it seems clear that Jesus wanted to show that He was the peaceful king of Zechariah 9:9, not the triumphant Davidic conqueror (Schweizer). The *colt* therefore, although the animal is unspecified in the text

247

sent must already have been friends or followers of the Lord, or else the words, put by Jesus into the mouth of His disciples, would have fallen upon deaf ears. But the actual circumstances described to the disciples in either case required prophetic fore-knowledge, of the type sometimes granted to prophets of Old Testament days (*cf.* 1 Sa. 10:1–6). It is of course possible, and has been claimed by some scholars, that what we have here is not an instance of prophetic foreknowledge, but evidence of a prior arrangement: this might fit this instance, but is less likely.

6. Here is a good example of the power committed to the disciple of acting in the Master's name[1] and asking at the Master's bidding. At His word, the disciple may do as Elijah did for Elisha, and claim another for the Lord's service (1 Ki. 19:19). The sole justification needed is that the Lord needs such a one (verse 3): even if we translate *ho kyrios* as 'his owner' instead of 'the Lord' (which seems banal in this context), the point can still be maintained. Compared with the claim that Jesus makes, the rights of all those who stand in the position of the 'owner' in the text shrink into insignificance; not even father and mother have the right to withhold one whom Jesus calls to His service.

7–8. The first few pieces of clothing laid on the donkey's back by the disciples were no doubt strictly utilitarian, to serve as a rough saddle, but those *garments* hurled recklessly on the road, like the leafy branches, were purely in His honour as a king.[2] So a Davidic conqueror should be greeted, on his triumphal ride

---

here, would be a donkey's foal (always more common than the horse in Palestine). There is probably no need to link the *tied* with Gn. 49:11, though the early church Fathers did.

[1]This is assuming that *ho Kyrios* (3) refers directly to Jesus (or at least to God) and that we are therefore justified in translating *The Lord has need of it*. To take the meaning, with Taylor, quoted by Cranfield, as 'Its owner needs it' seems somewhat banal, as Anderson sees. In any case, the owner could not have been Jesus, though he might have been a friend of His. If *kyrios* refers to Jesus, however, it is the only place in Mark that it is so used as a title for Him, though it was common later.

[2]To Anderson, this waving of branches looks like the Feast of Tabernacles, and would suggest autumn as a date: Taylor and Nineham, on the other hand, have suggested the Feast of Dedication, with December as a date. But the Passover is a spring festival, and there would be plenty of leafy branches available around Jerusalem, although any palm branches (Jn. 12:13) would need to have been brought up by pilgrims from Jericho and the Jordan Valley. For the spreading of clothing as a makeshift 'throne', *c.f.* the coronation of King Jehu (2 Ki. 9:13).

into his capital. That day, all had a share, however small, in the sacrifice associated with such a ride; for if one gave the donkey, others sacrificed their clothing; and, on this day at least, none spoke of such sacrifices as being waste. Love's extravagance in self-giving always goes unrebuked by Jesus, though not always by others (14:4), as the woman of Bethany was to find to her cost. The reason for this is to be found in the self-giving of Jesus for our sake (2 Cor. 8:9): that is why 'God loves a cheerful giver' (2 Cor. 9:7).

9–10. The song of the pilgrim crowds (not necessarily the same as the Jerusalem mob that called for the crucifixion of Jesus within a few days, 15:14), made the meaning of the identification of Jesus with the Son of David clearer. To the crowds, Jesus was 'the Coming One' (*cf.* John the Baptist's wording, in 1:7), the expected king of David's line, about to establish His earthly kingdom there and then. This was still an expectation of the disciples even after the resurrection (see Acts 1:6). If the word *hosanna* was anything more than a pious liturgical exclamation at that time (*cf.* 'amen' and 'hallelujah'), then it was a cry to this Davidic King, pleading for immediate salvation: 'save us, now, we beg.' Bartimaeus had called Jesus 'Son of David' and begged for help: were these crowds doing the same? But history would show that, unlike Bartimaeus, their blindness remained.

That certain of the Pharisees took grave exception to the theological implications of such an attribution is clear from the other gospels (*e.g.* Lk. 19:39). In Mark, however, we have no reference to this opposition as yet, until after the cleansing of the temple (verse 18).

ii. The return to Bethany (11:11)

Mark alone makes clear that Jesus made a preliminary inspection of the temple on the evening of arrival in Jerusalem, but that, probably owing to the lateness of the hour, nothing further was done until the next day. This, again, is a small piece of factual information, maybe derived from the Petrine reminiscences, which was lost in the other traditions, overshadowed in them by the magnitude of the actual cleansing of the temple on the next day. It also gives one of the little details of the domestic life of Jesus: He did not sleep in Jerusalem itself, crowded with pilgrims for the festival and full of His enemies, but at a welcoming home in Bethany,[1] (presumably that of Mary and Martha, Jn. 11:1). Even Bethany, with all the other surrounding 'outer suburbs', was probably crowded with pilgrims over festival time, so that the presence of Jesus and the twelve would not arouse particular comment. Is it symbolic that Israel's Messiah could find no place within Jerusalem, but must lodge outside the walls at Bethany (Minear)?

iii. Cursing the fig tree (11:12–14)

The resources of a Bethany household may have been somewhat strained by this extra group of Galilean fishermen and peasants. To be hungry at such an hour in the morning would be quite unusual. Unless we realize that this whole event was an acted parable we shall be puzzled by all sorts of irrelevant questions. The tree gave outward promise of fruit but nothing more: so its punishment was to remain eternally barren. In a sense, this withering of the tree was only a perpetuation of its present fruitless condition. The fig tree and the vine are two time-honoured symbols of Israel (cf. 12:1–12 for the symbol of the vine), to whom God's Son had now come, looking for fruit and finding none, though there was outward religious profession in plenty. Henceforth, Israel was to be withered and fruitless; the physical judgment of AD 70 was only an outward sign of this. Immediately below the fig tree passage, in verses 15–19, there comes the further acted parable of the cleansing of the temple. God came to His temple looking for spiritual fruit and found none; so it was inevitable that the judgment of 13:1–2 be pronounced, that, of the temple in all its splendour, not one stone would be left standing upon another.[2] Like tree, like

---

[1]Cranfield points out that this does not contradict Luke 21:37, for Bethany could be regarded as lying on the slopes of the Mount of Olives; see Grollenberg. But to seek for mechanical consistency in every tiny detail of a story like this is unfair.

[2]Lightfoot, amongst others, points out that the connection is made clear in this gospel by placing the narrative of the cleansing of the temple between the two halves of the fig tree incident, the application of which is therefore made obvious: it can only mean judgment on Israel. Schweizer well says that this is clearly not a 'prophecy after the event', for in AD 70,

temple; like temple, like nation; the parallel is exact. But Mark's Gentile audience would have no cause to rejoice in this, for Paul warns us that all this is to make us tremble and search our hearts (Rom. 11:21), lest God have cause to do so to us Gentiles as well.

Not the season for figs (13). As it stands, the Greek clearly means 'It was not the right time of the year for figs', and it would be unfair to translate 'its season for figs', as if referring to this tree only, just to avoid a difficulty. But it is fair to say that presumably Jesus was hoping for the small 'early ripe' figs, small protuberances that ripen with the leaves, before the main fig crop, and are considered a great delicacy (Ho. 9:10). It is absurd to suggest that a country person like Jesus would not have known at what time figs were ripe. See 13:28 for the leafing of the fig tree as a sign of summer's coming, indeed, the first sign.

The Greek particle *ara, if,* suggests that the finding of figs was only an unlikely possibility contemplated by Jesus. He was therefore in no sense surprised by the tree's unfruitfulness, as He would have been had it been the time of the regular fig crop. This 'nature miracle' is unusual in that it is the only one of a destructive nature performed by Jesus, unless we include the drowning of the Gadarene swine. This was necessarily so, in the case of the fig tree, if it was to be a 'sign' of coming judgment on God's people. Like all such 'nature signs' in the gospel, it is performed by Jesus Himself and not by a disciple acting on His behalf, as in the case of healings and expulsion of demons.

B. THE CLEANSING OF THE TEMPLE (11:15-19)

In a context like this, it is important to notice how different were the aspects of the situation which angered the Pharisees and priests from those which angered Jesus. Both had a high concept of the nature of the temple; but their concepts were fundamentally different. The Pharisees, according to the other gospels at least, had been shocked beyond measure by the words of the children calling out in the temple (Mt. 21:15), but

---

the temple was merely burnt; it was not until after the AD 135 revolt that it was completely razed to the ground.

were not in the least perturbed by the uproar of the merchants and the money-changers. After all, they may have reasoned, these services were for the furtherance and convenience of the ceremonial worship, that outward religious form which meant everything to them. There is plenty of early evidence to suggest that the priests also benefited financially by this traffic; the high priest in particular seems to have owned shops in the temple area, presumably around the 'Court of the Gentiles', the only area into which non-Jews might enter. They were doubtless also shocked by the prediction by Jesus of ruin to the holy place (13:2), of which they must have heard, and certainly scandalized by His prediction, as they thought, of building the temple again in three days (14:57). But for Him, the supreme blasphemy was that this place, which was to have been in God's purpose a place of prayer for non-Jewish people of every nation, instead of being exclusively a Jewish national sanctuary, should have become a business-house, and for dishonest business at that (11:17). Those familiar with such markets can easily imagine all the petty cheating and haggling that took place in the very shadow of the temple that symbolized God's presence. It is natural that Mark, a gospel written for the Gentiles, should record the passionate concern of Jesus that Gentiles should be able to worship God in the temple.[1]

15-16. The vigour with which Jesus dealt with these previously tolerated retailers and financiers left a vivid impression not only on the Pharisees, but also upon His disciples; to them, 'the wrath of the Lamb' was a new experience (Rev. 6:16).[2] But,

[1]Mark is the only one of the synoptists to have the clause *and he would not allow anyone to carry anything through the temple* (16). Best (IOM), while allowing this to be original, sees it as a superfluous retention: but surely it highlights the concern of Jesus for the possibility of Gentile worship in the outer courts of the temple, where alone it was permitted. Best's phrase is a shrewd observation, however, 'wherever we see the commentators in confusion, this is a sign of the preservation of tradition.' Carrying vessels through the temple came in fact under a rabbinic prohibition, though apparently it was often ignored, since the temple was a 'short cut' for many, who lived nearby.

[2]It is unfair of Lightfoot to refer to this as the only act of violence recorded of Jesus: it need not be construed as an act of violence at all. It was certainly not the violent demonstration by a posse of 'burly Galileans', hailed by some politicizing modern commentators. See Carmichael, quoted in Anderson. The cleansing of the temple is not a political or revolutionary act, any more than the feeding of the five thousand was a 'Zealot' act (Manson, in Anderson).

if His own followers were amazed, so was the whole crowd: this was new teaching as far as they were concerned, especially at the time of a great Jewish festival like Passover. There is no evidence that they objected, however; it was left to the chief priests and scribes to plan His death from that moment (verse 18). Did they see already a threat to the exclusiveness of Judaism, with the inclusion of the Gentiles in worship?

The attitude of Jesus to the temple is an interesting study, although we must look at other gospels to find the details. The temple (and indeed Judaism) is not a central concern of Mark in the way that it is of Matthew, for instance. His world is that of the synagogue and the overseas mission of the church among the Gentiles, with Galilee rather than Judea as its focus: to that extent at least, Marxsen is correct.

The scale of commercial operations in the temple courts was staggering, by any standards. According to Schweizer, a single merchant once offered three thousand sheep for sale in one day. This very scale has led some commentators to suggest that Jesus performed only a token cleansing of one particular area. But this is not the picture in Mark, and would scarcely have roused the anger of the authorities to such a degree (verse 18).

It seems that the view of the temple here expressed by Jesus was not primarily as a place of sacrifice, still less as a static dwelling-place for God, but a place of prayer and teaching, and an outward reflection to humankind of God's very nature. Jesus neither despised nor minimized the temple, as we can see from the wrath that its profanation aroused within Him. It is in the light of this unexpected side of His character that we can see how He appeared to some of His contemporaries as an 'Elijah returned' (6:15): see Malachi 3:1–4 for the prophecy of the purification of the temple, and, for the return of Elijah, Malachi 4:5.

It is not strange that this concept of the temple taught by Jesus continues to be exactly that of the early disciples; they go to the temple at what is to them the 'hour of prayer' (Acts 3:1), though it is actually the hour of the evening sacrifice. The colonnades of the temple are where the teachers of the new 'sect' sit expounding the 'way' exactly as Jesus had done before them (Acts 3:11), until expelled by the parent body of Judaism. This concept of the temple is indeed, far closer to that of the synagogue than that of the temple proper; for synagogues were, by definition, places for prayer (Acts 16:13), and instruction (Acts 13:15). But non-Jewish people must still wait to find a place of acceptance in the temple (Acts 21:28). Within the synagogue, on the other hand, the non-Jewish proselyte was always welcome. Seeing that, while the temple may have given a picture of the church theologically, the synagogue was almost certainly the pattern upon which the local church was organized, this point has vast theological implications.[1]

17. The Greek verb *edidasken, taught* (*i.e.* 'continued teaching'), implies a deliberate teaching programme adopted by Jesus rather than a casual pronouncement, uttered in the heat of anger, amid the wreck of the temple stalls. After the event, Jesus is giving scriptural justification for His action, as any rabbi would. The Scripture quoted by Him is Isaiah 56:7, telling how foreign proselytes will one day be welcomed to the temple.[2] It is noteworthy that Jesus here quotes only the clause in Isaiah about prayer, and omits that about offering sacrifice, for He Himself was soon to be the sacrifice that would unite Jew and non-Jew in one (Jn. 11:51–52). With Isaiah 56:7 is joined here Jeremiah 7:11, a verse which comes in the midst of a searing indictment of the Jews of Jeremiah's day, whose lives were in utter contradiction to the outward worship which they offered. The quotation would gain force from the fact that Jeremiah, too, had preached it in the temple of his day. It came with a warning about the destruction of Shiloh, and the prophecy that, as God had abandoned Shiloh, so He would abandon Jerusalem and His temple there (Jer. 7:14).

18. Small wonder that the chief priests and scribes now began to plot His death; His meaning was only too plain and they

---

[1] For a detailed examination of the whole question of the temple, and its place in Christian thought, see the present writer's *The New Temple*, IVP, 1951.

[2] 'For Mark, it is the revelation to the Gentiles that is decisive' (Schweizer, IOM). This is natural, if Mark is indeed a gospel for Gentiles: but we have no reason to suppose that this was not in the mind of Jesus also, as He taught. For His teaching during this last week, see Anderson: 'The weapons Jesus carries on the eve of his passion are certainly not those of the freedom fighter or revolutionary political agent, but those of the uniquely authoritative teacher.'

feared him. The amazement of the crowds of pilgrims as they listened to His teaching was not without some fear, too, to judge from the strong Greek verb used, *exeplēsseto, was astonished.* Not since the days before the fall of the first temple had they heard such explicit words of doom; one wonders how many of them lived to see the great stones topple over, one by one, into the fire in AD 70 some forty years later. Few of the generation who had heard Jesus preach would outlive that disaster, except the infant church, which took its Lord's advice and fled to Pella in Transjordan (13:14). It is fashionable in some quarters today to deny this flight, but otherwise it is hard to see how the church of Jerusalem would have survived in the general turmoil.

19. It would scarcely have been safe for Him to have spent the night in the city now, with so many foes actively plotting His death; but Bethany was still safe, and so there He presumably returned (*cf.* verse 12).

C. EXHORTATION AND DEBATE (11:20 – 12:44)

i. The meaning of the withered fig tree (11:20–26)

Jesus does not explain to the disciples why He had cursed the barren fig tree; that we must infer from the passage above (verses 12–14). Instead, He uses the incident here as an illustration of the effectual nature of prayer. Only the Marcan account records that it was Peter who observed the withering; this may possibly show a Petrine source. It is typical of Mark's style that he 'sandwiches' the prophecy of the destruction of the temple between the two halves of the story of the cursing of the fig tree, thus making the application of the parable perfectly plain to his readers.

The disciples did not, as we might today, find any moral problem in the cursing of the fig tree; indeed, if this is seen as an acted parable with reference to Israel, it drops into place at once. Their only reaction was amazement that the cursing by Jesus has been so effectual (11:21) and so immediate. Blessing (10:16) and cursing (14) may both come fittingly from the lips of Jesus, but not from ours (Jas. 3:10). Our human cursing would be light and unthinking; His was of the nature of the pronouncement of a solemn sentence, in a prayer that would be fulfilled. This is a reminder to us that prayer is not simply asking God for the pleasant things which we may desire, but an earnest yearning for, and entering into, the will of God, for ourselves and others, whether it is sweet or bitter. This was the prayer of Jesus in Gethsemane (14:35-36), and such prayers will always be answered by God.

22-24. Jesus is, in addition, rebuking their lack of faith in Him, shown by their utter astonishment when His cursing of the fig tree produced such sudden and drastic results. Wither a fig tree? Given faith, they could uproot mountains (a common rabbinic phrase), and hurl them into the sea. It is obvious, then, that this need for faith when praying was a constant point of the teaching of Jesus which He reiterated to His disciples in various forms to fit different occasions. Faith is not chosen arbitrarily as a condition of prayer: it is the basic condition of all our relationship with God (Heb. 11:6), including prayer. Even on the basis of this faith, however, we may not generalize and think that we can remove any 'mountains' and wither any 'fig trees' at will. Mountains will truly be removed, but at God's will, not ours (1 Jn. 5:14). The metaphor is not of course to be taken literally; we never read of Jesus moving mountains physically, although, as Creator-God, He calmed the storm (4:39) and fed the crowds (6:41) and here withered the fig tree (11:21).

25. There is another 'condition' of prayer stated by Jesus here, and that is forgiveness of our fellows. This, too, is not arbitrary; we have no inherent right to be heard by God; all is His grace and undeserved favour. But, unless we forgive our fellows freely, it shows that we have no consciousness of the grace that we ourselves have received and need, and so it shows that we are expecting to be heard on our own merits, which cannot be. Mark does not record the 'Lord's prayer' (Mt. 6:12), for whatever reason, but this certainly reiterates one of its clauses.

26. This verse is omitted in several important MSS and may have entered from the very similar saying in Matthew 6:15. In any case, whether properly belonging here or not, the verse not only expresses a logical deduction from verse 25, but also a solemn theological truth. This is not an arbitrary refusal by God to forgive us. We, by our own unforgiving spirit, have made it impossible to accept the forgiveness freely offered by God, since we refuse to adopt the only attitude in which it can be appropriated.

ii. By what authority? (11:27-33)

The rumblings of the coming storm grow louder. As Jesus continued to teach the crowds in the temple (see verse 17), the authorities came, angrily demanding to know 'in whose name' this Galilean Rabbi taught; whose disciple was He, or what official commission had He to show? Only such rabbinic authority or commissioning could warrant and justify to them His cavalier way of dealing with the temple vendors.[1] True, Jesus taught in His own name, unlike the scribes, with their continual quotation of precedents (1:22): but He also claimed, and clearly displayed, God's direct authority in so doing. It was a realization of this divine authority that drew His disciples to Him (4:41): it was failure to see it, or rather unwillingness to admit it, that condemned the Pharisees. So Jesus, instead of giving them a direct answer, tells them that His authority stems from the same source as that of John the Baptist. Their greatest condemnation is that they do not seem to have considered this question as a moral probe, but purely as an intellectual trap. Their query as they sought to reply was not 'true or false?' but 'safe or unsafe?'. Similarly, the popular conviction (verse 32) that John's authority was of God was seen by them, not as an example of a truth hidden from the wise and revealed to the simple, but only as a possible personal danger, if they dissented from it. So, as a crowning irony, they blandly said they did not know (verse 33), whereupon Jesus showed what He thought of such deliberate pretended ignorance by saying, *neither will I tell you*. The root of the trouble lay not in their intellect, but in their

---

[1]Cranfield claims, perhaps rightly, that their question is not limited to rabbinic authorization: but surely, in view of official scorn of the 'unlettered rabbi' from Galilee (Jn. 7:15), this would be a natural question to ask.

stubborn wills: they stood self-condemned. The question of Jesus to them was not a trap; it was yet another opportunity for them to realize and confess their blindness, and to ask for sight. Theirs was the unforgivable sin, that constant wilful opposition and blindness that is the sin against the Holy Spirit (3:29). If it is true that there is a way to hell from the gates of heaven, as Bunyan has it, then it is equally true that there is a way to heaven from the gates of hell: yet here were those who contemptuously refused to take it.

iii. The wicked tenant farmers (12:1–12)

The parable of the wicked tenant farmers follows very naturally upon the final refusal by the Pharisees to consider seriously the source of the authority of Jesus. In so doing, they refused to admit the obvious fact that they knew its source already. This next parable is, in consequence, a parable of judgment. It is more properly the parable of the rejection of the landlord's son, than the parable of the wicked tenant farmers, although his rejection is at once the logical result and the supreme proof of their wickedness.

1. As soon as Jesus began to speak, seeing that the Old Testament 'back-cloth' of the parable was Isaiah 5:1–7, everyone would know that He referred to Israel – referred to them, in fact – and that this was yet another parable of judgment. All the details of the landowner's care and preparation of the vineyard are borrowed from Isaiah, though the concept of the tenant farmer is new.[1] Whatever the mistakes of the Pharisees, one common mistake of ours they did not make. Their very anger showed their realization that the words of Jesus were directed to them personally (verse 12) and not innocuously aimed at some third party. They did not need to be told that such a parable was 'paraenetic': they knew it at once.

2–5. Even the maltreatment of the prophets by their forebears was readily admitted by later Israel (Mt. 23:29–32), for this did

---

[1] The hedge, as Anderson sees, was probably a loose stone wall. But the tower is probably

not compromise them. Indeed, they prided themselves on their superior spiritual insight, and on showing their piety by building fine tombs for these ancient martyrs. As Jesus drily said, this only showed their identification with their ancestors: one generation killed the prophets, while another generation buried them, as if consenting to the crime (Lk. 11:48). Every generation can always see the spiritual blindness of its forebears, but never its own.

6–8. As often in the New Testament, *agapētos, beloved,* probably here has the force of 'only', a sense which is more specifically brought out in this context by the use of *hena, one.* The uniqueness of the position of Jesus and the extraordinary exhibition of the grace of God in sending Him, are alike manifested in this word. There is a pathos in the owner's phrase *they will respect my son,* but it also contains a truth, for the one who wants to receive the Father not only will but must receive the Son (9:37). The position of Jesus is both similar to, and yet very different from, that of the prophets who came to Israel before Him, for there is a finality in His coming. God can, as it were, do no more. Christ is God's last word to humanity. So judgment is at once passed on the wicked tenant farmers, although the execution of that judgment may be stayed as, in a sense, it is stayed throughout this present age, in spite of a temporal judgment falling upon the Jerusalem of that generation. From now on, the demand made is repentance for our share in that crime (*cf.* Acts 2:23, 38). This is very different from the message brought by the earlier 'servants' the prophets, whose demand was for that spiritual 'fruit', which alone could justify the 'tenant farmers' in the 'landowner's' eyes. It was not through their failure to recognize the Son that they killed Him; that would have been pardonable. It was, as in the parable, precisely because they recognized Him for who He was (verse 7): they said, in essence, *'This is the heir; come, let us kill him, and the inheritance will be ours'* (see verse 7). We reject the claims of

---

not the 'lookout' suggested by him, but a 'villa' (the late Greek meaning of the word), built by the absentee landlord. See Schweizer for the unpopularity of this group, especially common in fertile Galilee with its many large estates.

Christ not because we misunderstand them, but because we understand them only too well, in spite of all our protestations to the contrary.

9. Mark simply records here the judgment of Jesus on the tenant farmers. Matthew 21:41 contains a graphic addition, making clear that the 'sentence' pronounced was the spontaneous verdict of the crowd, carried away by the graphic parable. This is very true to the third world: in open air preaching, preachers soon learn not to ask rhetorical questions, or they will assuredly get rhetorical answers from their uninhibited local congregation, as here. Once again the spontaneous moral judgments of unsophisticated folk are vindicated, as against the blindness of the self-styled 'wise'.

The item in the condemnation that seems to have enraged them beyond all bounds, was the promised giving of the vineyard to others. This struck a blow at the position of Israel as 'the most favoured nation'; the reference to the Gentiles was plain, and they could not stomach it, as is shown by their reaction in verse 12.

10. This quotation is from Psalm 118:22, the very Psalm from which, at the triumphal entry, the earlier pilgrim cry of 'hosanna' (11:9) had been taken,[1] as well as the 'Blessed is he who comes in the name of the Lord' (11:10). The Lord's coming is for judgment as well as salvation, as the tenant farmers will find to their cost.

Jesus is Himself the rejected stone, now become, in God's good purpose, the keystone of the building which is the new temple, the Christian church, His body. But in a sense the Gentiles too, once despised by Israel, yet now finding a place as 'living stones' in God's plan (1 Pet. 2:5), may also be included in the wider meaning of the verse. Contemptuously rejected they might have been, but yet they are chosen by God. This was the miracle that the Lord had done and which was truly marvellous in Gentile eyes (verse 11), among whom Mark's readers must surely have been numbered.

---

[1] Of course, as a regular Passover Psalm, it would be much in their minds at this season: but for another interesting and possible reason for the exclamation at the triumphal entry, see Cranfield. For the philology of the word, see BAGD and articles quoted there.

11. All that we can do, as always, is to bow our heads in reverence and marvel at the plan of God, as the Psalmist does here. The quotation from the psalter is to show us that this plan is nothing new, but God's eternal way of working; there is a divine consistency in God's dealing with us (Mal. 3:6). *Have you not read this scripture* is ironic, directed as it is to those whose whole business and indeed profession was the study of the Old Testament.

12. The Pharisees regarded Jesus from now on as a dangerous revolutionary, deliberately intent on arousing the crowds against them. Later the same charge would be brought against His disciples (Acts 17:6 and 24:5), with just as little reason or justification. Did Gentile Christians at Rome see any parallel to their own case, when they were made the scapegoats and persecuted by Nero after the great fire of AD 64?

iv. Tribute to Caesar (12:13-17)

Now begins the terrible game of 'cat and mouse', the endless Pharisaic manoeuvring that will end in the death of Jesus. The first question about the source of His authority had left them helpless (11:33), but perhaps He can be caught in the same way Himself, and be condemned on a political charge. If Jesus had placed them upon the horns of a dilemma, where either answer was unsafe because of the crowd, they will try to do the same with Him. The *Herodians* do not seem to have been a coherent sect in the sense that Pharisees or Sadducees were, but probably were a political pressure group, cutting across other divisions, made up of those who saw in the support of the unscrupulous but outwardly orthodox Herod the hope of Israel; and that meant acceptance of Rome as overlord. As there is no reference to the Herodians outside the New Testament and dependent literature, however, certainty is impossible. Clearly to Mark and his sources, they were an identifiable group, and equally clearly they were opposed to Jesus: more we cannot say with confidence.

14. Nothing is more horrible than the smooth plausibility of the approach, as though they could flatter Jesus into abandoning all

caution and compromising Himself. The point is that any religious teacher who was a regarder of *the position of men*, who looked on outer show and not inner reality, would certainly be afraid to say or do anything that could be construed as an insult towards Caesar. Into this political trap they sought to lead Him. Yet if He avoided this trap, and lent His authority to the payment of tribute to the hated Roman, the Zealots of hot-tempered Galilee would certainly be alienated: and did not Jesus number at least one such among His disciples (see 3:18)? More, the bulk of the non-Judaean pilgrims, who had so tumultuously escorted into Jerusalem their prophet from Nazareth (Mt. 21:11), were likewise Galileans, always suspect at festival time (Lk. 13:1) as likely to riot. If their support was removed, Jesus would be isolated and outwardly helpless.

15. Such *hypocrisy*, or play-acting, did not deceive Him, and He did not conceal the fact from them. From such hollow sham the Son of God must have turned with loathing; the strongest charge that He brought against teacher of the law and Pharisee was that they were utterly insincere (7:6). Jesus was therefore aware of their trick from the start.

16. The production of a coin as an illustration was a typical rabbinic touch, but the use made of it here was new. It is significant of His poverty that Jesus had no coin Himself, but had to ask for one. By the acceptance of the imperial coinage, marked by the head and title of the reigning emperor, the Jews had already shown their acceptance of imperial rule, even if unwillingly. There is a world of bitterness in the terseness of their one-word reply, *Caesar's*: not even Pharisees or Herodians would have chosen that position.

17. So came the reply of Jesus, with its irresistible logic, which is: the coin already belongs to Caesar: give it back, then, to him. Translated into theological terms, it becomes the Christian acceptance of the state, as an institution ordained by God; this is strongly advanced by Paul (Rom. 13:1–2) and Peter (1 Peter 2:13–14). If we accept the amenities of the state, in law and order, expressed in a guaranteed coinage as in other things, then we have no right to seek to escape the burdens imposed by the state. But this lesson Jesus would leave His audience to infer. If He had spoken so openly here, the Pharisees would have used it as a handle against Him, to stir up the Zealots. The Zealots probably did not yet exist as a coherent party (the evidence is conflicting), but certainly Zealot elements were in existence since 6 BC at least. Jesus consistently rejected the path of violence chosen by Sicarii and Zealots, though He may have striven for some of the same goals by peaceful means (so Belo).

To any listening Zealot, the first clause *render to Caesar the things that are Caesar's* would have been the sting in the answer.[1] But the true sting for the Pharisee was in the tail, *and to God the things that are God's*, for none of them would dare to say that they were already giving God His full due. Even those trained lawyers were baffled by such an answer; there was no handle that they could use against Jesus, so *they were amazed*. And yet it may be that we have here one reason why the Galilean pilgrim crowd made no attempt to rescue their prophet at a later stage; did they perhaps suspect that He was somewhat pro-Roman after all? But even so, the chief priests still feared a violent reaction if Jesus was arrested openly at the time of a festival (14:2), so He cannot have completely lost the sympathy of the crowds.

There may well be also here a note of rebuke addressed to the political aspirations of the Herodians, or any other groups so occupied with their little local 'Caesar', the temporal power, that they had altogether forgotten God and His prior claims. In that case, as often in the New Testament, the *kai and* is not so much a conjunctive participle as an adversative particle, meaning 'and yet, for all your doing the first, yet do the second as well'.

v. The Sadducean question (12:18-27)

So the political attempt to snare Him had failed; but perhaps a theological question would succeed. For different reasons, both

[1] Many modern commentators try to explain away the plain sense of these words, but it corresponds too closely to a whole pattern of theology in the New Testament to be lightly rejected: see 1 Pet. 2:13-17. We may not reject a biblical doctrine just because it is unpopular. See Anderson for the absurdity of using this saying to justify political subver-

Pharisees and Sadducees[1] alike saw in Jesus a dangerous enemy, although it is unlikely, owing to their bitter antagonism (*cf.* Acts 23:6), that they ever acted in conscious collaboration here. The Sadducees were attempting, in this instance, to make spiritual truth look ridiculous by interpreting it with the grossest of literalism. By doing this, they hoped that the whole concept of the resurrection would be laughed out of court. The case they presented was doubly absurd, since they themselves did not believe in any such thing. To present an unfair caricature of a view, and then to demolish it, is an old pastime. Nevertheless, they held as strongly to the law of Moses as any others in Israel, and so they began their argument with the Mosaic principle of Levirate marriage.[2] In a sense, the Sadducees were the most 'conservative' group of all in Israel, accepting only the Law and rejecting, as they did, the Prophets and the Writings, the two later divisions of the Hebrew Bible. They had refused to accept God's further revelation in the Old Testament: now, they would refuse to accept God's final revelation in Jesus.

The case brought forward so solemnly by the Sadducees was obviously only a hypothetical instance. The symbolical number *seven* (20) in itself suggests this, although 'seven sons' seems to have been much more common in New Testament times (*e.g.* Acts 19:14) than in modern 'nuclear' families. For those interested, the Pharisees had already decided that such a wife would belong in the resurrection to her first husband (Schweizer).

24-25. The reply of Jesus is a marvel of patience and forbearance, although He rebukes the Sadducees for two things. The first is their failure to understand the very revelation of God

sion, or indeed, we might add, of imputing any particular political philosophy to Jesus at all. In any event, there is no doubt that the second statement takes precedence over the first (Schweizer).

[1]Johnson points out that the Sadducees are mentioned in Mark only here, and very little in the other gospels. Outside the N.T. little is known of them, since they died out after the fall of Jerusalem in AD 70, and therefore any rabbinic references would come from their Pharisee enemies. Once the temple had been destroyed, there was no place for a priestly aristocracy.

[2]This rule of marrying the childless wife of a dead brother was of course Mosaic (Dt. 25:5-10): the Sadducees were therefore in no sense attacking the custom, although they adduced an extreme instance of it to discredit the doctrine of resurrection.

upon which they claim to lean by thus quoting Moses. The second is their failure to appreciate God's power, supremely manifested for Bible writers both in the resurrection of Jesus Christ from the dead (Rom. 1:4) and ultimately in the general resurrection (1 Cor. 15:20–26). This Jesus will prove from the very law of Moses upon which they lean.

Jesus first, then, demonstrates the patent absurdity of the hypothetical case, showing that the question is meaningless in the form in which it is put by the Sadducees, because marriage ceases to have any sexual significance in heaven.[1] There is an irony in the way in which He shows that the particular concept of resurrection cannot be grasped apart from a whole general 'universe of belief', already rejected by the Sadducees, comprising the spiritual world of which 'angels' form part. In other words, such a question is a problem only to the Sadducees, not to the Pharisees, and that is because they have already in advance rejected the only terms upon which a solution could be found. There is therefore a subtlety in the statement that those resurrected are *like angels in heaven* (25), which does not appear on the surface, but which would scarcely be lost on either Pharisee or Sadducee, for different reasons. Verse 28 seems to show that at least one Pharisaic scribe heard it with approval.

26–27. But, having dealt with the Sadducees on their own terms, Jesus as usual proceeds to give a far deeper proof of the resurrection, and one which would be incapable of being caricatured. He has already explained what He meant by their ignorance of God's power; now He will explain what He meant by their ignorance of the Scripture, by basing Himself upon that very Moses on whom, rejecting what they regarded as later accretions, they relied. In God's self-revelation made to Moses at the burning bush (Ex. 3:6), God describes Himself as the God of Abraham, of Isaac and of Jacob. Now to talk of Himself as being a God of the past experience of these men, as a western philosopher might describe Him, would be nonsense to a Hebrew mind: for where is the experience apart from the person?

[1] As Minear well points out, resurrection is transformation, not just re-animation. Paul makes this very clear (1 Cor. 15:35–50).

Assuredly the experience is not within God; if it was so, God would have described Himself simply as 'I AM', as he did elsewhere (Ex. 3:14). But to describe Himself as Abraham's God, Isaac's God and Jacob's God is obviously felt to be adding a further revelation. Therefore, if God can still so describe Himself to Moses centuries after the death of these two men, their spiritual experience must still be existent. If so, these three patriarchs must still be in existence; and the guarantee of their 'eternal life' is not the nature of their experience of God, but the nature of the God whom they experienced.[1] He is the *God of the living* because He is the living God Himself (Mt. 16:16). So too, it was that, even in the physical realm, contact with Jesus brought new life to the dead (*cf.* 5:41); while to know God, and the Christ whom He sent, is the definition of eternal life (Jn. 17:3). Here is a great bridge between gospel and Pauline theology (*cf.* Rom. 6:1-5), although not necessarily a pointer to direct influence by Paul on Mark, as claimed by some commentators.

vi. The greatest commandment (12:28-34)

Now comes the question, perhaps genuinely intended, as to which is the greatest commandment of all. The first questioner of Jesus seems to have been either a Pharisee or a Herodian (13ff.), the second a Sadducee (18ff.). Mark simply tells us that this third questioner was a scribe, but, from his approval of the last answer, it seems likely that this was a Pharisaic move. Certainly, of all the three questioners, this scribe was the most honest, and alone received commendation from Jesus. It appears from verse 28 that he was already conscious of the theological strength of the reply of Jesus to the Sadducees; and from his words in verse 32, he was even more deeply struck by the reply here. The 'Christian Pharisees' were a group not unknown later within the Christian church (Acts 15:5), but the 'Judaizers' of the early church showed the dangers inherent in such an ambiguous position.

[1] Nineham well quotes Loisy here as saying that still, in the twentieth century, one of the most powerful arguments for the resurrection is the experience of communion with God.

29–31. Jesus' summary of Israel's duty was a junction of the famous Deuteronomic *Shema*, the 'Godward' command to Israel recorded in Deuteronomy (Deut. 6:4–5), with the 'human' command recorded in Leviticus (19:18).[1] It has often been remarked that many of the most telling sayings of Jesus (as in the temple cleansing) were derived from a creative combination of two or more separate passages from the Old Testament; this is another example.

In this summary, the heart of true religion is seen to lie, not in negative commands, but in a positive loving attitude to God and others. This is the Pauline 'liberty'[2] of the New Testament (Gal. 5:1). This is what St Augustine means by saying 'Love and do as you like', for such love towards God and others will in itself keep us from licence. If we love others, we will do nothing to work them hurt and, if we love God, what we like and choose will be to do God's will and pleasure (Ps. 40:8). That is why Paul can say 'love is the fulfilling of the law' (Rom. 13:10).

32–33. The law, the temple and the favoured position of Israel were the three great 'planks' of Judaism, as we can see from the fierce reaction to any challenge to them perceived in early Christian preaching (Acts 21:28). The second and third had already been challenged by Jesus since His arrival in Jerusalem: this scribe had intended to test His orthodoxy on the first and greatest, the law. This was no doubt the point where Jesus was most suspect by the Pharisees ever since the earlier controversies. One can almost hear in these two verses the trained lawyer weighing the Lord's answer clause by clause, with almost pedantic repetitiveness. 'A good answer – a true answer – a scriptural answer', he agrees, perhaps not without a slightly

---

[1] It is fashionable nowadays to place the 'great commandment' beside the 'great commission' (Mt. 28:19) as denoting the social responsibility of the church (*love your neighbour as yourself*) alongside its evangelistic responsibility. No-one would deny the social implication of the gospel, but, in fairness to biblical exegesis, it should be remembered that the 'first and great commandment' as recorded here is total love for God: the 'second great commandment' of love for neighbours stems from it, and is set within this theological context. If we lose this balance, we are left with a shallow humanitarianism without any deep theological roots, as Anderson sees clearly.

[2] Kierkegaard (quoted in Anderson), well says 'If we are to love our neighbour as ourselves, then this commandment opens, as with a masterkey, the lock to our self-love, and snatches it away from us.'

patronizing air towards this theological layman. He gives his verdict finally; in Scripture, obedience is indeed better than sacrifice (1 Sa. 15:22), and so to love God and one's fellows is more than all the observances of the law. This was not of course a new view: it was the heart of the prophetic message to Israel.

34. The lawyer had weighed and appraised the answer that Jesus had made; but to his surprise and the consternation of the bystanders, he found that, even as he was answering, Jesus had been appraising him. When humans dare to sit in judgment on the claims of Christ, they find instead that Christ is sitting in judgment on them: they stand either self-condemned or justified by their attitude to Him. It is not surprising that, after this, no-one dared to ask Jesus any further question. We are nowhere told that this scribe, so close to the kingdom, ever actually entered it. We know that there were some believers in Jesus, however, even among the ruling Sanhedrin group at Jerusalem (15:43), and priests and Pharisees within the church later. Nevertheless, this is the only 'teacher of the law' who appears in a favourable light in Mark (Schweizer).

vii. The son of David? (12:35–37)

Now follows the last of the series of 'hard questions'. As the series had begun with a baffling question put by Jesus to the chief priests on the source of John's authority (11:30), so it would end with an equally baffling question put by Him about the identity of the son of David.[1] The Marcan context aims this question directly at 'the law teachers', as being propounders of the last conundrum. Of course 'scribe' did not denote a separate 'party', as Pharisee did, but a profession: but some at least of these 'writers' were certainly Pharisees. It may be that the cry of the pilgrims at the triumphal entry (11:10), had brought this particular messianic title into prominence, with the phrase 'the kingdom of our father David'. It was widely agreed that the kingly Messiah destined to re-introduce David's kingdom was

[1]There seems, in the light of this, no need to assume that here we have only the end of a final conflict-story (so Cranfield, following Gagg), rather than a topic introduced freshly and deliberately by Jesus Himself.

to be 'David's son', but this would have been understood as being merely by physical descent, and applicable to the earthly deliverer, for whom all Jews looked, and for whom extremists at least worked actively.

36–37. Yet an earthly messianic king could not be the full theological meaning of the title, as Jesus illustrated by an argument which they could not well refute. As usual, He first shows them that, even on their own premises, they are inconsistent. Psalm 110 was accepted both as Davidic and as messianic by every orthodox scribe. But if David is speaking here, and speaking of the coming Messiah, how can he possibly call Him *my Lord*? How is the use of such a title consistent with David's own occupation of a superior position, that of physical ancestor compared with physical descendant? Mark simply records that Jesus put the question: but the context makes plain that the scholars could find no answer, and that this marked the end of attempts to trap Jesus in His speech, at least until His trial (15:1–5). We today, in the light of the rest of the New Testament, can see clearly how the Christ can both be born of David's physical line, and yet still be David's Lord, because He is identical with God Himself; but Jesus made no attempt to explain this as yet even to His disciples. It was enough that He was hailed as 'Son of God' (5:7; 15:39), or 'the Son' (13:32). Whether or no this Psalm can have another historical interpretation is beside the point; the above interpretation was accepted by every orthodox Jew, and so the question asked by Jesus was unanswerable, as far as the scribes were concerned.[1] The large crowd of listeners seem to have greeted this discomfiture of the scribes with delight (verse 37): but even greater discomfiture was to follow for the scribes.

---

[1] Lane says 'Here only among the sayings of Jesus is the authority of an O.T. passage traced to its inspiration': but surely the point is only made explicit here to make the argument still more unanswerable, as far as the scribes are concerned. All orthodox Jews accepted without question that the Old Testament was inspired, and therefore authoritative: Jesus was not alone in His views.

viii. The warning against the scribes (12:38-40)

Beware of the scribes:[1] the *scribes* or 'writers' had now been effectively silenced, just as the politically-minded Sadducees had been silenced before (12:27). Such plain talk undoubtedly increased the antagonism of the religious circles towards Jesus, but it is unlikely to have been unpopular with the crowd (cf. *gladly* at the end of verse 37). In preaching to a western Gentile audience, Mark omits here many details of the fuller account in Matthew. On the whole, only that of obvious practical teaching value is likely to have been preserved, and this would involve only the main principle.

These scribal teachers of the law liked all the fame and outward honour that their unquestioned intellectual mastery of Scripture brought to them. They were, by this date, professional biblical expositors and commentators, and devoted to the biblical text as few others have been; they were conservative and reverent in their approach to the Bible as they knew it. But the gospels often warn against them, as here. Had they rejected the authority of Scripture, their conduct would have been explicable; as it was, they were left without excuse. For those who accept the Bible as a rule of faith and conduct, there is no excuse for disobedience.

40. The law teachers not only loved the outward show and empty glory of religious observance, which is the sin of pride;[2] they also loved money, which is the sin of covetousness. Yet all the time they did this under cover of lengthy prayers, a fact which invested all their other sins with the new and awful quality of hypocrisy. The widow and orphan should above all others have been the objects of their compassion and prayer because they are the objects of God's special concern (Ex. 22:22; Ps. 146:9) and instead, they robbed them. It is precisely because

[1] Perhaps 'professional copyists' would give the meaning better, though NIV uses 'teachers of the law' as a 'dynamic equivalent'. It was originally as 'copyists of the law' that the scribes had attained their great knowledge of it. They proudly looked back to Ezra as their spiritual ancestor (Ezr. 7:12), and as the first of their line, just as the Sadducees may have looked back to Zadok (1 Ki. 2:35).
[2] It matters little whether we read here *stoais*, 'porticos', or *stolais*, 'long robes', though the second is preferable in sense. In either case, scribal ostentation is the point.

they pray, that their condemnation will be the more terrible, more than that of a rogue who robs outright without pretence of prayer or religion. So comes the irony that Jesus preached love to the sinner, but judgment to the religious, not of course because they were religious, but because they were inconsistent and indeed hypocritical. Greater knowledge and greater opportunities only bring greater responsibility, which can, if rejected, bring greater condemnation.

ix. The widow's gift (12:41–44)

Now comes, appropriately enough after this warning, the story of the widow's gift. Avarice and nominal religion, with all its pomp and show, have just been castigated. Here by contrast is one of the very group who are made a prey by the scribes, a widow who, out of poverty and true devotion to God, makes an offering unseen and unnoticed, except by Jesus. Together, the pictures are a matching pair, emphasizing the strong contrast. Jesus, of course, did not deny that the rich gave *large sums*; he merely said that the widow gave still more, for theirs was only a contribution, generous though it might be, while hers was a total sacrifice. It is well to remember that God measures giving, not by what we give, but by what we keep for ourselves; and the widow kept nothing, but gave both coins, all that she had (verses 42 and 44). As Anderson well says, she could so legitimately have kept one for herself, but she did not.

D. THE 'LITTLE APOCALYPSE' (13:1–37)

i. The doom on the temple (13:1–4)

With chapter 13 we come to the so-called 'little Apocalypse',[1] the gospel core of the material which is amplified in the book of

---

[1]The use of this convenient descriptive title does not of course convey a distrust of the dominical nature of the contents, although many modern editors take this position. But Cranfield's is a healthier approach. Beasley-Murray still remains the best guide, in seeing the chapter as 'notes' on an authentic discourse or discourses of Jesus, that circulated before Mark's Gospel, although he has more recently modified his position. Of course, a well-remembered complex of oral tradition would serve as well as a written source. While it is not, as sometimes claimed, 'a meditation upon the Book of Daniel', there is no doubt that

Revelation (*cf.* 1 Thes. 4:13–17 for a similar passage). It is noteworthy that Jesus makes no attempt to gratify mere curiosity here; instead, His aim is practical and ethical. Indeed, wherever the disciples expressed such idle curiosity, He at once heartily discouraged them (verse 4). As it stands, the chapter is a fitting introduction to the passion narrative (Lightfoot). On the whole section see David Wenham, *The Rediscovery of Jesus' Eschatological Discourse*, quoted in the footnote below.

This opening section deals with the destruction of the temple. The whole of the 'little Apocalypse' seems designed to warn the disciples against four great spiritual dangers. The first danger is that of reliance upon the outward symbols of religion, venerable and loved though they may be (verse 2). The second danger (verses 5, 6) is that of deception by false Messiahs; the third (verses 7, 8) is that of distraction by world turmoil around us; the fourth (verses 9ff.) is that of being 'tripped' because of the unexpected severity of the persecution for our faith. To be forewarned, in each case, is to be forearmed: we must *take heed* (verse 5). From now on, we move into a climate of increasing violence, and a sense of impending catastrophe (Lightfoot).

1–2. There is a ring of patriotic pride in the words of the unnamed disciple here. Built by the hated Herod it might be, but the 'third temple' was one of the architectural wonders of the Roman world, unfinished at the date of its destruction. The 'fox' (Luke 13:32) built well, with the help of his borrowed Roman engineers: Herodian masonry is noted for its excellence everywhere in Palestine. So, too, there is a note of sadness in the reply of Jesus: for nothing in all Jerusalem could match the temple for splendour and apparent permanence (Minear). Jesus was here preparing His disciples for the days when every

---

much of the imagery is drawn from Old Testament apocalyptic, which Jesus must have known. There is much discussion today as to whether this discourse is an integral part of the Lord's teaching, or only peripheral [Pesch, quoted in Telford, IOM). The first would seem to be the answer. Otherwise the ending of Mark is inexplicable and incomplete: with this chapter, the future is already sketched, at least in outline. On the whole matter, see most recently Wenham, *The Rediscovery of Jesus' Eschatological Discourse*, Sheffield, JSOT Press, 1984, even if Blomberg is not convinced of all the details of Wenham's reconstruction (*The Historical Reliability of the Gospels*, Leicester and Downers Grove: Inter-Varsity Press, 1987, p. 143).

familiar and outward religious help would be taken away from them, in the expulsion of the Christian 'sect' from the parent body of Judaism, when the danger was so great that the infant church would waver or even go back to the well-loved institutions of Judaism (see Heb. 6:4–6). Later still, the sack and burning of the earthly temple, while almost a death-knell to Palestinian Judaism (the final blow came later, after Bar-Cochba's revolt in AD 135), must have had a great 'evidential' value to the Christian church as fulfilling the word of Jesus. After that, there was little danger of going back to the outward forms of Judaism, for there was nothing to which to go. No sacrifice has since been offered in Israel; how could there be sacrifice, without a temple? Some rabbis found the answer in Hosea 14:2, presumably in the sacrifice of praise, but a Christian could offer this as readily as a Jew: there was no temptation to return here.

3. This is an interesting verse, unique in Mark, in that *Andrew* is joined to the usual three who receive special instruction from Jesus. The real problem is not why Andrew was joined with the others on this occasion (when the four of them sought Jesus out), but why he was omitted on other occasions. John's Gospel makes more mention of Andrew than Mark does (see Jn. 1:40; 12:22), and so, if we want to know more of Andrew's attractive personality, we must learn it from John, not Mark. He seems to have been a less forceful character than his brother Peter, just as James seems to have been less forceful than John, to judge from the scantiness of reference to him. But all alike played their part in the purpose of God, and all alike were called by Jesus.

4. Perhaps this question of the four disciples as to the date of the coming judgment is an example of that somewhat unhealthy spiritual curiosity mentioned above. The chapter that follows is an example of the way in which Jesus at once translated all such abstract enquiries into the personal and moral realm. No theological problem can be considered in isolation, for it does not exist in isolation; it has immediate practical relevance to our present position, beliefs and conduct. Interest in God's ways which is purely intellectual becomes morbid in that it is unnatural and divorced from reality.

ii. The signs of the end (13:5-8)[1]

In reply, Jesus does indeed give to the disciples some signs of the end, although they are not signs that enable either them or us to give detailed chronological predictions. Nevertheless, some of them were precise enough to assure the survival of the Jerusalem church, if, according to tradition, it took warning and fled to Pella in Transjordan before the Roman ring of steel had tightened round the doomed city in AD 70.[2] So, as a sign of the times, Jesus gives the second warning, against false spiritual leaders, whether or no they call themselves by the actual name of Christ (*in my name*). Of course, there were literal fulfilments enough of this in the next century; Bar-Cochba at least claimed full messiahship. But in a wider sense and in a later age, to worship Christ with false beliefs about Him is to worship a false Christ, by whatever name we call Him; the disciples must not be led astray by this. Even before the close of the New Testament period, the wave of Gnostic heresy, with its false teaching about Christ, had struck the church, threatening to engulf it.

Broadly, then, a crop of false teachers will be one sign of the end, as will be a steady worsening of the political world situation. This introduces the third danger, and also the third warning; we must *not be alarmed* over international crises, as the non-Christian may be. The Christian's heart must not be *troubled* (see Jn. 14:1), for these troubles are only a necessary stage. All this is the beginning of the world's labour pains; the *telos, the end*, the goal and aim of history which is the final establishment of God's rule, is yet to come. Paul has a similar concept when he describes all creation as moaning in labour, waiting for God's consummation (Rom. 8:22). Paul apparently sees these *birth pangs* as a continuous, present, this-worldly experience, though aimed at one future point of time, an interpretation which may help in the understanding of this passage.

---

[1] The diligent have found seven distinct signs here, and traced a broad correspondence with Revelation 6 (Schweizer). This detail may however be somewhat artificial, while a general correspondence is only to be expected.

[2] This tradition is often challenged today, but without sufficient reason. Pesch (in Telford, IOM), now considers this apocalypse to be the very 'oracle' mentioned by Eusebius that led to the flight of the Christians to Pella, though he holds it to be post-dominical in nature.

8. If a local and temporary 'primary' fulfilment is to be sought, as distinct from a continuous or even final one, then the 'year of the four emperors' (AD 69), as the imperial throne at Rome changed hands with astonishing rapidity, while all the time the fortified cities of Galilee were falling, would fit well. In a wider sense, this is a continual picture of the present age of turmoil, in the midst of which the church must live and witness. It is to be noted that neither the 'primary' nor 'continuous' interpretation rules out a final eschatological fulfilment in addition. If Mark's original readers were situated largely in Rome, these references would be very meaningful and indeed encouraging.

iii. The beginning of the troubles (13:9–13)

The greatest danger is lest any Christian should be led *astray* (verses 5 and 22) or 'tripped up'[1] by the bitter persecution they will assuredly suffer for their faith: again, this would be a special word for a Roman church in the first century. At this time, as the disciples saw the mounting tide of hostility against their Master, they must have begun to understand what was to come, although the full force of persecution did not strike the church until the days of Acts (Acts 8:1). Each of these 'testings' cuts closer to the bone than the testing before it, for such is God's way of dealing with His children (Jb. 1:9 to 2:7). This last test is no exception; the persecution is now to be so bitter that it destroys the closest natural ties known to humans (verse 12). But even this must not make us stumble, for Jesus has warned us beforehand just so that this stumbling on our part may be avoided (13:23).

9. The mention of *councils* and *synagogues* must have struck a responsive note in early Christians, who remembered the bitter persecution of the church by Saul of Tarsus (Acts 8:1–3). It was doubly fitting that Paul, who had already unconsciously fulfilled the first half of the verse by his hostility, should also consciously

---

[1] This is the meaning of the Greek word *skandalizo*, used in the parallel passage in Mt. 24:9–10, translated by RSV as *fall away*. But, in Mark, *lead astray, planaō*, is the preferred word.

fulfil the second by his witness before men in authority, like Felix, Festus, Agrippa and perhaps even Caesar himself (2 Tim. 4:16, 17). It would however be absurd to think that this passage was written on the basis of Paul's career: it is too general for that. The Greek *hēgemonōn*, rulers, is a technical term in the New Testament, used of Roman officials ranging from provincial governors to Pontius Pilate, the lowly procurator (or prefect, in one inscription) of Judea. *Basileōn, kings,* covers all royal rulers from local petty tetrarch to emperor. Typically Marcan is the injunction given here to 'watch out' (Schweizer).

The wording *to all nations* does not convey the full meaning:[1] 'to all the non-Jewish peoples' would be better. Once again comes the axe-blow at Israel's position of 'most favoured nation': the worldwide proclamation is of primary importance to Mark (Schweizer), and here he finds its justification in the words of Jesus Himself. All nations must have the opportunity of hearing the good news of the kingdom.

11. *It is not you who speak, but the Holy Spirit.*[2] There are numerous instances of extempore Christian defence in Acts, although naturally none in Mark: the speech of Peter before the Sanhedrin is only one example among many (Acts 4:8ff.). But we may not trade on this, and put God to the test (Lk. 4:12). This promise is specifically given for those who are dragged unexpectedly into courts by their persecutors, not for those who have time to pray and prepare for some known Christian opportunity lying ahead.

12-13. Here, in outline, is the great biblical doctrine of *hypomonē*, sometimes called in theology 'the perseverance of the

---

[1]Though Cranfield so takes it, as indicating the *extent* of the preaching even if not the extent of the response. In a sense, it is Mark's version of the 'great commission', even if we reject 16:15 as being post-Marcan. But those like Pesch (quoted in Telford, IOM), may be right who see in it basically a warning against an early expectation of the end, rather than a charter for world evangelism.

[2]Marxsen: 'It is . . . not quite the persecuted who speak, rather, the preaching content is given to them by the Holy Spirit'. For the role of the Spirit in Mark, and the guarantee of the Spirit that Jesus is indeed God's emissary, see Weeden, in Telford. This is one of the few uses of the full phrase 'the *Holy* Spirit' in Mark (Anderson). Luke, in the parallel passage, does not speak of the Holy Spirit as supplying the words, but Christ Himself (Lk. 21:15); this

saints': the one *who endures to the end will be saved* (13). By *saved* cannot be meant merely 'will be rescued from physical death', for there has already been warning of possible *death* in verse 12, suffered in Christ's cause. The 'salvation' promised here must mean something deeper, reaching beyond the grave. There is therefore the same eschatological paradox as in Revelation 2:10, 'Be faithful unto death, and I will give you the crown of life'. The disciple, says Jesus, must hold fast right to the end in order to be saved: but, as Paul says, true Christians will in fact hold fast, because God will hold them fast (Rom. 14:4). Here is another biblical paradox which we do well to hold reverently. Its solution, like that of similar theological paradoxes, is to be found not, as with mathematical problems, at infinity, but at eternity, and in God. Matthew 10:22 gives this same saying of Jesus in another context; it was therefore not merely a casual utterance on one particular occasion, but represented an integral part of His teaching.

iv. The 'desolating sacrilege' (13:14–20)

Now comes the reference to *the desolating sacrilege* (14), better, if more loosely, to be paraphrased 'the idol that profanes'. As in all apocalyptic, particularly that produced in troubled times (as most apocalyptic naturally is), the wording was deliberately guarded, lest it fall into the wrong hands; the book of Revelation provides numerous instances of this. Daniel (9:27; 11:31; 12:11) shows the Old Testament background to the phrase. Initially, the word probably referred to the statue set up in the temple by Antiochus, so profaning it, and the sacrifice of swine's flesh on the altar. In this passage, it fairly certainly refers to the encirclement of Jerusalem by Roman armies (so Luke 21:20 understands it). The Roman 'eagles', the standards of the legions, were held by the Zealots to be sacrilegious 'abominations', being 'idols', and as such forbidden in the ten commandments. In AD 70, Roman standards, often bearing images of Caesar, stood on the site of the ruined temple. Later, of course, after the revolt of AD

---

is an illustration of how closely Christ and the Spirit were associated in the early church (Acts 16:7).

135, when a statue and temple of Zeus stood on the ruined site of the temple in Aelia Capitolina, as rebuilt Gentile Jerusalem was called, the horror was complete: for the orthodox Jew, the ultimate desolation had come.

The phrase *let the reader understand* cannot, by definition, be part of the original spoken saying of Jesus. Contrast the frequent 'he who has ears to hear, let him hear' (4:9, *etc.*), which by its form as well as by its rabbinic ring, must belong to the original spoken words of Jesus. But the words 'the reader' certainly suggest an editorial comment made in some early written collection, perhaps made by Mark himself. It was necessary to add some such explanatory phrase, for Mark is the most cryptic of the gospels, in saying *set up where it ought not to be*, in place of Matthew's blunt 'standing in the holy place', *i.e.* in the temple itself (Mt. 24:15). If the gospel is early, and written at Rome, this secrecy is understandable, particularly if the Jewish war is still under way.

These verses supply a good illustration of prophetic 'foreshortening' of history. Prophecy is basically proclamation or a 'forthtelling' of God's ways and mind, as we are constantly reminded by modern scholars. But it undoubtedly included in addition a foretelling of God's purposes, even if this is a stumbling-block to scientific antisupernaturalism today.[1] This foretelling is done in a 'two dimensional' manner, in that the perspective of time is usually either lacking or vague. This may well be because time has no independent existence outside our temporal order; but to argue this would take us into philosophy. This prophetic 'foreshortening' often passes over in silence, in the sequence of the several events, the vast stretches of time that separate them, and so joins closely events which are actually far apart.

Here God's immediate judgment on His people at one particular point in history is almost imperceptibly dovetailed into

[1]The re-emergence of prophecy in the days of Acts illustrates this aspect. While this New Testament 'prophecy' certainly included exhortation, perhaps as its main function (Acts 15:32), yet men like Agabus equally certainly foretold the future on occasion (Acts 11:28; 21:11), as apparently did other nameless prophets (Acts 20:23). Whether the gift of 'prophecy' in the Corinthian church (1 Cor. 12:10) included this futuristic aspect, we cannot say: and Christians are divided as to whether such a distinct gift is given today. Most modern 'prophets' seem to give general assurances of God's activity, rather than detailed predictions of definite events, but perhaps this was equally true of most New Testament prophets. Certainly, 'prophets' are most closely associated with 'teachers' (Acts 13:1), in lists of spiritual gifts and functions, which may give a key to understanding their task.

His universal judgment on all humanity at the last day. Since both are manifestations of God's continual ongoing judgment on human sin and rebellion, the whole makes sense. Here, then, in the first place are portrayed the devastations of the Roman armies. Here, too, is pictured the flight of the Jerusalem church to Pella, as the Roman legions purposely delayed their attack on Jerusalem, hoping to persuade this great stronghold to surrender voluntarily. It must indeed have seemed, in the final mopping-up operations of the war, as if the entire population of Palestine was to be extirpated; but God, *for the sake of the elect* (20), would cut short those days. Imperial Rome had greater interests now, in the form of the sudden scramble to establish the new Flavian dynasty at Rome: many of the troops would be hastily withdrawn. The Christian church would now see a new and deep meaning in the use of *whom he chose* (20), for the word could not now refer to Israel, coming as it does in the context announcing God's judgment on the nation. The infant church at Pella, in Transjordan, had survived: here is God's new chosen people, Jew and Gentile alike.

v. False Christs and false prophets (13:21–23)

False Christs and false prophets (22) will appear. This is really a return to the theme of verse 6 and the reference to *signs* may be drawn from Deuteronomy 13:1–3, with its solemn warnings against signs and wonders performed by misleading prophets. The primary reference may be to the numerous 'religions' and pseudo-messianic Jewish rebellions that both preceded and followed AD 70. But for the Christian church, the relevance here may equally well be to the many Jewish-Christian (especially Gnostic) heresies of the first century, although the application could be widened to cover all ages.[1]

22. *Signs and wonders.* This is a reminder that, as in the Old Testament, false prophets can perform *signs and wonders*, as well as true prophets (Ex. 7:11). It is important to realize this today,

---

[1] It is quite gratuitous to see here a reference to a supposed *theios anēr* ('divine man') Christology, as against a 'suffering Messiah' Christology. For the curious, the position is summarized by Weeden in IOM.

where there is a renewed interest in these manifestations. Miracles were undoubtedly performed by the apostles in Acts (see for example Acts 2:43). Paul lists them among the gifts of the Spirit, even if not at the top of the list (1 Cor. 12:10). In themselves, even if performed by true prophets, 'signs and wonders' are ambivalent. They are only 'signs' of the far greater working by God in Christ which we must accept by faith or not at all.

To lead astray, if possible, the elect. Once again, as in 20, we have a reference to 'the chosen ones', with a 'Johannine' reminder that to succeed in deceiving *the elect* would be a contradiction in terms (1 Jn. 2:26, 27). Equally 'Johannine' is the reminder in verse 23 that the Lord has warned His disciples in advance of these things (*cf.* Jn. 13:19). Mark has fewer 'Johannine' touches than either of the other synoptists; but enough remains even in matter-of-fact Mark to show that he is drawing upon a common 'bank' of tradition upon which John also drew.

vi. The coming of the Son of man (13:24-27)

Next comes a clear foretelling of the coming of *the Son of man* in a passage which is a veritable jigsaw of quotations from the apocalyptic books of the Old Testament, especially in verses 24 and 25. Verse 26 seems to mark the break, if there is a break, between the immediate judgment of God on His chosen people and His ultimate judgment on all creation. Political stirrings on a world scale are here described in terms of astronomical phenomena, a pattern derived particularly from the book of Isaiah (Is. 13:10; 24:23). This is typical of all eschatological usage and might refer just as much to toppling first-century Roman rulers as to a twentieth-century clash of 'north' and 'south', 'haves' and 'have nots'. But verse 26, with the clear imagery of the return of the Son of man to judgment (Dn. 7:13), can refer only to one event in history, the second coming of Christ. In view of Jesus' constant use of the title 'Son of man' as a title for Himself, His disciples cannot have failed to see that He referred to Himself here also, although they may well have failed to understand how such a thing could be, or indeed what it meant.[1]

[1]Some scholars maintain that this eschatological *Son of man*, seen here as coming in

27. In Daniel 7, the coming of the Son of man immediately follows the description of the sitting in judgment of the Ancient One, and initiates the establishment of an everlasting kingdom. Daniel 7:10 has reference to countless bands of heavenly ministrants, and so the reference to angelic 'gatherers' here in Mark, while owing something to other Old Testament passages, also fits the context of Daniel. In 27 comes the third Marcan reference in this passage to *his elect*, the 'chosen ones' (*cf.* verses 20 and 22). From the 'remnant' concept of the old covenant to the 'church' concept of the new covenant is only a short step, for it is a logical development: both are God's *elect*.

vii. The parable of the fig tree (13:28-29)

It is unnecessary to read into the parable of the fig tree in this context a reference to the subsequent earthly history of the Jewish nation. It is true that vine and fig are traditional symbols of God's people in the Old Testament, and that the fig tree cursed by Jesus (11:12-14) seems to have been an acted parable of contemporary Judaism. Nevertheless that does not prove that every biblical mention of the fig tree conceals a reference to Israel, or that we can predict the date of Christ's second coming from political events in Israel's life today, like the 'return' to Palestine. This saying of Jesus seems to be merely a general countryman's parable; compare the shrewd piece of weather-lore in Matthew 16:2, 3. When the trees burst into leaf, summer is coming – and very quickly in Palestine, as Schweizer notes. In the same way, says Jesus, these happenings will warn us that the second coming is at the very door (verse 29).

viii. The date of the coming (13:30-32)

In the midst of many details that are puzzling, two main

---

judgment, is quite different from the 'Son of man' as the title by which Jesus often described Himself (a usage which more extreme groups would deny). But if we accept the evidence of the gospel, it is clear that Jesus used this title of Himself, and He seems to have used it of Himself in at least three different senses. In the present passage, two of these usages appear side by side, so that, since nothing is said to distinguish them, they must both apply to the same person. To suggest anything else is to distort natural exegesis in favour of a theory, and to reject the plain evidence of Mark.

principles are clear. First, the Christian is to avoid unhealthy interest in the actual date, and secondly, we are to see the very uncertainty as to the date as a strong stimulant to ceaseless watchfulness. In other words, like every other Christian doctrine, that of the second coming has a moral and spiritual goal; we must be watchful, lest our Master, when He returns, finds us sleeping (36). As Schweizer says, every description of the end time is also an exhortation to the church.

30. *This generation* must surely be the generation of Jesus' earthly ministry, some of whom would indeed have lived to see the awful days of the siege of Jerusalem. But the generation of the ministry would not of course see Christ's second coming, so some have striven, rather unnaturally, to interpret *genea* as meaning 'people', and refer it to the whole Jewish nation, which will not pass away before that time. Undoubtedly, the delay in the second coming of the Lord (the *parousia*) was a puzzle to the early church, many of whom seem to have expected it in their lifetime, and were therefore saddened and troubled when, one by one, death carried them away before it (2 Pet. 3:4). It is therefore better to restrict the reference in *these things* to the temporal judgment of AD 70. But, in anticipating the Lord's return at any moment, the infant church was making no mistake, for every generation should continually be eagerly looking for and expecting the coming (2 Pet. 3:12). In the purpose of God, no event now stands between Christ's ascension and His second coming, and so it is eternally near.

31. *Heaven and earth will pass away*, presumably in the shaking of all things, which is to introduce the second coming: the reference may be to Isaiah 34:4. *Pass away* is probably the link between this and the previous saying. The emphasis here, however, is not on the apocalyptic prediction, but on the permanence of Christ's words (Anderson): that means that they are equated with the words of Yahweh in the Old Testament (Is. 40:8). Revelation 21:1 may be taking up this saying of Jesus: the first heaven and earth (*i.e.* to the Hebrew, the totality of all things) will go, so that the new may come.

32. *No one knows*; this is a wise warning that, if we calculate to our own satisfaction the date in time upon which Christ will return, we shall certainly be mistaken. This should strike caution into the most daring modern exponent of prophecy. At a deeper level, it teaches that there are certain things hidden even from the Son, in the omniscience of the Father. Compare the statement of Jesus to James and John (10:40), that to sit on His right and left was not in His power to grant. This is the only place in Mark where Jesus refers to Himself absolutely as 'the Son' (Anderson). It has been claimed by some that a familiar later title for Jesus is here being used by the evangelist: but such an 'absolute' usage is not impossible on the lips of Jesus Himself in the light of the use of *my son* in the parable of the tenant farmers (12:6), clearly referring to Jesus.

ix. The end of the discourse (13:33–37)

The final verses underline the moral and spiritual incentive provided by the doctrine of the second coming. Much of this brief parable appears to be 'back-cloth' in the particular context, so that there is no need to press the details. Here, it is the watchfulness of the door-keeper that is the main point of the parable; we must stay awake and on duty, a constant emphasis in Mark.

34. *The doorkeeper*: some feel that *the doorkeeper* is only part of the 'scenery' of the parable, and therefore requires no special exegesis. But there is some evidence to show that the simile of the 'porter' was used by the early church for those engaged in Christian ministry. The master of the house, when he arrives after his long absence, must not find us sleeping, but doing our duty and carrying out the particular task which he has left to us. True, the doorkeeper must keep special watch, because that is his special task (Ezk. 3:17), and perhaps therefore this has special relevance to those in pastoral positions who are 'watchmen' in the church.

37. *I say to all: Watch*: this verse nevertheless shows us that the command is generalized, not directed only at the Christian ministry or indeed at any group or class within the church. Further, it may be a clear indication that Jesus Himself did not necessarily expect that His second coming would be in the near future, as many modern expositors assume rather than prove. The whole tenor of this parable suggests a long absence. From this solemn last word, *watch* (Greek *grēgoreite*, 'be wakeful'), comes the favourite later 'Gregory' used as a Christian name.

VI. THE PASSION NARRATIVE (14:1 – 15:47)[1]

A. THE LAST SUPPER (14:1–25)

i. The death of Jesus is decided (14:1–2)

With chapters 14 and 15 we come directly to the passion story in Mark, although both Matthew and Luke record more parables first. This may be taken as showing that the teaching of Jesus in and around the temple was both more detailed and more extensive in those final days than we should gather from Mark alone. As usual, Mark uses 'shorthand', omitting what is not essential to his purpose. Also, as on other occasions (*e.g.* the cursing of the fig tree), he 'sandwiches' the story of the anointing at Bethany between his first mention of the plot against Jesus, and its carrying out (Anderson). This is not merely for dramatic suspense, although the love shown at Bethany will highlight the hatred at Jerusalem: the anointing at Bethany is, in a sense, an explanation of the death of Jesus.

Verse 1 introduces the most definite decision so far made by the religious leaders. Jesus must die, and as soon as possible; all that the chief priests now lack is an opportunity. Even their objection to this judicial murder at Passover time is not a moral hesitation because of its incompatibility with the nature of a religious ceremony, but purely prudential, lest a riot should

---

[1] Although, as mentioned in the introduction, most scholars (at least until recently) considered the passion narrative as a 'block' of material that had come down to Mark, and was embodied in his gospel, it is certainly true that 'virtually all the major Marcan themes converge in 14–16' (Kelber, quoted in Telford, IOM). But this would not necessarily show that Mark constructed the passion story: it may only show that he constructed his whole gospel along the themes already present in the passion story.

break out among the excitable Passover crowds. The exact chronology of the crucifixion has long been in dispute, and the discussion has been revived in recent years. At least the crucifixion clearly took place in the general period of Passover, whether or no it corresponded in time to the actual moment when the Passover lamb was being killed.[1]

ii. The anointing at Bethany (14:3-9)

It has been seen in 11:11 that Jesus spent each night among unnamed friends in *Bethany*. John 12:1-8 makes it probable that this was the home of Eliezer (of which 'Lazarus' is the shortened Aramaic form), Miriam ('Mary') and Martha. But who then is *Simon the leper*, whose household it is, according to both Matthew and Mark? We may dismiss the suggestion that he was only a former owner of the house, giving his name to the building even when it passed to subsequent owners. Also it seems unlikely that Jesus was 'eating out' in another house that night. It may well be that the father of the house, though still alive, was a leper, and that control of his household had therefore passed, for all practical purposes, to his children. So Uzziah lived in splendid isolation in the basement of his palace, while his son Jotham ruled in his stead (2 Ch. 26:21).[2]

To equate this anointing at Bethany with that anointing which is described in Luke 7:36-50 raises at least as many problems as it solves: for one thing, the lesson drawn from the act is completely different, apart altogether from the timing. It is best, as in the case of several of the miracles of Jesus, to assume that we have separate accounts of different, though similar, incidents here. Schweizer points out how irregular the woman's act was:

[1]So John undoubtedly seems to take it, from his careful dating. Whether or not sectarian Judaism, such as the Essene community at Qumran, observed Passover on a different date, following a different calendar, it is most unlikely that Jesus and His disciples did. Because the Passover was set by the moon, a wide divergence would seem to be impossible, although conceivably a day or two either side would be possible.
[2]Minear sees spiritual significance in the fact that Jesus stayed in the home of the ritually unclean leper, not of the clean. But, although Jesus certainly was willing to touch lepers, and so incur defilement (1:41), this seems over-exegesis here. Whoever he was, Simon the leper must have been well known to the early disciples, or he would have been more closely identified (Anderson). Was he perhaps a leper who had been healed by Jesus? If so, there is no reference to the fact in the gospel narrative, although of course this does not disprove it.

but, if she was a member of the household, it was explicable. John is quite clear that the woman involved was Mary, although Mark may possibly have been ignorant of this. Mark very rarely records names in any case.

4–5. *There were some*: other evangelists (Mt. 26:8; Jn. 12:4) are more specific than Mark is here, naming those who objected to the wastefulness of the woman's act of devotion as being the disciples, among whom John mentions Judas specifically. That Mark cannot have been ignorant of this is shown by the fact that he moves straight from this incident to the offer by Judas to the temple authorites to betray his master (verses 10–11). Judas obviously thought that the attitude of Jesus to money was quite inconsistent and unrealistic. First had come the appraisal of the widow's gift (12:43), and now came the acceptance of the sacrifice of the alabaster jar of ointment: it did not make sense.

Yet the attitude of Jesus both to this costly gift and to the widow's slender gift was fundamentally the same. He regarded both gifts as priceless, but accepted such giving, whether directly to God or indirectly through Him, as right and natural. This was a strange reversal of earthly values; and although Mark does not record either that Judas was the apostolic treasurer or that he was dishonest (Jn. 12:6), it is understandable that on this basis, Judas felt misgivings. The world despised the widow's mite as too small, while it criticized the anointing of Bethany as wasteful, exhibitionist and unrealistic. What the disciples said about the value of the ointment and the need of the poor was perfectly true, but Jesus looks for uncalculating devotion to Himself rather than fine wisdom and balanced judgment in giving. The Lord, as Paul says, loves a cheerful giver, not a carefully calculating one (2 Cor. 9:7). A year's wages were involved here (Anderson), however: it was no small sum to be written off. Perhaps the poverty of the disciples increased their indignation at what to them was a senseless waste of good money.

6. Their sharp criticism must have stung the woman like a whip-lash. Mark uses in verse 5 the verb *enebrimōnto* (they 'reproached her'), which philologically means 'snorted at her', but in emotional content comes closer to modern English 'glo-wered at her'. Jesus saw how troubled she was: she must have wondered whether after all, she had made a foolish mistake. Many of those similarly criticized for their own self-offering for Christ's service know a similar qualm: and to them as well as to her comes the word of comfort. Ultimately Jesus looks, not at the human wisdom of our acts, but at the love to Him which prompts them. Note that He does not commend her for practical wisdom, though He is quick in her defence against the taunts of the worldly-wise.

7. Here is the Christian scale of priorities, the ability to choose out of many pressing needs that which it is God's will that we should seek to meet at one particular moment. We cannot in ourselves meet all the world's needs, nor indeed is it God's will that we personally should. This knowledge brings the tranquil-lity that characterized Jesus amid His manifold activity. Nervous strain is, after all, only a symptom of lack of faith in God, for it springs from the belief that nothing will be done by God unless we do it ourselves. The biblical picture is very different: one plants, another waters, but it is God who gives the increase (1 Cor. 3:6). The reference to the continual presence of the poor, in verse 7, is a quotation from Deuteronomy 15:11. It does not of course mean that we should accept poverty as an inevitable fact, and therefore do nothing to try to abolish it, for the whole Law is aimed at doing that. It is simply a practical recognition that, whatever we do, in this fallen world, there will always be some in need, whom we may and should help, as Deuteronomy also points out.

8–9. This does not necessarily mean that she had plumbed the whole secret of the coming death of Jesus, although already she may have heard some saying that had solemnized her. Jesus may have meant that, at His burial, loving hands would lavish costly spices on Him, as Mary had done; and if it was not waste then, it was not waste now. Both at the beginning and end of the life of Jesus, costly treasures were lavished on Him (Mt. 2:11): no doubt some thought that both gifts alike were wasted.

iii. The betrayal by Judas (14:10–11)

With that, *Judas*, or 'Judah' (we often forget the noble Old Testament associations of his name), went to the priests, determined to betray Jesus. The Bible has no hint of the view, popular in some quarters today, that Judas merely wanted to force the hand of Jesus, to make Him exhibit His divine power, if He were unwilling to do it unprompted. The mention of a promised sum of money in verse 11 makes it clear that Judas was motivated by sheer love of money: he had apparently decided that there would soon be no more money to be gained by following Jesus, if Jesus continued to encourage 'wastefulness' like that of Mary's. From that moment Judas, too, like the religious leaders, only sought an opportunity to betray Him (*cf.* verse 1). The worldly-wise priests must have nodded their heads, confirmed in their beliefs; even among the disciples of this other-worldly Galilean, money talked loudly. If the name 'Iscariot' is indeed derived from the Aramaic *sheqarya*, 'deceiver' (see Anderson), it was peculiarly appropriate, as we think of this treachery. It is striking that Levi, the converted tax collector, was not tempted by money, while Judas was: perhaps Levi had learned the emptiness of wealth long before, when he left it to follow Jesus.

iv. The owner of the upper room (14:12–16)

The story of the finding of the upper room bears many resemblances to the finding of the donkey used at the triumphal entry. Jesus must have had many unknown disciples or friends, upon whom He could rely at such moments to render unquestioning service. This in itself should be an encouragement to those with small or prosaic gifts; the Lord has need of them, too (11:3). We have only one record in the whole gospel story of the use by Jesus of either donkey or room; but that one use was strategic, essential at the moment to God's whole plan.

12. The plain reading of the text of Mark here would suggest that this was the very day on the evening of which the Passover was killed and eaten, but the question is a difficult one,

especially in view of the Johannine evidence.[1] In either case, both the last supper and the crucifixion were in the general context of Passover, and that is the only important point theologically, whether or not the last supper was a Passover meal.

13. Jesus here shows a combination of supernatural knowledge and practical preparation, as in the events surrounding the triumphal entry. In view of the fact that the upper room of verse 15 was ready for them, it suggests that Jesus had already made some prior arrangements to keep Passover at the home of this resident of Jerusalem. This was apparently a common practice of country pilgrims. But it needed supernatural foreknowledge, again of the kind manifested by Samuel and other prophets (1 Sa. 10:2-6), to tell His disciples of the signs that would lead them to the right house. Perhaps, even when Mark was writing, it was still unsafe or unwise to divulge the householder's name; it must have surely been known to him, if the writer was indeed John Mark with his Jerusalem connections. It is over-exegesis to see, in the sign of a man doing what was normally a woman's task (water-carrying), the mark of a disciple, or to see in the earthen 'jar' of water, rather than a 'leather skin', another 'sign' (Anderson). Jars were simply larger domestic containers than skins. In any case, the man was only a servant, the sign and the guide to the right home. It was with *the householder* that the disciples had to deal, and whether the servant was a disciple of Jesus or not, the master certainly must have been.

14-15. The very simplicity of the statement, *the teacher says* (Greek *didaskalos*, 'teacher', *i.e.* 'rabbi'), shows that Jesus was too well known to the man to need further identification, and that His disciples were probably known by sight to him. It is just possible that this was in fact the home of John Mark in Jerusalem, for later Christian tradition held that the last supper

[1]The best recent summary of evidence is in Cranfield, but the question cannot be said to have been solved. John, as often, seems to be deliberately writing, probably at a later date, to correct an unconscious misunderstanding of the earlier accounts. This is the only passage in Mark where the supper seems linked with the Passover, but it cannot be said to be certainly equated.

took place there. That would then, by the usual rule of early anonymity, account for the namelessness of the householder in the Marcan account. See Acts 12:12 for later use of this house by the disciples as a place of meeting; but as the house is there named from Mary, we must then assume that John Mark's father, presumably *the householder*, was dead by the date of Acts. The Passover, in origin a household festival (Ex. 12:1-12), at least since Josiah's reign (2 Ki. 23:23), must be kept within Jerusalem itself, to allow for the slaughter of the Passover lamb within the temple precincts. By New Testament times it was held within strictly defined city limits; it could not be observed, for instance, in Bethany, which would otherwise have seemed an obvious choice, with its friendly household.

16. As in the case of the tethered donkey, one can almost hear the wonder of the disciples, in the wording of this verse; *they found it as he had told them.* But such divine provision did not absolve them from strictly practical duties such as preparing the lamb, the bitter herbs and the wine, that were needed for the meal, if it was Passover. There is no contradiction therefore between the first half and the second half of this verse: Jesus works in 'natural' and 'supernatural' ways alike, at His sovereign will.

v. The prophecy of the betrayal (14:17-21)

All the gospels show the knowledge of Jesus that one of the twelve would betray Him; the quotation in verse 18 of Psalm 41:9 makes plain some of the agony which this created in His heart. As so often, if we note the Old Testament Scriptures either quoted or paraphrased by Jesus, we can see by what biblical types and analogies He understood His own experience, and thus we, in our turn, can comprehend it more deeply.

18-20. *One of you.* Mark has already prepared us for the coming treachery of Judas (10), but the reference to the betrayer here is general, not specific (verse 18). Even if Jesus knew who His betrayer was, His disciples did not: it is interesting that they seem to have had no suspicion as yet that it was Judas, or they would not have asked the question in verse 19. In Mark's account, Jesus does not further identify His betrayer: He merely reiterates the warning, making the deed more awful by emphasizing the closeness of the fellowship (verse 20). If this was indeed an actual Passover meal, the *dipping bread in the same dish with me* may even be a reference to the dipping of either bread or meat (so Lagrange) in the 'bitter sauce' that was a feature of the Passover meal. Does it refer to the 'morsel' of John 13:26?

21. *The Son of man goes.* Here again is a paradox. The Son of man will go, betrayed by a close friend, in fulfilment of prophetic Scripture; and yet His false follower is fully culpable for the act and cannot escape individual responsibility for what he does. Such an enigma cannot be resolved in human terms, but that does not mean that it cannot be solved at a higher level. But disciples are not necessarily called to the solution of this theological problem: instead they are called to the solemn heart searching of verse 19, 'Is it I?' (NIV 'Surely not I?'). This is the 'paraenetic' or 'pastoral' approach so typical of Mark's Gospel that it is hard to believe that it is not intentional: see Tannehill in IOM, approaching the question from the angle of literary criticism. Minear well points out that all of this incident is an illustration of Romans 5:8, 'while we were still sinners, Christ died for us', for it was for disciples as weak and sinful as this (18–21) that Jesus instituted that last supper.

vi. The Lord's Supper (14:22–25)

Whether or no the Lord's Supper was an actual Passover meal we cannot be sure; that depends on the exact time of the crucifixion. But even if the true Passover was taking place at the time when Jesus was hanging upon the cross, and the Lord's Supper was therefore only a *qiddūsh*, a lengthened 'grace' before the ordinary meal of a religious fraternity, the thought of Passover would still have been prominent in the minds of the disciples.[1] Verses 12 to 14, however, seem to make clear that in Mark's mind this was an actual Passover meal.

[1]Cranfield denies the possibility of a *qiddūsh* in these circumstances, but the point seems debatable.

22. *This is my body.* See Anderson for a reminder that Aramaic has no word for *is*: there is no thought therefore of material identity of *body* and *bread*.[1] What then would the meaning of the words of institution have been for the disciples? Even if they failed to understand them at the time, they certainly remembered them and reproduced them later. If they pondered them at all, they must surely have seen a reference to the eating of 'the Passover', especially if the occasion was an actual Passover meal. If it was, it is interesting to note that Jesus did not use the flesh of the actual lamb or kid to symbolize His body, but only the broken bread. If it was not a Passover, then of course there would have been no lamb, but merely bread and wine throughout, and the question would not have risen. It is only in John's Gospel that Jesus is described as 'the Lamb of God' (Jn. 1:29), although 'Christ our Passover' is a fully Pauline phrase (1 Cor. 5:7), familiar to the church later. (RSV, correctly, has paschal lamb).

In a sense, the taking, blessing and breaking of the bread is a deliberate recalling of the usual action of Jesus at the miracles of feeding (6:41; 8:6); but it is also a picture of His taking common human flesh, blessing it and allowing it to be 'broken' for mankind. To Belo, it is primarily a picture of Christ's (and therefore the Christian's) concern for the hungry of the world: but this, while true, by no means exhausts the meaning, missing, as it does, the deeper significance.

23. If this was a Passover meal, then the breaking of the unleavened biscuits (the *matzōth* of Exodus 12:8), is an integral part of the Passover service, although the symbolism of the breaking is unexplained, in modern rites at least. The drinking of the wine is an equally integral part, although the two actions are not directly related, as they are here. Nowadays, four times during the service a cup of wine must be drunk, and three times bread must be broken, so it would be idle to try to equate the actions of Jesus with any particular one of these occasions. In

---

[1]See also Anderson and Cranfield for the possibility that the word used by Jesus in the original Aramaic was not *bisri*, 'flesh', but *gūphi*, 'body', in the sense of 'self': Jesus is giving Himself for the life of the world. This is interesting and may be true, but we must deal with the Greek before us where, although all texts read *sōma*, 'body', not *sarx*, 'flesh' (in contrast to Jn. 6:51), yet *sōma* does not have this extended sense of Greek.

view of the singing of the *Hallēl* immediately afterwards (verse 26), it would seem to have been an occasion towards the end of the meal, but we know too little of first-century Jewish liturgical practices to be dogmatic. The meaning of the action of Jesus would have been unaffected by its position in any case.

24. *My blood.* The wine stands for the shed *blood* of Jesus, which is described here as 'covenant blood', that is blood inaugurating a solemn agreement between God and people as that at Sinai did (Ex. 24:8). Whether or not *new* should be read here, as an adjective qualifying 'covenant', is a question of little importance, for while this covenant is parallel to that inaugurated by Moses, it is obviously not the same covenant. Therefore, whether or not the word 'new' belongs here texually, it certainly belongs theologically. This 'new covenant' was a familiar prophetic concept in Old Testament times (Je. 31:31; the 'new heart' and 'spirit' of Ezk. 37:26). 'Covenant blood' is already a slightly different concept from 'passover blood', so here again there is a creative fusion of ideas.

The wording *for many* is a direct link with the interpretation of the Messiah's work and office in terms of Isaiah 53:12, in spite of Nineham's view that this is only a Semitic commonplace. But Nineham is right in emphasizing that 'many' in Hebrew is 'inclusive', not 'exclusive' and therefore virtually equivalent to 'all' in English.

Christ's death is here seen in terms of the Passover; it is seen as the inauguration of a new covenant; and it is seen as a sacrifice, presumably a sin offering (Is. 53:10). All three are distinct, though all three are sealed by bloodshed; but, while it may be academically possible to isolate one concept from another for the purpose of study, yet to gain a clear picture of the work of Christ, we must combine all three into one.

25. This is the eschatological, the forward-looking, emphasis in the Lord's Supper. There is no Lord's Supper in heaven, for there it is 'fulfilled' in the marriage-feast of the Lamb (Rev. 19:9), the messianic banquet, to use Jewish terminology familiar from the parables (Mt. 22:2). In modern Judaism, even the Passover itself has been set in an eschatological context, though it has largely become a temporal and material eschatology. It is hard, however, to see how the physical history of the nation of Israel has any relevance here: the consummation of the kingdom of God lies in eternity, not in time.

B. THE AGONY IN GETHSEMANE (14:26-42)

i. *The road to Gethsemane (14:26-31)*

At the end of the meal, the customary *hymn*, the *Hallēl*, or closing section of the Psalter, was sung, and the group went out, but this time not to Bethany. This was presumably because of the lateness of the hour, and because they wanted to remain near Jerusalem itself, over the actual festival season. Instead, they camped for the night among the trees of the Mount of Olives, as doubtless other pilgrims did also. Now the denial by Peter is prophesied, and the universal flight of the disciples, just as the betrayal had already been foretold: this conversation may well have taken place on the walk from the city to Gethsemane. This, says Schweizer, shows that God is still sovereign, even in this defection: all is foreknown, and in fulfilment of Scripture.

27-28. Jesus here used another quotation from Zechariah to illustrate the coming dispersal of His disciples, consequent on His death (Zc. 13:7), as well as their immediate flight from Him in the garden. He saw this scattering, not as a result of persecution, but owing to a 'stumbling' on their part. Their faith will be staggered by all that happens to Him, in spite of all His previous warnings. But this same chapter of Zechariah ends in a promise of mercy to the tested remnant; and so here, in verse 28, Jesus ends with yet another prediction of His resurrection, and a promise of a reunion in familiar Galilee. This promise in 16:7, will be taken up in the words of the angel to the women, after the resurrection.[1]

---

[1] There are so few resurrection appearances recorded in the other gospels as having taken place in Galilee (although see Mt. 28:16), that this must be a genuine tradition. No-one would ever have invented it after the event, since most of the recorded resurrection appearances were in or near Jerusalem. But it is a mistake to spiritualize 'Galilee' here, or to see the promise as referring to the spiritual presence of Christ in the hearts of His disciples,

29. *I will not.* All the gospels show the same picture of impetuous Peter, full of false pride in his own fancied strength, and scorn for the weakness of the others; he had no difficulty in believing the words of Jesus to be true of his fellow disciples. But it is well to remember that all the other disciples protested their own strength too (31); they too were proud and self-confident. Peter may have distinguished himself from the others, but he has not succeeded in isolating himself.

30. As Peter had distinguished himself by boasting, so he was to distinguish himself by failure, so that others, as well as he, might learn distrust of natural strength. As often, Jesus adds a prophetic 'sign', for the cock crowing is more than a note of time, although it certainly includes that. This sign was doubtless given so that Peter might be reminded of the forewarning when the incident occurred (see verse 72). Only Mark records the second cock-crow (Schweizer). 'Second cock-crow' is a definite point of time in the early morning, very distinct from the sleepy first cock-crow at midnight; but whether Jesus meant this, or just two cock-crows in quick succession, it is idle to speculate. Cocks and hens were not supposed to be kept in Jerusalem, according to Schweizer: if so, the regulation was obviously in vain.

31. Peter's guilt is certainly not minimized here, but Mark makes plain that it was a guilt shared by all the apostolic band: *they all said the same.* Peter was here, as always, only the representative disciple, the mouthpiece of the apostolic band, possibly because of his very impulsiveness and outspokenness. So it had been at Caesarea Philippi (8:29), that day when the blinding discovery made him the 'proto-Christian', and, in a sense, a 'representative' of the whole body (Matthew 16:17–18). This verse is a reminder that he is a representative of them in all their weaknesses as well as in their spiritual strengths. The walk down from the Old City to the Garden of Gethsemane would take some twenty minutes, as those will know who have joined

---

or even to His expected *parousia* or 'second coming' in Galilee, as various editors do. Galilee is not equivalent in Mark to 'Gentile Christianity', though many Gentile Christians may well have lived there later.

the procession in Jerusalem which still winds its way down through the darkened streets each Thursday night. It is during this time that we must imagine the above conversations taking place.

ii. The agony in the garden (14:32-42)

They now move on into the Garden of Gethsemane, where Jesus, as it were, surrounds Himself with two rings of supporters, to stand with Him in His hour of need. At the outside, near the garden entrance, were the eight, for Judas is no longer with them; further in, the chosen three remained closest to Him. To the three Jesus revealed something of the inner struggle that was His (verse 33). This is one of the points of His life at which we can see how real must have been the temptation in the wilderness (1:12-13), and why He rebuked Peter so sternly at the suggested avoidance of the cross (8:33). In the next verse (34) Jesus shows how deep and real is His anguish at this time: He is not portrayed as a Stoic who cannot suffer (Schweizer). Pagan philosophers may mock at this: to the Christian, it is the glory of the cross. The suffering of Christ is not 'docetic' and make-believe: it is real and costly.

34. The quotation from Psalm 42:5 or 11 is doubly suitable. This Psalm not only expresses the soul's deep longing for God, but also contains in the last clause of each of these two verses an affirmation of faith, and a promise of God's deliverance. So at the very moment when Jesus seems most perplexed, He is yet most conscious by faith of God's ultimate vindication.

Watch. The verb used here, *grēgoreite*, may have reminded His disciples of the parable of the doorkeeper, told them just before (13:34-37), for the task of the doorkeeper was to watch, and Jesus has rounded off the parable by giving this as a general injunction to all His disciples. Minear reminds us that the Passover was to be 'a night of watching' (Ex. 12:42): this cannot have been far from their thoughts at this season of the Jewish liturgical year.

35. Standing was the usual posture for prayer in ancient times, with the hands lifted heavenwards (11:25); prostration in prayer was indicative of extreme spiritual anguish (*e.g.* Nu. 16:22). *If it were possible*: here again is a divine paradox, seen in the repetition of the adjective *dynaton, possible*, in the next verse. All things are by definition possible to divine omnipotence; but it was not possible for Jesus to be the Christ, and yet to avoid drinking the cup. To do this would have been only a verbal, not an actual, possibility, for it would have been a contradiction in terms. So, in 15:32 the priests will challenge Jesus to come down from the cross, if He is the Christ. But, if He had come down from the cross, He could not have been the Christ, for the Christ, by definition, must suffer.

36. Only Mark here has preserved the intimate *Abba, Father,*[1] from the original Aramaic prayer. Romans 8:15 and Galatians 4:6 show the quasi-liturgical use of this linguistic survival in the early church. As in the saying to James and John (10:38), *cup* is here a symbol of suffering, not of joy, although the two meanings are blended in the words of institution at the Last Supper. But the thought may well go far deeper than a mere general symbolism of suffering, to the particular Old Testament concept of the cup of the wrath of God, designed for the foes of God (Ps. 75:8), which Jesus was to drink at Calvary. The last clause, *not what I will, but what thou wilt*, is a summary of the earthly life of obedience of the Christ; such obedience was only perfected when it was 'unto death' (Phil. 2:8). This is not a helpless victim of fate decreed, but One who struggles towards God's will (Anderson).

But what caused Him such anguish? To speak of a natural human shrinking from betrayal, mockery, scourging and death, all heightened by full foreknowledge, is too shallow an answer, while these no doubt were factors. All of these Jesus had not only foreseen, but also foretold to His disciples (*e.g.* in 10:32–34). During all of His earthly life He had been conscious of a steadily

[1]It is a mistake, however, with some editors, to see this admittedly colloquial term as a 'nursery-word'; what other Aramaic word for 'Father' could Jesus have used? By this date, 'emphatic' forms like *Abbā* were used very freely in Aramaic, with little appreciable difference in meaning from 'absolute' forms like *Aḇ*. See also the comment on 5:41. Nevertheless, it does seem to be true that orthodox Jews of the first century avoided the familiar term in prayer (Anderson), as many old-fashioned Christians still avoid calling God 'You' in prayer today.

mounting pressure, from which He was not finally released until the cry of triumph from the cross (15:37–39). Jesus had already used the parallel pictures of baptism and the cup to describe this inner constraint (Lk. 12:50), as He had done in the conversation with James and John (10:38). We must seek the reason for His anguish in 15:34 in the experience of separation from God which was to come. This was the 'cup', this was the 'baptism', which He would have avoided if it had been at all possible.

37–39. Jesus' words of rebuke, though applicable to all, are addressed directly to Peter, using *Simon*, his old 'natural' name (1:16), not 'Cephas' (Peter) his name 'in grace' (3:16). But they are not merely a rebuke: they are also to prepare Him for the coming test in the judgment hall. But Peter and his fellows were warned in vain, for they failed to take the only steps which could have saved them from falling into temptation: earnest prayer and continual watchfulness (verse 38). This again is not arbitrary; such prayer is, at one and the same time, a confession of the weakness of our *flesh* (38) and a showing forth of the readiness of our *spirit* (38), joined with a realization of the power of God to whom we pray. So prayer is one expression of Christian faith, as obedience is another. Peter's rebuke from Jesus is that he had not the strength to 'watch' even for one hour. The Greek verb *ouk ischusas, could not,* is the same verb as that used in 9:18 to describe the powerlessness of the disciples to heal the boy at the foot of the mountain of transfiguration, again on that occasion, as Jesus said, a powerlessness brought about by prayerlessness (9:29).

40. The language is again reminiscent of that used to describe the three at the mountain of transfiguration (9:6), where even talkative Peter was finally lost for words. Here in the garden, the shamefaced disciples were utterly abashed, and could find no words to say.

41–42. The mention of a third return of Jesus to the disciples, gives the idea of finality and completeness; so there is a fitting finality in the words of His disciples, *Are you still sleeping?*[1] Their

[1]Unless, with AV, we should take it as a command, 'sleep on now'. The next word, *apechei*, is a puzzle; RSV says *It is enough!* This fits the context, but for other suggestions, less convincing, see Schweizer.

failure has been complete, the crisis is over, and the betrayer is near. In the words of Jesus here there is no hint of bitterness, but there is a world of sadness. By *the hour has come*, Jesus means, not only that God's time has come, but that the matter over which He had prayed has been settled (Lane), and God's sovereign will has been revealed.

C. JESUS IS TAKEN PRISONER (14:43-52)

43. *Judas came.* Judas has not been specifically mentioned since verse 10, but verse 20 shows that he had still been present at the supper. We must assume that he had slipped away from the supper earlier that evening, presumably as soon as he had found out what place in Jerusalem was to be the camping place for that night. He had then waited until the group of disciples might be safely assumed to be asleep; and the verses above show how right Judas was in this judgment. He was not lacking in worldly wisdom; it was indeed through worldly wisdom as well as avarice that Judas fell (11). So, too, he had brought a well-armed company of temple police and younger priests, with *swords and clubs* respectively (not, with Anderson, a city mob of 'toughs'), prepared for resistence to the arrest. Judas knew his impetuous fellow disciples; and Peter's violent reaction showed how wise Judas had been in this also (47), although Mark does not actually give Peter's name as the attacker.

44-45. Judas had even made the identification of Jesus by the temple police certain amid the uncertainties and half light of the garden with its olive trees. Jesus was to be marked out to the authorities by the usual *kiss* of peace and the salutation of *Master*, 'Rabbi', both natural signs between disciple and master. Here is the proof of utter moral blindness. Judas did not see the condemnation that would be eternally his for using the very signs of affection as a means of betrayal. His sole concern was that the arrest should go smoothly; and again, his wisdom and efficiency were the snares that caught him. The miracle is that Judas could live so close to Jesus for three years, and yet could steel his heart against Him like this.

46. *Seized him.* As usual, Mark merely reports the blunt facts. The other gospels give a fuller account of what happened in the garden. Cranfield is right in saying that the traitor's kiss had so imprinted itself on their memory that even Mark recounts it in detail, in contrast with his 'scrappy' description of other events. But it is typical of Mark to give only the 'bare bones' in a narrative: he is moving forward to the cross as quickly as possible.

47. *Drew his sword.* The disciple involved is anonymous here. But which of the disciples carried the 'two swords' mentioned in Luke 22:38? Peter, the two 'sons of thunder', and Simon the Zealot, would seem to be likely candidates: the disciple must therefore be one of them. Only John 18:10 finds it safe to mention Peter's name,[1] writing possibly after Peter's death (Jn. 21:19); he also is the only evangelist to mention the name of the servant concerned (Jn. 18:10). In a gospel as early as Mark, such a circumstantial detail might have been dangerous. Mark does not mention either the healing of the ear or the rebuke to Peter, though he records the rebuke of Jesus to the armed arrest (48). To meet force with force was not the way of Jesus, even if it seemed natural both to the high priests and to Peter.[2]

48–49. This deserved rebuke must have stung the priests. They had not arrested Him by day in the temple; not for fear of His disciples, but for fear of the crowds, unblinded by the prejudice that theological learning had brought, who would have protested against such an outrage (12:12).

Such a violent arrest of the Messiah was a fulfilment of many prophetic *scriptures* (49). The passage especially in mind here may be that quoted in Luke 22:37, 'and he was reckoned with the transgressors'; especially since it is also taken from Isaiah

---

[1]Lagrange, quoted by Cranfield, seems right in maintaining that Mark's *heis tis, one of them*, 'a certain man', implies that, although Mark knows well who struck the blow, yet, for reasons of his own, he will not give the name.

[2]Although Mark does not mention the saying at this point, recording in Mt. 26:52, 'All who take the sword will perish by the sword', he is equally clear that Jesus had rejected the path of physical violence as a way of establishing His kingdom. Jesus was no violent 'Zealot', as even left-wing commentators like Belo freely admit. If He rejected even angelic help to rescue Him from His enemies (Mt. 26:53), why should He use earthly force to do it?

53:12. Those who have seen secret police at work in any part of the world will understand this passage well. Arrests are usually made at night, for two reasons; the victims are liable to be confused and offer less resistance, and the neighbours are not likely to gather and protest. Life changes little over the millennia.

50. *Fled.* So was fulfilled the prophecy of Jesus about their 'stumbling' (14:27, 'fall away'). If they had accepted God's way without stumbling, they might have grieved, but they would have stood faithfully by their Lord as He was arrested. But to do this is not 'natural', and that is why Christ's way always makes natural humanity stumble (1 Cor. 2:14). Peter was probably representative of all the disciples, and the stumbling block greater, in that he had always advocated the natural path for Christ (8:32). To be 'offended in Christ', to 'stumble at him', in biblical language, means to be utterly staggered by His ways, to lack the spiritual key that alone opens our understanding, something that God's Spirit alone can bring (1 Cor. 2:10–16).

51–52. The Greek word *neaniskos, young man,* might denote one in late adolescence, in his teens. This man is often taken as being John Mark of Jerusalem, in whose family home the last supper may have taken place (as later tradition maintained), and where the later Christians certainly met for prayer and worship (Acts 12:12). This in itself is a reminder of the strong physical link and continuity between the world of the gospels and the world of Acts chapters 1–12, a factor which we often forget today. It is only after that date, with the great Gentile expansion of the church, that the break comes, a break which does not become final till the sack of Jerusalem in AD 70. Whoever it was, it was a lad, hurriedly aroused from sleep, with a sheet wrapped around him; presumably one of the frightened disciples had dashed back with the news to the house where the last supper had been held. Of course this detail may have simply been an irrelevant vivid memory, a trifling incident stamped upon the mind, not by its own importance, but by the importance of the events surrounding it. If the young man was indeed John Mark, his anonymity here is perfectly explicable. It might, it is true, be any other youth, and not Mark: but if so, it is hard to see either the reason for the mention, or who else it could have been. In any case, it must have been some young disciple, closely associated with Jesus, and probably also closely associated with the house of the last supper. It seems unnecessary and unfair to spiritualize an incident like this; it is stated as a plain fact, and as such it should be accepted, whatever spiritual lessons we may then draw from it.[1] Some branches of Gnostics made great use of the incident, for their own heretical purposes, but we may safely reject their interpretation as utterly inconsistent with the gospel. The curious may consult *IDBS* on the matter. Any hint of homosexuality is impossible (Rom. 1:27).

D. THE FALL OF PETER (14:53–72)

53. In this account of Peter's denial, the exact chronology of the trial is uncertain; it is even uncertain how many separate court hearings are recorded. As this does not affect the main issue, however, we may leave it for lengthier works to consider: at the very least, there is one appearance of Jesus before the high priest, and one before Pilate, recorded in Mark.

On the face of it, the time would still seem to be late at night. This impression is heightened by the mention of the fire in verse 54. Fires are for light as much as for heat in any simple society, even today. But Jerusalem lies nearly a thousand metres above sea-level, and spring mornings can be cold, so the fire in itself would not be conclusive evidence of time. True, Peter was warming himself at the fire (verse 54), but he seems to have been recognized by the fire-light (verse 67), so either explanation is possible. It is interesting to note (with Anderson), that Mark is once again 'sandwiching' the account of the fall of Peter

[1] Tannehill (IOM), for instance, wants us to see the specially shameful flight of the young man as symbolizing the shameful flight of all the disciples, and his 'linen garment' as signifying his original readiness for martyrdom. This is, too far-fetched: fleeing naked, if it symbolizes anything in biblical eyes, symbolizes not shame but terror (Am. 2:16), as often pointed out. To see liturgical (especially baptismal) significance in the story is equally wide of the mark; that would be to invest the early church with a modern interest in liturgiology. See Anderson for the implausibility of any connection between this figure and the young man at the empty tomb (16:5).

between accounts of the trial of Jesus: the faithfulness of Jesus to death and the unfaithfulness of Peter are thereby contrasted vividly.

54. *Followed him at a distance.* Why? Was it out of mere curiosity (Mt. 26:58), or had Peter some wild idea of rescuing Jesus by force? His lies told to the girls in the courtyard need not have arisen altogether from cowardice; they might have been part of some perverted strategy, though Scripture admittedly gives no hint of this. But if this was so, he was still (as in 8:32) thinking human thoughts, and so still came under condemnation from Jesus (8:33). Nevertheless, this line of interpretation seems over-subtle, like the interpretation which would impute good, though warped, motives to Judas in his betrayal of Christ. Probably Peter had no plan at all, but was merely thunderstruck. From whatever motive he *followed*, he still stands condemned in Scripture as the one who denied Jesus after all his boastfulness. But he is also the one who will be singled out by the love of God to hear the good news of the resurrection (16:7). Even for Peter, there is to be a way back; for those later Christians who had denied their Lord in time of persecution, this would bring hope.

55. *Sought testimony.* This appears to have been a sort of preliminary fact-finding commission of the Sanhedrin.[1] While they had long ago decided on the death of Jesus (3:6), they had still to formulate a legal charge, adequate to justify the death penalty; they had no desire simply to assassinate Him, lest it provoke a bloody riot and consequent Roman action. A proof of their moral blindness was their failure to see that, in God's eyes, there was no difference between the quick knife of the 'sicarii' or

[1] One reason for this view is that, if it was a 'trial', it broke so many of the regulations laid down in the tractate 'Sanhedrin' (trials might not be at night, nor might they be in the high priest's house, *etc.*). But the problem has been made worse by well-meaning scholars who wish to absolve the Jewish religious authorities of all blame for the death of Jesus, and make the Romans fully responsible. The anti-semitism of the Christian church in past centuries has been inexcusable (see introduction), and to base it on the death of Christ is a distortion of the gospel; but all four evangelists are clear that the leaders of his own people handed Jesus over to the Romans (compare Acts 2:23). To deny the historicity of the appearance before the Sanhedrin is to reject the plain evidence of Scripture.

'dagger-men', who abounded at festival time (see Acts 21:38), and such judicial murder as they contemplated. But even if the high priests could find some clear breach of the Torah, sufficient in Jewish eyes to warrant a death sentence, their task was still only half done. They also had to produce some political charge, adequate in Roman eyes to warrant the carrying out of the death sentence. Both Pilate (Mk. 15:14) and Gallio (Acts 18:14–16) show Roman reluctance to condemn a provincial on purely religious grounds, especially when that religion was to them an offensive oriental cult, practised by an unpopular subject people. The Mishnah makes frequent bitter reference to the fact that the Romans had taken away the cherished power of capital punishment from the Jewish courts, even when dealing with their own people (cf. Jn. 18:31, where this is made explicit).[1] Especially in explosive Jerusalem at passover time, with the city tense and full of milling throngs of nationalistic Jews, the Romans were on their guard. Such legal murder, especially if it provoked an uproar (14:2), might have dire consequences for the Jewish leaders, if not to the whole Jewish state (Jn. 11:48), as they knew well.

56. For this whole section on the nature of the charges laid against Jesus, see the author's *The New Temple*, where the question is discussed at some length. The trouble on this occasion was not lack of evidence, but too much; doubtless the money that bought Judas also bought these willing helpers also, as can still be done outside the law courts of many another city. But, as usual, it was harder to agree on a consistent lie than to tell the simple truth. It is obvious that none of the early charges against Jesus about sabbath-breaking would hold water, or they would have been produced at once. Common Jewish equity would not allow someone to be put to death for healing a sick man on the sabbath day, any more than for watering his animals on the sabbath; and the Pharisees, grumble as they might, knew this too well to proceed with that charge.

---

[1]See Johnson and Anderson for a detailed discussion of this somewhat disputed point. Various lynchings, actual or attempted, recorded in the New Testament do not disprove the point made above.

57–59. Of all the synoptists, Mark contains the fullest version of the content of this charge.[1] This accusation at least was a substantially true (if misunderstood) report of a saying not recorded in full by Mark, but preserved in John 2:19. Indeed, without the Johannine reference, we should be at a loss to explain the charge except as a pure fabrication. Mark does, however, contain a general prophecy by Jesus of the destruction of the temple (13:2), although not of its 'rebuilding' by Him.

From John, we see that this saying, understood by the disciples only after the resurrection, was a reference to the dissolution and raising up again, three days later, of the Lord's body; and from this springs the whole 'New Temple' concept. This metaphor was apparently freely used in Christian catechesis within the early church, of which space will not allow a full discussion here (*e.g.* Eph. 2:21).

But if this charge against Jesus were taken literally, which is unlikely, it could be understood only as a claim to possess supernatural or even magical powers; and Jesus could not be condemned for that alone, for the source of His power might still be good or evil. The Talmud is full of stories of miracle-working rabbis. The bitter Pharisees might say that Jesus performed demon expulsions through Beelzebul (3:22), but the common people would scarcely believe that, let alone a charge that He was about to destroy and rebuild the temple by demonic powers. But such wild charges could not justify a legal death sentence, the more so if the same saying of Jesus contained a prophecy of rebuilding it.[2] Also it is hard to see how anybody could have a taken such a saying literally. Herod had performed this vast task over a period of many years, demolishing Zerubbabel's old temple down to ground level, and laboriously rebuilding, with great blocks of Herodian masonry, the temple which they saw now; could any Pharisee seriously believe that Jesus intended to repeat this process in three days?[3]

---

[1]See Cole, *The New Temple*, IVP, 1951, for a full discussion, with attempted explanation.

[2]Lightfoot is therefore quite correct when he says that the charge against Jesus was not one of promising to destroy the temple, but of promising to transform it, even if this 'rebuilding' was wrongly understood in a literal sense.

[3]See Cranfield, but he goes too far in abandoning all hope of discovering the original form of the saying.

60. Even if the charges themselves could neither be agreed upon (59), nor substantiated, perhaps Jesus could be goaded by them into some utterance that would incriminate Him. But He remained silent; there was no need for Him to deny such flimsy charges. Even to the priestly court, they were worthless, except as make-weights. The silence of the Christ was in itself a prophetic sign (Is. 53:7), as Peter saw later (1 Pet. 2:23).

61. The high priest must have known that Jesus had at least accepted the title of *Christ* (Messiah) from those around Him (8:29), even if, by the 'Messianic secret', He had avoided making such a claim openly in presence of His enemies, until God's time had come. Matthew 26:63 makes clear that this was no casual enquiry by the high priest, but a question put 'under oath', as it were, in the solemn name of God.

But would He deftly extricate Himself from this ensnaring question, as He had from their well-planned trap about paying tribute to Caesar (12:14)? As with a modern Moslem, for Jesus to claim to be Messiah, the Anointed, God's Prophet, would be no blasphemy, although it might be hotly contradicted and a sign would be demanded. But to claim to be *the Son of the Blessed* would be to them intolerable blasphemy, and, for such a blasphemy, He could be condemned to death by the Sanhedrin, as He indeed was, in spite of the doubts of Anderson as to whether this charge had sufficient weight (verse 64). The bitterness of their taunt at the cross (15:32) again shows that Messiahship was a well-known claim of Jesus, whether enunciated in these exact terms or not. At the cross, His Messiahship and kingship of Israel are mentioned by them, but not Sonship of God: that must wait for the declaration by the centurion (15:39), although Matthew 27:40 has it.

62. It may be significant that Jesus replies with the very Name of God, *I am* (Ex. 3:14), thus putting Himself on an equality with God, which we know to have been a long-standing grievance on their part (2:7). In Luke, His answer is more ambiguous, though Jesus accepts the title 'Son of God' (Luke 22:70). But the phrase is reported only by Mark; even Matthew, with all his Jewish interests, does not record it.[1] The form of the saying may therefore be more accidental than significant theologically, although John seems to develop the same point in his gospel on another occasion (Jn. 18:6).

Jesus, while accepting the title suggested by the high priest, defines it further in terms of *Son of man*, His special self-chosen title. This is explained by another 'creative fusion' of Psalm 110:1 with Daniel 7:13. But, if the high priest had ears to hear, there was a solemn warning in this choice of a title, for this is the Son of man vindicated and enthroned, and returning in judgment, as Stephen saw Him before his death by stoning (Acts 7:56). The priesthood stood on trial that day, although the execution of sentence was yet to come, on the terrible day in AD 70 when the priests were cut down by the Roman soldiers at the altar, as they steadily continued with their sacrifices to the last.

63. *Tore his garments.* This was the true condemnation of the religious leaders of Israel themselves: the high priest had asked not for information, but only to trap Jesus, for he must have known the claims long before he asked. Of course, had not such a claim been true, it would have been either madness (3:21) or blasphemy. But the condemnation of the high priest is not simply that he did not believe the claim, but that he did not even ask himself whether it was true or false. He was wilfully and culpably blind, for he had closed his eyes in advance to the truth.

The symbolic tearing of garments, by now traditional on hearing blasphemy, was in origin a sign of grief, as is plain from the Old Testament (*e.g.* Lv. 10:6). Here it had become distorted into a sign of joy at a wicked purpose successfully accomplished. Joyfully, the worthless witnesses are now dismissed: the high priest hastily calls the *bêth dîn*, or court, to be themselves witnesses, and he formally asks for their opinion (64). Just as formally they give it: Jesus of Nazareth is liable to the death penalty for blasphemy. The agony is that, had His claim been false, it would indeed have been a blasphemy of such magnitude as to deserve the death sentence; but what if He were right?

---

[1]See Stauffer, under *egō* (TNDT). Weeden (IOM) well points out that 'I am' is not only a title of God, but, in the Christian community, a specific identification for Christ. This latter

65. With this condemnation, away went all restraint; no longer did the judges trouble to observe even the outward forms of legal impartiality. Peter at least never forgot the patient endurance of Jesus amid the taunts and blows (1 Pet. 2:21–23), a fulfilment of Isaiah 50:6. The derisive call, *Prophesy*, is a further gibe at His claim to Messiahship, which would at the least involve prophethood, and had been shown above to involve Sonship of God. But 'prophet' was in any case a popularly used title for Jesus (6:15), even when He was not recognized as Messiah.

66–71. The whole account of Peter's fall leaves the reader helpless, powerless to intervene, as the story develops, stage by stage, until Peter has passed the point of no return. His rash self-confidence and scorn of others (29); his failure to discipline himself in the garden (37); his panic and flight (50); his following at a distance (54); his close association with the enemies of Jesus (54): all these in turn made the actual denial the logical and indeed almost inevitable result. No doubt Peter was sincere in his initial desires and protestations (31), but the battle against temptation in the high priest's palace had been lost long before; the time for a Christian to fight temptation is before it is encountered (38).

This girl (66–67) may have seen Peter before, in the company of Jesus, and so recognized him as one of the disciples; the Jerusalem bystanders (70) concluded that he must be one because of his Galilean accent. There were many Galileans in the capital at passover time, but not among the servants of the high priest. The tragedy is that each step downward might have been a step upward; on each occasion, Peter was being forced to declare himself openly. On the first occasion, as Anderson says, he could have said 'yes' to the girl without too great risk. But Peter chose, deliberately, three times to say 'no'; and so these promptings of grace became occasions of condemnation, as they must always be if they are refused.

It is the fashion nowadays to make excuses for Peter, as some

---

point is of course made much clearer in John's Gospel with the sevenfold 'I am' statements of Jesus.

do for Judas; and in so far as it means that we see our own weakness in him, that may be good. But unless we see the seriousness of his sin, we cannot understand the bitterness of his remorse (verse 72), nor the depth of his repentance, nor the grace of his restoration. Our task is not to analyse by what easy steps Peter's fall came, but to realize the terrible nature of it.

72. It has been suggested above (on verse 30) that 'second cock-crow' is a definite point of time, not merely a prophetic sign. It denotes true dawn, as against the midnight of first cock-crow; 15:1, 'as soon as it was morning', supports this. But be that as it may, it was as a fulfilled sign that 'second cock-crow' recalled to the mind of Peter the words of Jesus; and so his cup of remorse was full. *Broke down*, in Greek *epibalōn* (for which see BAGD), could also be translated 'on thinking it over', or 'he set to and thought', or simply 'he began to think'.[1] *Broke down and wept*, however, is certainly the best 'dynamic equivalent' of the whole phrase. 'Pulling his cloak over his head' is also possible, but less likely.

E. THE TRIAL BEFORE PILATE (15:1–15)[2]

i. The stage is set (15:1)

This reads as if the previous night's proceedings had been only an attempt by a 'steering committee' to clarify the charge with the legal experts. Now a plenary session of the Sanhedrin formally bound Jesus, and brought Him before the Governor. So begins, not the trial before Pilate, but the trial of Pilate, for he stands self-revealed as he attempts in vain, first to avoid the issue, and then to escape responsibility for the decision. But as in the case of Peter, Pilate is pushed inexorably to a verdict, and his verdict is condemned every time that we repeat in the creed the clause 'suffered under Pontius Pilate'. The decision of the

---

[1] So J. H. Moulton, *Grammar of New Testament Greek*, Vol. 1 (Edinburgh: T. & T. Clark, 1906) p. 131, quoting a Ptolemaic papyrus, also mentioned by BAGD.

[2] Many modern commentators (like Anderson, for instance) are excessively critical in their approach to the story of this trial: but the account, if taken at its face value, is perfectly consistent throughout.

Sanhedrin had already been made, but Pilate was no more compelled to carry it out than Judas was compelled to betray Jesus.

ii. Pilate condemns Jesus (15:2–15)

The trial proper begins (as we can see from other gospels), with a confused mass of general accusations (*many things*, or *many charges*, 3 and 4), designed to paint Jesus in a black light politically as a revolutionary, a trouble maker, one who forbade the payment of Caesar's taxes and one who claimed to be an earthly ruler Himself. At this period the word *basileus, king*, was used generally of tetrarchs, subject kings, and the emperor (1 Pet. 2:13), although the latter might also be called *sebastos*, corresponding in meaning to the Latin *augustus*. The crime in this court would have to be one of sedition against Rome, and so any and every flimsy charge was added as a make-weight; but at the mention of the claim to be another petty Jewish kinglet, Pilate jumped to action.[1] That charge might well have some substance, and, if so, imperial Rome would take notice of it. No 'client king' must rule except with Rome's consent. To Pilate's abrupt question, Jesus gave a tranquil answer which was a full admission (2), not evasive, as some translations would suggest. In Mark's Gospel, the nature of Christ's kingship is not defined, as it is in John 18:36, but it is just as central an issue in the crucifixion story (9, 12, 18, 26).

3–5. Still the list of charges continued, and still the Lord did not answer them, to the marvel of Pilate. It is at this point that Luke inserts the story of the despatch of the prisoner to Herod, under whose immediate jurisdiction Galilee lay (Lk. 23:6). This episode is omitted in Mark, as not affecting the main movement of the trial. In fact, the whole account in Mark is brief and 'telescoped'; were it not for the other gospels, we might well miss some of the complexity of the sequence of events. But Mark, for all his brevity, covers all the main points; Pilate is still

[1] It has often been noted by commentators that *king of the Jews* is a title which would be used only by foreigners (18). *The king of Israel* was what Hebrews would have said among themselves, and did indeed say, in mockery (32).

cynical, still knows that the Jews accuse Jesus only out of envy (10), still desires to please them (15). Turbulent Palestine was to be the grave of many an ambitious administrator's career; high priests had influence at Rome. Finally, Pilate knowingly frees the guilty, and condemns the innocent (15): that is his own condemnation.

6. There was still one possibility of escaping the responsibility of a final decision, by the time-honoured custom of releasing a political prisoner amid a time of general rejoicing. Many of the new nations of today have similarly celebrated their post-war independence by some kind of general amnesty of political prisoners. Verse 6, *he used to release*, however, suggests that either the custom had already ceased at the date of writing, or, more likely, that it was unknown to Mark's Gentile readers, and therefore needed explanation. It is most unlikely that it was simply a practice unique to Pilate, which lapsed on his recall.

7. There is some MS evidence for the possibility of the criminal's full name being 'Jesus bar-Abba', or possibly 'bar-Rabba'. Jesus, or Joshua, was a common first-century Jewish name, so the reading may be correct. If the name was equally borne by both,[1] it would heighten the contrast between the two figures. Some exegetes have made further play with the possible meaning of 'bar-Abba', 'son of the father', as another parallel. But as the Gospel of the Hebrews (quoted by Jerome on Mt. 27:16, the synoptic parallel to this verse) has the spelling 'bar-Rabba', 'son of the great one', the point seems untenable linguistically, however helpful devotionally, unless of course the second element here stands for a divine name. At all events, the man seems to have been a Zealot, captured after some brush with the authorities in which there had been deaths (7), and whose doom was thus sealed, but whose popularity with the nationalists was also assured. The outcome of such a choice was obvious even from the start; but the high priests made it doubly certain, by their open canvassing for Barabbas at this point (11).

[1]Cranfield has an interesting explanation of Pilate's attitude, based on this coincidence of name: but it is too conjectural to be convincing: the MS evidence may be artificial.

8. Pilate may possibly have thought that this request would give him a chance to escape from a difficult situation. But Mark prefaces the verse by verse 7 to show that this way was already blocked; the chief priests already have another candidate for amnesty in view.

9–12. Attention is often drawn to the fickleness of crowds by comparing the cheering crowd at the triumphant entry (11:9–10) with the hostile courtroom crowd here. But, although such rapid change is quite possible, yet, right up to the trial, the popularity of Jesus with the crowd was undoubted (12:37). Indeed, it was precisely because of this popularity that the religious leaders dared not arrest Him openly (14:2). The simple answer is that these were two different crowds involved. The crowd at the triumphal entry was made up of pious pilgrims, no doubt many from Galilee, and an equally pious group from Jerusalem which met them (Jn. 12:12ff). These last may themselves have been earlier arrivals among the pilgrims. But, as Luther found, when he made his famous pilgrimage to Rome, piety is apt to flourish more away from a Holy City than in it; and doubtless there were many residents of Jerusalem who were far from pious. We know from the other gospels that, even among the ordinary people of Jerusalem, there was much strife concerning Jesus (Jn. 7:43). This crowd at the trial must have been composed, in part at least, of the followers and servants of the high priests, seeing that all had moved apparently together from the high-priestly hall to Pilate's palace. So we are probably dealing here with a mere section of the Jerusalem mob, a section specifically stated in verse 11 to have been deliberately inflamed by the high priests. Pious pilgrims had more to do at Passover time than to gape at Roman trials; indeed, even the priests themselves had scruples about incurring ceremonial defilement at such a time (Jn. 18:28). As Schweizer says, Mark places the blame on the authorities for the crucifixion of Jesus. This includes both the Roman and Jewish authorities equally.

9–10. The perversity of human nature is clearly seen here. On the one hand, Pilate genuinely wishes to escape from a difficult position by releasing Jesus. On the other hand, he cannot resist 'getting his own back', on the Jewish leaders, who have placed him in such a difficult situation. His way of petty vengeance is to taunt them with the accusation of kingship admitted by Jesus (9 and 12), although he must have known how galling this would be to them (10). Yet this petty vengeance by Pilate only made it the more certain that what he most desired could not take place, for it only increased their bitterness against Jesus. We cannot say that such perversity is impossible, for it is a factor of daily experience; and the particle *for* in verse 10 makes nonsense unless we take some such common sense explanation. Pilate was no unnatural monster; he was a man in so many ways like all others. This is what makes his story such a warning, and also so credible.

13–14. Even allowing for a natural preference for the freeing of Barabbas, the 'patriotic' figure, it is hard to see why the crowd should then shout, demanding a Roman death for Jesus, unless the priests had deliberately inflamed them, perhaps by stories of His supposed blasphemies (*cf.* verse 11). Beheading was the Roman death for a citizen, as traditionally for Paul; crucifixion for a slave or foreigner, as traditionally for Peter (Jn. 21:18); stoning was the normal form of Jewish death-sentence, from the earliest days (Jos. 7:25). After death by stoning, the criminal's body might be displayed hanging upon a 'tree' until the evening (Jos. 10:26; Dt. 21:22–23). This to the Jew was a sign that the one who so died was under the wrath and curse of God (Dt. 21:23). So, in God's providence, the cross, besides its Roman associations of shame and a slave's death, had the deeper Hebrew meaning of God's curse (Gal. 3:13), borne for us.

15. Nothing could be more cynical than the total disregard for truth and justice in this man who, knowing Jesus to be innocent (14), yet flogged and crucified the Son of God, simply through a desire to ingratiate himself with the Jews (15). As usual, Mark does not 'highlight' the picture, either by making excuses for Pilate, or by passing judgments on him. He simply states the facts; that is sufficient condemnation. No doubt Mark's readers could think of parallels from their own experiences in time of persecution.

313

F. THE CRUCIFIXION (15:16–47)

i. *The mockery (15:16–20)*

Now comes the callous mocking by the soldiers (see 14:65 for the mocking by the priests). We may note here, with many commentators, the extreme reserve and economy of language with which Mark describes the events of the crucifixion. There is neither description of, nor stress on, the physical sufferings of Jesus, great as they were: Mark knew that there was greater suffering at a deeper level to be endured on the cross.

16. *The soldiers.* Even we, who have grown used to atrocities in wars, may be surprised by the venom of Pilate's men here, who may not have been full Roman citizens, but were certainly pro-Roman in sentiment. If the 'Italian cohort' (see Acts 10:1) was stationed in Judaea in those days, there must have been inhabitants of Italy among them, with the half-way gift of 'Latin rights'. None of these long-service regulars would have been locally raised in Palestine. Many were doubtless wild auxiliaries drawn from other frontier provinces of the empire; the one common loyalty that bound them together was the Roman soldier's oath to the Caesar and the Eagles. Towards the Jews, a despised subject people, they would have no sympathy.

The one charge that they understood (which was probably that under which in Roman eyes Jesus had been condemned) was that this prisoner claimed to be a king Himself, and was therefore a potential rival to Caesar, despicable though He might seem to them. Hence the point of the rough mockery – the *purple cloak*, or scarlet cape of the Roman cavalryman, the crown, the sceptre, like those worn by the great commander-in-chief himself, to whom alone they bowed *in homage* (19). All condemned criminals were regarded as fair game for cruel mockery, but there was a special pent-up bitterness being released here. As Anderson sees, the parallels to this sort of mockery in secular literature do not disprove the historicity of the account here: rightly viewed, they only confirm it.

The Roman military exasperation against the 'cloak and dagger' patriots of first-century Judaism was growing, until it found terrible outlet in the massacres of AD 70, when easy-going Titus

314

tried in vain to save prisoners from the wrath of the legionaries. Those who have seen 'regular' troops, long subject to such 'pinpoint' civilian guerrilla activities, will know the exasperation which it breeds in a regular army: hence the atrocities that so often occur.

Jewish nationalism led to the arrest of Jesus and Roman nationalism to His mockery and His cross: so deep in all things human is the 'old nature'. Patriotism is not enough, as more than one patriot has found at the last; it is only too easy to give national or class struggles a quasi-Christian significance.

ii. Carrying the cross of Jesus (15:21)

Simon of Cyrene might be taken figuratively as a picture of every disciple, bearing the Lord's cross for Him.[1] His Greek name may mean 'snub-nosed' (the form *simos* certainly does), but as, in the case of the apostle, it may represent the good Hebrew name 'Simeon' (*cf.* Acts 15:14 for the full form). If so, he was probably a Cyrenian Jew; they had their own shared synagogue in Jerusalem (Acts 6:9). He may have been a visitor to Jerusalem for the Passover, although his entry from *the country* at such an early hour might suggest that he was a resident of Jerusalem, as might the fact that his sons Alexander and Rufus seem to have been known personally to the early Christians (21), even if he himself was not. Certainly the indefinite Greek particle *tina*, 'somebody called Simon', does not suggest personal knowledge of Simon himself[2] by the Christian community.

It is tempting, in view of the tradition that Mark's Gospel originally took shape at Rome, to see a possible reference here to the Rufus of the Roman church mentioned in Romans 16:13,

---

[1]Of course, there is an important difference: Simon did not carry the *patibulum* or 'crosspiece' of Christ's cross willingly, but only under compulsion (Anderson). The Gnostics (and some Moslem groups later) went much farther: they claimed that Simon, not Jesus, was crucified at Golgotha (Schweizer). This is a distortion of the biblical account, arising from the belief that God could not allow a sinless person to die on the cross: but this paradox is the very heart of the gospel, as well as being its greatest stumbling-block.

[2]See Best (IOM): he regards this as an example of 'unnecessary retention of names', and therefore as a proof of retention of original source material completely untouched. He is undoubtedly right but, even so, the names of the sons must have been meaningful to Mark's sources, the earliest Christian community.

although there only the mother, not father, of Rufus is mentioned. Such an identification is too tenuous to press; and of Alexander we can say nothing, for none of the three New Testament candidates appears to be likely (Acts 4:6; 19:33; and 1 Tim. 1:20 with 2 Tim. 4:14). In any case, disciple himself or not, Simon was 'conscripted' (*compelled*) by the Roman Government for this unpopular piece of state service, which acerbated feelings still further among the provincials.

iii. The cross (15:22–32)[1]

Whatever the exact site of the crucifixion, the meaning of *Golgotha* is well translated by the Latin *Calvarium*, suggesting a smooth rounded hilltop devoid of vegetation, giving the appearance of a bald head, or skull. With deference to some topographers, who see plainly the two staring 'eye sockets' in 'Gordon's Calvary' at Jerusalem as proof of identification, to Hebrew and Greek minds, the chief impression left by a 'skull' was its roundness and smoothness, to judge by etymology. In any case, the two 'eye sockets' of Gordon's calvary were probably only caused by later subsidence or collapse of the walls of water cisterns, cut into the rock on the site. The true site of the crucifixion is almost certainly that now occupied by Holy Sepulchre Church, although now altered beyond recognition: see Smith in *IDB Sup*.

23. The sour local *wine* which they gave Him was 'laced' with *myrrh*; this would give it a bitter taste, but a soporific effect, and was an act of mercy. Jesus, however, would not take any such anaesthetic; all His faculties must be unclouded for what lay before Him.[2] Such drugged wine, tradition tells us, was provided by pious women of Jerusalem for condemned criminals, to dull the pains of execution: whether 'incense' (so the Talmud) or *myrrh* was used, makes little difference.

---

[1]For comparison and clarification of many details, see the article 'Crucifixion, method of' in the *IDB Sup.*, by Strange, based upon the finding in Jerusalem of the bones of a crucified person.

[2]Cranfield also suggests a second reason: it would break the vow of Jesus made at the last supper, recorded in 14:25, that He would not drink wine again until He drank it in God's kingdom. But Jesus did accept a drink of sour wine later, while on the cross (36), so this reasoning is doubtful.

24. Although Mark makes no specific reference to the fulfilment of prophecy in this verse, yet his choice of wording shows
that both he and the other evangelists see in this gambling by
the soldiers for Christ's clothing, a fulfilment of Psalm 22:18.
There was therefore a divine prophetic appropriateness, not
only in the death of Jesus, but in its manner; and not merely in
the manner of His death, but even in the incidents associated
with it. This prophetic appropriateness the disciples apparently
failed to see until after the resurrection; perhaps that is why
Mark makes no reference to it here, although other evangelists
will. It is nonsense to reject the story of the gambling, with some
editors, on the grounds that we have no evidence for this
method of disposing of the clothing of a condemned criminal,
always by tradition the property of the executioners. How else
would soldiers divide objects of unequal value, even today?

25. The exact time of the crucifixion is a problem; normally *the
third hour* would be understood as nine o'clock in the morning.
The three hours of darkness would then be from noon until
three o'clock in the afternoon (33). If the day was reckoned as
beginning at nine o'clock, then of course the darkness would
have been from three o'clock to six o'clock: see commentators on
John's account for a full discussion of the point.

26. *King of the Jews*: this ironical and no doubt sarcastic
wooden identification-tag nailed to the cross was Pilate's last
revenge on those who had forced him into such a difficult
position. To the disciples, it was no irony, but God's own
vindication of His Son, even in the hour of His death. Later,
hymn writers delighted to use the concept of the King, crowned
at last, reigning from the tree. For the apparent survival of
fragments of an identification tag of this type, see under 'Crucifixion' in *IDB Sup.*: archaeological discovery of the skeleton of a
crucified man has illustrated many points, including this.

27. This suggests that an execution had been impending in
any case, and that Jesus was only taking the place of Barabbas,
as the third victim. The just dies for the unjust, the innocent for
the guilty (1 Pet. 3:18). Mark simply gives the general statement

that even these two criminals heaped insults on Jesus (verse 32): for more detail, we must turn to other gospels.

As in the case of the 'wise men', the Old Latin text has preserved names for the criminals. *Zoathan* and *Chammatha* are one MS reading amid several; both names have a Semitic ring, so are possible. The Old Latin and the Old Syriac between them preserve several similar traditions which are undoubtedly early, but as to whose truth, there is no independent test. Nevertheless, there was no need to invent these names, any more than there was to invent names for the wise men (Mt. 2:1); so the survival of any name in a MS is an argument for its genuineness, even if the exact spelling is uncertain. Dysmas and Gestas are the names for the criminals preserved in the apocryphal gospels, but they, by definition, are less trustworthy.

28. *The Scripture was fulfilled.* This verse, with its quotation of Isaiah 53:12, is missing in many MSS. It is easy to see how it could have been added as an explanatory comment on the fact of the crucifixion of two criminals with Jesus, for besides being an undoubted truth, it takes up the reference made to Isaiah 53:12 by Jesus in the upper room, before the group left for Gethsemane (*cf. for many*, 14:24). Whether or not it should be read in the text here is not really important, for it corresponds to a deep theological insight to which allusion is also made in 14:48–49. Jesus was treated by the authorities as an evil-doer, true; but this was only an outward picture of the far deeper truth that He was treated as an evil-doer by God upon the cross for our sakes (2 Cor. 5:21). More, all of this was in God's purpose: it was a 'fulfilment' of Scripture; as this verse says.

29–30. The shaking of heads in mockery, and the blasphemy, like the gambling for His clothing (24), are all described in the language of the Psalter. Again, it is the same Psalm as before which is used (Ps. 22:7), and by which the significance of these events is interpreted. The climax comes with the loud 'cry of abandonment' (34), which is again a direct quotation from Psalm 22:1. This further quotation of Psalm 22 shows that not only did the disciples use this particular Psalm as a means of understanding the suffering of their Lord; Jesus Himself so used it, which is no doubt why the disciples extended its use. The mockery of the crowds, and especially of the priests, at the cross is the strongest possible psychological proof of the reality of the various claims of Jesus. They virtually prove the veracity of the saying about the destruction and rebuilding of the 'temple', for instance (29); that He spoke of saving others, that is, He used this particular word in connection with His work on their behalf (31); that He indeed claimed to be the Messiah, and Israel's King (32). All these claims they undoubtedly disbelieved; but, if Jesus had never made them, then the taunt would have lost all its sting. Their basic error, as Schweizer sees, was that they assumed that the primary objective of Jesus would be to save His own life: they wanted some 'superman' exhibition of power, whereas to die upon the cross was His whole purpose.

31. There was prophetic truth in these bitter words. If Christ wanted to save others, then He could not come down from the cross; that temptation He had rejected first in the wilderness (1:13), then at Caesarea Philippi (8:33), and lastly in the garden of Gethsemane (14:36). To descend from the cross was not indeed a physical impossibility, but it was a moral and spiritual impossibility for the Messiah. If He did so, He would cease to be God's Christ, treading God's path of Messiahship; instead, He would become a mere human Christ, and such a Christ could never save the world. The only path by which to save others was to refuse to save Himself: in a way totally unexpected by them, the priests were correct.

32. Their demand was impossible, for *see and believe* is not God's order of working, but ours. It would be a reversal of the rule of faith, which is that 'all things are possible to him who believes' (9:23). It was impossible, too, because even if the miracle were to be granted to them, they still would not have believed. The resistance to God lay in their stubborn will, not in their intellect; they were determined not to believe, for their concern, like Pilate's, was not with truth. Against such opposition, God's judgment is clear (Rom. 1:18). *Those who were* *crucified with him*: Mark does not tell of the one terrorist who turned to God at the last, but he does tell of Joseph of Arimathea, a member of the Sanhedrin, who did believe (43).

iv. The death (15:33-41)

As mentioned above (25), the usual interpretation of the indicated time would be that darkness – as in the plagues of Egypt, a sign of God's curse (Ex. 10:22) – fell on the land from noon till three o'clock in the afternoon. Mark simply records darkness without specifying the cause: if there was a Passover full moon at the time, it could hardly have been a solar eclipse (see Morris, *Luke*). The exact cause used by God is of course immaterial: it is the symbolism which is important here. Darkness at noon, by its paradoxical nature, was a fitting sign for God the Creator to give to those who had rejected the light of the world. To Minear, the darkness signified the darkness of 'the Day of the Lord' (Am. 5:18): this is quite possible. Certainly, in Amos 8:9, there is a prophecy of the sun going down at noon, as a manifestation of God's judgment. Was the darkness a sandstorm?

34-35. Linguistically, if *sabachthani* be read, with most MSS, this is not the Hebrew form found in the Old Testament, but the Aramaic form contained in the Targum, while the *zaphthanei* preserved by two MSS is the true Hebrew. Here we must tread reverently. As Anderson says, the gospel writers do not supply us with materials with which to study the psychology of Christ: but it seems probable that Jesus, in this hour, was staying Himself upon the Scriptures, not in the sacred Hebrew, but rather in the colloquial paraphrase of His own Aramaic mother-tongue.[1] This verse therefore belongs to those few where we have the very words of Jesus preserved; for, while He may well have conversed freely in colloquial Greek, yet with His disciples he presumably used Galilean Aramaic.[2] There are similar

[1] See also comment on 5:41, for the use of Aramaic by Jesus.

[2] There is still much argument as to the linguistic situation in first-century Palestine, for which there is little literary evidence, since Greek, as elsewhere in the eastern half of the empire, was the normal language of literacy. But the Bar-Cochba letters show that Hebrew, as well as being the tongue of the scholars, was (perhaps artificially), the tongue of the

linguistic variations on the form of the word used for *God* in the first part of the quotation, but unless the form *Eli* be read, not *Eloi*, it is hard to see how the crude pun upon the name *Eliyahu* (*Elijah*, 35) could be sustained. For the connection in scribal tradition between Elijah and the Messiah, see 9:11; the appearance of Elijah with Jesus on the mount of transfiguration (9:4) shows that this was no misconception.[1]

But what was the meaning of this cry? Had God indeed deserted Him? No, clearly not, for this was God's path, and not what the Son would have chosen for Himself, if it had not been God's will; this is the whole meaning of the agony in the Garden (14:36). More, it was God's path as made plain to the Son from the commencement of His ministry, as the threefold prediction of His death to the disciples makes plain (see 8:31, 9:31, 10:33). It has been well said that the opening words of the cry, *My God*, are in fact in themselves an affirmation of faith.[2] Since this same Psalm 22 from which they are quoted ends in a cry of triumph, it is reasonable to suppose that Jesus chose it with this in view also. Otherwise, there were many suitable passages (*e.g.* in Lamentations) which express the endurance of suffering without any final consciousness of victory, and any of these Jesus might well have used. So here we have the agony of one suffering the experience of abandonment by God, and yet certain by faith of ultimate vindication and triumph. But to what, and why, was He abandoned? To betrayal, mockery, scourging and death – yes: but to limit the explanation to these things would be superficial exegesis, for all of these He had faced and foretold for years. There was a far deeper spiritual agony which Jesus

---

patriots and Zealots, and was possibly still spoken around Jerusalem. In Galilee, although Greek may have been written by all, and may have been the tongue of many Gentiles, Aramaic was clearly spoken among the Jewish population, and possibly among many of the Semitic population.

[1]The crowds presumably had in mind the familiar late tradition of Elijah appearing to work miracles for pious Israelites in their hour of need: this was a commonplace of later rabbinics, but was obviously used here in mockery alone.

[2]Anderson will have none of this. To him, the cry 'plumbs the depths of . . . doubts', as well as of clinging to God. He sees it as akin to the credal belief that Christ 'descended into hell' (*Hades*). But this explanation is psychological, not theological, in spite of Anderson's own warnings on the matter. Also *Hades* is not *Gehenna*: Christ descended to the realm of the dead, not to a place of punishment. The 'harrowing of hell' is a late theological idea, presumably based on 1 Peter 3:19.

endured alone in the darkness, an agony which we can never plumb and which, thanks to His endurance of it on the cross, no created being need ever now experience. No explanation is adequate other than the traditional view that, in that dark hour, God's wrath fell upon Him. Because wrath is no abstract principle, but a personal manifestation, this means that His unclouded communion with the Father, enjoyed from all eternity, was temporarily broken. Some commentators have held that Christ suffered all the pangs of hell in that time; and if hell is at root a separation from God, then He certainly did. But on such mysteries Scripture is silent, and Mark tells us nothing here. If there was a barrier between the Father and the Son at that moment, it could only be because of sin; and the Son knew no sin (2 Cor. 5:21), so it could only be our sin that cost Him such agony. Here is the heart of the cross; here is the mystery which no painting or sculpture, with distorted face, can ever begin to show, because we fail to realize the true nature of the punishment for sin, as separation from God, and therefore the true nature and depth of the agony borne by Him. Both spiritual punishment and reward are ultimately to be seen in terms of God and our relationship to Him, either utter severance from Him or the closest communion with Him; all else is consequent definition. This is not to minimize the seriousness of the concept of eternal punishment and reward; instead, it projects them on to a far wider screen, and gives them a moral depth unthinkable otherwise.

36. The *vinegar* (Greek *oxos*, Latin *posca*) was the sour wine not only of the soldier's rations, but of everyday use.[1] Those who travel or live in countries where such cheap wine is the common local drink, everywhere sold, will know it well. This is quite a different occasion from the offering of the drugged wine in verse 23 before the crucifixion. There may even have been a touch of rough kindness in the deed in spite of the coarse jest which accompanied it, especially if, as John 19:28 says, it was brought in response to a request from Jesus. The *vinegar* of this verse is

---

[1]Although Anderson makes the interesting observation that, as commonly drunk by the Roman soldiers, it was commonly a mixture of sour wine, water and egg.

taken from Psalm 69:21, another messianic Psalm which begins in sorrow and ends in triumph. This Psalm too must therefore have been in the mind of Jesus, and helps us to understand His thoughts at this time.

37. *Loud cry.* Whatever the motives of the bystander who gave the drink, Jesus certainly neither asked for it nor drank it through a mere desire to fulfil the wording of Scripture, but in order to gather His strength for the loud cry that followed, immediately before He died. Mark does not particularize the cry, other than noting how it rang out (37) and noting its effect on the Roman centurion on duty at the execution (39). Indeed, the only saying on the cross that Mark records in detail is the 'cry of abandonment' (34), in keeping with his usual clipped style. Schweizer points out how incomprehensible is this final cry if no explanation is given: but both the effect on the centurion and the evidence of the other gospels show that it was a victor's cry of triumph. It would of course be most unusual for a dying man to shout with such strength, especially after an ordeal like crucifixion. For the wording of the cry, see the other evangelists.

38. This tearing in two of the great woven *curtain of the temple*, allowing anybody to look at will into the holiest place of all (the 'Holy of holies'), is recorded in all three synoptic gospels. The symbolism of this is used later in the New Testament to illustrate the tearing down of the barrier between Jew and Gentile, in the broken body of Christ, by which all barriers between God and man were abolished (Heb. 10:20; Eph. 2:14). Both Jewish priesthood and Jewish temple had ceased to have any future religious significance, as shown by the tearing of this curtain, since now there was direct access for all to God through Christ. Jerome reports that the 'Gospel of the Hebrews' does not mention the torn curtain, but says that the great lintel of the temple cracked and fell.[1] An earthquake could produce both results,

[1] The chief priests might mock Jesus by saying that the prophecy of the destruction of the temple was unfulfilled: but here was a sign of coming destruction at least. So, apparently, Schweizer, in IOM, though the point is not made clearly. Other Jewish traditions mention the great temple gates bursting open of their own accord: an earthquake could have produced this effect also.

and an earthquake is specifically mentioned by Matthew in this context (Mt. 27:51). Mark, as usual, simply mentions the fact of the torn curtain without any explanation, physical or theological.

39. For the puzzled Roman *centurion*, or non-commissioned officer, on duty with his squad at the cross, the evidence had been overwhelming. He must have watched and wondered until this point: now at last, he was convinced. What he, a pagan, really meant by the title *the Son of God*,[1] has been much disputed. It may not have been by any means the unique position that such a title conveys to the Christian. But for Mark, writing for a Gentile public, this is one of the two high points of his whole gospel. As Jewish Peter had already recognized Jesus as Christ (8:29), so now a Gentile centurion had recognized Him as Son of God: as Peter had denied Him, so now the centurion would confess Him.

Whatever of others, the later Christian church certainly saw in this utterance of the centurion a statement of faith, whether conscious or unconscious. Jesus demanded little knowledge and much faith as initial steps, in those who first came to Him, so that the centurion may well have become a true believer later. So Christian tradition assumed; for, true or false, elaborate stories about this centurion circulated in later days. The tradition is not without suspicion, however, when we find him travelling overseas in company with Joseph of Arimathea, who also appears in this context (verse 43). That, however, does not affect the issue of the possible conversion of the centurion to Christianity.

40–41. *Women looking on.* Here Mark specifically mentions the group of women disciples, some of them wealthy, who had followed Jesus from Galilee, and had apparently supported the apostolic group from their worldly wealth (41). They were watching the cross *from afar* (40), as both safety and Jewish

---

[1]Moule discusses this passage, and seems right in following Colwell, thus allowing us to translate the phrase as '*the* Son of God' equally with '*a* Son of God'. Of course, '*a* Son of God' would be of very general meaning to a Gentile, but it could still have been taken up by Christians as an unconscious expression of the truth, and thereby filled by them with deeper meaning. This general sense, however, is certainly not how Mark takes it (Schweizer).

convention demanded. They seem to have corresponded roughly to the 'inner circle' of the twelve, as distinct from the larger number of 'followers' (men or women) in the metaphorical sense, who remained living at home. This same group of women was to share in the witness to the burial of Jesus (47), to bring loving gifts of spices to the tomb (16:1), and to hear the first news of the resurrection (16:5–6) and the command to witness (16:7). In the current debate within the church on the ministry of Christian women, it is interesting to see this group, roughly the counterpart of the twelve, already engaged in a distinct, but just as real, ministry. Mark, as often, does not theorize: he simply records the fact that two at least of these women were 'witnesses' of Christ's death, His burial, and the empty tomb, even though official Judaism would not accept as legal the evidence of women (Lane). This cannot be accidental: God has accepted, indeed, chosen them as witnesses for the most important events of history.

v. The burial (15:42–47)

The agony in Gethsemane is over, and the suffering on Golgotha past; now comes the burial in the tomb, described in these verses. True, the Easter story is not complete until that tomb is empty; but the great atoning sacrifice has already been made, and the dividing curtain has been torn apart. That was the meaning of the final cry of triumph from the cross (37). Now there is a lull after the storm: it is as though, after all the tenseness of the packed sequence from Gethsemane to Calvary, there was need for a pause in the narrative.

42. It was now the evening of Friday, as Mark carefully explains for the benefit of his Gentile audience. Quite irrespective of the question as to the relative timing of the Lord's death and of the Passover, Jesus certainly died on the day before a Jewish sabbath (John 19:31). The time was now therefore just before sundown on Friday, when sabbath actually began for the Jew, since for them a day was reckoned from sunset to sunset. This accounts for the haste in removing the body of Jesus from the cross, lest the sabbath be profaned, if the body was left hanging there. A pious Jew would have removed a body at nightfall in any case (Dt. 21:23), especially in the case of one regarded by the public as a convicted criminal.

So, if the body of Jesus was hastily buried with temporary arrangements (verse 46), no proper burial would be possible until after sunset on the sabbath (Saturday night). In point of fact, no action was taken by the women until early morning on Sunday, for the various preparations would require both time and daylight to carry out. After sunset on Saturday, the spices and linen could be bought (16:1), for it is unlikely that costly spices were ready to hand in any but wealthy circles: but for the actual embalming, the women must wait for the dawn of Sunday (16:2).

While Mark does not record the 'parable of Jonah' (Mt. 12:40), he does record on three occasions the prophecy by Jesus that He would rise again 'after three days' (see the commentary on 8:31). To talk of 'coincidence' in timing, if one is already prepared to accept the far greater manifestation of divine power expressed in the actual resurrection, is ludicrous. There is no real difference between the 'after three days' of Mark (in the better text), and the 'on the third day', of the other evangelists: both can refer to the same period of time, by Semitic idiom.

But besides being a prophetic 'necessity' (for Ho. 6:2 was clearly seen by the early church as a prophecy of the resurrection), there were various other aspects making resurrection on the third day appropriate. The symbolism of the number three for completeness is clear, throughout the Bible. The 'third day' could thus be taken to denote perfection and culmination, almost inevitability in God's working.

Any lingering suspicions, sometimes artificially revived by modern commentators, that Jesus had merely fainted, and was restored by the coolness of the tomb, would be banished by the length of such a period.

As to the reported Jewish belief that the soul lingered near the body for two days, but finally fled on or before the third day, it would only increase the evidential value of the resurrection as a miracle, by proving conclusively that this was indeed a true raising of the dead. The resurrection of Jesus was no mere re-uniting of a hovering soul with a waiting body, but an act of mighty power (Rom. 1:4).

43. Joseph of Arimathea, mentioned in passing here, is often overshadowed in our eyes by his fellow-councillor Nicodemus, who appears with him in the Johannine account (Jn. 19:39). Nicodemus appears to be known only to John, however, while all the synoptists know of Joseph, the wealthy member of the Sanhedrin, although he appears only in the context of the burial of Jesus. The text, here, reading *euschēmōn, respected*, suggests an influential and highly honoured man: in popular parlance, it meant 'well to do' as well as influential.[1] He was one yearning for, and looking for, the establishment of God's reign upon earth, doubtless through the earthly Jesus of Nazareth. It showed real courage, for a man of his position to confess an association with a leader already fallen and thus apparently incapable of benefiting him further. But even Joseph's loving care for the dead body of Jesus showed that he had no immediate expectation of a resurrection. The 'linen shroud' and the stone rolled against the door of the sepulchre are too final for that (verse 46). There may be, however, an implied contrast between the denial of Peter and the confession of Joseph.

Note the failure of the disciples to come forward even now, when all was over. The only exception is the group of women (47), who would prepare the spices for Christ's burial, who were watching the entombment (47). Pilate would have almost certainly refused to grant the body to such humble disciples, for it was the property of the Roman Government, as that of any other condemned and executed criminal was, while to a man of wealth and position like Joseph, he might well be prepared to hand it over as a favour. See Schweizer on the usual disposal of the bodies of those executed. Scientific investigation has now shown conclusively that the so-called 'Turin Shroud' cannot be the shroud mentioned here.

44. Pilate's surprise at the news of the death was genuine;

[1] This probably arose in the Hebrew mind because of the common connection in the early part of the Old Testament between piety and wealth. This concept was slowly corrected (or rather, 'balanced'), by the prophets of the Old Testament by pointing out that it was only too possible to obtain wealth by injustice and oppression of the poor, and the introduction of the concept of the 'righteous sufferer' who is not necessarily rewarded in this life at all (see Hab. 3:17). It is interesting, if alarming, to see the rise in modern times of a 'prosperity cult' within Christianity, which promises worldly wealth to those who follow Christ. Needless to say, this is quite foreign to the teaching of the New Testament. When Jesus tells

men might, and often did, linger for days under the torture of crucifixion, before dying of exposure and thirst under the pitiless sun, or of asphyxiation from the strained hanging position. In the granting of the request, is there perhaps some stirring of Pilate's conscience? In the quick question as to whether the prisoner is already dead, is he trying to turn attention away from himself? Note the variant reading, *whether He had been some time dead*.

45. One wonders what answer the centurion gave to Pilate; but although it is tempting to speculate, it was probably only the bare military question and answer, certifying that death had actually taken place. A Roman sergeant had seen too many deaths to be in any uncertainty about such a fact. This, indeed, had been the very reason why a responsible officer had been posted with the squad on duty, in order to certify that the execution had been carried out as commanded. Common soldiers were not above the temptation to accept bribes on such occasions (Mt. 28:12–15).

46–47. Burial was necessary lest people said Christ's was not a real death: hence the creed says with finality 'dead, and buried'. Nevertheless, this burial was only temporary; Joseph must have hurriedly wound the *linen shroud* of fine gauze (Greek *sindon*), which he had just bought, around the body. He then laid the body in the tomb, hewn out of the rock near the site of the crucifixion, and rolled across the blocking stone that served as a door to secure it. After this, he must have departed in haste, for it cannot have been far from the legal commencement of the sabbath.

The kings of Judah had been buried in this way, in garden tombs and with spices (*e.g.* 2 Ki. 21:26), although the modern attributions to royalty of the old rock-hewn tombs of Jerusalem are by no means certain. Nevertheless, sufficient examples of such rock-hewn tombs remain from the turn of the first century to give a fair idea of the type that Mark is describing. The so-called 'Garden Tomb', near 'Gordon's Calvary', while almost certainly not the tomb in question, reproduces very well the

His disciples that they will 'receive a hundredfold' as much (10:30) in return for anything sacrificed for Him, He is speaking neither in quantitative nor materialistic terms, though every Christian would agree on the spiritual truth of what is said.

atmosphere and appearance, much more indeed than the traditional and probably correct site of 'Holy Sepulchre'. Wherever the exact site of the tomb was, the two Marys *saw where he was laid* (47) and then returned home to prepare spices (16:1), ready to return after the sabbath and to complete the process of embalming the body; that was strictly a women's task in Israel custom, not men's, as in Egypt (as Herodotus records). It was very necessary that they should witness where Jesus had been buried, lest they be later accused of mistakenly coming to the wrong tomb on the morning of the resurrection, a charge made in ancient as in modern days by opponents. The witness of women might not be accepted in Jewish law, but it was essential to the plan of God: the disciples themselves could not act as witnesses, for they had all fled.[1]

VII. THE THIRD DAY: THE RISEN LORD (16:1–20)

A. THE RESURRECTION (16:1–8)

1–2. It was very early on Sunday morning, before full daylight (2). Now sabbath was over, with its agonizing forced inactivity; now at last the women could do something, even if it was only embalming the dead, for which they had already bought the spices (1). Nineham is right in stressing their utter unpreparedness for the event that lay ahead; this is a sure proof of the veracity of the narrative. Here was love and deep devotion; but it was only an adoration of a dead Christ, and that was not yet true Christian faith. The women looked for the familiar loved figure of the past, so the first result of the resurrection message was only the fear produced in them by the news of this new divine Christ (8). A past chapter in God's dealings with them had closed, and they, like us, were such cowards that they would rather cling to the old familiar past than venture out continually into the new and unknown with God; yet this is the present and continual meaning of the walk of faith, as Abraham

[1] There is no need to assume, with Schweizer, that they had all fled to Galilee already, though they may possibly have gone there after receiving the message of the angel to the women in 16:6–7.

329

found. They did not want to lose their earthly Jesus: yet Paul sees this transference of faith from the incarnate Lord to the risen Lord as necessary (2 Cor. 5:16). The disciples had always, even in His earthly life, shrunk from their beloved familiar Lord when He displayed supernatural powers (4:41). This only goes to show that, for all their closeness to Him, they had not yet fully understood Him (9:32), nor indeed could they until after His resurrection, as the gospels reiterate.

3. The stone which had been placed in position by Joseph (15:46), would have rolled down its sloping groove and slid into place, precisely to guard against any such unauthorized entry by individuals, so the anxiety of the women was well founded. The priests might be afraid of a smuggling away of the body by the disciples (Mt. 27:64), but Joseph would have equally feared common tomb-robbers, at whom so many tomb-imprecations of early centuries are directed. There were numerous cases of tombs being re-used by others for a second 'pirate' burial, after the throwing away of the first body or bones. But in confessing their own complete helplessness, they had come the first neces- sary step; God would act, and indeed, had already acted. To Schweizer, the question of the women depicts the 'human' approach: our whole human predicament is summed up in these few words.

4. If they had only known it, the resurrection had already made all their cares and anxieties unnecessary; that which they themselves could never do, God had already done, for the stone (*very large*), has already been rolled away. Mark does not men- tion the earthquake and the angelic visitation which had moved the stone according to Matthew 28:2: as usual, he restricts him- self to the bare facts necessary for his story. It does not of course necessarily mean that he was ignorant of these points: indeed, his reference to the 'young man dressed in a white robe' sug- gests otherwise (5), since angels have already played their part in Mark's story (1:13).

6. To dovetail the various resurrection appearances of Christ, or indeed the order of early visits by disciples to the tomb, is not

as easy as might appear at first sight, although the gospel accounts are in rough general agreement. Full discussion of this point, however, is more relevant to a commentary on other New Testament books, for the text before us is quite straightforward, as far as it goes, at least in these first eight verses. In subsequent verses, the account seems to be simply an attempted harmonisation of material contained in the other gospels. It is obvious that here as elsewhere, much is omitted in Mark's Gospel, either because it was felt irrelevant to the main 'run' of the story, and therefore irrelevant to direct gospel preaching, or else because the author did not have the necessary close contact himself with any primary eyewitness of the resurrection events, although this is hard to believe, if the author was John Mark as already suggested.

Whatever the explanation, it is still a remarkable fact that Mark did not include any direct account of a resurrection appearance of Christ to his disciples.[1] This is one of the 'Marcan omissions' which puzzled the early church as greatly as they puzzle us, and to which we are no nearer a solution today.

But whatever the reason for this omission, it must be considered in the light of the similar omission of any full account of the restoration of Peter, to which verse 7 contains a passing reference only. In view of the stress laid on Peter's denial, this is somewhat strange, but is probably to be explained by Mark's 'economical' story-telling style.

If the longer ending of Mark is genuine (see section B below), then several points expressed in the above sentence must be reworded. Among other things, there is here a general reference to the restoration of all the apostolic band in verses 14–18, where Peter would be included. We have seen before (8:33) how Mark sets Peter in a wider context, so that he can stand in 'theological shorthand' for the whole body. In Peter's denial and restoration he is the representative disciple, and so it could be argued that there is no need specially to single him out here: all had fled, all had denied their Lord, all were restored, except only Judas.

5. Mark does not directly identify the *young man* as an angel,

---

[1]For a good discussion of the matter, see Anderson; an equal number of arguments can be put forward on either side.

although his supernatural character is clear from the ensuing narrative.[1] The realm of spiritual reality which we loosely call 'angels' is revealed to humans in the Bible in various forms. At times, they appear as living non-human creatures (Ezk. 1:5–14); at other times, as abstract mathematical forms (Ezk. 1:16). But the usual form of revelation is as celestial beings who have assumed human shape, at least temporarily. Youth and gleaming whiteness of garments probably symbolize heavenly perfection and glory (cf. 9:3, for the transformation in the garments of Jesus at the mountain of transfiguration).[2] In spite of this accommodation to human vision and understanding, the women were still alarmed before these beings of pure spirit, as often were others in the New Testament account (Lk. 1:12; 1:29; 2:9).

6. So here, too, as in other biblical instances (e.g. Lk. 2:9), the first task of the angel is to reassure, by confirming to the women that the purpose of this appearance is mercy, not judgment. Here was not only angelic announcement of the glad news, but also clear visible evidence, in the empty tomb: *Jesus of Nazareth* (a familiar title), who had been crucified, has risen from the dead. Again, Mark stresses the reality of the hard facts of His death. Even the manifestation of the angel, however, and the sight of the place where Jesus had lain did not convince the women completely, to judge from their subsequent actions. That the ordinary word *neaniskos, young man,* is used here in Mark, and not the specific *angelos,* 'angel' or 'heavenly messenger', probably only implies that, apart from the sense of awe which he inspired, there was nothing compelling about the appearance of the heavenly visitant. It is to the eye of faith that angels appear, for the unbelieving do not see them; and furthermore, it is the eye of faith that interprets angels for what they are. Whenever God acts, it must always be with sufficient ambiguity for us to

[1] It is therefore quite gratuitous to identify this supernatural messenger with the very earthy 'young man' who fled in Gethsemane (14:51): it is not even likely that there is an implied theological contrast between the two 'young men', as might have been the case had this been in John's Gospel. See Telford in IOM for various theories on the matter.

[2] Lane points out here what is made explicit in the account of the transfiguration (9:3), that brightness, not colour, is the point of the reference. But this is broadly speaking true of all adjectives of colour in the ancient world: see *IBD* under the entry *colours.*

need the interpretation of faith if we are to see the happening as an act of God. Christian faith is, in the last resort, an understanding by faith of every event as the activity of a God who is at once all love, all holiness and all power. So, without the key of faith, which is the means of interpretation, even the news of the resurrection would be opaque. But faith is not subjective self-deception, for it does not create the fact which it interprets. Only God creates the fact or event, in this case, the event of the resurrection of Jesus. Faith is an appropriation for oneself of the act of God, a grasping hold of that which is real, even if at present unseen (Heb. 11:1).[1]

7-8. If the women had fully believed the message, we might have expected them to witness boldly and immediately. But, in fairness, the women had merely had a momentary encounter with an angel: so far, they had not met the Lord Himself. Those who have themselves met the risen Lord face to face 'cannot but speak' of those things that they had heard and seen (Acts 4:20), as we can see from the accounts in the other gospels, summarised in verses 9 to 12 below, in the 'longer ending'. But even believing testimony by witnesses does not necessarily lead to faith on the part of the hearers.

Further, it is not clear from Mark that it was only unbelief that closed the mouths of these potential witnesses to the resurrection. They were certainly afraid, but also *astonishment* was theirs (verse 8), and *ekstasis* may contain a note of joy as well: awe, rather than fear, filled them (Lightfoot). This news was too great and wonderful to grasp at once, and it may be that only the abrupt ending of Mark at verse 8 stops us from hearing of a subsequent report to the eleven apostles, as in the other gospels.[2]

---

[1]Even if Mark's Gospel had originally ended at 8 (which is uncertain), there can be no doubt that Mark, like all other early Christians, believed that a physical resurrection of Jesus had taken place. That is the whole point of the witness of the angel, and the sight of the empty tomb (6): Mark is too matter-of-fact to allow us to spiritualize these away. Whatever the views of some modern theologians as to the possibility of a Christianity based purely upon a 'spiritual' resurrection of Christ, it is unknown to the New Testament, whether in the gospel accounts (as here), or in the epistles (as in 1 Cor. 15:12-20).

[2]Tannehill (IOM) sees the failure of the women to witness as on a par with the continual failure of the disciples in Mark to understand; even after the resurrection, there has been no change. As contrast, he sees Joseph of Arimathea and Simon of Cyrene: but this is a false

Whether it was obeyed or not, the commission to bring the news was certainly given to the women, with the specific inclusion of *Peter* (verse 7) as one recipient of the message. For the Lord's promised preceding of the disciples to Galilee, see the promise of 14:28, and the comment on that verse. Other gospels mention resurrection appearances in Jerusalem, but certainly do not exclude an appearance in Galilee, to which indeed Matthew specifically refers (Mt. 28:16). We do not need to follow Marxsen here in seeing a reference to the Gentile Christian church of later days in Galilee: as Minear says, the Lord is simply gathering together in Galilee the 'sheep of the flock' earlier scattered in Gethsemane.

B. THE LONGER ENDING (16:9–20)

This section contains the so-called 'longer ending' of Mark, omitted in some MSS, and rejected as spurious by most early authorities, such as Eusebius and Jerome. Certainly the style is quite unlike that of the rest of Mark. This poses a problem which may be put briefly as follows. To end the gospel with verse 8 is not only abrupt linguistically, but also abrupt theologically.[1] Nevertheless, this so-called 'longer ending' is not found in some important manuscripts, and seems to be deliberately excluded. In addition, between verses 8 and 9, several early MSS and versions read 'But they told Peter and his group briefly all the things that had been commanded them. And after these things Jesus himself appeared to them, and sent out through them from east to west the holy and incorruptible proclamation of everlasting salvation.' This reads like an early attempt to tidy loose ends; the last clause in particular does not sound Marcan in its expression. One MS actually ends with this summary, omitting verses 9–20 altogether, which is even more suspicious.

---

contrast, for neither of them has any faith in a resurrection. It is only Pentecost that will mark the real difference in the readiness of the disciples to witness.

[1] With due respect to Lightfoot and other modern scholars, they have proved only the *possibility* of such an abrupt ending, but certainly not its *likelihood*. It is only fair to say, however, that most commentators today accept the ending at verse 8 as original, except for those who would add 16–20 as part of the original account. Few would now argue for verses 9 to 15 as being part of the original text, even if they believe the contents to be accurate.

As regards the longer ending itself, it may be fairly described as showing knowledge of the subject matter of John 20:1–8 (the story of Mary Magdalene), along with that of Luke 24:13–35 (the story of the Emmaus road), and Matthew 28:18–20 (the great commission). If so, it must be later than these other gospels, and therefore later than Mark.

It is, in fact, a short harmony of resurrection appearances, a skeleton outline which can be easily filled in from the other gospel narratives. But verse 9 itself seems to be introduced without reference to verse 1 above, virtually as a fresh beginning, which is suspicious. Indeed, the whole summary seems to have been drawn up independently of Mark's Gospel, without reference to any of the preceding verses.

Therefore it seems reasonable to see the longer ending as an attempt, known at least as early as Irenaeus, to 'round off' a gospel whose original ending was either felt to be inadequate or had been lost; that several such attempts were made is obvious from the different versions circulating. Further general textual uncertainty is shown by the addition of another long saying added to verse 14 by one authority. Jerome knew of its existence in several MSS of his day, but as it is, from its content, obviously non-canonical, it will not be further mentioned here except as evidence for a general textual dislocation at this point in Mark's Gospel.

What, then, is the theological value of this longer ending? It may be compared with the story of the woman caught in adultery, in John 8:1–11, as an example of a Christian tradition which may well be genuine and is undoubtedly early, but does not belong to the actual gospel text as it stands. In the case of the Marcan ending, we can go further; the contents are in any case authentic, even if perhaps derived from other evangels, and there is even the strong possibility that this is an 'official ending', added by the early church to a sort of 'second edition' of Mark. We know so little about the actual circumstances of the primary composition and first written forms of the gospel that it is unwise to be dogmatic. We shall therefore comment briefly upon it, even if it is only a patchwork of pieces from the other gospels. It would be unwise, however, to build a theological position upon these verses alone; and this no responsible Christian group has ever done.

9. This resurrection appearance of Christ is clearly not the appearance of the angel in the garden to Mary, along with the other Mary, as mentioned in verse 5 above (Jn. 20:1). It perhaps refers to John 20:16, Mary's second visit to the tomb, when she met the Lord Himself. Luke, who is presumably the other source here, also mentions in connection with Mary of Magdala the 'seven demons'[1] (Lk. 8:2), a number which is probably figurative for total possession by the powers of evil. Some have suggested that this Mary was the anonymous woman who anointed the Lord's feet in the house of Simon the Pharisee (Lk. 7:38), since she is described there as being a 'sinner'. In any case, the thought is clearly that Mary, to whom much had been forgiven, 'loved much' (Lk. 7:47).

10–11. Even if the other women *said nothing to anyone* because of their fear (8), Mary Magdalene here spreads the good news. But, even when she did, the disciples refused to believe (11), in spite of their sorrow (10). There is nothing more tragic than the refusal of the disciples to receive such witness, even when it was the answer to their problems. The unbelief of the disciples has been a constant theme of Mark's Gospel: they are still the same, even after the resurrection of Jesus, showing that the picture given is true.

12–13. So it was not surprising that two of these same disciples failed at first to see, in the stranger of the Emmaus road, the risen Christ (Lk. 24:16). That seems to be the story indicated by *in another form* here: usually Jesus was recognized by His disciples at once, during His resurrection appearance to them. Again, it was poetic justice that those who had initially disbelieved the women's witness should now find themselves disbelieved by the other disciples, when they returned to Jerusalem, to tell how they had met the Lord.

---

[1] The expulsion of demons is frequently mentioned in the gospels, more sparingly mentioned in Acts, and not at all in the epistles. Neither is there any special 'gift' of demon-expulsion mentioned in the epistles, though there are several references to gifts of healing (*e.g.* 1 Cor. 12:9). While there is no doubt that to be 'demonized' describes a theological reality, it is possible that metaphorical or popular language is sometimes employed here. The position seems exactly analogous to influence by, or possession by, the Holy Spirit: all

14. This must refer to the appearance of Christ to the whole body of the disciples, chronicled in John 20:19ff. It almost seems as if the disciples, in the stubbornness of their sorrow, had actually preferred unbelief and despondency to God's joyous truth of resurrection. Unbelief and hardness of heart had long been the besetting sins of the disciples (9:19), and nowhere were these more apparent than in this refusal to believe in the resurrection. There is a consistency in the portrayal of the disciples throughout which is very remarkable. Yet, by God's law, these two very sins would be the greatest obstacles to the apostolic preaching of the gospel to others. To understand the blindness and perversity of those outside Christ, they need only look at their own hearts to understand and be humbled.

15–16. This is a form of the 'great commission' which, according to Matthew 28:16–20, was delivered on a mountain in Galilee, where so much of Christ's earlier teaching had been given.[1] This appearance fulfilled His expressed intention to precede His disciples to Galilee (7). Until the disciples had met the risen Lord for themselves, and were truly convinced of His resurrection, they had no gospel to preach, and so it was fitting that only now should they receive the great commission. Indeed, so far from generalizing the evangelistic mission, during the days of the earthly ministry of Jesus, the scope of His healing and teaching work, though widespread, had been deliberately restricted by Him to Israel, and work among the Gentiles was not sought by Him (7:27). In Mark's 'Gentile' Gospel, while he does not record any prohibition by the Lord of preaching by His disciples to Gentiles (Mt. 10:5), as is natural, yet equally he nowhere records any command to them to preach 'to the nations', during His earthly ministry. In view of Mark's strongly Gentile interest, this is a remarkable fact, confirming the truth of the picture given in the other gospels. If this is so, a very remarkable extension of the scope of evangelism has taken place after the cross and

---

sorts of 'degrees' of influence seem possible, ranging at one extreme from resistance to the Spirit (Acts 7:51) to filling by the Spirit (Acts 4:8) at the other extreme.

[1] Some scholars (*e.g.* Linnemann and Schmithals, quoted in Telford, IOM), while rejecting the earlier verses, accept 16–20 (but not 15), as the original ending of Mark; however, this seems an arbitrary judgment.

resurrection of Christ, although the full effects will not be seen until after Pentecost.

Schweizer sees a peculiar appropriateness in the fact that the missionary commission follows immediately upon the denunciation of unbelief. Faith will lead to proclamation: unbelief will seal the lips of the disciples.

16. As always in God's dealings with humanity, it is faith that justifies and unbelief that condemns, and Christian faith is to be henceforth to be symbolized and sealed in baptism. We have no mention of Christian baptism elsewhere in Mark, though John 4:1–2 seems to mention it during the ministry of Jesus. Nor does the longer ending, in this commandment, specify either the manner of baptism or the formula to be used. This may be either because these things were not held to be of importance, or because both were so familiar at the time of writing that no need was felt to detail them here.

17–18. Here again is a great rule of the spiritual life; signs are to be given to those who believe, not primarily in order that they may believe. This was the ceaseless battle between the Pharisees and Jesus, with the Pharisees reiterating their demands for a sign, and Jesus equally adamant that no sign would be given to unbelief (8:11–12). Incidentally, the word used for 'sign' here is not used by Mark of Jesus' miracles, although it is so used by John (Anderson): this may also show a later date, and certainly suggests non-Marcan authorship for the longer ending.

This promise is a word for the church; it is for those within, not for those outside. Every one of these evidential 'signs', except possibly the drinking of lethal draughts, is recorded in the history of the early church in Acts. The speaking of *new tongues* for instance, is frequently found from Pentecost onwards (Acts 2:4). For the rest, in Acts 16:18 Paul expels a demon; in Acts 28:5 he shakes off a snake into the fire; in Acts 28:8 he lays his hand on sick and heals them. Whether or not such spectacular manifestations were intended to be continuous in the life of the church, or to be restricted to this period, or sporadic throughout church history, must be decided in the light of the rest of the New Testament. In view of the uncertain

338

textual evidence for this longer conclusion, and therefore its doubtful canonical status, no dogmatic assumptions should be made from this particular passage alone.[1] If, as suggested, these verses are a sub-apostolic attempt to restore a lost ending to Mark, then we must assume that there was some known extra-biblical case of Christians drinking lethal draughts without harm; otherwise, there would have been no point in including the phenomenon here amid a list of other well attested miracles.[2]

19. This verse clearly describes the ascension (Lk. 24:50–51), in phraseology borrowed from the Old Testament, although it is difficult to speak of any specific quotation. The verse seems a combination of 2 Kings 2:11 (the ascent of Elijah), with the messianic Psalm 110:1. So the early Christian interpretation of the Lord's ascension is clear; it is a triumphal ascent, to be followed by an 'enthronement', awaiting God's ultimate vindication of His Christ. Psalm 110 is the great messianic Psalm, where Melchizedek's priesthood is promised to the Lord; it is also the very Psalm quoted to the scribes by Jesus when He asked them His 'hard question' about the identity of David's Son, who was also David's Lord (12:37).

20. This is the peaceful closing verse, like Luke 24:53; but Luke leaves the disciples at worship in the temple, while the longer ending of Mark shows the church expanding on all fronts. The reason for this may be that Luke's Gospel is only the first volume of his church history; there is a sequel to come in the book of Acts. Not so here; the whole of Acts is covered for the author in this single verse; and it may be more than an accident that the style of this last verse is much closer to that of Acts.

[1] All three views have been held by equally respected and equally conservative biblical scholars: but those who adopt the second or third position should at least consider seriously the re-emergence of many of these signs in the church of our day. Anderson wisely points out that the writers of this longer ending obviously belonged to a group which held that these 'signs' were intended to be ongoing features of church life.
[2] Eusebius 3:39, does mention this as occurring in the case of Justus Barsabbas (cf. Acts 1:23), but tells the story only on the authority of Papias, for whom he has very little respect. Still, it may well represent an early tradition: if so, this incident may lie behind the mention here.

There can be no going back to the old; the church must move forwards, with her Lord. In this, the anonymous author speaks truly, and, even if he is not Mark, he is a worthy successor to the writer of the earliest gospel, for he shares fully Mark's goals and interests. Lastly, as in the gospel itself, the *signs* do not constitute the message: they but *confirmed* it. So we may add our *Amen*.

COMMON JAPANESE PHRASES

COMMON
JAPANESE
PHRASES

Compiled by
Sanseido

Translated and adapted by
John Brennan

KODANSHA INTERNATIONAL
Tokyo · New York · London

Distributed in the United States by Kodansha America, Inc., 114 Fifth Avenue, New York N.Y. 10011, and in the United Kingdom and continental Europe by Kodansha Europe Ltd., 95 Aldwych, London WC2B 4JF. Published by Kodansha International Ltd., 17-14 Otowa 1-chome, Bunkyo-ku, Tokyo 112, and Kodansha America, Inc.

First edition, 1997
97 98 99 00 10 9 8 7 6 5 4 3 2 1
ISBN 4-7700-2072-4

CONTENTS

Preface

Early on in my own education in Japanese (a process that may conclude in time for the colonization of Uranus), I witnessed something that alerted me to the prominent role reserved for established phraseology. It was during my first few months in Tokyo, long before I could really speak the language, and the outfit I was working for was hosting a daytime gathering to celebrate the opening of a new branch. Other than me almost everyone in attendance was Japanese, except for a foursome of business school types from the United States who had apparently sneaked out of the office upstairs where they were interning for the summer. Before the drinks were served, we all had to stand around in a big circle and introduce ourselves—in Japanese, naturally. As it happened, the MBA boys from upstairs were up first, and I was more than curious to see what they would say. I myself did not yet know how to introduce myself in Japanese. The first American cruised through his brief introduction; he had the routine down pretty well, I thought. I probably smirked a bit, though, when the second one simply repeated the words used by the guy before him, changing only the name. When the other two Americans followed suit, rattling off the very same phrase their colleagues had, I glanced around to see if any of the native speakers found this as fishy as I did. None did. In fact, to a man they used exactly the same phrase to introduce themselves—so I did, too. By the time my turn came around, I had my introduction down cold—*Burenan desu. Dōzo yoroshiku onegai shimasu*. I even pulled off the bow that went with it.

Now, outside of the military or the realm of comedy (and

not counting that scene near the end of "Spartacus"), it's pretty hard to imagine two dozen English speakers using exactly the same phrase, one after the other, to introduce themselves. That Japanese speakers do so as a matter of course not only points up the very different roles that words can serve in different cultures, but also holds an immediate implication for anyone hoping to communicate in Japanese: Learn that phrase!

The introduction, naturally, is only the beginning. There's a whole storehouse of expressions that have become entrenched in Japanese-language behavior through endless repetition and are now all but automatically employed in certain situations and exchanges. This book invites English-language readers inside that storehouse to browse around and sample some of the stock.

There are two groups of readers for whom this book will be particularly useful. The first group comprises serious students of Japanese, those who are already familiar with Japanese grammar and with the various structural inflections designating polite, honorific, and humble language. None of these points are explained here; that's a job for other books, some of which the serious student has likely read. For those readers, this book serves up a host of pointers for pursuing the Japanese language further down the timeworn paths traced and retraced by its native speakers, whose behavior defines conventional usage.

The other group for whom this book will have special value consists of people who don't know any Japanese and don't care about the underlying linguistic details. They just want a few words they can memorize and deliver in given situations to show that, even if they can't always express it, they're clued in and are onto the spirit of the thing. Such readers will find in these pages not only the right words to say but also abundant guidance on when and how to say them.

Beyond the utility of the phrases presented, both serious students of Japanese and more casual readers are apt to be interested in the observations about the social and psychological contexts in which these expressions are used. Language conventions often reflect a set of tacit assumptions about the world that permeate—though they may not be shared by—the entire society, and this is conspicuously prevalent in Japanese. The editors at Sanseido, whose 1992 *Kimari Monku no Jiten* ("Dictionary of Common Phrases") is this book's source, made a point of enlivening their remarks on Japanese phraseology with little object lessons on the social graces, drawn from a very characteristic worldview. Wherever possible, this approach has been preserved in the translation here, with certain adjustments for the benefit of English-language readers. Suffice it to say that the worldview represented here isn't necessarily my own.

I've done my best to translate all the phrases and accompanying commentary into natural-sounding standard American English, whenever necessary forgoing a literal decoding of the components of a phrase or sentence in order to be faithful to the meaning of the whole. To some extent I've tried to approximate in English the level of formality, politeness, or humility that's usually explicit in the Japanese, but American English has such variable standards for these dimensions of expression that any given interpretation is sure to sound odd to somebody. Japanese phrases or sentences that contain what are considered exclusively female or exclusively male speech forms are designated by the symbols Ⓕ and Ⓜ, respectively. The conventions for transliterating Japanese are those observed in the other books in the *Power Japanese* series.

***

I'm deeply grateful to Michael Brase of Kodansha International for his (almost) infinite patience and sagacious counsel, and also to KI's Shigeyoshi Suzuki for keeping a sharp eye on the Japanese text. My heartfelt thanks to the great Tom Gally for getting me through the door.

John Brennan

まえがき

　どんな言語にも「決まり文句」というものがあります。人間が言葉を用いて社会生活をする以上、決まり文句は通貨のごとく日常ひんぱんに使われています。ある程度外国語の学習が進んでくると、決まり文句という通貨がいかに便利か分かるときが必ず来ると思いますが、本書はまさにそうした学習者に読んでいただきたい本といえます。

　外国語の学習にとって文法を学ぶことはたしかに必要なことではありますが、コミュニケーションという点からは、どうしても決まり文句なくしてはスムーズに会話を運ぶのはむつかしいようです。それは決まり文句が意味内容もさることながら、むしろ世の中の"潤滑油"として話し手や聞き手の気持ちを伝えるシグナルとしての役割を大いに担っているからに他なりません。「つまらないものですが……」という有名な日本的フレーズはそのシグナルの端的な例です。贈り物を贈る側も受ける側もこの決まり文句のおかげでずいぶん気が楽になります。贈答の習慣のある日本では、まさに贈り物とセットになった大切なサインというわけです。ですからこの表現をそのまま字義どおり英訳して「日本人はヘンな言い訳をする」というのはまったくの見当違い。日本社会、文化への理解を欠いていると言わざるを得ません。

　本書では日本語学習者のために日常よく使われる決まり文句を場面別にとりあげています。簡単なものから多少むつかしいと感じられるものまではば広く取り上げ、学習者が意味だけでなく使うときのコツやタイミングなども感じ取れるよう例文も豊富に用意しています。

　尚、本書は『決まり文句の辞典』（三省堂）に基づき、海外の読者に読んでいただけるよう若干のアダプテーションを行ったもので、語学書としてばかりか日本の社会を知るための参考書として気軽に読んでいただくとおもしろいと思います。

講談社インターナショナル編集局

❦

Best wishes on the beginning of a New Year

あけましておめでとうございます。

Akemashite omedetō gozaimasu.

Best wishes on the beginning of a New Year.

This is the standard expression for greeting people for the first time in the New Year, the celebration of which is the most significant and ceremonially observed holiday period in the Japanese calendar. A complete formal New Year's greeting begins with these words and continues with an expression of gratitude for the other person's kindness (or patronage) over the course of the previous year:

旧年中はお世話になりました。

Kyūnen-chū wa osewa ni narimashita.

I appreciate your kindness throughout the past year.

The speaker then expresses the hope that the New Year will see the continuation of good relations, communicating this desire in the form of a request:

本年も相変わりませず、よろしくお願いいたします。

Honnen mo aikawarimasezu, yoroshiku onegai itashimasu.

I humbly ask your continued favor in the coming year.

Even such a formal greeting, however, will have the hollow ring of a memorized formula if your delivery is rushed or if the words are tossed off in a monotone. It is essential to deliver your greeting at a measured pace, be attentive to the reply, and bow once respectfully upon concluding the greeting.

Among friends, from whom an extended and formal New Year's greeting would sound stilted and unnatural, a shorter and less formal alternative is preferred:

あけましておめでとう。今年もどうぞよろしく。

Akemashite omedetō. Kotoshi mo dōzo yoroshiku.

Happy New Year! Don't forget me this year!

While the general trend is toward less formality, this is an excellent opportunity to represent yourself as a solid, serious person to people in your neighborhood, for example, or to higher-ups at the office, by extending a scrupulously proper formal New Year's greeting, as described above. These few phrases, skillfully executed, could actually help to restore a less than impeccable public image, if need be. After all, New Year's time is the season for making fresh starts. The key to making a good impression is the delivery: enunciate each word clearly to the very end of the greeting, finishing with a crisp *onegai itashimasu*. The big finish is a sure crowd-pleaser.

Congratulations on this happy day

本日はおめでとうございます。

Honjitsu wa omedetō gozaimasu.

Congratulations on this happy day.

For a guest attending a celebration or special event—a wedding, a piano or dance recital, a party celebrating the publication of a book or commemorating the founding of a company—this standard congratulatory greeting is the very first thing to say to the hosts or to any of the participants in the event.

When you attend a celebration or similar event, your primary social duty is to express your heartfelt congratulations—*omedetō*—to the appropriate people. By using this expression when greeting your hosts at the reception table or the entranceway, you clearly identify yourself as an invited guest. This paves the way for the reply, which is likely to be something on the order of:

> ありがとうございます。恐れいりますが、こちら
> にご記帳をお願いいたします。
>
> *Arigatō gozaimasu. Osoreirimasu ga, kochira ni gokichō o onegai itashimasu.*
>
> Thank you very much. May I trouble you to sign the guest book, please?

Depending on the occasion, guests at a celebration may greet one another with the standard congratulatory expression *omedetō gozaimasu*, communicating the same sort of mutual felicitation as when people wish one another a Happy New Year (see *Akemashite omedetō gozaimasu*). In such cases, *omedetō gozaimasu* can be an especially convenient way to greet people you don't know—a brief, friendly expression that you deliver with a smile, and one that does not automatically lead to the more complicated business of formal introductions.

In case you have been asked to make a toast or give a speech at such an event, you should preface your remarks with an earnest:

> 皆さま、おめでとうございます。
>
> *Mina-sama, omedetō gozaimasu.*
>
> Ladies and gentlemen, I offer my congratulations.

This has two distinct advantages: it properly communicates

your good wishes to all those assembled, and it also serves notice that you are now going to speak and everyone should pipe down and listen up.

❧

May even greater success lie ahead

ますますのご発展を祈っております。

Masumasu no gohatten o inotte orimasu.

May even greater success lie ahead.

This expression may be employed on celebratory occasions like the founding of a new business enterprise, the opening of a new establishment, or the winning of a prize or an election, and it can also apply to a commemorative event such as the tenth anniversary of a firm's founding. It serves as a standard ending for a message of congratulations, a sort of closing salute.

When extending congratulations for the success of a business, the word *hatten* (literally, "development," but translated here as "success," and in this usage preceded by the honorific prefix *go*) is frequently replaced with such words as *han'ei* ("prosperity"), or even *katsuyaku* ("activity") or *seikō* ("success")—all of which must be preceded by the honorific *go*. Thus, for such occasions any of the following variations are also appropriate:

ますますのご発展を祈っております。

Masumasu no gohan'ei o inotte orimasu.

May even greater prosperity lie ahead.

ますますのご活躍を祈っております。

Masumasu no gokatsuyaku o inotte orimasu.

May even more enterprising activity lie ahead.

ますますのご成功を祈っております。

Masumasu no goseikō o inotte orimasu.

May even greater success lie ahead.

To congratulate an individual on his or her personal accomplishments, you will never go wrong with the old standby:

ますますのご発展を祈っております。

Masumasu no gohatten o inotte orimasu.

May even greater success lie ahead.

For a business-related occasion, it is essential to include in one's remarks some words of praise for the efforts of those involved. If you are offering congratulations on the progress or success of a particular company, for example, you applaud the hard work of the *shain*, or "all the employees" (everyone up to, but not including, the *shachō*, or "president"). For this purpose the following are useful:

並々ならぬご努力とご苦労の結果と……

Naminami naranu godoryoku to gokurō no kekka to ...

As a result of your extraordinary efforts and hard work ...

山田さんの実行力には頭が下がります。

Yamada-san no jikkōryoku ni wa atama ga sagarimasu.

I bow my head to your ability to get the job done, Mr. Yamada.

社員一丸となって、ここまで盛り立てて、……

Shain-ichigan to natte, koko made moritatete, ...

All the employees, working together as one, having brought you this far, ...

A great deal of importance is attached to recognizing the diligence and the sacrifices of employees and to expressing a sense of empathy. If you convincingly demonstrate an understanding of the struggles and hard work that preceded the day's celebration, you are likely to win the hearts of the celebrants. In addition, it is important to communicate your own pleasure over the accomplishments of those being honored. This is perhaps best done in simple and direct language, as in:

自分のことのようにうれしく思っています。
Jibun no koto no yō ni ureshiku omotte imasu.
I feel as happy as if I myself had achieved your great success.

In any case, whether at the end of your remarks or the beginning, you are expected to offer words of encouragement and to emphasize your expectations for the future.

Congratulations on the birth of your child

ご安産でおめでとうございます。
Goanzan de omedetō gozaimasu.
Congratulations on the birth of your child.

This is the standard formal expression for congratulating the mother of a newborn baby or any of the immediate family. Such congratulations are traditionally regarded as falling within the domain of conversation among women— the mother of the child and her female well-wishers. In the past it was customary to wait until the mother had completely recovered from the delivery (up to a month or so after the actual birth) to call on her and offer congratulations, but these days felicitous sentiments are commonly expressed less formally, usually over the telephone. A typical example of informal congratulations from a woman might go:

おめでとう、よくがんばったわね。ゆっくり体を
休めて、早く赤ちゃんの顔を見せてちょうだい
ね。Ⓕ

Omedetō. Yoku gambatta wa ne. Yukkuri karada o yasumete, hayaku akachan no kao o misete chōdai ne.

Congratulations! It must have been hard. Take good care of yourself now, and let us see the baby real soon!

When you see the new baby for the first time, you'll be expected to note a specific resemblance to one parent or the other, or perhaps to remark on some praiseworthy facial feature. In this situation, the following expressions may come in handy.

口もとがきりっとして、お利口そう。Ⓕ

Kuchimoto ga kiritto shite, orikosō.

Looks like quite an intelligent baby, with that determined-looking mouth.

おかあさまに似て、やさしそうな顔立ちね。Ⓕ

Okāsama ni nite, yasashisō na kaodachi ne.

She looks like her mother, with those gentle features.

おとうさまに似て、男らしい顔だちですね。Ⓕ

18

Otōsama ni nite, otokorashii kaodachi desu ne.

He looks like his father, with those masculine features.

目鼻立ちがはっきりして、しっかりした赤ちゃんだこと。Ⓕ

Mehanadachi ga hakkiri shite, shikkari shita akachan da koto.

Such a fine-featured little face. That's certainly a healthy-looking child.

お人形さんみたい。Ⓕ

Oningyo-san mitai.

She (He) looks like a little doll.

While there are certain descriptive terms, like *marumaru to* ("chubby") and *tamago no yō* ("like an egg"), that are still apt to be applied to baby boys rather than baby girls, it is no longer generally considered appropriate, as it was in the past, to suggest that the birth of a male heir is a more auspicious event than that of a girl.

Thanks to everyone, mother and child are both fine

おかげさまで、母子ともに元気です。

Okagesama de, boshi tomo ni genki desu.

Thanks to everyone, mother and child are both fine.

This standard line is indispensable for fathers and others

announcing the good news immediately after the birth of a child. The first thing that everyone wants to hear—be it the grandparents, siblings, other relatives, or friends—is that the delivery was successful, that the child is sound and healthy, and that there were no post-delivery complications; this simple sentence delivers the goods. The phrase *okagesama de* (an often-heard, nonspecific expression of appreciation here translated as "thanks to everyone") communicates in a natural-sounding way a sense of gratitude—for the consideration the mother received from others during her pregnancy, for the kindness of fate, for the benevolence of the gods. This sentence provides a succinct, convenient response that any father can trot out whenever he is congratulated on the birth of a child, and it is also useful when replying to the various phone calls and cards from well-wishers that are likely to accompany the arrival of a new baby.

Beyond this standard formula for saying "All's well, thank heavens," it is also customary (and quite natural) to tell people whether it's a boy or a girl, to report the date and time of the birth, and—depending on how interested your listener really is—perhaps to report the baby's weight at birth. The idea is that these details, beyond their informational value, will more vividly communicate a sense of your own happiness.

It's not considered necessary or even appropriate to make a point of announcing a new baby to the entire neighborhood and to all one's friends and acquaintances, but it is important to convey the good news to people who were particularly helpful during the mother's pregnancy and to those who showed concern for her welfare. For couples who were married in the traditional way, it is essential to inform the *nakōdo*—the older couple who played the role of matchmakers or sponsors during the courtship and at the wedding. The new parents, with infant in tow, often pay a formal visit to the *nakōdo* soon after the child is born, out of respect and to show off the fruits of their happy union.

❧

Please accept my condolences on this sad occasion

このたびはご愁傷さまでございます。

Kono tabi wa goshūshōsama de gozaimasu.

Please accept my condolences on this sad occasion.

Often heard at both wakes and funerals, this short expression is the one most commonly used for extending one's sympathy to the bereaved. Because it is so widely used, some people consider it trite, too formulaic, or simply inadequate to effectively communicate a sense of sincere condolence. Nevertheless, in certain situations—such as when signing in at the reception table at a wake—you may find these words extremely useful.

A word about delivery: while it is generally regarded as polite to speak such formal words distinctly and at a deliberate pace, mourners customarily begin this expression by clearly articulating the words *kono tabi* (translated here as "on this sad occasion") and then deliver the rest of the sentence (*goshūshōsama de gozaimasu*, or "please accept my condolences") in hushed, practically inaudible tones deemed appropriate to the unspeakably painful event being observed.

Depending on the circumstances—when addressing a close relative of the deceased, for example—it may be appropriate to add a word or two, such as:

さぞお力落としのことと存じます。

Sazo ochikara-otoshi no koto to zonjimasu.

I'm sure this has been a terrible blow.

心からお悔やみ申しあげます。

Kokoro kara okuyami mōshiagemasu.

Allow me to offer my heartfelt sympathy.

These or similar words having been said, decorum dictates that you face the bereaved directly and execute a deep bow from the waist (about 60 degrees) with arms held straight at your sides and eyes forward—don't bend your neck! Next, raise your eyes slightly without lifting your head. Then lift your head (but don't stand up straight) to complete your first bow. Finally, bow deeply a second time.

At a funeral, you are likely to be invited to light an incense stick and place it in an urn in front of a photo of the deceased, which is displayed on an altar. You may be invited to do this with an expression such as:

ご霊前にお供えください。

Goreizen ni osonae kudasai.

Please offer a prayer for the soul of the deceased.

This brief ritual has its own explicit protocol. When your turn comes, take an incense stick and light it with one of the matches provided for the purpose, but don't blow the match out! Gently wave it back and forth until the flame goes out. Place the incense stick, lighted end up, in the urn and bring your hands together in front of your face, head down, in an attitude of prayer. After a moment, bow deeply, then turn and leave the altar.

Before you leave either a wake or a funeral, a member of the bereaved family will probably make a point of thanking you for coming. You are likely to hear:

お忙しい中を、さっそくお悔やみいただきまして
　ありがとうございます。

Oisogashii naka o, sassoku okuyami o itadakimashite ari-
　gatō gozaimasu.

Thank you for taking the time, on such short notice, to offer your condolences.

❧

It was such shocking news that I rushed right over

あまり突然のことで、驚いてとんでまいりました。

Amari totsuzen no koto de, odoroite tonde mairimashita.

It was such shocking news that I rushed right over.

In the unfortunate event that a relative or friend suddenly dies, this is a useful expression of sympathy. Whatever the cause—a traffic accident, a sudden illness, or a fatal condition not previously revealed—the sad news comes as a shock, and your words should show how hard it is to accept such a thing.

ついこの間お会いしたときは、あんなにお元気だったのにと思いますと、信じられない気持ちです。

Tsui kono aida oai shita toki wa, anna ni ogenki datta no ni to omoimasu to, shinjirarenai kimochi desu.

To think I saw her just the other day and she seemed perfectly fine. It's unbelievable.

このたびは思いもかけない災難で、ご心中をお察しいたします。

Kono tabi wa omoi mo kakenai sainan de, goshinchū osasshi itashimasu.

This is such an unthinkable tragedy, I can imagine how you must feel.

さぞかしお嘆きのことでしょう。

Sazokashi onageki no koto deshō.

You must be heartbroken.

これからというところでしたのに、本当に残念です。

Kore kara to iu tokoro deshita no ni, hontō ni zannen desu.

It's truly a pity, he had such a bright future ahead of him.

If the death was due to some extraordinary cause, such as suicide, you must be circumspect in your choice of words so as not to exacerbate the grief of the bereaved survivors.

このたびは本当に思いがけないことで、さぞおつらいことでしょう。ご冥福をお祈りいたします。

Kono tabi wa honto ni omoigakenai koto de, sazo otsurai koto deshō. Gomeifuku o oinori itashimasu.

This is such an unexpected tragedy, it must be terribly painful for you. I'll pray for her happiness in the next life.

At such times, inquiring into the circumstances of death is, of course, quite out of the question.

Sensitivity is also required when addressing parents who have lost a child. The right words are often difficult to find, but you might try these:

なんと申しあげてよいかわかりません。

Nan to mōshiagete yoi ka wakarimasen.

I simply don't know what to say.

お気持ちは痛いほどわかります。

Okimochi wa itai hodo wakarimasu.

I share your grief.

❧

I know this is painful, but don't let it get the best of you

おつらいでしょうが、気をしっかりお持ちになっ
てください。

Otsurai deshō ga, ki o shikkari omochi ni natte kudasai.

I know this is painful, but don't let it get the best of
you.

Offering words of encouragement to those who are in
mourning is a tricky matter. Carelessly spoken, otherwise
appropriate words may come off as insincere or even smug,
and even when they are tactfully delivered the gesture may
seem pointless. Unless you are a close friend, it may be just
as well to offer your condolences and leave it at that. For a
longtime friend of the survivors or a member of the family
circle, however, it's natural to make the attempt to keep people's spirits up.

お嘆きはごもっともですが、お体をいたわって、
一日も早く元気な顔を見せてください。

*Onageki wa gomottomo desu ga, okarada o itawatte, ichi-
nichi mo hayaku genki na kao o misete kudasai.*

I know you must be feeling terrible sorrow, but do
take good care of yourself and try to get over it.

あなたがしっかりした方と結婚なさったからおか
あさまもご安心なさったと思いますね。

*Anata ga shikkari shita kata to kekkon nasatta kara
okāsama mo go-anshin nasatta to omoimasu ne.*

I know your mother rests in peace, knowing you
married such a good man.

25

初孫の顔を見せてあげられて、それが何よりよか
ったですね。

*Hatsumago no kao o misete agerarete, sore ga nani yori
yokatta desu ne.*

He lived to see his first grandchild, and I know that
must have been a great consolation.

あまりお嘆きの深いのも、故人の障りになりまし
ょうから。

*Amari onageki no fukai no mo, kojin no sawari ni nari-
mashō kara.*

He wouldn't be happy knowing you were suffering
so much.

あとに残ったあなたがしっかり生きてゆかれるの
が、何よりのご供養ですよ。

*Ato ni nokotta anata ga shikkari ikite yukareru no ga,
nani yori no gokuyō desu yo.*

The greatest thing you can do in her memory is to
go on living a good life.

The use of expressions like these at such a painful time
must, of course, reflect the depth of one's friendship and
empathy; if not, they may sound overly familiar or even in-
trusive.

❦

I'd like to offer a few words
if I may

ひと言ご挨拶申しあげます。

Hitokoto goaisatsu mōshiagemasu.
I'd like to offer a few words if I may.

An experienced public speaker may regard such a standard opening line as painfully unimaginative, but for those unaccustomed to making speeches it's reassuring to have a familiar expression at hand to start off with, and this one will suit almost any formal occasion. A simple self-introduction should follow:

ただいまご紹介にあずかりましたジョン・ブラウンでございます。

Tadaima goshōkai ni azukarimashita Jon Buraun de gozaimasu.

My name's John Brown, and I've been asked to say a few words.

Or simply:

ジョン・ブラウンでございます。

Jon Buraun de gozaimasu.

My name's John Brown.

Even though you may have just been introduced, it's a good idea to give your name once more, since it will help ensure that the audience remembers it (they are apt to need help remembering a non-Japanese name), and it will also give you a moment to remember what you are going to say next. For that matter, it will probably be to your advantage to have memorized a string of stock phrases, thus sparing yourself the awkward moment when you search for the right word and find you don't know it.

When the occasion is a celebration, you can always lead off by congratulating the guest of honor:

田中さん、おめでとうございまする。

Tanaka-san, omedetō gozaimasu.

Tanaka-san, please accept my congratulations.

The size of the audience will help determine which expressions are most suitable. While larger gatherings, since they tend to be more formal, call for the formal-sounding *hitokoto goaisatsu* opening with which we led off, it is permissible to greet a smaller crowd in much more familiar language:

今日はうれしいですね。

Kyō wa ureshii desu ne.

Well, this is certainly a happy day, isn't it?

Whatever the content of your speech or toast, nothing is more important than getting the names right. Many a Japanese wedding speech has been made and then instantly forgotten by all concerned, but the speaker they never forget is the one who, from start to finish, calls the groom or bride (or both!) by the wrong name. This actually happens, and more often than you might think.

❖

Thank you for taking time out of your busy schedules to join us today

本日はご多忙中お集まりいただきまして、ありがとうございます。

Honjitsu wa gotabō-chū oatsumari itadakimashite, arigatō gozaimasu.

Thank you for taking time out of your busy schedules to join us today.

This familiar greeting, spoken by the host or chairperson, is used to signal the opening of a formal meeting, conference, or lecture. It is rarely used, however, at more informal gatherings, such as internal business meetings or regularly scheduled meetings.

Among the harried denizens of today's hectic business world, one is forced to assume that no one has a lot of free time, or at least that no one would ever admit it. Even people who once were thought to have plenty of leisure time—housewives and retirees, for example—can often be seen hustling around at a strenuous pace, clutching their appointment books. In smaller communities and outlying areas, local governments have sponsored luncheon programs for presumably solitary elderly people, on the assumption that a great many older people suffer from loneliness and boredom. The programs have not, however, been very successful; it seems most older people are too busy to attend. But when people do show up for events of this sort, it is imperative to greet them by properly expressing appreciation for their presence. The following is an appropriate way:

万障おくりあわせの上、ご参集くださいまして、
ありがとうございます。

Banshō-okuriawase no ue, gosanshū kudasaimashite, ari-gatō gozaimasu.

Thank you for taking the trouble to join us today, in spite of the inconvenience.

When the people being greeted have had to brave inclement weather or other specific hardships in order to be present, this must be duly noted in the greeting:

雨の中をお集りいただきまして、ありがとうござ
います。

Ame no naka o oatsumari itadakimashite, arigatō gozai-masu.

Thank you for taking the trouble to come, in spite of the rain.

While the often-heard *honjitsu wa gotabō-chū* greeting with which we began is certainly a reliable selection, it would suggest a remarkable lack of resourcefulness if every formal assembly were to begin with this very same line. In practice, the opening greeting is often tailored to the occasion:

年の瀬もおしつまって、世の中あわただしくなってきましたなか、お集まりいただき、ありがとうございます。

Toshi no se mo oshitsumatte, yo no naka awatadashiku natte kimashita naka, oatsumari itadaki, arigatō gozaimasu.

With the year drawing to an end and the world having grown that much busier, we thank you for taking the trouble to be with us today.

折悪しくアメリカ大統領来日と重なりまして駅や道路の検問が煩わしかったかと思われますが、お集りいただき、ありがとうございます。

Oriashiku Amerika daitōryō rai-nichi to kasanarimashite eki ya dōro no kenmon ga wazurawashikatta ka to omowaremasu ga, oatsumari itadaki, arigatō gozaimasu.

Since this event unfortunately coincides with the arrival of the U.S. President, I'm afraid many of you may have been inconvenienced by security checks at train stations or on the streets. Thank you for putting up with all the bother it has taken to be here.

You are more likely to win favor with an audience of schedule-jugglers if you specifically note the effort that was required to attend and express your gratitude.

❦

How quickly time passes

月日のたつのは早いものでございます。

Tsukihi no tatsu no wa hayai mono de gozaimasu.

How quickly time passes.

When people gather for a commemorative event—a memorial service for a departed friend, a golden wedding anniversary, or the anniversary of the founding of a company—it is natural for a speaker to preface his remarks by inviting those assembled to reflect on the passage of time. This short sentence fulfills that function.

Next come the specifics:

思いおこせば5年前……

Omoiokoseba gonen mae ...

As you may recall, it was five years ago that ...

おかげさまで父の一周忌を迎えることができました。

Okagesama de chichi no isshūki o mukaeru koto ga deki-mashita.

Through the kindness of everyone (who helped us get through it), a full year has passed since my father died.

Tsukihi no tatsu no wa hayai mono de gozaimasu (our opening expression above) is also used when formally expressing thanks—in person or in writing—to someone who has helped a son or daughter get accepted at the right school or find a job. Along with parental affection and pride, these words evoke the particular poignancy of seeing one's children grow up.

The formal Buddhist memorial service for a deceased person is held on the anniversary of the date of death. Exactly which anniversaries are observed depends to some extent on the age of the deceased and other considerations, but memorial services are almost always held on the first and second anniversaries. Presumably, the purpose of such a gathering is to dissipate the lingering sorrow of the survivors by recounting various memories of the deceased. At memorials held prior to the first anniversary—these customarily include a gathering on the forty-ninth day after death (called *shijūkunichi*) and another during *niibon*, or the next observance of the annual Festival of the Dead—it is not advisable to engage in reminiscences about the deceased unless prompted to do so by the survivors, as the bereaved may be as yet too mindful of their loss.

For lighter occasions, such as the anniversary of a firm's founding, a variety of useful expressions are available:

長いようで短い15年でした。
Nagai yō de mijikai jūgo-nen deshita.
While it sounds like a long time, these fifteen years have passed quickly.

顧みますれば、今日にいたる10年間……
Kaerimimasureba, konnichi ni itaru jūnen-kan ...
Looking back, ten years have already passed ...

継続は力なりと申しますが……
Keizoku wa chikara nari to mōshimasu ga ...
To endure is to grow stronger, as they say, but ...

幾多の山坂をこえて……
Ikuta no yamasaka o koete ...
Having overcome numerous challenges ...

苦しいときもございましたが……

Kurushii toki mo gozaimashita ga ...

While it has been a struggle at times ...

Whatever the anniversary celebrates, whether the perseverance of an enterprise or the endurance of a family or household, the speaker should emphasize the sustaining efforts of all the individuals who made such an event possible.

This is a poor thing, but ...

つまらないものですが……

Tsumaranai mono desu ga ...

This is a poor thing, but ...

This odd-sounding locution is the conventionally approved way to signal that you are offering a gift. Often heard in Japan, where both gift-giving and linguistic self-deprecation are highly ritualized, expressions such as this can sometimes elicit a puzzled response from a non-native speaker. After all, you might reason, if they think it's a poor gift then why are they giving it to me? In fact, since in addition to "trifling" *tsumaranai* can also be translated as "boring" or "useless," a little knowledge can really leave you confused. Needless to say, the phrase does not mean that the speaker actually believes the gift to be boring or worthless (she might think so, but she probably wouldn't tell you). This is simply a verbal ritual of humility, presumably intended to steer the receiver of a gift away from any sense of obligation or intense gratitude.

Interestingly, even though no native speaker of Japanese

could ever mistake the intent behind a phrase like this one, nowadays one often hears people dispensing with such ritualized utterances in favor of more transparent language. Younger people in particular, when giving someone a gift, might actually give it the old hard sell:

これ、とてもおいしいんですよ。
Kore, totemo oishii n' desu yo.
It's really delicious.

きっとお似合いだと思いまして……
Kitto oniai da to omoimashite ...
I thought it would look good on you.

Another humble-sounding phrase for gift-givers is:

珍しくもございませが……
Mezurashiku mo gozaimasen ga ...
This is nothing special, but ...

This is a handy expression when the offering is the sort of practical household item—soap, towels, fruit, coffee, beer, or the like—often given as a midsummer present (*ochūgen*) or year-end present (*oseibo*), in which case it is not only properly humble but accurate. This is not to say that such gifts aren't highly appreciated anyway, incidentally. This and the other phrases below are often followed by the word *dōzo* ("Please [accept it]"), spoken as the gift is proffered.

When the gift is something you made by hand, you are expected to humbly deprecate your own handiwork.

お恥ずかしいのですけれど……
Ohazukashii no desu keredo ...
I've done an embarrassingly poor job of it, but ...

うまくできなかったんですけど……

Umaku dekinakatta n' desu kedo ...
This didn't turn out very well, but ...

Some expressions both downplay the value of a gift and emphasize the spirit in which it is given.

心ばかりの品ですが……
Kokoro bakari no shina desu ga ...
This is just a small token of my appreciation.

A phrase like this communicates something more than mere formal courtesy, and is useful when the gift itself is meant to express more than just good manners.

It may not be to your liking, but ...

お口に合いますかどうか……
Okuchi ni aimasu ka dō ka ...
It may not be to your liking, but ...

This standard phrase can be used whenever you present a gift of food, as often happens when paying a visit to someone's home. It can also used by a host or hostess when serving food to a guest, and by a housewife bringing a few helpings of a home-cooked specialty over to the neighbors.

Everyone has his own tastes when it comes to food, of course. The mere fact that something was expensive or comes highly recommended is no guarantee that any given person will like it. Therefore, notwithstanding that you yourself believe the item to be a scrumptious morsel, you should make allowances for a different reaction when you offer it to another.

お口に合いますかどうか、おひとつどうぞ。
Okuchi ni aimasu ka dō ka, ohitotsu dōzo.
This may not suit your taste, but please try one.

These days one does sometimes hear less cautious language:

わが家では大変好評ですので……
Wagaya de wa taihen kōhyō desu no de ...
This is quite popular at our house, so ...

先日食べてとてもおいしかったので……
Senjitsu tabete totemo oishikatta no de ...
I had this the other day and it was really good, so ...

私のおはこ料理なんです。
Watashi no ohako-ryōri nan desu.
This is my specialty.

This type of approach, though, is best reserved for close friends and relatives.

When you offer food to guests at your home or invite them to start eating, you are expected, as a matter of course, to belittle the merits of the food being served:

何もございませんが、どうぞ召し上がってください。
Nani mo gozaimasen ga, dōzo meshiagatte kudasai.
It's nothing much, but please go ahead and have some.

あいにく召しあがっていただけるようなものがなくて、……
Ainiku meshiagatte itadakeru yō na mono ga nakute, ...

Unfortunately we have nothing worth serving to a guest ...

A well-mannered guest will say, just prior to tucking into the victuals:

いただきます。　　　　　　　頂戴いたします。

Itadakimasu.　　or perhaps　　*Chōdai itashimasu.*

Both are expressions of gratitude for what is about to be received.

At the end of the meal, a polite guest compliments the hosts.

たいへんごちそうさまでした。おいしゅうございました。

Taihen gochisōsama deshita. Oishū gozaimashita.

Thank you for the great meal. That was superb.

The host or hostess just as politely demurs, again dismissing the quality of the food offered.

お粗末さまでした。

Osomatsusama deshita.

It was a meager offering.

Occasionally, the standard *okuchi ni aimasu ka dō ka* may seem a bit too commonplace to express the feeling behind the thing being offered. If so, you might offer a reason for offering this particular thing.

暑いときは冷たいものがよいかと思いまして……

Atsui toki wa tsumetai mono ga yoi ka to omoimashite ...

I thought something cool might be nice in this heat ...

Hearing this, the listener will perhaps be more likely to appreciate your consideration.

🐦

This is a token of my good wishes

お祝いの気持ちでございます。

Oiwai no kimochi de gozaimasu.

This is a token of my good wishes.

This is what you say when you present a gift to mark a special occasion. The custom of a previous era dictated that gifts given in celebration of a particular event be handed to the person being honored on the morning of an auspicious day (as determined by the traditional lunar calendar). These days, few people observe such restrictions, but certain other points of protocol do remain in effect.

When you give a present that has been gift-wrapped, it may well not be opened on the spot but instead be put aside to be opened later. If so, it's a good idea to say what's inside and why you chose it, thus providing the recipient with an opportunity to say something gracious like this:

ちょうど欲しかったものです。

Chōdo hoshikatta mono desu.

It's exactly what I wanted.

This is also a way of enabling the recipient to thank you specifically for your particular gift.

When you are presenting someone with a gift of cash—no checks please!—here is a useful expression that seldom fails to draw a smile:

軽いものにかえさせていただきました。

Karui mono ni kaesasete itadakimashita.

Here's a little something that's not too heavy.

When the occasion for celebration is entry into or graduation from school, gifts often go to the parents, who will accept them on their child's behalf (you might give the child a card as well, if you're looking to win hearts), but this is only advisable for younger children. The situation may vary depending on your relationship with the principals, but in general children of middle school age or older are better off collecting their own presents—they certainly think so—and you will be fondly regarded for respecting their autonomy.

As a rule, it is best to be prompt with celebratory gifts for all occasions other than the birth of a child. Just what to give, of course, depends on the occasion. Certain celebrations are traditionally associated with specific gifts: a vase or a potted plant for a housewarming, baby clothes for a new baby, a decorative figurine for the opening of a store or the launching of a business. Not surprisingly, this usually produces an oversupply of the traditional selections, so it's just as well to find out, if you can, what the intended recipient really wants.

This is nothing special, but it happens to be a specialty of the area I come from

珍しくもございませんが、私どもの国の特産物でして……

Mezurashiku mo gozaimasen ga, watakushi-domo no kuni no tokusan-butsu deshite ...

This is nothing special, but it happens to be a specialty of the area I come from.

When you present people with a local specialty from back home, whether it's a formal midsummer or year-end gift, a present for someone you're visiting, or simply something to share with the neighbors, this phrase will come in handy. Thanks to Japan's booming home-delivery services, regional delicacies from all over the country can be now be enjoyed at home wherever you live, making such items—imports included—popular as gifts.

For the recipient, the main point isn't so much that your gift is difficult to obtain but that it came from the same place you come from, a point that is likely to enhance the flavor of even the most commonplace cuisine:

ほう、あの人の故郷のワインか。

Hō, ano hito no furusato no wain ka.

Hmm, so this is the wine he drinks back home.

You yourself may duly comment on the difference:

外国のワインなど珍しくもございませんが、故郷のワインを飲みますと、私などはひと味ちがうように思いまして……

Gaikoku no wain nado mezurashiku mo gozaimasen ga, furusato no wain o nomimasu to, watashi nado wa hitoaji chigau yō ni omoimashite ...

Imported wine is nothing special nowadays, but to me the wine from home somehow tastes just a little bit better.

There is every chance your companion will agree with you (at least publicly).

A brand-name gift is considered a safe bet by a lot of people, since both the giver and the receiver can presumably be assured of its quality and the value of the gift is beyond dispute—everyone knows how much it cost. Still, as a present, a little something special from back home probably says more than any brand-name item ever could. At the same time, such a gift is likely to invite all kinds of questions about your origins, leading to discussions that may well strengthen the bonds between you and the beneficiary of your generosity.

🐟

This is very kind of you. I'm honored

これはご丁寧に、恐れいります。

Kore wa goteinei ni, osoreirimasu.

This is very kind of you. I'm honored.

When you receive a gift, you must be mindful of the proper form for showing gratitude—a casual word or two of thanks won't do. It's common, for example, to indicate that you are simply overwhelmed, even to the point of apologizing (for the trouble the giver has gone through to select it) and hinting that you really couldn't possibly accept it.

こんなことをしていただくと申し訳なくて……

Konna koto o shite itadaku to mōshiwake nakute ...

Oh, this is so very kind of you, but I'm afraid, really ...

祝ってくださるお気持ちだけで十分ですのにこんなものまで頂戴して……

Iwatte kudasaru okimochi dake de jūbun desu no ni konna mono made chōdai shite ...

41

> Your good wishes alone are precious enough, but to receive such a lovely gift as well ...

The gift-giver, playing his part in this ritual, will deprecate his gift as a way of urging you to accept it.

いいえ、大したものでもありませんから……

Iie, taishita mono de mo arimasen kara ...

Oh, hardly. It's really nothing to make a fuss over.

At this point it would be possible to end the drama by simply saying you'll park your good manners and take the loot.

それでは遠慮なく頂戴します。

Sore de wa enryo naku chōdai shimasu.

In that case, I'll dispense with the formalities and accept it.

You will communicate more of a sense of gratitude, however, if you emphasize your pleasure rather than your capitulation.

それでは喜んで頂戴します。

Sore de wa yorokonde chōdai shimasu.

In that case, I happily accept your gift.

Finally, you are actually ready to say thanks, and you should do so in way that lets the gift-giver know you fully appreciate the feeling behind the gift.

お心のこもったお品をありがとうございます。

Okokoro no komotta oshina o arigatō gozaimasu.

Thank you for such a thoughtful gift.

Traditionally, gift-giving and gift-receiving have been linked in a quid pro quo arrangement that is still widely observed, to the extent that even now people often automatically associate the act of accepting a gift with the obligation to give one in return. Owing to this aspect of the transaction, there are actually plenty of people who would just as soon not receive gifts at all. There are also occasions when you are not expected to (and should not) give a return gift: when you are given a present to take home from a reception or banquet; when you receive a farewell gift, a get-well present, a graduation present, or the like from someone older or in a senior position; or when you receive a midsummer gift, a year-end gift, or a present given in thanks for a favor you did from someone younger or in a lower position.

Some people feel obligated to give gifts in return for get-well gifts or presents given to them to celebrate a family occasion. In the former case, since the fact of one's recovery is presumably being celebrated by all one's friends, it's not necessarily good form to give presents only to people from whom you received them, and in the latter case return presents are simply unnecessary.

🐦

You're always so very thoughtful. I do appreciate it

いつもお心にかけていただいて、ありがとうございます。

Itsumo okokoro ni kakete itadaite, arigatō gozaimasu.

You're always so very thoughtful. I do appreciate it.

If you regularly receive presents—midsummer gifts or year-end gifts, for instance—from a particular person, it is essential to emphasize that person's continual generosity, and this is one way to do so. An expression of gratitude may often take the form of an apology (usually *sumimasen* "I'm sorry"; literally, "There's no end to it"), presumably for putting the gift-giver to so much trouble:

いつもいつも、すみません。

Itsumo itsumo, sumimasen.

You're always so generous. I can't thank you enough.

To someone who makes a point of giving you a different gift every time (not everyone does), you might say:

いつもお珍しいものを、ありがとうございます。

Itsumo omezurashii mono o, arigatō gozaimasu.

Your gifts are always so special. Thank you.

結構なものを頂戴いたしまして、ありがとうご
　　います。

Kekkō na mono o chōdai itashimashite, arigatō gozaimasu.

Thank you for such a lovely present.

In thanking someone who is in the habit of giving you practical gifts—these customarily include staples like *miso* (fermented soybean paste) and *nori* (dried seaweed), as well as cooking oil—you can emphasize how useful they are:

いつも重宝させていただいております。

Itsumo chōhō sasete itadaite orimasu.

They always come in so handy.

To thank a regular visitor to your home who always brings along a gift, you may, as above, express your gratitude in words of apology:

いつも気を遣っていただいてすみません。

Itsumo ki o tsukatte itadaite sumimasen.

You always go to such trouble. I really appreciate it.

In this situation, presuming your guest is someone with whom you are fairly close, you can open the gift on the spot (after making a brief show of polite refusal). If the gift is food (and it very likely will be), you might serve some of it immediately, sharing it with your guest. Similarly, when you are visiting someone else and have brought along a gift of food or drink, you might present it with an expression such as:

いっしょにいただこうと思って……

Issho ni itadakō to omotte ...

I thought we might all enjoy this together.

This makes it all the easier for your host to graciously accept your gift, perhaps with an expression such as:

では喜んで。

De wa yorokonde.

Well then, I accept with pleasure.

While the customs of previous eras were quite explicit about the proper way to accept a formal gift—a present was supposed to be received on a tray, which had to be placed at the head of the table, the seat of honor, while an elaborate show of gratitude took place—rigid adherence to protocol is no longer the norm. Nevertheless, it is still considered polite to accept a gift by receiving it with both hands, arms slightly extended, and then raise it toward one's head in a ritual gesture of gratitude.

🐦

I'm afraid I hardly deserve such kindness

過分なお志を頂戴いたしまして……

Kabun na okokorozashi o chōdai itashimashite ...

I'm afraid I hardly deserve such kindness.

When calling on someone who is recovering from an illness or an injury or when visiting the family of someone who has died, it is customary in Japan to present a gift, usually a gift of money. This expression is one standard form of expressing gratitude for such a gift—but *don't* use it right away!

When you receive a birthday present or the like from a good friend, there's nothing wrong with opening it on the spot and showing your pleasure. But when you are presented with an envelope containing cash by someone attending the funeral of a member of your family or by someone visiting you in the hospital, it would be highly irregular to open it then and there. At such times, you may graciously accept the offering by saying:

ご丁寧なお志をいただきまして、ありがとうございます。

Goteinei na okokorozashi o itadakimashite, arigatō gozaimasu.

It's gracious of you. Thank you for your kindness.

To someone who visits you at your sickbed, you might be more emphatic:

お顔を拝見しただけで元気がでるような気がいた

します。その上こんなものまで頂いて……

Okao o haiken shita dake de genki ga deru yō na ki ga itashimasu. Sono ue, konna mono made itadaite ...

Your company alone is enough to make me feel better. To receive a gift on top of that, why ...

When the occasion is a funeral or memorial service, less is more:

ご丁重なお供えをいただきまして、ありがとうございます。

Goteichō na osonae o itadakimashite, arigatō gozaimasu.

It's gracious of you. Thank you for this offering.

or perhaps:

ありがとうございます。さっそく供えさせていただきます。

Arigatō gozaimasu. Sassoku sonaesasete itadakimasu.

Thank you. I'll present your offering right away.

Only after several days have passed—when you next see the gift-giver or when (as custom also requires) you communicate your gratitude in writing—should you make use of the formal expression of thanks with which we began. You might begin by saying:

先日は丁寧なご弔問をいただきまして、ありがとうございます。

Senjitsu wa teinei na gochōmon o itadakimashite, arigatō gozaimasu.

It was kind of you to come and offer your sympathy the other day. Thank you.

or possibly:

先日は丁寧なお見舞いをいただきまして、ありがとうございます。

Senjitsu wa teinei na omimai o itadakimashite, arigatō gozaimasu.

It was kind of you to come and visit me (when I was bedridden) the other day. Thank you.

Now you're ready to make your full-blown formal statement of gratitude:

過分なお志を頂戴いたしまして、恐縮いたしております。

Kabun na okokorozashi o chōdai itashimashite, kyōshuku itashite orimasu.

I'm afraid I hardly deserve such kindness, but I deeply appreciate it.

When the occasion for generosity was the death of someone close to you, you might also add something like:

亡くなりました父も、さぞ喜んでいることと思います。

Nakunarimashita chichi mo, sazo yorokonde iru koto to omoimasu.

I'm sure my late father would also be very pleased.

❦

Going out?

お出かけですか。

Odekake desu ka.

Going out?

Here is a perfectly polite way to hail a neighbor or an acquaintance who, judging by her appearance or hurried pace, is obviously going out. This expression is not the same as a proper greeting, which would require more elaborate language, but it implies a courteous respect for the fact that the other person is in a hurry. Although grammatically a question, this is really an observation. It should not be confused with a direct question, such as:

どちらにお出かけですか。
Dochira ni odekake desu ka.
Where are you going?

To abruptly pose such a question would definitely be overstepping the established (if tacit) conversational boundaries.

Since *Odekake desu ka* is not really a question, the person thus greeted is by no means obliged nor necessarily expected to state his destination. Instead, he can answer vaguely, as people commonly do:

ええ、ちょっとそこまで。
Ee, chotto soko made.
Yes, I'm just stepping out for a minute.

Should you encounter someone who won't settle for this vague reply and who seems intent on getting you to state your itinerary, feel free to cut the conversation short without mincing words. Politeness does not require you to suffer prying questions, and it is considered distinctly impolite to detain someone who has places to go with a lot of idle chatter. Common courtesy (and common sense) dictates that the other person keep the conversation brief, ending it after a moment or two with a polite send off:

では、お気をつけて。
De wa, oki o tsukete.
Well, take care.

or

いってらっしゃい。
Itte 'rasshai.
Goodbye for now.

The phrase *Odekake desu ka* has another, common but somewhat different usage. You may hear someone who comes to your door or calls up on the telephone say:

スミスさんはお出かけですか
Sumisu-san wa odekake desu ka.
Has Mr. Smith gone out?

With these words the visitor or caller is simply requesting, in a politely oblique manner, to speak with the person named—the implied assumption is not that the person named has gone out but that he is present. When employed this way, the sentence *Murata-san wa odekake desu ka* is virtually synonymous with the more direct (and slightly more common) but still very polite form:

村田さんはいらっしゃいますか。
Murata-san wa irasshaimasu ka.
Is Mr. Murata in?

How are you?

ごきげんいかが。
Gokigen ikaga.
How are you?

As you might expect, the polite thing to do when you see someone you know is to inquire about his health and frame of mind, and this common expression performs that function quite succinctly. The term *kigen* (here preceded by the honorific prefix *go*) is conveniently broad in meaning, taking in the other person's situation, well-being, or mood. This expression is considered slightly more refined than some of the more commonly heard alternatives, including:

お変わりありませんか。

Okawari arimasen ka.

How have you been?

(Literally, "Have there been any changes?")

お元気ですか。

Ogenki desu ka.

How's everything?

In addition, *gokigen ikaga* is among the preferred forms for politely asking someone who has been ill or injured about his condition when you visit him.

Standard replies to these greetings include:

おかげさまで、とても元気にしています。

Okagesama de, totemo genki ni shite imasu.

I'm happy to say I'm just fine.

and the shortened form:

おかげさまで。

Okagesama de.

Very well, thank you.

Courtesy dictates that your reply be followed by a return form of the same query:

おかげさまで、とても元気にしています。そちらは。

Okagesama de, totemo genki ni shite imasu. Sochira wa.

I'm happy to say I'm just fine. How about you?

おかげさまで。あなたのほうは。

Okagesama de. Anata no hō wa.

Very well, thank you. And you?

An expression similar in form to but different in meaning from *gokigen ikaga* is:

ごきげんよう。

Gokigen yō.

Take care, now.

which is a kind of all-purpose salutation used as both a greeting and as an expression of farewell. It is derived from *gokigen yoku* (literally, "your good health"), which could be construed as either a congratulatory or a hopeful message with which to greet or see someone off. Both *gokigen ikaga* and *gokigen yō* could conceivably be used in similar situations, so keep in mind that *gokigen ikaga* is a question requiring an answer, while *gokigen yō* is merely another way to say hello or goodbye.

In addition to asking people how they are, it is also extremely common to remark on the season or the weather when you run into someone you know. Here you have your choice of a whole litany of innocuous observations:

寒くなりましたね。

Samuku narimashita ne.

It's gotten cold, hasn't it?

涼しくなりましたね。

Suzushiku narimashita ne.

It's gotten cool, hasn't it?

暑くなりましたね。
Atsuku narimashita ne.
It's gotten hot, hasn't it?

しのぎやすくなりましたね。
Shinogiyasuku narimashita ne.
It's gotten nicer, hasn't it?

あいにくのお天気ですね。
Ainiku no otenki desu ne.
Awful weather, isn't it?

Chance meetings between acquaintances, of course, don't call for much more pithy meteorological commentary than this—the more insipid the remark, the easier it is to agree with, so you can both get on about your business.

Have you got a moment?

ちょっといいですか。
Chotto ii desu ka.
Have you got a moment?

With this expression you can get someone's attention or consent to enter into a conversation, usually so that you can ask a question or make a request. This is an abbreviated form of what was once—and still is, in some cases—a more elaborate display of verbal courtesy. For example:

ちょっとお時間をいただきたいのですが。
Chotto ojikan o itadakitai no desu ga.

I'd wonder if I could have a moment of your time.

今、ご都合はいかがですか。

Ima, gotsugō wa ikaga desu ka.

Would this be a convenient time to have a word with you?

These longer, more formal expressions, however, would sound overly delicate if used among peers or people who know one another well. In such company, the informal shorter form cited above—or the even shorter form *chotto ii*—sounds more appropriate and is thus much more commonly used, for example, by office colleagues talking to each other or summoning a peer over the phone.

Since this is an informal expression, you would not use it when addressing a superior at work or anyone other than a colleague or friend. Instead, to make the sort of crisply polite impression considered ideal in more formal transactions, you would say:

失礼します。		失礼ですが……
Shitsurei shimasu.	or	*Shitsurei desu ga ...*
Excuse me.		Excuse me, but ...

恐れいります。		恐れいりますが……
Osoreirimasu.	or	*Osoreirimasu ga ...*
I beg your pardon.		I beg your pardon, but ...

If you're addressing someone you've never met in order to ask a question, you can add an extra courteous touch by declaring your intentions.

少々お尋ねいたします。

Shōshō otazune itashimasu.

I'd like to ask a question if I may.

Having received your answer or taken in whatever reply your interlocutor makes, you should properly excuse yourself for the presumption:

お引き止めして申し訳ありませんでした。
Ohikitome shite mōshiwake arimasen deshita.
I apologize for detaining you.

Perhaps the most commonly heard forms used to get someone's attention are:

すみません。		すみませんが……
Sumimasen.	or	*Sumimasen ga ...*
Pardon me.		Pardon me, but ...

These everyday expressions are most useful for situations in which neither formality nor familiarity is the reigning principle—when you ask a railway employee about the correct fare, place an order with a waitress, or ask a police officer for directions, for example. In such cases, an expression like *osoreirimasu* would sound unnaturally formal, while *chotto ii desu ka* would sound overly familiar.

❁

Is is all right if I take this seat?

こちらの席、よろしいでしょうか。
Kochira no seki, yoroshii deshō ka.
Is is all right if I take this seat?

When you're looking for a place to sit in a dining hall, at a drinking place, or anywhere else where strangers share (and sometimes compete for) seating or table space, you'll make a better impression on other people if you politely confirm the availability of a seat rather than peremptorily claiming it for your own. This expression is the ticket. Speaking of tickets, you're also likely to find it useful in movie theaters and on trains and buses, where these magic words are usually sufficient to get an otherwise available seat cleared of any luggage parked on it.

A possible alternative is:

こちら、空いていますか。

Kochira, aite imasu ka.

Is this seat empty?

Although this more direct approach is by no means impolite, it does lack the delicacy of the expression cited above. After all, when you ask "Is this seat empty?" you're really saying, "This seat is empty, isn't it?" and implying that you don't need anyone's blessing or permission to take it. In the same way, when you want people to make room for you, you could simply ask directly:

ちょっとつめてくれませんか。

Chotto tsumete kuremasen ka.

Could you make a little room, please?

But it would be much more courteous to frame your request in words that don't sound quite so demanding, such as the expression we began with:

こちらの席、よろしいですか。

Kochira no seki, yoroshii desu ka.

Is is all right if I take this seat?

Or you could be more elaborate:

恐れ入りますが、少々おつめ合わせいただけない
　　でしょうか。

Osoreirimasu ga, shōshō otsumeawase itadakenai deshō ka.

Pardon me, but I wonder if you wouldn't be kind
enough to make a little room.

Speaking of making room, it often happens that people
entering a party or a banquet hall linger in clusters near the
entranceway, causing congestion and blocking the way for
subsequent arrivals. At such times you are likely to hear
someone in charge say something like:

ご順に中ほどまでおつめ合わせください。

Gojun ni naka-hodo made otsumeawase kudasai.

Would everyone kindly make way and move along
inside?

There is a special form of this same basic request reserved
for occasions when people are sitting (or kneeling) on
tatami:

お膝おくりをお願いいたします。

Ohiza-okuri o onegai itashimasu.

Would everyone move closer together and make
room, please?

Given the relative infrequency of events held on tatami
floors these days, this expression is seldom heard anymore.

I've let too much time pass since I saw you last

ご無沙汰いたしました。

Gobusata itashimashita.
I've let too much time pass since I saw you last.

This is the polite way to greet someone you haven't seen in a long time, whether you happen to be visiting the person at home or meeting her elsewhere. The literal meaning of the message is that you haven't been passing along news and information the way you should, but in conventional usage it has the effect of an implicit apology for not staying in closer touch with someone you consider to be a benefactor.

Another expression that appears quite similar in form actually has a very different usage.

どうもご挨拶が遅れまして……
Dōmo goaisatsu ga okuremashite ...
I really should have been in touch sooner.

This phrase is employed when a tentative business transaction has heretofore been sketched out by telephone or fax, and the party initiating the deal has appeared to make his proposal in person. By using this expression, he conveys the sense that, by all that is proper, this formality should have been observed much sooner.

By way of comparison, consider two very common expressions that are used in the same sorts of situations as *gobusata itashimashita*:

しばらくでした。
Shibaraku deshita.
It's been a while.

お久しぶりです。
Ohisashiburi desu.
It's been a long time, hasn't it?

Unlike the first two expressions introduced above, neither

phrase carries any sense of apology. These are much more casual forms that—not unlike "Long time, no see"—are perfectly appropriate for greeting people you know well but probably too casual for mere acquaintances and definitely too offhand for your elders or superiors at work.

When you meet an acquaintance you haven't seen for some time, it's naturally considered courteous to talk about how things have been. Several standard lines are available for this purpose:

お変わりありませんか。

Okawari arimasen ka.

How have you been?

(literally, "Have there been any changes?")

ちっともお変わりになりませんね。

Chitto mo okawari ni narimasen ne.

You haven't changed a bit.

お変わりなくてけっこうですね。

Okawari nakute kekkō desu ne.

You're looking well, as ever.

お元気そうでなによりです。

Ogenkisō de nani yori desu.

You look well, and that's the important thing.

The latter three expressions are, of course, logical choices when the other person actually does look well, but even if that is not the case, these words may still be appropriate. It may be, for example, that the other person has been ill or has suffered some misfortune, which you have heard about from other sources, and you may wish to cheer him up by using expressions such as these.

I hope you get well soon

一日も早いご回復を祈っております。

Ichinichi mo hayai gokaifuku o inotte orimasu.

I hope you get well soon.

There are a variety of concerns that must be attended to when you pay a visit to someone who is bedridden, the first of which is whether or not you should be visiting in the first place. Many people have no desire to entertain visitors when they're not at their best, or simply don't want anyone to see them in an incapacitated state, so you cannot assume it's all right to go visit as soon as you hear that someone is sick or in the hospital. This also holds true for people who are hospitalized after being injured. The best policy, whenever possible, is to find out about the person's condition from someone who knows and to pay a visit—once you know visitors are welcome—during the patient's convalescence.

It may be that hospitalization is required to treat an illness or condition of a private nature, such as hemorrhoids or a gynecological condition, that the person in question would rather not disclose. In such a case, any inquiries on your part are likely to be met with vague reassurances that it's nothing serious, and the most courteous course you can follow is to drop the subject.

These caveats notwithstanding, for someone in the midst of a long and tedious recovery, or someone, especially an older person, getting over a relatively minor illness, a visit from a friend or an acquaintance can be the best medicine there is. Rather than fretting over what kind of get-well gift to send, the kindest thing may be simply to put in a personal appearance now and then. Since your host is unwell, of course, you must take care not to wear him out, so it's best to keep your visits brief. You should also be mindful of the other person's concern for her appearance—it may be embarrassing to entertain visitors while dressed in pajamas or while wearing no makeup.

The sentence with which this section began is an appropriate expression of farewell with which to end a visit to a sick friend. Some alternatives are:

お大事になさってください。

Odaiji ni nasatte kudasai.

Please take good care of yourself.

どうかあせらずに養生なさってください。

Dō ka aserazu ni yōjō nasatte kudasai.

Just take it easy and let yourself get better.

天の与えた休養だと思って、このさい英気を養っ
てください。

Ten no ataeta kyūyō da to omotte, kono sai eiki o yashi-
natte kudasai.

Consider it a heaven-sent rest and use the opportunity to build up your strength.

These days a lot of people, especially people in the business world, seem to be learning the limits of their endurance
only by suffering some sort of physical collapse. In addition to your wishes for a speedy recovery, you might want
to add a note of caution when visiting a fallen corporate
warrior:

会社も困ってるでしょうが、我が身が大事ですよ。

Kaisha mo komatte 'ru deshō ga, wagami ga daiji desu yo.

The office will have to struggle along without you
for a while, but you really ought to be thinking
about your health.

I feel much better now that I see you looking so well

お元気そうなので安心いたしました。

Ogenkisō na no de anshin itashimashita.

I feel much better now that I see you looking so well.

Here is a standard line employed by visitors to cheer up an acquaintance who has been hospitalized due to an illness or injury. Once you've greeted the patient, it's quite natural to inquire about her condition (it's also perfectly polite, provided you don't pry). You might try one of the following:

どうなさいました。

Dō nasaimashita ka.

How did all this come about?

いかがですか。

Ikaga desu ka.

How are you doing?

After hearing the reply, you might trot out the standard cheer-up line introduced above, or you might use slightly different words:

心配していましたが、お顔の色がいいので安心しました。

Shinpai shite imashita ga, okao no iro ga ii no de anshin shimashita.

I was worried about you, but now that I see you looking so healthy I feel better.

Whichever way you say it, the point is to strike a note of cheerful reassurance, but a measure of caution is advisable as well. Depending on the person and the situation, intentionally uplifting remarks of this sort may not be particularly welcome (they may sound trite or insincere). If this should appear to be the case—if your bedridden friend seems hard put to respond—the best thing is probably to move briskly on to another topic.

In some cases it may seem absurd or even cruel to compliment someone on how good she looks when the opposite is all too obvious. On these occasions you might take a different tack:

明るくてきれいなおへやですね。

Akarukute kirei na oheya desu ne.

This is a nice cheerful room, isn't it?

窓から外の景色がよく見えて、晴れ晴れしますね。

Mado kara soto no keshiki ga yoku miete, harebare shimasu ne.

You have such a nice view from the window, it's quite refreshing.

You should try to be sensitive to the mood of the person you're visiting. It's relatively easy for someone enduring a protracted convalescence to get depressed, and at times it might be appropriate to sound a note of slight reprimand in order to steer someone away from self-pity.

もうしばらくの辛抱ですから、無理をしないでがんばってください。

Mō shibaraku no shinbō desu kara, muri o shinai de ganbatte kudasai.

You're just going to have to be patient a little while longer, so try to accept that and don't overdo things.

病気に負けてへこたれてはいけませんよ。

Byōki ni makete hekotarete wa ikemasen yo.

You can't get depressed and let this thing get the best of you.

思うようにならないでしょうが、わがままを言わないで、しっかり療養してください。

Omou yō ni naranai deshō ga, wagamama o iwanai de, shikkari ryōyō shite kudasai.

Things may not be going the way you'd like them to, but you just have to do what you're told and let yourself heal.

Whether or not you would actually say such things, of course, depends entirely on your relationship with the person and on the person's character.

An illness or injury often affects not only the individual but the family as well, and it may be well to offer your encouragement to them when you have the chance. If you are a friend of the family, you might offer your services in support:

私にできることならいたしますから……

Watashi ni dekiru koto nara itashimasu kara ...

If there's anything I can do to help ...

Even if there's nothing particular to be done, such words of encouragement are usually highly appreciated.

This was certainly
an unexpected misfortune

とんだ災難でしたね。

Tonda sainan deshita ne.

This was certainly an unexpected misfortune.

The formal custom of calling on people to provide support in times of trouble extends beyond illness and injury; one also visits friends and acquaintances whose lives have been disrupted by fires, floods, or earthquakes. This sentence is a useful expression of concern for occasions when disaster—large or small—has struck. Others include:

びっくりして、とんできましたよ。

Bikkuri shite, tonde kimashita yo.

I was so shocked that I rushed right over.

突然で大変でしたね。でも大事にいたらなくて何
よりでした。

Totsuzen de taihen deshita ne. Demo daiji ni itaranakute nani yori deshita.

This was so sudden, it must have been quite a shock. Thank heaven no one was seriously hurt.

事故と伺ったときは私も血が下がるような気がし
ましたが、命に別状なくて本当に不幸中の幸い
でした。

Jiko to ukagatta toki wa watashi mo chi ga sagaru yō na ki ga shimashita ga, inochi ni betsujō nakute hontō ni fukō-chū no saiwai deshita.

When I heard about the accident, it bowled me over.
Bad as it is, though, it's a blessing that everyone survived.

It's courteous to offer assistance, especially when the
damage is limited to material loss:

ご不自由でしょう。お手伝いできることがあった
ら、何でもおっしゃってください。

*Gofujiyū deshō. Otetsudai dekiru koto ga attara, nan de
mo osshatte kudasai.*

You must be having a tough time of it. If there's
anything I can do to help, just say so.

ご家族みなご無事で何よりでした。ご無事ならば、
なくしたものはまたなんとでもなりますよ。私
もできるかぎりお役に立つようにしますから。

*Gokazoku mina gobuji de nani yori deshita. Gobuji nara-
ba, nakushita mono wa mata nan to de mo narimasu
yo. Watashi mo dekiru kagiri oyaku ni tatsu yō ni shimasu kara.*

Thank heaven everyone in the family is all right.
That's the important thing—you can always replace
whatever you lost. You can count on me to do
anything I possibly can.

お力になれることがあったら、何でも遠慮なくお
っしゃってください。

*Ochikara ni nareru koto ga attara, nan de mo enryo naku
osshatte kudasai.*

If there's anything I can do to help out, no matter
what, just let me know.

Given the nature of a disastrous event like a fire or an
earthquake, one cannot expect those coping with the aftermath to waste time waiting on visitors. If you intend to lend

a hand, make sure you arrive adequately prepared to do so. If it looks as though you'd only be in the way, though, it's best to hand over whatever gift you have brought and take your leave without further ado. As to a gift, cash is always welcome at such times, but you might also consider practical items, such as bottled mineral water, canned food, or a portable gas burner. The gifts that will be most appreciated are those that are most urgently needed.

We're really lost without you

あなたがいなくて本当に困っています。

Anata ga inakute hontō ni komatte imasu.

We're really lost without you.

When you visit someone who has been ill, especially a colleague, words of encouragement are a standard part of the protocol. This expression conveys particular appreciation for the value of the other person's efforts on the job, to reinforce what may be a flagging sense of self-worth.

If the person you're visiting is in a supervisory position and gets the impression that everything back at the office is humming right along without him or that his absence has gone unnoticed, he is likely to feel that his role is superfluous—an anxiety lurking in the minds of many people in the business world nowadays. Such worries are hardly conducive to recuperation; to dispel them you might say something like:

課長がいないと、職場がなんだかピリッとしないんですよ。

*Kachō ga inai to, shokuba ga nandaka piritto shinai n'
desu yo.*

With you (the section chief) away, the office seems
to have lost some of the old drive.

主任が入院中だというと、お得意さんが、じゃ退
院してから出直すかって言われるんですよ。

*Shunin ga nyūin-chū da to iu to, otokui-san ga, ja taiin
shite kara denaosu ka tte iwareru n' desu yo.*

Regular clients don't want to talk to anyone but
you—when they hear the chief is in the hospital,
they say they'll call again when you're back.

なんとかこなしてはいるんですが、鶴のひと声が
あるのとないのとじゃ大違いなんですよ。

*Nantoka konashite wa iru n' desu ga, tsuru no hitokoe ga
aru no to nai no to ja ōchigai nan desu yo.*

We're managing to get by, I guess, but it's nothing
like when you're around to lay down the law.

If you're visiting someone who works under you, you
might cheer him up by conveying the idea that everyone at
work is looking forward to his recovery:

みんなで手分けして仕事はさばいているんだが、や
っぱり君独自のノウハウというのがあってね。Ⓜ

*Minna de tewake shite shigoto wa sabaite iru n' da ga,
yappari kimi dokuji no nohau to iu no ga atte ne.*

Everybody's pitching in to get the job done, but nobody really has your special touch.

In the event that recovery is expected to be a lengthy
process, the prudent course is to avoid saying anything to
make the patient impatient—overeager, that is, to get well
and back to work. Instead, focus on the long term, as in
this extended sample:

この際じっくりといいアイディアを練ってくれた
まえ。こんな機会はめったとないから、禍転じ
て福となす、という気分で、仕事とまったく関
係のない本を読んだり、病院内を観察するのも、
案外次の仕事につながるかもしれないよ。Ⓜ

*Kono sai jikkuri to ii aidia o nette kureta mae. Konna
kikai wa metta to nai kara, wazawai tenjite fuku to
nasu, to iu kibun de, shigoto to mattaku kankei no nai
hon o yondari, byōin-nai o kansatsu suru no mo, angai
tsugi no shigoto ni tsunagaru ka mo shirenai yo.*

Use the time to let some good ideas develop. You
don't get many chances like this, so think of it as
a way to get some benefit out of a bad break. Read
a few books that have nothing to do with work,
take a look around the hospital. You never know—
it could help you on the job later on.

When it's time to leave, it's a good idea to leave on a
cheerful note, such as the promise of another visit:

またお見舞いに寄らせてもらいます。

Mata omimai ni yorasete moraimasu.

I'll come to see you again soon.

You were very kind to come and see me. Thank you

ご丁重なお見舞いをいただき、ありがとうござい
ました。

Goteichō na omimai o itadaki, arigatō gozaimashita.

You were very kind to come and see me. Thank you.

The customs involved in thanking someone for visiting you in the hospital have various stages, the first of which is simply expressing your gratitude in suitable words at the time of the visit:

さっそくのお見舞い、ありがとうございます。

Sassoku no omimai, arigatō gozaimasu.

Thank you for coming to see me so soon.

あなたの顔を見ただけでうれしくて、元気がわい
    てくるようです。

*Anata no kao o mita dake de ureshikute, genki ga waite
    kuru yō desu.*

I'm really happy to see you. I feel better already.

お顔を見せてくださるだけでうれしいのに、お心
    遣いいただいて、ありがとうございます。

*Okao o misete kudasaru dake de ureshii no ni, okokoro-
    zukai itadaite, arigatō gozaimasu.*

I'm so glad you've come to see me, and thank you
    for the gift.

If you received a get-well present from someone while in the hospital, it's customary to thank them again once you've returned home.

入院中は何かとお心遣いありがとうございました。
    おかげさまで予定より早く退院することができ
    ました。あと少し、自宅で体力をつけるようが
    んばります。

*Nyūin-chū wa nani ka to okokoro-zukai arigatō goza-
    imashita. Okagesama de yotei yori hayaku taiin suru
    koto ga dekimashita. Ato sukoshi, jitaku de tairyoku o
    tsukeru yō ganbarimasu.*

Thank you for the gift you brought me while I was in the hospital. I'm happy to say that I've gotten well enough to leave the hospital sooner than expected, and now it's just a matter of recuperating at home for a little while.

Then, when you've finally returned to ordinary life, you should once again thank those who facilitated your recovery. You might say:

休んでいるあいだはお世話になりました。

Yasunde iru aida wa osewa ni narimashita.

Thank you for all you did while I was indisposed.

But you needn't make it quite so brief; this is one time when people tend to pour it on. For example:

みなさんにご迷惑をおかけしました。そのうえお
忙しいのにお見舞いに来てくださってありがと
うございます。元気になれたのも皆さんのおか
げです。いい経験をしたと思って、これからの
仕事に励んで、ご恩返しをするつもりです。

Minasan ni gomeiwaku o okake shimashita. Sono ue oiso-gashii no ni omimai ni kite kudasatte arigatō goza-imasu. Genki ni nareta no mo minasan no okage desu. Ii keiken o shita to omotte, kore kara no shigoto ni ha-gende, go-ongaeshi o suru tsumori desu.

I regret having put you all to so much trouble. I'm grateful to you for taking time out of your busy schedules to visit me—your kindness was the key to my recovery. I will look upon this as a positive experience and apply my very best efforts to my work, in the hope that I can someday repay all you have done for me.

日頃忘れていた健康のありがたさを身にしみて知
ったというのが収穫でした。それにつけても療

71

養中のあたたかいお見舞いには勇気づけられ、
つくづく友人のありがたさを再発見しました。

Higoro wasurete ita kenkō no arigatasa o mi ni shimite shitta to iu no ga shūkaku deshita. Sore ni tsukete mo ryōyō-chū no atatakai omimai ni wa yūki-zukerare, tsukuzuku yūjin no arigatasa o sai-hakken shimashita.

The realization that good health is a great blessing—something I had lost sight of—has now become acutely clear. Moreover, as one who drew strength from your kind visits during my convalescence, I have realized anew what a great blessing it is to have good friends.

It is customary, once you have returned to ordinary life or have recovered sufficiently, to celebrate the return of good health by sending return gifts to those whose good wishes (and get-well presents of cash) have sustained you. There is no need to spend lavishly on these presents, however, especially in light of the expense of hospitalization and convalescence. Something simple will suffice, and it's also nice to send a note announcing that you're back in action.

❧

How good of you to come!

ようこそおいでくださいました。

Yōkoso oide kudasaimashita.

How good of you to come!

Here are some gracious words with which to welcome a visitor to your home. The first part of the word *yōkoso* is, in fact, derived from *yoku*, which literally means "well," and you could say that this expression performs the same literal functions that the term "welcome" does in English. It is somewhat more emphatic, perhaps, than the more familiar expression

いらっしゃいませ。
Irasshaimase.
Welcome!

which is used in a wider variety of contexts—to welcome customers to a store or restaurant, for example—and not merely to greet visitors to one's home.

Alternatives to *yōkoso oide kudasaimashita* include:

お待ちしておりました。
Omachi shite orimashita.
I've been looking forward to seeing you.

これはお珍しい。
Kore wa omezurashii.
Isn't this a nice surprise!

The first of these applies to situations in which the visitor was expected, while the second can be used when someone drops by without giving advance notice, particularly when the surprise visitor is someone who is usually too busy to come around. Unannounced visits are, of course, something out of the ordinary for most people and can be disruptive for those being visited. For this reason, the caller may well offer a brief excuse for any inconvenience:

ご近所まで参りましたもので……。
Gokinjo made mairimasita mono de ...
I just happened to be in the neighborhood, so ...

Once you have initially welcomed someone who has come

for a visit, your next job is to invite him into your home, usually by saying something like:

どうぞお上がりください。

Dōzo oagari kudasai.

Please come in.

Having led your guest into the room where you'll be entertaining him, you should encourage him to take a seat.

どうぞお楽になさってください。

Dōzo oraku ni nasatte kudasai.

Please make yourself comfortable.

When you serve the tea or coffee or snacks, you should do so with a suitably humble-sounding invitation to partake:

何もございませんが、どうぞごゆっくり。

Nani mo gozaimasen ga, dōzo goyukkuri.

It isn't much, but please help yourself.

The guest, for his part, deferentially resists such favored treatment, saying:

どうぞお構いなく。

Dōzo okamai naku.

Please don't go to any trouble over me.

or

どうぞお気遣いなく。

Dōzo okizukai naku.

Please don't worry about me.

If the guest has brought along a gift for the host, he might present it at this point, or if it's a gift of food or drink, even earlier. In this connection, it should be noted that the odd-sounding phrase

つまらない物ですが。
Tsumaranai mono desu ga.
I'm afraid this isn't much of a gift.

seems to have gradually lost currency among visitors, perhaps due to the decidedly negative implications of the word *tsumaranai* (literally, "poor" or "trifling"). Instead, many people now prefer such expressions as:

心ばかりのものですが。
Kokoro bakari no mono desu ga.
This is just something to show my appreciation.

☽

Oh, look at the time!

おや、もうこんな時間。
Oya, mō konna jikan.
Oh, look at the time!

When you visit the home of a friend, it is generally left up to you as the guest to bring the visit to an end. One time-honored pretext for doing so is to remark on the lateness of the hour, for which purpose this expression works wonderfully. When you feel the time has come to be leaving, wait until the conversation begins to flag or some other convenient opening appears, then consult your watch or a clock and utter the magic words as you rise to go. According to the rules of politeness, this is the signal for your host to insist that it's too soon to depart, saying something like:

まだよろしいじゃありませんか。

Mada yoroshii ja arimasen ka.
You don't have to leave already, do you?

You shouldn't take this literally—your host is merely performing a role as required by courtesy. Besides, it's considered very bad manners to overstay your welcome, so feel free to firmly resist the (ostensible) invitation to linger:

いえいえ、すっかり長居してしまいました。
Ie ie, sukkari naga-i shite shimaimashita.
No, I've already imposed on your hospitality far too long.

Presuming there are no further politely forceful attempts to detain you (if there are—be strong!), you can prepare to take your leave, but first offer some appreciative comment, like:

今日はとても楽しかったです。
Kyō wa totemo tanoshikatta desu.
I had a wonderful time today.

Should you find yourself tiring of the old checking-your-watch routine, another other useful expression for signaling your imminent departure is:

そろそろおいとまを……
Sorosoro oitoma o ...
Well, I'd best be getting along.

There are more elaborately polite expressions that make use of the term *itoma* ("leave-taking," here preceded by the honorific prefix *o*), some of which have been immortalized in *rakugo* routines and the like; you could really make an impression on your hosts if you were to say, for example:

あまり長居をいたしましてはかえってご迷惑でございますから、これでおいとまを。

*Amari naga-i o itashimashite wa kaette gomewaku de go-
   zaimasu kara, kore de oitoma o.*

I would be imposing on you if I were to dawdle any
   longer, so I'd better be going.

If you have been treated to a meal by your host and
then decide that you have stayed just about as long as courtesy requires, you can make your departure in style with
this somewhat antiquated bit of verbosity:

いただき立ちで申し訳ございませんが、そろそろ
おいとまを。

*Itadaki-dachi de mōshiwake gozaimasen ga, sorosoro oi-
   toma o.*

I apologize for having to eat and run, but I'm afraid
   I have to be going.

As you say this, keep in mind that rude though it is to eat
and run, it's still worse to abuse your hosts' hospitality by
overstaying your welcome.

○

I wish I'd had more to offer
by way of hospitality

何のおもてなしもできませんで……

Nan no omotenashi mo dekimasen de ...

I wish I'd had more to offer by way of hospitality.

This is perhaps the expression most widely used by people
seeing off someone who has been visiting them at home.
The term *motenashi* (here employed with the honorific pre-

fix *o* and translated as "hospitality") literally means "treatment" in a very general sense, but it is usually understood to refer to the digestible components of hospitality: food and drink. In other words, the host is apologizing for only providing tea instead of a full meal, or for only providing a meal instead of a grand banquet; the implication is that whatever was offered wasn't good enough for you. This show of humility is, of course, a ritual dictated by courtesy—actually, you may have been treated like visiting royalty.

Alternatives to the above expression include:

何のおかまいもできませんで……

Nan no okamai mo dekimasen de ...

I'm afraid I've been a poor host.

なんのお愛想もございませんで……

Nan no oaiso mo gozaimasen de ...

I'm sorry I couldn't be more hospitable.

The departing guest, meanwhile, does his own apologizing:

今日はかえってご迷惑をおかけしまして……

Kyō wa kaette gomewaku o okake shimashite ...

I'm sorry for imposing on you today.

Here, then, is a paradigm of politeness, Japanese style: each of the principal parties to a perfectly harmless social transaction finds something to apologize for, permitting a balanced mutual show of humility.

There are various polite ways for a host to invite a departing guest to come again:

ぜひまたお立ち寄りください。

Zehi mata otachiyori kudasai.

By all means, stop over again sometime.

近いうちにまた遊びにきてください。

Chikai uchi ni mata asobi ni kite kudasai.

Come and see us again soon, okay?

今度いらっしゃるときは、もっとごゆっくりして
　　いってください。

Kondo irassharu toki wa, motto goyukkuri shite itte kuda-
　　sai.

The next time you come we'll have a good long visit,
　　all right?

これからも時々お顔を見せてください。

Kore kara mo tokidoki okao o misete kudasai.

Drop by when you have a chance—don't be a stranger.

これを機会にちょくちょくお出かけください。

Kore o kikai ni chokuchoku odekake kudasai.

Any time you feel like getting out, just come right
　　on over.

According to custom, the host accompanies his guest to the
front gate (more often the front door nowadays), where he
bids his guest farewell:

ごきげんよう。

Gokigen yō.

Take care, now.

The guest might reply on his way out (making one last
show of apology, since this phrase·literally means "I beg
your pardon"):

ごめんください。

Gomen kudasai.

Thank you and goodbye.

❀

I hope that you will favor me with your guidance and advice

ご指導ご鞭撻を賜りますよう、お願いいたします。

Goshidō gobentatsu o tamawarimasu yō, onegai itashimasu.

I hope that you will favor me with your guidance and advice.

This formal request is most often employed, as a salutation of sorts, in connection with either marriage plans or the quest for employment. It has the ring of old-fashioned abject humility—to request *bentatsu* (here preceded by the honorific *go*) is to literally ask for a whipping—and so is reserved for occasions that require explicit self-deprecation.

There are other, slightly less submissive-sounding ways to say basically the same thing:

一所懸命やっていくつもりでございますので、今後ともどうぞよろしくご指導くださいますようお願い申しあげます。

Isshō-kenmei yatte iku tsumori de gozaimasu no de, kongo tomo dōzo yoroshiku goshidō kudasaimasu yō onegai-mōshiagemasu.

I ask your guidance in the days to come. I intend to do my very best.

ベストを尽くしてがんばるつもりでおります。

Besuto o tsukushite ganbaru tsumori de orimasu.

I'll make every effort to do my very best.

なにぶんにも未熟者でございますから、どうぞこ

80

のうえともご忠告ご指導くださいますよう、お
願い申しあげます。

*Nanibun ni mo mijuku-mono de gozaimasu kara, dōzo
kono ue tomo gochūkoku goshidō kudasaimasu yō, onegai mōshiagemasu.*

Since I'm still somewhat inexperienced, I ask that
you favor me with your advice and guidance.

ふつつか者どうしですが、今後ともよろしくご指
導ください。

*Futsutsuka-mono dōshi desu ga, kongo tomo yoroshiku go-
shidō kudasai.*

Unschooled as I am in the ways of the world, I ask
that you guide me in the days ahead.

The parents of the bride or the groom are also sometimes
called upon to request the favor of others on behalf of their
children. For example:

これからも末永くお見守りいただき、厳しいご叱
正、ご指導を賜りますよう、心からお願い申し
あげます。

*Kore kara mo suenagaku omimamori itadaki, kibishii
goshissei, goshidō o tamawarimasu yō, kokoro kara onegaimōshiagemasu.*

We ask that that they may always enjoy your protection, and that you favor them with strict guidance
and sound advice.

or perhaps:

まだまだ足取りのおぼつかない未熟者ですので、
折にふれて皆さまのお力添えをいただきたくお
願い申しあげます。

*Mada mada ashidori no obotsukanai mijuku-mono desu
no de, ori ni furete mina-sama no ochikarazoe o itadaki-
taku onegaimōshiagemasu.*

As they are just starting out and don't know much of life, we ask you all to grant them the favor of your support from time to time.

At a formal wedding reception, it's customary for the father of the groom (occasionally the father of the bride) to bring the festivities to a close by saying a few words, often conveying this same sort of message. It's considered good form for the bride and groom to say a word or two also, giving them a chance to speak for themselves and perhaps elicit a sense of support among the guests. At such times, although the entire (and often astronomical) expense of the wedding is invariably borne by the parents, no mention is made of this nor is gratitude explicitly expressed.

❀

Make it so / Say hello, etc.

よろしく。

Yoroshiku.

Make it so / Say hello, etc.

The multiplicity and variety of functions that this word serves make it not only one of the most useful terms in the language but also one of the most ubiquitous (not to mention practically impossible to translate bereft of context). When used to seal an agreement or formalize a request, it represents an abbreviation of the more formal expression

どうぞよろしくお願いします。

Dōzo yoroshiku onegai shimasu.

I ask that you please make it so.

For most informal transactions and situations, *yoroshiku* alone will suffice.

Let us consider some of the uses to which this term is commonly put. Suppose you wanted to ask someone you know to give your regards to a third person whom you both know. The standard informal expression to use is:

中田さんによろしく。

Nakada-san ni yoroshiku.

Say hello to Mr. Nakada for me.

Or let's say you've been introduced for the first time to someone of roughly your own age and status. To formalize the introduction you would probably say:

どうぞよろしく。

Dōzo yoroshiku.

Pleased to meet you.

In neither case does the use of *yoroshiku* necessarily imply a strict commitment to any specific arrangement. Rather, the term as used here is merely a standard form of greeting.* It is also sometimes used to end conversations, including telephone calls, especially when business has been discussed (the word *hitotsu*, literally, "one," lends a lighter, more familiar tone to a request for favor):

ひとつよろしく。Ⓜ

Hitotsu yoroshiku.

Do whatever needs doing, okay?

It should be noted, though, that this is merely a business-like way to say goodbye and doesn't actually commit anyone to anything in particular. The point is, although it is a term usually associated with requests, the informal use of *yoroshiku* often has nothing at all to do with making a request.

Yoroshiku acquires much more gravity when you address

someone who is considered your elder or a superior at work. If you present a request in such circumstances, you risk your reputation as someone who knows the rules unless you scrupulously punctuate your request with a carefully delivered

よろしくお願いします。

Yoroshiku onegai shimasu.

I ask that you make it so.

On occasion you might be asked to take responsibility for some job by a superior at work, who explains what needs to be done and then says:

あとはよろしくやってくれ。Ⓜ

Ato wa yoroshiku yatte kure.

As for the rest of it, do what you think is best.

In this context *yoroshiku* means something like "appropriately" or "to a sufficient extent," indicating the sort of conveniently vague standard that bosses often demand and seldom seem to elucidate.

*Interestingly enough, *dōzo yoroshiku* as a first-time greeting appears in inverted form as term of farewell in business-related telephone calls: *yoroshiku dōzo.*

✺

I have a big favor to ask you

折り入ってお願いがございます。

Ori-itte onegai ga gozaimasu.

I have a big favor to ask you.

The first part of this expression, *ori-itte* (literally, "earnestly"), is the part that packs the punch—this word alone will tip off the listener that you want her to listen closely because you've got some truly pressing business on your mind. For this very reason, you should observe a measure of discretion before using this expression, lest you suffer the same fate that befell the boy who cried wolf. This is a sentence to be reserved for occasions of serious need and is not to be trotted out whenever an itch wants scratching. When you begin with these words, you can expect the person you're addressing to straighten up and pay serious attention.

A similarly ominous-sounding expression, and one useful for similar occasions, is:

ほかにお願いできる方もございませんので……
Hoka ni onegai dekiru kata mo gozaimasen no de ...
You're the only person I can ask this of.

The suggestion here is not, of course, that you have already run through a list of potential candidates before getting to this person, but that this person alone, owing to her power or ability, is in a position to be able to help you with a very serious need, and therefore should give sympathetic consideration to the request that you so urgently wish to make.

If you do find yourself in a situation in which you desperately require assistance, it's probably a good idea to present your case to someone other than those you tend to hit up for ordinary favors. Notwithstanding the fact that both of these expressions will have great impact on the proper person, it's not advisable to try springing either of them on someone you still owe a favor to from the week before, or someone whose generosity (or patience) you have already tested; your plaintive words are likely to be greeted with rolling eyes and muted sighs rather than the sympathetic attention you were hoping for. In the main, people tend to reserve these expressions for those they consider their standby saviours in times when all else fails—special relatives, former teachers, mentors, or certain bosses—and only then to ask for help with matters of a personal nature.

❀

I'm happy to be of service

喜んでつとめさせていただきます。

Yorokonde tsutomesasete itadakimasu.

I'm happy to be of service.

This is a standard expression of consent to a formal request, particularly useful when the request comes from someone to whom you are indebted and therefore can't refuse—a sponsor or patron, or the person who acted as go-between or master of ceremonies at your wedding, for example. Possible alternatives include:

私のような者でお役に立てるなら……

Watashi no yō na mono de oyaku ni tateru nara ...

If you think I could be of any assistance to you, of course.

及ばずながら、尽力させていただきます。

Oyobazunagara, jinryoku sasete itadakimasu.

I'll do my best, however humble my efforts may be.

いや光栄です。私でよければ、喜んでおひきうけ しましょう。

Iya kōei desu. Watashi de yokereba, yorokonde ohikiuke shimashō.

I'm honored. It would be a pleasure, if you really
think I'm the man for the job.

ほかならぬあなたのお頼みですから。

Hoka-naranu anata no o tanomi desu kara.

It might be different if it were someone else asking,
but for you—of course.

こんなことでご恩返しができるなら喜んで。

Konna koto de go-ongaeshi dekiru nara yorokonde.

It would be a pleasure to have the chance to repay
your kindness.

お安いご用ですよ。

Oyasui goyō desu yo.

That's hardly asking much of me (in return for the
service you've done me).

Since you are in fact agreeing, and with (ostensible) enthusiasm, to the request, and thereby rendering satisfaction,
it may not seem important to be too concerned about just
what words you use. Nevertheless, you shouldn't give the
impression that you are agreeing in haste or without giving
due consideration to what is expected of you. Depending
on just what the favor involves, the person asking may have
thought a great deal about who to ask before settling on
you—so you are expected to take such a request seriously.
Giving your consent too breezily or rushing too eagerly
into a commitment in the manner of Tora-san from the
movies, for example, may actually undermine the other person's confidence in you, leaving him to wonder if the job
will really get done. Better to reassure the other person by
conveying a realistic sense of your limitations and soberly
declaring your intention to honor the request to the best of
your abilities:

どこまでご希望にそえるかわかりませんが、でき
るかぎりつとめさせていただきます。

Doko made gokibō ni soeru ka wakarimasen ga, dekiru kangiri tsutomesasete itadakimasu.

I'm not sure I can live up to your expectations, but I'll give it my very best effort.

Should an occasion arise when you simply cannot comply with a formal request from someone to whom you owe a favor, you have a way out. There is an all-purpose formal expression of refusal—to be used sparingly, if at all—that will close the matter for good:

そういったご依頼は一切お受けしないことにして
おりますので、悪しからずご了承ください。

Sō itta goirai wa issai ouke shinai koto ni shite orimasu no de, ashikarazu goryōshō kudasai.

It's my standard policy not to accept this type of request. I hope you'll understand without taking offense.

Needless to say, once you've rejected a request from someone in this manner, you not eligible to comply with a similar request from someone else.

❀

Only because it's you who's asking

ほかならぬあなたの頼みですもの。Ⓕ

Hoka-naranu anata no tanomi desu mono.

Only because it's you who's asking.

If someone makes a request and you decide to accept it, you have your pick of a number of common expressions to communicate your consent. For example, if you wish to acquiesce humbly to the other person's wishes, you can choose from the following:

私でよければ、喜んで。
Watashi de yokereba, yorokonde.
Certainly, if you're sure I'm the right person.

私にできることなら、喜んで。
Watashi ni dekiru koto nara, yorokonde.
Sure, if you think I'd be equal to the task.

お役に立つかどうかわかりませんが……
Oyaku ni tatsu ka dō ka wakarimasen ga ...
All right, although I'm not sure how much good I can do.

While these are all familiar and polite expressions, none of them sounds too old-fashioned or too formal for use in casual speech. On the other hand, if you want to emphasize that it would be no trouble at all to grant the request, you might use one of these:

お安いご用ですよ。
Oyasui goyō desu yo.
No problem at all.

ご安心ください。
Go-anshin kudasai.
Don't trouble yourself—I'll take care of it.

そんなことなら、いつでもおっしゃってくだされ
　ばいいのに。

Sonna koto nara, itsu de mo osshatte kudasareba ii no ni.

That's all? Of course, any time you like.

If the other person was worried that he might be imposing
on you, this type of reply has the advantage of putting his
worries to rest. There's another expression that promotes
this sense of reassurance more vividly:

大船に乗ったつもりで万事私におまかせください。

*Ōbune ni notta tsumori de banji watashi ni omakase ku-
dasai.*

Just hop on board my ship and leave everything to
　me.

There may be occasions when you are either reluctant or
ill-equipped to take on whatever favor is being asked of
you, although you feel you must. Then again, there may be
certain people for whom you would be willing to do just
about anything. In both such cases, the sentence at the beginning of this section will come in handy.

ほかならぬあなたの頼みですもの。

Hoka-naranu anata no tanomi desu mono.

Only because it's you who is asking.

By saying this you are implicitly agreeing to do what is
asked of you, but exactly what you mean depends on which
kind of situation you find yourself in. On the one hand,
the person making the request may be someone who, for
reasons of honor or obligation, you simply cannot refuse;
in that case, you mean that you'll do what is asked because
you are obliged to—you would not do it otherwise. In this
situation, you are subtly putting a negative spin on your
reply. On the other hand, the person asking the favor may
be someone for whom you'd gladly brave both fires and

floods; in that case you mean that it's not the favor that counts, but the person who is asking. Here the message has a strongly positive cast.

❁

I regret that
I can't be of any help

お力になれなくて残念です。

Ochikara ni narenakute zannen desu.

I regret that I can't be of any help.

When you are presented with a request from someone to whom you're not particularly close, you can use this expression to politely decline, if you wish. A similar alternative expression is:

お役に立てなくて残念です。

Oyaku ni tatenakute zannen desu.

I'm afraid that I won't be able to be of any assistance.

If someone asks you to take charge of a neighborhood project or to accept some other position of responsibility, you may well feel you're not qualified for the job. In such cases as this, a popular strategy is to plead a lack of ability:

私には荷が重すぎて……。

Watashi ni wa ni ga omosugite ...

I don't have what it takes.

力不足で、とてもご要望にお応えできそうにもあ
りません。

Chikara-busoku de, totemo goyōbō ni okotae dekisō ni mo arimasen.

I just don't have the ability—I couldn't do a satisfactory job of it.

A similar gambit is to point out the trouble that would likely result from rashly accepting responsibilities that one is ill-equipped to perform:

せっかくお声をかけていただきましたが、なにぶ
ん仕事が忙しく、お引き受けしてもかえって皆
さんにご迷惑をおかけするだけですので……

Sekkaku okoe o kakete itadakimashita ga, nanibun shigoto ga isogashiku, ohikiuke shite mo kaette mina-san ni gomeiwaku o okake suru dake desu no de ...

I appreciate your asking me, but I'm already so busy with work that if I were to accept I'm afraid I'd only end up causing everyone a lot of trouble.

Some situations call for more a forceful way to turn down a request. Let's say that you have shown an interest in or even tentatively agreed to a request, only to find that the favor asked has suddenly grown bigger or more complicated than anything that was originally discussed. Your response is to emphatically opt out, but rather than imply that anyone was trying to take advantage of you, you might simply say:

この話はなかったことにしてください。

Kono hanashi wa nakatta koto ni shite kudasai.

Let's just forget that this subject ever came up.

This expression conveys a strong and unmistakable rejection of the proposal. Since the situation is not what you were led to believe and no further discussion will make it so, you can use these words to put an end to the subject. A sightly different but related expression is:

おろしてもらいます。
Oroshite moraimasu.
Deal me out.

When you have previously agreed to a request but later wish to withdraw your consent, you can use this expression, though it won't in any way shield you from hard feelings on the other side.

❖

There's no time like the present

善は急げ
Zen wa isoge.
There's no time like the present.

This is an abbreviation of an old proverb:

善は急げ、悪は延べよ。
Zen wa isoge, aku wa nobeyo.
Hasten the good deeds, postpone the bad.

In contemporary usage, the second half of the proverb tends to be omitted, but the first part (here translated outside the context of the whole proverb as "There's no time like the present") is often cited in the effort to persuade someone to take what will clearly be a beneficial action. If you have a friend who is considering such a course of action but wavering, you might say something like:

善は急げというじゃないか。Ⓜ

Zen wa isoge to iu ja nai ka.

As the saying goes, there's no time like the present.

With these words you can help incite your friend—for her own good and in a manner not at all coercive or preachy (well, maybe a tad preachy)—to forge ahead without delay.

Suppose you are in a position of authority and someone working under you comes up with a plan for tackling some task or another. If you approve of the plan and decide to adopt it, you could simply say, "Okay, put this plan into action immediately." But if you seize the opportunity to quote the saying cited above—fleshing it out with a few details, of course—you can avoid sounding too bossy and instead strike a pleasing note of praise and encouragement.

In a similar way, these three little words can provide you with a convenient and succinct means of lighting a fire under a friend who's dithering or taking an overly leisurely approach to things. As the examples above suggest, this expression works best when spoken by someone in a position of authority or by a friend or peer—probably not the sort of quip to try out on the boss.

Another phrase often used in conjunction with this expression is

思い立ったら吉日。

Omoitattara kichijitsu.

Strike while the iron is hot.

The meaning (literally, "The day you make up your mind to do something is the best day to do it") is basically the same as that of the phrase *zen wa isoge,* and the function—to promote action or discourage procrastination—is also the same.

◐

Have you thought it over?

考えていただけましたか。

Kangaete itadakemashita ka.

Have you thought it over?

Occasionally you may ask a favor or make a request of someone and find that you can't get an answer on the spot—the other person is unable or unwilling to say yes or no right away and wants time to think it over. Under normal circumstances, you simply have to be patient. After a suitable interval (just how long depends on what you're asking), you can feel free to broach the subject again, saying:

例の件、考えていただけましたか。

Rei no ken, kangaete itadakemashita ka.

About that thing we talked about, have you thought it over?

You could also say something like:

例の件、どうなりましたか。

Rei no ken, dō narimashita ka.

About that thing we talked about, what did you decide?

Unless the person you're dealing with is someone to whom you're very close, this is a decidedly familiar way of putting the question, though, and not likely to be well received. It may seem like a fine distinction, but when you're addressing someone other than a close friend or a subordinate at work, it is within the realm of moderation and politeness to ask if the person has thought it over (as in the two expressions above), and outside that realm to ask for a decision.

On the other hand, if it is a very close friend or someone working under you, you probably don't have to observe such niceties. You can simply say:

例の件、いいでしょう？

Rei no ken, ii desshō?

About that other thing, it's okay, right?

In this case, you're even allowed to resort to steamrolling if
you still can't get a straight answer:

まだ考えているの？　絶対迷惑はかけないからウ
ンと言ってよ。

*Mada kangaete iru no? Zettai meiwaku wa kakenai kara
un to itte yo.*

You're still thinking it over? Come on, there's absolutely nothing to worry about. Just say yes.

Among close friends, as long as the person asked didn't cat-
egorically reject the request outright, all manner of nagging,
wheedling, and begging is generally considered permissable
in the effort to win consent to a request. With surprising
frequency, the situation actually ends up in a sort of role-re-
versal, with the person who asked the favor berating his
would-be benefactor for indecisiveness and saying things like:

いつまで待たせれば気がすむのよ。Ⓕ

Itsu made matasereba ki ga sumu no yo.

How long do I have to wait before you make up
your mind?

Often enough, the other person capitulates just to get back
on his friend's good side. Not always, though, and then the
person asking has no choice but to abandon the cause, but
not before one last parting shot that both signals the end
of the struggle and conveys his exasperation:

もうあなたになんか頼まないわ。Ⓕ

Mō anata ni nanka tanomanai wa.

That's the last time I ever ask you for anything.

◈

Has your situation improved at all lately?

その後、ご都合はいかがですか。

Sono go, gotsugō wa ikaga desu ka.

Has your situation improved at all lately?

You're bound to feel reluctant to remind or persuade people to repay money that you lent them. Even so, there's no point in fuming and fretting as you wait and wait for money that doesn't appear to be on its way back to you. Sometimes people simply (even if conveniently) forget, and if that's the case the surest way to ensure you'll see your money again is by providing a polite reminder. Perhaps the safest and least objectionable expressions for the purpose would be something like:

以前ご用立てしたお金のことですが、その後、ご
都合はいかがですか。

*Izen goyōdate shita okane no koto desu ga, sono go, gotsugō
wa ikaga desu ka.*

or

以前お貸ししたお金のことですが、その後、ご都
合はいかがですか。

97

*Izen okashi shita okane no koto desu ga, sono go, gotsugō
wa ikaga desu ka.*

About that money I lent you, has your situation improved at all recently?

With these words, you are clearly giving the other person
the benefit of the doubt—maybe it did just slip his mind—
and are merely calling his attention to the subject in a neutral way. The term *tsugō* (translated in this expression as
"your situation" and employed here with the honorific prefix *go*) is a deliberately ambiguous choice of words, but in
this context it clearly refers to the other person's manage-
ment of his finances; *tsugō* is often used when the subject of
money comes up to refer obliquely to someone's financial
affairs (although it is also widely used to refer to "convenience" or "inconvenience" in a general sense). Someone
might say, for example, talking about herself:

今は都合が悪くて……
Ima wa tsugō ga warukute ...
I'm a little short at the moment.

In another context, you might hear someone, perhaps a
banker, say:

いろいろご都合もおありかと存じますが……
Iroiro gotsugō mo oari ka to zonjimasu ga ...
We all have our own particular financial worries, I
suppose.

If you are really serious about getting your money back
without further delay, there is one fairly reliable way to obtain repayment of a loan without giving offense to the bor-
rower. If you explain that you urgently need the money
yourself, the other person can hardly refuse.

突然こんなことを申しあげるのは心苦しいのです

が、先日お貸ししたお金、私のほうでも急に必
要になりまして……

*Totsuzen konna koto o mōshiageru no wa kokorogurushii
no desu ga, senjitsu okashi shita okane, watashi no hō
de mo kyū ni hitsuyō ni narimashite ...*

I'm really sorry to have to tell you this so suddenly,
but something has come up and I really need that
money I lent you the other day ...

Needless to say, both the borrowing and lending of money
can lead to tangled webs.

Something's not quite right

何か違うんじゃない。
Nani ka chigau 'n ja nai.
Something's not quite right.

This is the sort of thing you might say to express doubt or
dissatisfaction, to indicate that the situation has gotten
mixed up or gone wrong somehow and all is not as it
should be. The main part of the sentence, *nani ka chigau*
(translated here as "something's not right") is conveniently
vague; this expression is especially useful when it's hard to
pinpoint exactly what the problem is. It is often used in
preference to more definitive statements such as:

それは間違っている。
Sore wa machigatte iru.
That's wrong.

The preference for vagueness, which applies to many other

types of expressions as well, seems to be based on a common aversion to the risk involved in making stronger statements—especially contrary ones. If you use the expression *sore wa machigatte iru*, for example, you run the risk of directly offending someone, and at the least you're likely to be put on the spot and have to justify your objections in detail, when someone else replies:

それではお前はどう考えるんだ。Ⓜ

Sore de wa omae wa dō kangaeru n' da.

Okay, then suppose you explain to us how you see the situation.

It is to avoid this very situation that people tend to stick to cracks like *nani ka chigau n' ja nai,* which sound more impressionistic and don't convey any strong message for which they might be held responsible.

Suppose you encounter a couple out shopping, the woman trying to put together an outfit while the man looks on and tries to act helpful. You might hear the following exchange:

この色とこの色を組み合わせるのはどう？

Kono iro to kono iro o kumiawaseru no wa dō?

What do you think, does this color go with this other color?

うーん、何か違うな。Ⓜ

Uun, nani ka chigau na.

Hmm, something's not quite right about it.

The man, who isn't very taken with the combination of colors, avoids the possibility of hurting the woman's feelings (she might like the combination) while implicitly suggesting that she keep looking.

Another example: a photographer is trying valiantly to get a model to pose in a manner suitable for the picture he needs. He tells her what he wants and she tries one pose after another, but none of them is quite on the mark. Tacitly, what the photographer wants to say is, "You really don't have any idea what I'm looking for here, do you?" Ever the diplomatic professional, though, he actually says:

どうも違うな。

Dōmo chigau na.

I don't know, something's not right.

These days one often hears a different expression used, particularly by young women, to express essentially the same meaning as those above:

ちょっと変。

Chotto hen.

Kind of weird.

This expression conveys a strong sense that the objection is more subjective than objective and thus not necessarily explainable in logical terms.

Stop trying to stand in the way

足を引っ張るのはやめてください。

Ashi o hipparu no wa yamete kudasai.

Stop trying to stand in the way.

Sometimes an objection can take the form of a scolding, in which case this expression might come in handy. The phrase *ashi o hipparu* (literally, "to trip up," here translated as "stand in the way") refers to such ill-considered behavior as deliberately trying to hinder someone's progress or undermine someone's success. It is often heard in contexts like the following:

人が一所懸命努力しているのに、足を引っ張るよ
うなことはやめてください。

Hito ga issho-kenmei doryoku shite iru no ni, ashi o hipparu yō na koto wa yamete kudasai.

I'm doing the very best I can—stop trying to stand in my way.

This expression is generally used to deliver a forceful rebuke to someone whose actions are motivated by malice or envy, and it often implies that the speaker has reached the limits of endurance and will tolerate no more such behavior. To drive home this point, the speaker often follows up with phrases like:

もうこりごりです。

Mō korigori desu.

I've had enough!

いいかげんにしてください。

Ii kagen ni shite kudasai.

You've taken this far enough!

Such language represents the utmost degree of protest or criticism; these words should be used with extreme discretion.

Consider the example of a local governmental council that convenes to discuss a certain proposal. On one side of the issue is the majority, which favors the proposal, and on the other side is a hostile minority. The minority stoops to underhanded tactics, outright fabrication, and overall demagoguery in an attempt to bring down the majority's leaders and reverse the vote—until someone representing the majority is sufficiently outraged to take the members of the minority to task. This is a case in which the use of the harsh language cited above would probably be considered justifiable.

In addition to *ashi o hipparu*, there are several other related idioms in which *ashi* ("leg" or "foot") figures prominently. One such phrase is:

揚げ足を取る
ageashi o toru
literally, "grab a raised leg"

which refers to trapping someone in a slip of the tongue, pretending to mistake someone's meaning, or just being sarcastic and generally picking on people. Another interesting specimen is:

足をすくう
ashi o sukuu
literally, "to trip"

which means to catch someone off guard or take advantage of inattentiveness.

It may seem impolite for me to say this

ぶしつけを承知で申しあげます。
Bushitsuke o shōchi de mōshiagemasu.
It may seem impolite for me to say this.

While it's usually a good idea to couch your objections in mild language, you may occasionally find yourself in circumstances where there's no point in mincing words. By prefacing your remarks with this expression, you serve notice that you're going to dispense with delicacy for a change and frankly speak your mind. Although the term *bushitsuke* literally means "rudeness," this expression doesn't, of course, communicate an intention to be rude (nor will it excuse a subsequent display of bad manners) but only an intention to speak openly and unambiguously. Another expression that can be used the same way is:

この際、忌憚なく申しあげます。

Kono sai, kitan naku mōshiagemasu.

I'm going to be candid with you.

Both sentences lend themselves to use in more formal exchanges—conversations with people whom you either don't know well or who are in positions of authority. Less ceremony is required to prepare a close friend for a frank opinion; to a friend you can simply say:

この際、はっきり言うけど……

Kono sai, hakkiri iu kedo ...

If you want to know the truth ...

Another standard expression that is similar in meaning to those cited above but different in usage is:

遠慮なく言わせていただいたほうが、おたがいの
ためと思いまして……

Enryo naku iwasete itadaita hō ga, otagai no tame to omoimashite ...

It will be better for both of us if I speak frankly.

The difference is that this is not something you can say to an elder or to anyone in a position of authority over you.

No matter what unreasonable or absurd position such a person takes, the use of phrase *otagai no tame* (here translated "for both of us") implies that you know what's best—an impermissible act of presumption when dealing with authority figures. This sentence, then, is to be reserved for use with peers or people over whom you have authority.

Whomever you're addressing, merely warning people you're going to be candid does not grant you a license to rant and rave. As in virtually every other conversational context, you are expected to behave with composure and restraint, and particularly so when you publicly disagree with someone. Intemperate remarks can lead straight to a quarrel, and that really would be rude.

It probably just slipped your mind, but ...

ついうっかりなさったんだと思いますが……
Tsui ukkari nasatta n' da to omoimasu ga ...
It probably just slipped your mind, but ...

In cities like Tokyo, residents are supposed to take their garbage out only on certain days of the week, when municipal garbage trucks come around to collect the trash at designated neighborhood pick-up sites. But suppose the fellow who lives across the way from you is putting his garbage out on the street whenever he pleases, and this has become a nuisance. In this instance you might approach him at a convenient moment and say:

お忙しくてついうっかりなさったんだと思います
　が、ゴミの収集日は火曜日ですよ。

*Oisogashikute tsui ukkari nasatta n' da to omoimasu ga,
gomi no shūshū-bi wa kayōbi desu yo.*

I'm sure you're busy and it probably just slipped your
mind, but the pick-up day for trash is Tuesday.

By reminding him of the correct procedure in this polite
way, you can avoid the risk of causing needless offense. The
expression *tsui ukkari nasatta n' da to omoimasu* conveys the
message that you are not accusing the other person of
doing anything wrong, but simply pointing out something
that may have been forgotten or misunderstood. The phrase
clearly communicates a sense of open-minded consideration
for the other person's point of view—after all, anyone can
make a mistake—and thus can be highly useful for fostering
harmonious relations in a variety of situations. In order for
the expression to have the intended effect, however, it must
not be taken for sarcasm, so make sure to (at least) sound
sincere.

Let's say you want a neighbor to pay for certain dam-
ages for which he bears indirect responsibility. You might
present your case this way:

野球に夢中になって、ついうっかり方向がずれた
　んだと思いますが、おたくのお坊ちゃんがうちの
　窓ガラスにボールをぶつけてしまったらしく……

*Yakyū ni muchū ni natte, tsui ukkari hōkō ga zureta n'
da to omoimasu ga, otaku no obotchan ga uchi no
mado-garasu ni bōru o butsukete shimatta rashiku ...*

I'm sure he was caught up in the game and just happened to throw the ball in the wrong direction,
but it seems your son broke one of our windows
with a baseball ...

Or perhaps it's you who need straightening out: you
have been practicing the piano at night after work, and

someone in your apartment building has lodged a complaint. The landlord subsequently pays you a visit, saying:

> ついうっかりなさったんだと思いますが、このア
> パートでは夜9時すぎのピアノはご遠慮してい
> ただくことになっておりまして……

Tsui ukkari nasatta n' da to omoimasu ga, kono apāto de wa yoru kuji-sugi no piano wa goenryo shite itadaku koto ni natte orimashite ...

I'm sure you just didn't realize it, but we have a rule in the building against playing the piano after nine at night.

Here's one more example to show how potential disputes can be avoided through the diplomatic application of the indirect approach. Let's say the people who have moved into the apartment next door keep the volume on their television turned up so high that it's driving you crazy. Rather than complain to the landlord or, worse, march over there and demand that they turn it down, you might call on them the next day and say:

> このアパート、壁が薄いのでうちのテレビの音が
> お邪魔になっているんじゃないかと、前々から
> 気にしておりましたのよ。Ⓕ

Kono apāto, kabe ga usui no de uchi no terebi no oto ga ojame ni natte iru n' ja nai ka to, maemae kara ki ni shite orimashita no yo.

The walls in this building are so thin, I've been wondering for the longest time whether the sound from my television is bothering you.

No discerning person will mistake the real implication of your words, nor will anyone fail to appreciate your consideration for their feelings.

✛

For fear of intruding I'm afraid I've fallen out of touch

遠慮が無沙汰になってしまいました。

Enryo ga busata ni natte shimaimashita.

For fear of intruding I'm afraid I've fallen out of touch.

Now and then you may run into someone—a former colleague, say, or an old classmate—with whom you once had a long-standing acquaintance that has since lapsed. At such times, this polite expression will provide a smooth opening to what could otherwise be an awkward reunion. This sort of greeting will also serve you well if you have occasion to get in touch with a current acquaintance whom you haven't seen in a long while.

The meaning of the first part of this expression, translated here as "for fear of intruding," emerges from the key term *enryo*, the implications of which may be clearer from the following, more elaborate example:

あまりひんぱんにお訪ねしてはご迷惑かと思い、
遠慮しておりました。

Amari hinpan ni otazune shite wa gomeiwaku ka to omoi, enryo shite orimashita.

I was afraid I'd make a nuisance of myself by calling on you too often, so I was keeping my distance (out of respect for your privacy).

The use of *enryo* thus implies that it was neither negligence nor any disinclination on your part that caused you to fall out of touch (*gobusata*) but only a sense of propriety and respect, lending this handy expression the tone of an explanation (though not necessarily a truthful one) rather than an apology.

In general, such explanations or excuses tend to adhere to a basic pattern: you testify to your original intention to do whatever it was and then point out how fate or circumstances intervened to prevent you from following through. In delivering such an account, you are likely to find one or more of the following expressions useful.

kokoro narazu mo ("in spite of my best intentions"), as in:

心ならずも渋滞に巻き込まれ、到着が三十分も遅れてしまいました。

Kokoro narazu mo jūtai ni makikomare, tōchaku ga sanjuppun mo okurete shimaimashita.

In spite of my best intentions I got stuck in traffic and ended up arriving half an hour late.

yamunaku ("be forced"), as in:

病院で検査いたしましたところ安静にせよとのことで、やむなく出発を見合わせました。

Byōin de kensa itashimashita tokoro ansei ni seyo to no koto de, yamunaku shuppatsu o miawasemashita.

I had just had a checkup and they warned me to take it easy, so I was forced to postpone my departure.

It's not always advisable to lead off with an excuse, however. Suppose you have the bad luck to arrive late for a date—a severely regarded transgression. Your would-be companion is likely to be in a foul enough mood already, and for you to rattle off even a plausible excuse when you finally show up may well have the effect of trying to put out a fire with gasoline. Rather than trying straightaway to jus-

tify your lapse in punctuality, it would be much better to
lead off with an apology:

ごめんなさい。でも、せめて事情だけでも聞いて
　くれない？Ⓕ

Gomen nasai. Demo, semete jijō dake de mo kiite kurenai?

I'm sorry. But would you at least let me explain what
happened?

Apologies having been made, even if not gleefully accepted,
your best chance of salvaging the evening is probably to
proceed very slowly—timidly—into an account of how, in
spite of your best intentions, you were forced to be late.

I did no such thing

身に覚えのないことだ。

Mi ni oboe no nai koto da.

I did no such thing.

While it's bad enough to find oneself the object of ground-
less criticism or gossip, there is a danger in letting loose talk
run its course, since rumors often give way to more serious
misunderstandings and may even damage one's overall cred-
ibility. It is therefore considered advisable to publicly refute
unfounded criticism—to explicitly defend one's integrity and
silence the wagging tongues. This phrase is used to refute
accusations xor blame for a misdeed that the speaker is quite
certain—based on a clear recollection of the situation—he
did not commit. Consider this short dialogue, for example:

彼女を泣かせたのは君じゃないのか。Ⓜ

Kanojo o nakaseta no wa kimi ja nai no ka?
It was you who drove her to tears, wasn't it?

何を言う。身に覚えのないことだ。Ⓜ
Nani o iu. Mi ni oboe no nai koto da.
What are you talking about? I did no such thing.

The implication is that the person accused has not only done nothing wrong but is moreover taken aback at being held to blame. A similar expression is:

根も葉もないことだ。
Ne mo ha mo nai koto da.
There's no truth to that whatsoever.

Here, the emphasis is on the fact that the charge has no basis (the literal meaning is "That has neither roots nor leaves"); this expression is frequently employed to squelch ugly rumors.

Merely denying a charge does not necessarily disarm it or eliminate accumulated mistrust, however. This is perhaps most obviously true of politicians, whose frequent denials of equally frequent charges of corruption tend to be dismissed as self-serving fictions. Someone whose integrity is in doubt from the outset has little hope of refuting an accusation by simply insisting on his honesty—such protestations of virtue and innocence are apt to be ignored. The phrase used to describe such a case is:

身から出た錆
Mi kara deta sabi
As they sow, so shall they reap.
(literally, "It's rust from your own body.")

Sometimes the problem is not so much what's being said but rather who is saying it. Here is a strong comeback that will shoot down any loose-lipped busybody making intemperate accusations or insinuations:

あなたにそんなことを言われる筋合いはない。

Anata ni sonna koto o iwareru sujiai wa nai.

You have no business talking to me that way.

With this retort, you imply that whether or not the allegation is true is a separate matter and not one that you intend to discuss. The clear message is that the other party has his nose in your business and had better get it out fast. *Anata* ("you"), rather than the person's name, is purposely employed here as a kind of putdown; under normal circumstances, the speaker would use the other person's name or title. There is, incidentally, always some danger that the use of *anata* will come off sounding rude, for which reason it is studiously avoided by people addressing higher-ups and elders.

I'm speechless!

あいた口がふさがらない。

Aita kuchi ga fusagaranai.

I'm speechless!

Here, oddly enough, is familiar way to express what is ostensibly inexpressible—astonishment that surpasses words. Generally used to indicate one's utter stupefaction in reaction to some unthinkable act of stupidity by another person, this expression can be backed up by the following one, which means precisely the same thing:

あきれてものが言えない。

Akirete mono ga ienai.
I'm dumbfounded.

Only certain situations lend themselves to the use of such expressions, of course. To wit:

金魚が寒そうだから水槽にお湯を入れただと？ まったくあきれてものが言えない。Ⓜ

Kin'gyo ga samusō da kara suisō ni oyu o ireta da to? Mattaku akirete mono ga ienai.

You poured hot water in the fish tank because you thought the fish looked cold? I'm absolutely dumbfounded.

When someone does something so stupid that it departs entirely from the realm of common sense, it's not unreasonable to raise doubts about what goes on inside his head, for which purpose another familiar expression works very well:

いったい何を考えているのか……

Ittai nani o kangaete iru no ka ...

What in the world can you be thinking of?

For adults dealing with children who blithely persist in foolish behavior despite having been explicitly and emphatically instructed otherwise time and time again, the ultimate recourse is often a declaration of surrender:

もう勝手にしなさい。私は知りませんからね。Ⓕ

Mō katte ni shinasai. Watashi wa shirimasen kara ne.

Okay, do as you like. I'm not going to be responsible.

This sort of disavowal is often referred to by the term

匙を投げる
saji o nageru
to abandon hope

A literal translation of this familiar phrase might be "to throw down the spoon," which is aptly reminiscent of "to throw in the towel." Supposedly, the expression originally referred to the frustrated act of a physician confronting an incurable condition: in despair at his inability to save the patient, the doctor would seize his spoon for mixing up tonics and elixirs (he was also the pharmacist, apparently) and fling it. In fact, the phrase is often used in a medical context:

もうあの人には医者が匙を投げた。
Mō ano hito ni wa isha ga saji o nageta.
The doctors have given up on her.

When, after repeated demonstrations of buffoonery, someone is written off as an imbecile, an expression frequently employed is:

バカにつける薬はない。
Baka ni tsukeru kusuri wa nai.
There's no cure for a fool.

This one, however, is not recommended for parents dealing with errant children. Better to remain speechless.

It shows a lack of breeding

お里が知れますよ。
Osato ga shiremasu yo.
It shows a lack of breeding.

When someone's behavior is considered scandalous or dis-graceful—a serious breach of etiquette, a stunning display of ignorance, or any words or actions regarded as shamefully inappropriate—there is a tendency, apparent from the cur-rency of this and other similar expressions, to ascribe the misbehavior to a faulty upbringing.

年頃の娘が酔っぱらって上司にからんだり、服を脱いだり、まったくお里が知れるよ。Ⓜ

Toshigoro no musume ga yopparatte jōshi ni karandari, fuku o nuidari, mattaku osato ga shireru yo.

For a young woman to get drunk and hang all over her boss, shucking off her clothes—well, it sure shows lack of breeding.

そんなはしたない言葉を使うなんて、お里が知れますよ。

Sonna hashitanai kotoba o tsukau nante, osato ga shire-masu yo.

You're just showing off your lack of breeding, using vulgar language like that.

Here the term *sato* (here used with the honorific prefix *o*) which literally means "the home in which one was raised," connotes one's upbringing or lineage. Another phrase with essentially the same meaning is:

育ちがわかる。

Sodachi ga wakaru.

It shows a poor upbringing.

Both these expressions convey a caustic, if tacit, criticism of the way the person was raised by her parents and of the so-cial education she received at their hands. A similar expres-sion that more explicitly refers to parental failings is:

親の顔が見たい。

Oya no kao ga mitai.

I can just imagine his parents.

While the latter two expressions—*sodachi ga wakaru* and *oya no kao ga mitai*—are used in reference to either women or men, the phrase *osato ga shiremasu yo* is used all but exclusively in reference to a woman.

Whichever expression is employed, someone thus criticized probably won't submit lightly to having her parents disparaged or her upbringing called into question. Indeed, such remarks are likely to strike more deeply and painfully than if she herself were being directly censured. This may reflect the influence of what many consider to be a primary tenet of Japanese society, as expressed by the saying

子の不始末は親の恥。

Ko no fushimatsu wa oya no haji.

The sins of the children bring shame on the parents.

Quite often, parents reinforce this attitude when scolding their children, particularly in their frequent invocations of the term *seken*, which can be variously translated as "other people," "society," "what people think," or even "gossip."

そんなことをすれば世間がなんと言うだろう。

Sonna koto o sureba seken ga nan to iu darō.

What do you suppose people will think if you go and do a thing like that?

おまえは、親を世間の笑いものにしたいのか。Ⓜ

Omae wa, oya o seken no waraimono ni shitai no ka.

What do you want to do, humiliate your parents in front of the whole world?

The related compound *seken-tei* ("decency" or "public appearances") is also used in this context.

すこしは世間体を考えたらどうなんだ。Ⓜ

Sukoshi wa seken-tei o kangaetara dō nan da.

You might give a little thought to what people will think.

The attitudes reflected by the expressions considered in this section suggest that Japan is a tough place for offspring—at home their parents warn them to maintain appearances because the world is watching, and out in the world they're reprimanded for bringing shame on their parents.

He knows all the answers

ああ言えばこう言う。

Aa ieba kō iu.

He knows all the answers.

You're confronted with the need to reprimand somebody, but you no sooner broach the subject than he tells you that's not how it is at all, the situation is entirely different. You find he has a ready-made excuse for whatever complaint you might have. Such people can be maddening, and this expression applies to them.

ああ言えばこう言う。まったく口だけは達者なやつだ。

Aa ieba kō iu. Mattaku kuchi dake wa tassha na yatsu da.

That guy has an answer for everything. He's long on talk and that's about all.

An expression quite similar to this one in both usage and meaning is:

右と言えば左。
Migi to ieba hidari.
You say right and he says left.

Both of these phrases are used to describe a glib, evasive person, as opposed to someone who simply makes a point of contradicting others at every turn. The latter sort is often referred to as *amanojaku*, an epithet that implies a perversely contrary nature and that originally denoted demons who assail the gates of heaven.

A person who is very good at talking his way around problems but not much good at anything else—*kuchi dake wa tassha*—can also be called

口舌の徒
kōzetsu no to
a smooth talker

While this term (which literally means "an apostle of mouth and tongue") has a somewhat old-fashioned ring to it, it carries precisely the same criticism of the evasive verbalist as *migi to ieba hidari* and *aa ieba kō iu*.

Other disparaging expressions commonly applied to contrary or niggling types include:

口が減らないやつ
kuchi ga heranai yatsu
a guy who always has to have the last word
(literally, "someone with a mouth that won't wear out")

口から先に生まれてきたようなやつ
kuchi kara saki ni umarete kita yō na yatsu
a born yapper
(literally, "someone born mouth first")

While these are similar criticisms, the first is more clearly an indictment of someone who won't admit defeat or who insists on splitting hairs, while the second implies that, whatever his other failings, the person simply talks too much.

However one looks at it, there's nothing more vexing when trying to state your position than to be talked down or contradicted out of hand. It's all the more infuriating to encounter such willful opposition from a child or an underling, and at such times a good slap in the face might seem the most salient response. Naturally, any such impulse must be vanquished. As an adult, you must rely on the force of verbal, rather than physical, persuasion; if your first attempt meets with obstinate resistance, try another approach.

❦

I didn't recognize you

おみそれしました。

Omisore shimashita.

I didn't recognize you.

Originally, the message behind these words was the literal one—the phrase was employed as a sort of apologetic greeting by someone who had failed to recognize an acquaintance. Over time, people began using this expression as a form of polite hyperbole, to imply that the other person had undergone some transformation—due to a change in appearance, perhaps, or a display of unknown abilities—so wonderful as to render her unrecognizable. In this way, the phrase evolved into an expression of praise. If someone you know—someone whose everyday appearance you are accustomed to—turns up one day dressed to the nines, this phrase will be perfectly apt. To express the same sentiment, you could also say one of the following:

見違えた。

Michigaeta.

I thought you were someone else.

誰かと思った。

Dare ka to omotta.

Is that really you?

Whichever phrase you use, the effect is to exaggerate your reaction—in an implicitly complimentary way—to your friend's unfamiliar appearance.

Aside from the frequency with which they are employed to comment on someone's appearance, expressions such as *omisore shimashita* can also indicate how deeply impressed the speaker is with another person's skill or ability. Consider the example of one golfer complimenting another on his game; his companion having demonstrated abilities that far exceeded expectations, the speaker expresses his respect and admiration:

田中さんのゴルフの腕は大したものですな。いや、おみそれしました。Ⓜ

Tanaka-san no gorufu no ude wa taishita mono desu na. Iya, omisore shimashita.

You really have a wonderful talent for golf, Mr. Tanaka. I mean, I could hardly believe that was you.

A degree of caution should accompany the use of the phrases considered in this section. Although, as noted above, these are generally intended as words of praise in the form of hyperbole, they can have the ring of condescension, and may even be construed to suggest that the speaker has suddenly discovered redeeming qualities in someone who was previously held in low regard. The point is to celebrate the fact that the other person looks good or has done well—not to emphasize how amazing it is.

A useful alternative expression of praise, and one that is free from the potentially double-edged implications of those already mentioned, is:

さすがですね。

Sasuga desu ne.

which could be translated "Just as you'd expect" or "As usual" or "Isn't that just like you." In this case, the speaker clearly indicates that good things were expected from the other person all along.

❧

He's truly a man of honest character

竹を割ったようなお人柄ですね。

Take o watta yō na ohitogara desu ne.

He's truly a man of honest character.

Here is an expression of praise—this one customarily applied all but exclusively to males—that plays off that old cultural standby, the noble bamboo tree. The phrase implies that having a righteously honest disposition is like a length of bamboo that has split cleanly in two, something that bamboo does easily when cut from the top down. Literally rendered, *take o watta* means "split the bamboo." The man about whom these words are said is presumed to be that rare creature, an honest man, who has a completely forthright nature free from any hint of malice or perversity, as in this tribute, delivered by an older woman:

佐藤さんの息子さんは竹を割ったようなお人柄で、ほんとうに気持ちのいい好青年だわ。Ⓕ

Satō-san no musuko-san wa take o watta yo na ohitogara de, hontō ni kimochi no ii kō-seinen da wa.

Mr. Sato's son has such an honest character, he's really a fine young man.

Among the other stock phrases commonly used to express the speaker's positive appraisal of someone's character or qualities are 一本気な (*ippongi na*), as in 一本気な若者 (*ippongi na wakamono*), "a determined young man," or 筋のある (*suji no aru*), as in 筋のある若者 (*suji no aru wakamono*) "a young man with spunk."

The first of these, *ippongi na*, is most often used in a positive sense to salute someone's single-mindedness; keep in mind, however, that the same phrase is occasionally used in a pejorative sense to criticize someone for having a one-track mind. The second phrase, *suji no aru*, is similar to the first—it's used to express admiration for someone who is resolute or who doesn't easily admit defeat. This expression should not be confused with the phrase *suji ga ii*, which, in addition to "good character," can also mean that the person has a natural aptitude (for something specific) or that he acts in a particularly logical or well-thought-out manner.

We began this section with an expression of praise for honesty. Although there seems little risk of these words being overused, the world being what it is, it may help to have a couple of alternatives at the ready. One commonly heard phrase is:

裏表のない人

uraomote no nai hito

a straight shooter

The term *uraomote* can be literally translated as "front and back" or "two faces," so *uraomote no nai hito* can be read as "a person without two faces," or someone whose character is free from duplicity. As a tribute to honesty, it can conceivably carry the faint overtones of a backhanded compliment, since this phrase is no more than the inverse of the caustic epithet

裏表のある人

uraomote no aru hito

a two-faced phony; a hypocrite

A similar expressional—also potentially double-edged—is

かげひなたのない人

kagehinata no nai hito

someone who's on the level

This too is simply the contrary of a harshly critical expression:

かげひなたのある人

kagehinata no aru hito

a double-dealer

As noted above, the phrases *take o watta yō na* and *ippongi na* tend to be applied only to men, and moreover to relatively younger men; this is less true of the phrases *uraomote no aru (nai)*, *suji no aru*, and *suji ga ii*.

✿

You're just being polite

お上手ね。Ⓕ

Ojōzu ne.

You're just being polite.

Virtually every student of Japanese encounters the term *jōzu* (used above, as is generally the case, with the honorific prefix *o*) quite early on. Usually, it's used as a compliment or an expression of approval and refers to something done skillfully or to a skillful person. Thus, the immortal line also encountered early on by virtually anyone who can mangle a word or two of Japanese:

日本語がお上手ですね。

Nihongo ga ojōzu desu ne.

Your Japanese is quite good.

Obviously, the usage of *ojōzu* in this sense is not governed by strict standards of sincerity or accuracy. The synonymous term *umai* is employed in just the same manner, and with just as little compunction.

Compare this essentially standard usage of *ojōzu* with its usage in the following exchange, between a native speaker and a student of Japanese:

あなたの日本語はぼくたちよりうまいな。Ⓜ

Anata no nihongo wa bokutachi yori umai na.

You speak Japanese better than we do.

まあ、お上手ね。Ⓕ

Maa, ojōzu ne.

You're just being polite.

Here, *ojōzu* refers ironically to the first speaker's tactful words. The effect is of an oblique but effectively modest dismissal of base flattery. A slightly less respectful-sounding expression that is otherwise similar both in meaning and usage is:

口がうまい。
Kuchi ga umai.
You smooth talker (that's nonsense).

There are several other standard expressions that play on the term *jōzu*. Two of them,

お上手を言う　　　　　　上手を使う
ojōzu o iu　　　　　　*jōzu o tsukau*
to flatter; to lay it on thick

are similar to those discussed above—they connote the action of using words to curry favor with, fawn upon, or even grovel before someone. For example, the following response to unwarranted words of praise:

またそんな、お上手ばかりおっしゃって。Ⓕ
Mata sonna, ojōzu bakari osshatte.
This again. Stop trying to butter me up.

Sometimes the adverse reaction is elicited not merely by false praise but by the presumption of some ulterior motivation on the part of the other party. The term *ojōzu-gokashi* connotes self-interested behavior masquerading as kindness. This sort of conniving pretense—also called *otame-gokashi*—is typified by honey-tongued efforts to persuade someone to take an action that will ostensibly be to his advantage but in reality will benefit the persuader. Such efforts may be dismissed thus:

やめて、お上手ごかしはたくさんよ。Ⓕ

Yamete, ojōzu-gokashi wa takusan yo.

Enough! You're just trying to use me to feather your
own nest.

✿

I owe this entirely to Mr. Fukuda

ひとえに福田部長のおかげです。

Hitoe ni Fukuda-buchō no okage desu.

I owe this entirely to Mr. Fukuda (the section chief).

In the event you receive a promotion to a higher position
or your work is singled out for special recognition, you'll
be expected to respond by displaying appreciation and,
above all, humility. This expression exemplifies the ideal of
self-deprecation that is considered essential to social intercourse in Japan, particularly in the workplace. According to
this principle, when things go well you decline to take any
of the credit for yourself (at least publicly) and emphasize
instead the contributions of others. You might deflect
credit for a promotion toward a superior, for example:

このたび部長職を拝命いたしましたのも、ひとえ
に専務のお力添えのおかげです。

*Kono tabi buchō-shoku o haimei itashimashita no mo,
hitoe ni senmu no ochikarazoe no okage desu.*

My promotion to section chief is entirely due to
your own efforts (as director).

In such a case, it is incumbent on the boss—who must observe the same principle of overt modesty—to graciously

deflect the praise right back to you.

いやいや、君の実力が認められたのさ。Ⓜ

Iya iya, kimi no jitsuryoku ga mitomerareta no sa.

Nothing of the kind. It's your own abilities that have been recognized.

It may happen that you receive special recognition for your work as the head of a group or team, in which case you are obliged not only to fend off praise but also to thank the members of the group:

今度の昇進は私一人の手柄じゃない。君たちの惜しみない協力のおかげだ。ありがとう。Ⓜ

Kondo no shōshin wa watashi hitori no tegara ja nai. Kimi-tachi no oshiminai kyōryoku no okage da. Arigatō.

This promotion really isn't due to any special merit on my part. I owe it, rather, to the unselfish efforts of all of you. Thank you.

As for the members of the group themselves, they might variously reply:

おめでとうございます。これから責任重大ですね。バリバリやってください。

Omedetō gozaimasu. Kore kara sekinin-jūdai desu ne. Baribari yatte kudasai.

Congratulations. You'll be carrying a lot of responsibility from now on. Give it all you've got.

さすがですね。実力が認められて、私たちも嬉しいです。

Sasuga desu ne. Jitsuryoku ga mitomerarete, watashi-tachi mo ureshii desu.

One might have expected it. We're glad to see you get the recognition you deserve.

オレたちもがんばらなくっちゃね。Ⓜ

Ore-tachi mo ganbaranakutcha ne.

I guess we're gonna have to work hard and try to keep up with you.

Even in private conversations, you may wish to play up the unlikeliness of your good fortune, emphasizing that you never expected to be singled out:

内心、驚いているんだ。Ⓜ

Naishin, odoroite iru n' da.

To tell you the truth, it came as a complete surprise.

これも時の運ってやつかな。Ⓜ

Kore mo toki no un tte yatsu ka na.

This is just another case of dumb luck, I guess.

自信なんてなかったわ、本当よ。Ⓕ

Jishin nante nakatta wa, hontō yo.

I never expected this, honestly.

🦗

You've been a great help. It was very kind of you

ご親切に、助かりました。

Goshinsetsu ni, tasukarimashita.

You've been a great help. It was very kind of you.

If, as most speakers would probably agree, the most frequently used expression of gratitude in contemporary Japanese is *arigatō gozaimasu* ("Thank you"), then these are perhaps the next most commonly heard words of thanks. (Actually, as in the example below, the two expressions are frequently used in combination.) More so than *arigatō gozaimasu*, however, this phrase conveys a feeling of indebtedness. When another person has done you a favor at your own request or has simply provided a helping hand out of the goodness of her heart, this is the phrase to use. Equally useful are such variants as:

ご親切にありがとうございました。おかげさまで
助かりました。

Goshinsetsu ni arigatō gozaimashita. Okagesama de tasukari-mashita.

Thank you very much for your kindness. All's well now, thanks to you.

It should be stressed that these words convey a sense of gratitude more emphatic than you'd ordinarily show, say, to the waitress who brings you your coffee. Rather, this is the sort of thing you might say to a stranger who takes the trouble to give you explicit directions when you're lost, or who hurries after you to return the wallet you dropped unknowingly, or who volunteers to help you carry something heavy, or who rescues you from a drunken boor on the train. Naturally, the kindness of others is never so keenly appreciated as when it is needed most, and at such times it is important to make an appropriately elaborate—and sincere—demonstration of thanks.

Occasions may arise when some kind soul helps you out of a really tight spot and words simply aren't sufficient to communicate the depth of your gratitude. Imagine that a complete stranger has found your missing handbag and brought it to your home, with all the contents intact. In such a case, words of thanks delivered on the spot just aren't enough, so you might ask how to reach the person at his home:

> どうか、お名前とご住所をお聞かせください。
>
> *Dō ka, onamae to gojūsho o okikase kudasai.*
>
> Would you be so kind as to give me your name and your address?

You can then make a proper show of thanks by calling on your benefactor the very next day, usually bearing a small (and often edible) token of your gratitude.

The same course of action would be called for if, for example, you lost your wallet and a passerby lent you the train fare home. In this case, the kindly stranger might well decline the customary elaborate show of gratitude, saying something like:

> いや、名乗るほどの者ではありません。
>
> *Iya, nanoru hodo no mono de wa arimasen.*
>
> Look, it's no big thing (not important enough to take credit for).

At this point, the only gracious thing to do is to accept the favor gratefully and, with a solemn bow, sincerely state your thanks:

> ご親切は忘れません。
>
> *Goshinsetsu wa wasuremasen.*
>
> I won't forget your kindness.

When the person lending you a hand or doing you a favor is an acquaintance, rather than a stranger or passerby, it's considered appropriate to express your thanks with the words:

> いつもお世話になります。

Itsumo osewa ni narimasu.
I'm forever in your debt.

This expression is, however, perilously similar to the ubiquitous phrase *Itsumo osewa ni natte orimasu*, the formulaic phrase with which neighbors politely thank one another for being neighbors or business people greet their patrons and suppliers over the telephone, so a good deal of care should be taken to make it sound truly grateful rather than perfunctory.

✎

I've been wanting one for a long time

前からほしいと思っていたの。Ⓕ
Mae kara hoshii to omotte ita no.
I've been wanting one for a long time.

When a friend presents you with a gift, it is only natural to express your gratitude, and you can easily respond with a simple and heartfelt

どうもありがとう。
Dōmo arigatō.
Thanks very much.

Should you leave it at that, however, you will have inadvertently conveyed a distinct lack of courtesy.

It is considered far more gracious to call particular attention to the present itself, emphasizing its value to you and thus presumably returning a degree of pleasure to the gift-giver. For this purpose the first phrase introduced above will serve you well. If someone gives you a Gucci scarf, for example, you might say:

> まあ、グッチのスカーフ。これ、前からほしいと
> 思っていたの。どうもありがとう。Ⓕ
>
> *Maa, guchi no sukāfu. Kore, mae kara hoshii to omotte ita no. Dōmo arigatō.*
>
> Ooh, a Gucci scarf! I've been wanting one of these for a long time. Thanks a lot.

Since *mae kara hoshii to omotte ita* is a ready-made expression right out of the standard repertoire, it goes without saying that the actual truth value of these words in any given situation is far less important than the good manners (and good intentions) they represent. Even if you wouldn't know a Gucci scarf from a dishrag, by claiming to have yearned for one you are effectively showing appreciation to the gift-giver by subtly complimenting her on her good judgment and sense of taste—and that is the important thing. You can accomplish the same thing by saying:

> 私が欲しがってること、よくわかったわね。Ⓕ
>
> *Watashi ga hoshigatte 'ru koto, yoku wakatta wa ne.*
>
> You knew just what I wanted, didn't you.

Compared to *mae kara hoshii to omotte ita*, this expression may have a more transparently ingratiating ring to it, but the other person will probably ignore the obviousness of the strategy and receive your words in the spirit intended.

There are any number of alternative expressions representing variations on this recommended approach to public demonstrations of gratitude. What follows is a mere sampling.

To thank someone who takes you to a restaurant you've never been to:

前から食べたいと思っていたの。Ⓕ

Mae kara tabetai to omotte ita no.

I've been wanting to try this place for a long time.

To thank someone who takes you to a movie or play:

前から見たいと思っていたんだ。Ⓜ

Mae kara mitai to omotte ita n' da.

I've been wanting to see this for a long time.

To thank someone who takes you to a concert:

前から聴きたいと思っていたところだよ。Ⓜ

Mae kara kikitai to omotte ita tokoro da yo.

I've been wanting to go for a long time.

To thank someone who takes you somewhere you've never been:

前から行ってみたいと思っていたの。

Mae kara itte mitai to omotte ita no.

I've been wanting to come here for a long time.

Thus, what may be thought of as the *mae kara* strategy—which usually involves stretching the truth a little in order to show appreciation—is a multipurpose bit of phraseology that comes in handy on any number of occasions and helps establish your reputation as someone who knows how to express gratitude properly.

❦

I'm prepared to do whatever is required to make amends

いかなる償いもいたすつもりでございます。

Ikanaru tsugunai mo itasu tsumori de gozaimasu.

I'm prepared to do whatever is required to make
    amends.

This short sentence represents an extreme declaration of
formal apology. The Japanese language is said by some to
reflect a culture of apology, in the sense that the social act
most fundamentally enshrined in the language seems to be
the apology. Even the most ordinary transaction—asking for
information or making a minor request—usually incorpo-
rates such standard phrases as *sumimasen* ("I'm sorry") or *osoreirimasu* ("I beg your pardon"), expressions that, at least
on a literal level, convey apology. You might say that the
impact of such apologetic expressions has become diluted
through overuse. As a result, when the primary purpose actually is to formally and earnestly apologize for something
one has done, the language employed tends to be extreme.
What's more, people may literally get down on their knees
or even prostrate themselves to demonstrate the sincerity of
their words.

If you really want to reach back and humble yourself
the way they do in samurai movies, you might try this
(though you'll probably have to explain it after having used
it):

七重の膝を八重に折りまして、お詫びいたします。

Nanae no hiza o yae ni orimashite, owabi itashimasu.

I beg your forgiveness on bended knee.

A literal translation of this standard expression will provide an idea of the extreme attitude it expresses. *Nanae no hiza o yae ni orimashite* means forcing one's knees (which bend only in two) to bend seven ways (*nanae*) and then once more (*yae*, "eightfold")—as if this were physiologically possible—from which decidedly uncomfortable position one offers one's apology (*owabi itashimasu*).

Japanese society has long honored a sort of tacit understanding whereby a transgressor can effectively expiate his offense by making a sincere and sufficiently humble apology. In addition, a direct apology is considered the most reliable way to assuage the anger of the offended party. While both these functions have helped established the spoken apology as an essential social lubricant, it no longer necessarily holds the power it once did. These days, even the most sincere apology may be answered by a demand for complete financial compensation.

In the unfortunate event that you have caused an injury through your own negligence or carelessly started a fire that spread and damaged other people's property, no apology will be sufficient to undo the harm. Nevertheless, by conscientiously making the most humble kind of apology, you can at least demonstrate your sincere regret, and that is perhaps the first point to address. Should you commit the sort of offense that affects another person's reputation—calling off the wedding after the invitations have been sent out, for instance—be prepared to grovel your way through an apology that will surely be a once-in-a-lifetime lesson in public humility.

❧

I accept full responsibility for this

私の不徳のいたすところでございます。

Watashi no futoku no itasu tokoro de gozaimasu.

I accept full responsibility for this.

Occasionally, you may be required to apologize for something you didn't even do—for misconduct or carelessness by a subordinate or a family member, for instance. This is a standard form of apology for those occasions. Certain related expressions have lately fallen into disrepute as a result of being associated with shady politicians, who tend to rely on them in their efforts to double-talk their way past scandalous revelations. One of these is:

まことに遺憾に存じます。

Makoto ni ikan ni zonjimasu.

I consider this truly regrettable.

It should be pointed out, however, that there is no dishonesty inherent in the words themselves. Rather, what tarnishes their impact is the sanctimonious pose of feigned ignorance and the pretense, implicit in the use of these words, that someone else is responsible for the politician's own actions.

Suppose you recommended someone for a job, and she was hired but ended up making a mess of things. Or perhaps you played matchmaker for two people who subsequently got engaged, only to have one of them back out at the last minute. In such cases you really aren't to blame for the unfortunate outcome, but your fingerprints are on it. Your failing was that you didn't see trouble coming, so you might as well apologize for that:

私の不明から、このようなことになりまして申し
訳ございません。

*Watashi no fumei kara, kono yō na koto ni narimashite
mōshiwake gozaimasen.*

I'm deeply sorry that things have come to this pass,
all due to a lack of foresight on my part.

Needless to say, you meant well, and when the best of intentions produce unhappiness, who's to blame? Surely there's
no need to blame anyone, but the problem is that hard feelings often remain. Expressions like this are probably the
most effective way to deal with them.

If it's a case of misconduct or carelessness by someone
you're expected to be responsible for, here are two possible
approaches:

不行き届きで申し訳ございません。

Fu-yukitodoki de mōshiwake gozaimasen.

I apologize for this negligence.

至りませんで、とんだ粗相をいたしまして申し訳
ございません。

*Itarimasen de, tonda sosō o itashimashite mōshiwake goza-
imasen.*

Carelessness caused this awful mess. I apologize.

When delivering an apology such as this, you'll be more
likely to achieve the intended effect if you lower the tone of
your voice a degree or two and make a point of clearly enun-
ciating all the way to the end of the sentence. In such cases,
it's not advisable to start chanting *sumimasen*, as that may
very well only exacerbate the situation, laying you open to
the rebuke

すみませんですむと思うか。

Sumimasen de sumu to omou ka.

You think just saying you're sorry is going to make
   things right?

❦

I'm sorry about all the fuss

お騒がせいたしました。

Osawagase itashimashita.

I'm sorry about all the fuss.

As you might expect in a language that offers so many occasions for apology, there are many different ways to apologize. Just which way is appropriate in a given situation
depends on a number of factors, the first of which is the
identity of the person you're apologizing to. For example,
take the familiar form

ごめんなさい。

Gomen nasai.

Sorry.

This is a perfectly appropriate way to apologize to someone
in your family, a close friend, or a child. It would be a serious breach of etiquette and imply a lack of common sense,
however, to use this form with one of your elders or a superior at work. In that case you would probably best be ad-
vised to say:

申し訳ありませんでした。

Mōshiwake arimasen deshita.

Please accept my apologies.

If you make a mistake at work or somehow cause trouble for someone who is not part of your immediate circle, this type of apology will probably be appropriate. Later, once the dust has settled and the mistake has been rectified or the trouble resolved, you'll probably have an opportunity to say you're sorry once again—to perform a sort of follow-up apology. For that purpose, the form at the beginning of this section, *osawagase itashimashita*, is an excellent choice.

Let's compare *osawagase itashimashita* with a similar form that is often used in the same way:

ご迷惑をおかけしました。

Gomeiwaku o okake shimashita.

I apologize for causing you so much trouble.

Either form could be used for a follow-up apology. Generally speaking, though, *osawagase itashimashita* tends to be used when there really wasn't too much harm done or serious trouble caused in the first place. *Gomeiwaku o okake shimashita*, on the other hand, is more often used when the original matter was serious enough to possibly have a more lasting impact—when the water might not have all flowed under the bridge yet. Thus, you might consider three grades of apologies for circumstances like these: the first and most weighty is *mōshiwake arimasen deshita*; the second, not quite so grave, is *gomeiwaku o okake shimashita*; and the third and least somber is *osawagase itashimashita*. It's probably safe to use the latter expression if the person you're apologizing to seems glad to put the incident behind her. If you're lucky, your apology may even draw a smile.

❧

How thoughtless of me

私としたことが……

Watashi to shita koto ga ...

How thoughtless of me. For shame!

This phrase, an expression of mild self-criticism, is the kind of thing that might escape your lips if you were entertaining a visitor and suddenly realized you had forgotten to offer him a seat. This lightly apologetic expression is an abbreviated form of the longer phrase:

私としたことが、はしたない。

Watashi to shita koto ga, hashitanai.

How thoughtless of me!

In contemporary usage, the second part of this sentence, *hashitanai* ("shameful" or "disgraceful") tends to be omitted. The effect is to suggest that you have unintentionally committed a slight breach of courtesy, which you will now promptly rectify.

Often enough, the key phrase *watashi to shita koto ga* is followed by another expression that completes the sentence and drives the point home, as in the following examples:

私としたことが、気がつきませんで……

Watashi to shita koto ga, ki ga tsukimasen de ...

How thoughtless of me not to notice.

私としたことが、ご無礼いたしました。

Watashi to shita koto ga, goburei itashimashita.

How thoughtless of me, how rude!

私としたことが、とんだ粗相をいたしました。
Watashi to shita koto ga, tonda sosō o itashimashita.
How thoughtless of me to commit such a stupid
  oversight.

In each of these examples, the phrase that follows *watashi to shita koto ga* can itself be used as a form of apology, by itself or in a different combination. In fact, some people feel that an expression such as the last one, *tonda sosō o itashimashita*, actually sounds more properly submissive when not preceded by *watashi to shita koto ga*, in such sentences as:

まことに不調法でとんだ粗相をいたしました。
Makoto ni buchōhō de tonda sosō o itashimashita.
That was truly a rude and unforgivable oversight.

People who prefer to rely on slightly more formal expressions of apology such as this may feel that *watashi to shita koto ga*—the suggestion that one should (and generally does) know better than to do something impolite—sounds too much like an excuse rather than a sincere apology. On the other hand, there are those who find the use of this expression, and the spontaneous self-critique it implies, to be courteous and sometimes even charming.

❧

I'm sorry you had to witness such a disgraceful display

お見苦しいところをお目にかけまして……
Omigurushii tokoro o ome ni kakemashite ...

> I'm sorry you had to witness such a disgraceful display.

Ordinarily, protocol requires that visitors be entertained under controlled conditions; this means, among other things, that guests usually see only what they're supposed to see. Occasionally, however, the host slips up or something goes wrong, and the visitor gets an eyeful (or an earful) of something not intended for public display. This expression comes in handy at such times.

The first word of this expression, *migurushii* (appearing above with the honorific prefix *o*), means "unsightly" or "disgraceful." Suppose someone has come to visit and you're going to serve tea. The cupboard where the cups and saucers are kept is a disorderly mess, however, and in trying to get what you need you inadvertently trigger a clattering cascade of poorly stacked crockery. Or perhaps you have a photo you'd like to show your guest and you end up spending 20 minutes dredging up what seems like half your possessions out of closets and drawers trying to find it. In either situation you have exposed your guest to an unsightly spectacle, for which an apology is in order.

According to custom, the things that should not be exposed to view outside one's immediate circle—and there are surprisingly many such things—are covered by the term 内情 *naijō* (literally, "internal affairs"). These include such private realms as the contents of cupboards, drawers, and closets. Because they are private—and intimately associated with oneself—they are presumed to be *migurushii* from an outsider's point of view. Then again, displays of clumsiness (such as knocking over dishes) and time-wasting disorganization (such as the mess in the closet) may also be seen as disgraceful breaches of the *naijō* domain simply because that's not the way you're expected to act when you have company; apparently, that's the way you act when no one's around.

There are other ways in which private matters can encroach on the polite public domain in which guests are supposed to be received, leaving you in a position to apologize. It is unmistakably *migurushii* , for example, for a husband and wife or two colleagues to quarrel in front of a visitor. In such cases, a more proper apology mught be:

お聞き苦しいところをお聞かせしてしまいました。

Okikigurushii tokoro o okikase shite shimaimashita.

I'm sorry you had to hear such a disgraceful commotion.

決まり文句の辞典
COMMON JAPANESE PHRASES

1997年3月3日　第1刷発行

編　者	三省堂編修所
発行者	野間佐和子
発行所	講談社インターナショナル株式会社
	〒112 東京都文京区音羽 1-17-14
	電話：03-3944-6493
印刷所	株式会社　平河工業社
製本所	株式会社　堅省堂